Spirituality and Knowledge Dynamics

Management, Spirituality and Religion

Series Editor
Yochanan Altman

Volume 5

Spirituality and Knowledge Dynamics

New Perspectives for Knowledge Management and Knowledge Strategies

Edited by
Raysa Geaquinto Rocha,
Paulo Pinheiro,
Marcia d'Angelo
and Constantin Bratianu

DE GRUYTER

This publication was supported by the University of Essex's open access fund.

ISBN 978-3-11-100783-0
e-ISBN (PDF) 978-3-11-101041-0
e-ISBN (EPUB) 978-3-11-101142-4
ISSN 2700-7790
DOI https://doi.org/10.1515/9783111010410

Library of Congress Control Number: 2024937636

Bibliographic information published by the Deutsche Nationalbibliothek
The Deutsche Nationalbibliothek lists this publication in the Deutsche Nationalbibliografie; detailed bibliographic data are available on the internet at http://dnb.dnb.de.

Cover image: Ion Jonas, based on an idea by Yochanan Altman
Typesetting: Integra Software Services Pvt. Ltd.
Printing and binding: CPI books GmbH, Leck

MIX
Papier | Fördert gute Waldnutzung
FSC® C083411

www.degruyter.com

Acknowledgements

In crafting this acknowledgement section, we seek to convey our profound appreciation to the esteemed International Association for Knowledge Management (IAKM) for their unwavering support and invaluable contributions to advancing knowledge management scholarship. Their dedication to fostering a global community of researchers, practitioners, and thought leaders has been instrumental in shaping the intellectual landscape that has made this book possible.

We also extend our heartfelt gratitude to the University of Essex for their generous funding, which has enabled us to make this book openly accessible. By removing financial barriers, the university has demonstrated its commitment to democratizing knowledge and promoting scholarly discourse beyond traditional boundaries. This support has not only facilitated the dissemination of the ideas and research presented herein but has also amplified the potential impact of this book on the wider academic community and society.

The collective expertise, insights, and tireless efforts of the International Association of Management, Spirituality & Religion (IAMSR) membership have been a wellspring of inspiration and guidance throughout the development of this project. Their pioneering work in the Management, Spirituality, and Religion (MSR) field has laid the foundation upon which we have built, and their ongoing commitment to pushing the boundaries of our understanding has been a constant source of motivation.

As we present this book to the world, we do so with deep gratitude and appreciation for the IAMSR, IAKM, the University of Essex, and all those who have contributed to its creation. We sincerely hope this work will contribute to advancing knowledge management and MSR scholarship and serve as a testament to the transformative power of collaboration, support, and the shared pursuit of knowledge.

https://doi.org/10.1515/9783111010410-203

Foreword

This fine collection sets itself an important task: to revive the discourse between two epistemological fields – workplace spirituality and knowledge management. Both fields are foundational to the human experience, harking back to the antecedents of *homo sapiens*, at a time when work was a sacred undertaking requiring the blessing of the gods; whereas managing knowledge: the passing on of acquired know-how from one generation to the next, could make the difference between survival and extinction, and hence was imbued with sanctity. Indeed, spirituality and knowledge, *spiritual knowledge*, were two sides of the same coin.

The first decades of the twenty-first century evidence a renewed interest, a renaissance, in exploring ancient wisdoms, unveiling their mores as a means to informing our times, in which evolving knowledge creation technologies are the core of the zeitgeist of humanity.

Knowledge management and workplace spirituality share a tradition of scholarly pursuit alongside an applied enterprise emphasis. Combining theoretical excursions, empirical investigations, reflections, and case studies sourced from nine countries in four continents, this book serves as an essential guide for those wishing to understand key developments in these two pivotal fields of this day and age.

Prof. Yochanan Altman
WU Vienna Austria and University of Haifa Israel
Chair of the International Association of Management Spirituality & Religion
Publisher of the Journal of Management, Spirituality & Religion
IAMSR – De Gruyter Series Editor

https://doi.org/10.1515/9783111010410-204

Contents

Raysa Geaquinto Rocha and Constantin Bratianu

Introduction

Spirituality and knowledge dynamics are critical components of organizational development, well-being, and effectiveness. While the former is often seen as a personal, individualistic domain, it has an equally significant role to play in the workplace. This book brings together research illuminating how spirituality, wisdom traditions, and contemplative practices can positively influence organizational outcomes through knowledge dynamics.

The chapters explore the particularities of spirituality and knowledge dynamics within organizational settings. They offer invaluable insights for researchers, practitioners, and educators in the fields of management, knowledge management, and higher education. The book inspires readers to contemplate how spirituality can enhance their organization's effectiveness and well-being and provides fresh perspectives on how this can be accomplished. Its profound and thought-provoking content will surely leave a lasting impact on its readers.

This seminal book on spirituality and knowledge dynamics comprises an exquisite collection of eleven intellectually stimulating chapters authored by a distinguished panel of sixteen scholars hailing from fourteen nations across the globe. These countries include Austria, Brazil, Chile, the Czech Republic, Finland, Germany, Hungary, India, New Zealand, Portugal, Romania, Spain, and the United States of America. Notably, the contributors represent a kaleidoscope of fourteen distinct organizations, presenting an intricate tapestry of multifaceted viewpoints – including practitioners – and profound insights into knowledge dynamics and spirituality.

The book comprises an introduction followed by two sections on distinct aspects of spirituality and knowledge dynamics. The first section, *Unlocking Spirituality in Knowledge Dynamics*, is conceptual, the chapters focus on the theory of knowledge fields and knowledge dynamics, a spiritual knowledge management, and spirituality as a meta-story. The second section, *Exploring Spirituality in Knowledge Dynamics Across Contexts*, is empirical and explores Communities, Workplace, Higher Education, and Entrepreneurship.

Therefore, our book offers fresh viewpoints on spirituality and its role in knowledge management and strategies. Each chapter delves into the dynamic nature of spirituality and its impact on knowledge. Overall, the book provides thought-provoking insights on how spirituality and knowledge intersect.

Raysa Geaquinto Rocha, University of Essex, United Kingdom; NECE – Research Center in Business Sciences, University of Beira Interior, Portugal, e-mail: raysa.rocha@essex.ac.uk
Constantin Bratianu, Bucharest University of Economic Studies, Bucharest, Romania, e-mail: constantin.bratianu@gmail.com

https://doi.org/10.1515/9783111010410-001

I. Unlocking Spirituality in Knowledge Dynamics

The theory of knowledge fields and knowledge dynamics presents a new paradigm for understanding organizational knowledge dynamics. Based on the principles of thermodynamics and cognitive science findings, the first chapter addresses the theory positing that knowledge can be conceived as a complex field composed of three fundamental knowledge fields: rational, emotional, and spiritual. Knowledge from one field can be transformed into knowledge of any other, creating continuous dynamics. Knowledge dynamics contribute to wise managerial decision-making.

The domain of knowledge management has undergone a transformative change, and there is now a need to reflect on innovative ideas that can reshape its future role in a changing and dynamic world. One such idea, the second chapter, approaches Spiritual Knowledge Management, which involves enabling, managing, and organizing deep learning processes to develop the best version of oneself or an organization. This chapter focuses on defining and conceptualizing Spiritual Knowledge Management, which can contribute to theory-building in the field.

Moreover, spirituality has always been an enigmatic and dynamic phenomenon that is challenging to capture and analyze. Thus, the third chapter discusses that one way of accessing spirituality is through spiritual knowledge – a meta-story composed of stories about the self, relationships to others, and the relationship to the divine. Understanding and researching spirituality from this perspective can provide new insights into knowledge management and knowledge strategies.

II. Exploring Spirituality in Knowledge Dynamics Across Contexts: Communities, Workplace, Higher Education, and Entrepreneurship

Communities of Practice and Research

The Management, Spirituality, and Religion (MSR) group is an Interest Group of the annual Academy of Management conference. The fourth chapter applies relevant knowledge management literature to an opinion piece previously written about the MSR group. By taking a human-centered approach, the chapter centers around values in research, diversification of ways of knowing and research topics, and skill-building, with the aim of expanding KM's body of knowledge and providing impetus for further MSR group development and diversification.

The following chapter focuses on *Clear Sky*, a Buddhist-based meditation center in Canada, which serves as a petri dish for heart-based organizational practices. The chapter highlights three key dimensions: Karma Yoga, Dāna, and Shadow Integration. The authors explore how Karma Yoga bridges inner work and outer action and fosters a dynamic learning environment. Dāna highlights mutually generative exchanges and energy flows, while Shadow Integration uncovers and integrates shadow aspects to free up energy for doing good. The authors provide a template for organizations to experiment with heart-based, dynamic organizational practices through this analysis.

Workplace

Based on a mixed-method study, the sixth chapter delves into why leaders support organizational spirituality and how this support correlates with theoretical constructs. The thematic analysis indicates that leaders support spirituality to improve performance and well-being and enhance stakeholder connectedness. Moreover, leaders underscore the importance of knowledge management and organizational learning in disseminating spirituality. However, bureaucracy, legislation, and technology were identified as hindrances to developing spirituality in organizations. The correlation analysis found positive correlations between the elements of organizational spirituality and its influencers, such as knowledge management and the macro-environment.

The next chapter proposes a Human Flourishing organizational model that revises traditional human resource development for intrinsic value creation. The employee flourishing in knowledge management involves rational, emotional, and spiritual knowledge. While the spiritual dimension can appear as an abstract philosophical concept, empirical studies on Faith at Work demonstrate that spiritual knowledge and intelligence can be enacted in real-world examples.

Higher Education Institutions

The eighth chapter delves into how human development can be shaped by wisdom pedagogy in higher education. While universities focus on developing human beings, research on intellectual capital often ignores the role of spiritual capital. The author argues that the spiritual dimension of wisdom pedagogy needs more understanding and suggests the need for evolutionary and wisdom pedagogies. The chapter's theoretical framework shows the central role of the spiritual dimension of wisdom pedagogy in shaping values, attitudes, authenticity, and responsibility. The author presents practical implications for university educators, management, and curriculum developers.

The ninth chapter examines how Higher Education Institutions (HEIs) face issues related to knowledge management and spirituality in the workplace. Based on interviews with higher education teachers, the authors conclude that although most interviewees perceive the mission, vision, and values of HEIs, these were not explicitly disseminated. Regarding knowledge management, the authors suggest that the organizational culture of HEIs should promote the appreciation and recognition of tacit knowledge. Regarding organizational spirituality, there is a long way to go in HEIs as a whole. The authors suggest that HEI management should promote effective knowledge management and practices that contribute to a workplace guided by spiritual values.

Entrepreneurship

In the tenth chapter, you will better understand the different types of spiritual entrepreneurs and their conflicting personal beliefs. Contesting ideologies, defined in this study as personal cognitive logic that prioritizes individual egoistic interests over spiritual thinking, can significantly impact entrepreneurs' values and mindsets. Through examining the context of entrepreneurial reasoning, this study contributes to our understanding of how entrepreneurship is affected by spirituality and the values associated with it.

Finally, this book includes a practical eleventh chapter on spiritual entrepreneurship and creating an app that facilitates the practice and transmission of spiritual knowledge. This narrative unfolds the captivating yarn of three devoted individuals who have dedicated their lives to the pursuit of self-awareness and spiritual elevation. United by the synchronicity of time and space, their initial intention was to engage in reflective discourse centered around the transformative teachings of A Course in Miracles. It serves as a gateway, effortlessly bestowing upon seekers a comfortable and seamless avenue through which they may practice the profound teachings of the Course while also facilitating the transmission of spiritual wisdom. What was once perceived as a mere tool to undertake external endeavors, such as developing a mobile application, has become an instrument for enhancing the inward journey and collective growth through shared experiences.

I Unlocking Spirituality in Knowledge Dynamics

Constantin Bratianu

Chapter 1
How the Theory of Knowledge Fields and Knowledge Dynamics is Shaping Spiritual Knowledge and Wisdom

Abstract: This chapter explores the connections between the theory of knowledge fields, knowledge dynamics, and spiritual knowledge and wisdom within organizational contexts. The chapter presents the main ideas of the theory of knowledge fields and its new attributes in understanding organizational knowledge dynamics. The new paradigm is based on three assumptions: a) knowledge is a field; b) there are three fundamental knowledge fields: rational, emotional, and spiritual; and c) each form of knowledge can be transformed into another form. The theory of knowledge dynamics develops the third axiom based on thermodynamics principles and cognitive science findings. Both theories evidence the role of spiritual knowledge and its contribution to managerial decision-making and understanding wisdom.

Keywords: Knowledge Fields, Knowledge Dynamics, Spirituality, Wisdom, Wise Company

Introduction

Knowledge dynamics, including organizational spirituality, are essential to any corporate knowledge spectrum. Dynamics means variation in time and space, and knowledge dynamics metaphorically reflects that variation (Bratianu, 2021). In the extant literature, authors from different educational backgrounds and cultures interpret knowledge dynamics in many ways due to their metaphorical thinking (Andriessen, 2006, 2008; Lakoff & Johnson, 1999; Pinker, 2008). Knowledge dynamics can be seen as a process of knowledge variation in time for the same knowledge owners (Kianto et al., 2017), as a knowledge variation in space, considered as a knowledge flow (Nissen, 2006), as a transformation of tacit knowledge into explicit knowledge and vice versa (Nonaka & Takeuchi, 1995, 2019; Nonaka et al., 2008), and as a transformation of knowledge fields – rational, emotional, and spiritual knowledge (Bratianu, 2015).

In describing tacit knowledge, Nonaka and Takeuchi (1995) refer to its constituents. However, in doing so, they do not really explain their role or importance in knowledge

Constantin Bratianu, Bucharest University of Economic Studies, Bucharest, Romania,
e-mail: constantin.bratianu@gmail.com

https://doi.org/10.1515/9783111010410-002

dynamics adequately and deeply. In their view, "tacit knowledge is deeply rooted in an individual's action and experience, as well as in the ideals, values, or emotions he or she embraces" (Nonaka & Takeuchi, 1995, p. 8). That is because they used the iceberg as a metaphor, where we can quickly identify only two components: the visible part above the waterline associated with explicit knowledge and the hidden part under the waterline associated with tacit knowledge. Thus, tacit knowledge looks like a massive block of invisible ice to us without further description. Only by changing the knowledge metaphor Bratianu (2015) could reveal spiritual knowledge and its role in knowledge dynamics. Moreover, by developing the theory of knowledge fields and dynamics, he could show the power of knowledge dynamics in driving the managerial decision-making process and emerging organizational knowledge and spirituality.

This chapter aims to show the new horizon created by the theory of knowledge fields in understanding organizational knowledge and how spiritual knowledge and wisdom contribute to emerging organizational spirituality. The whole process is very complex, and its nonlinearity makes it challenging to describe it in linear logic, but we will try to reveal the critical aspects of that complexity. There is a spiritual dimension in any managerial process and an organizational spirituality that leads the organization toward performance or failure due to how the leaders' mindset is based on positive or negative values (Bratianu, 2015). As De Geus (1999) remarks, "Now we enter a third level: the level of *values and beliefs*. We do not need a crisis to reach this level; we can also get there through sustained reflection. However, once here, all our principles and attitudes are open to question in light of the values and attitudes of our environment" (p. 113).

The Theory of Knowledge Fields

Cognitive science demonstrated that our mind is integrated with our body (Varela et al., 1993), that thoughts are primarily unconscious, and that "abstract concepts are largely metaphorical" (Lakoff & Johnson, 1999, p. 3). We use metaphors to find meanings for abstract concepts and to construct their semantic domain. A good example is the concept of *knowledge*. "Knowledge is not a concept that has a delineated structure. Whatever structure it has, it gets through metaphor. Different people from different cultures use different metaphors to conceptualize knowledge. They may be using the same word; however, it can refer to totally different understandings of the concept of knowledge" (Andriessen & Boom, 2007, p. 3). No wonder in knowledge management, different authors formulated different definitions for knowledge due to using different metaphors. Bratianu (2015) extensively analyzed those metaphors and found three significant clusters. Each cluster generated a specific cluster of metaphors used to describe knowledge dynamics (Bratianu, 2021; Bratianu & Paiuc, 2022). We will explain all of these semantic clusters in the present chapter.

A metaphor is a structured analogy (Gentner et al., 2001) composed of three main elements: a source domain where we put the well-known concept, a target domain where we put the less-known concept, and a mapping function that transfers some attributes from the source domain into the target domain (Andriessen, 2008; Bratianu, 2011; Lakoff & Johnson, 1980).

In the first semantic cluster, knowledge metaphors are used in the source domain of physical objects. They are called ontological metaphors. The following are some examples used currently in the literature (italics added to underline the attributes mapped from the physical objects to knowledge).

(1) "The idea of dealing with *knowledge as an object* has been already exploited in a variety of areas across knowledge management and information technology" (Borgo & Pozza, 2012, p. 229).
(2) "The hope is that we will be able to *accumulate masses of knowledge*, control the flow of information, and access answers as quickly as we formulate questions" (Allee, 1997, p. 15).
(3) "Just as food and manufactured goods can be packaged and sold, there are ways *to package knowledge* for commercial benefit, using the intellectual property laws" (Sullivan, 1998, p. 143).

In example (1), the authors remark that *knowledge as an object* metaphor has been used extensively in the first wave of knowledge management. In example (2), the author shows how the metaphor transfers two material attributes of physical objects toward the concept of knowledge: the property of accumulation and that of having a mass. However, knowledge is an intangible entity and does not have any mass. Thus, the metaphor creates ambiguity concerning the real attributes of the concept of knowledge. In example (3), the author shows that the metaphor transfers the property of packaging objects toward the concept of knowledge, although knowledge does not have a physical body to be packaged. The metaphor *knowledge as objects* has as the main drawback the mapping attributes of the tangible objects to intangible knowledge. Also, we use linear operations like summation and multiplication for tangible objects, while we should use nonlinear operations for intangible objects.

The metaphors from the second wave of knowledge management introduced the idea of dynamics. Knowledge is not static but dynamic. The metaphors *knowledge as a flow* and knowledge as *stocks-and-flows* introduce the time dimension and dynamics attribute (Bratianu, 2011; Nissen, 2006; Nonaka et al., 2008). The basic idea is that knowledge is compared now with a fluid that is flowing through the channels and piping systems and can be accumulated in reservoirs. The concept of flow is simple and intuitive, inspiring many scientific metaphors. Nissen (2006) remarks that knowledge is not distributed uniformly through an organization, and thus, it must move from where it is created or stocked to where it is needed. "To the extent that organizational knowledge does not exist in the form needed for application or at the place and time required to enable work performance, then it must flow from how it exists and where it is located to how and where it is needed. This is the concept *knowledge flows*" (p. XX). The following are only some illustrative examples of using the knowledge flow metaphor (italics added).

(1) For this *free flow of knowledge* to prevail, the organizational culture must be extraordinary (Davenport & Prusak, 2000, p. 109).
(2) How *knowledge flows* in organizations is often a hidden process (O'Dell & Hubert, 2011, p. 29).
(3) With my broader view, I claim that managing *knowledge flows* can be applied and used in almost any type of organization (Leistner, 2010, p. 6).

In example (1), the authors recognize that in any organization, there is a free motion of knowledge from one place to another, like the free water flows in rivers. In example (2), the authors remark that knowledge flow is mostly a hidden process because the forces generating that flow are unknown. Thus, controlling the knowledge dynamics is a real issue for knowledge managers. In example (3), the author claims that managing knowledge flows is at the core of any managerial process. The *knowledge flow* metaphor introduces the idea of dynamics, but it keeps the limits imposed by tangibility and linearity. To illustrate the errors generated by these limitations, we present one of the most cited definitions for intellectual capital, which is constituted primarily of knowledge: "Intellectual capital is the *sum* of everything everybody in a company knows that gives it a competitive advantage ... Intellectual capital is intellectual material – knowledge, information, intellectual property, experience – that can be put to use to create wealth" (Stewart, 1999, p. XI). Dumay reformulates this definition, changing the concept of "wealth" with that of "value", but keeping the idea of that intellectual capital is "the *sum* of everything everybody in a company knows that gives a competitive advantage" (Dumay, 2016, p. 169). The fundamental concept of this definition is *the sum*, which emphasizes the property of linearity for intellectual capital, respectively, for knowledge. In Mathematics, the concept of *sum* and the operation of *summation* belong to the complex concept of *linear space*. However, knowledge is a nonlinear entity, and it should be defined using the concept of *integration* instead of *summation* (Bratianu, 2009, 2018).

The third wave of metaphors should overcome these limitations of tangibility and linearity, which generate semantic errors in interpreting and applying the concept of knowledge and all related concepts, like knowledge dynamics and intellectual capital. One of the best-constructed and explored metaphors to overcome these shortcomings is that of *knowledge as energy* (Bratianu, 2011, 2015). The concept of *energy* differs from physical objects because it is a field, an intangible and a non-substantial manifestation of matter. The metaphor's mapping function transfers three essential attributes of energy:

(1) Energy is a field → Knowledge is a field.
(2) Energy manifests in different forms, like mechanical, thermal, and electrical energy → Knowledge manifests in different forms, like rational, emotional, and spiritual knowledge.

(3) One form of energy can be transformed into any other form of energy (for example, mechanical energy can be transformed into thermal energy) → One form of knowledge can be transformed into another form of knowledge (for example, rational knowledge can be transformed into emotional knowledge).

These attributes change entirely our understanding of the concept of *knowledge* and open new horizons for research and practice in knowledge management. They are based on the Thermodynamics approach and cognitive science discoveries (Atkins, 2010; Chaldize, 2000; Damasio, 1999, 2012; Friedenberg & Silverman, 2016; Kahneman, 2011). Thermodynamics was created to explain and quantify the transformation of mechanical energy into thermal energy. Then, thermodynamics became a general science of changing phenomena due to its power to explain the transformation of any form of energy and use entropy to measure processes' irreversibility and the order of structural systems.

The Rational Knowledge Field

Rational knowledge results from rational thinking and using natural or symbolic language. Explicit knowledge can express rational knowledge (Davenport & Prusak, 2000; Nonaka & Takeuchi, 1995). Rational knowledge is objective, which is why it is used in science, technology, economics, business, education, and nearly all aspects of our lives. That explains the perception that rational knowledge is the only form of knowledge we deal with. Philosophers from ancient times sought *truth* and its justification. They ignore perceptions and emotions because they are subjective and cannot lead to finding the truth. For instance, explaining the view of Plato on knowledge, Russell (1972) remarks that "we cannot know things through the senses alone, since through the senses alone we cannot know that things exist. Therefore, knowledge consists of reflection, not impression, and perception is not knowledge" (p. 153). A good example is a mathematical equation resulting from a logical mind, not a given perception. In epistemology, knowledge is considered a valid and justified belief. Justification is the necessary condition for a belief to be considered knowledge. Audi (2011) asserts that "knowledge is at least justified true belief – that we know something only if we believe it, it is true, and our belief of it is justified" (p. 247). Descartes expressed metaphorically that idea with his famous expression "Cogito, ergo sum" and concluded that we should make a difference between mind and body (Russell, 1972, p. xx).

The Japanese philosophers opposed the Cartesian dualism of mind and body with the idea of the oneness of mind and body, the oneness of self and other people, and the oneness of people and nature. As Nonaka and Takeuchi (1995) remark, "The Japanese had failed to build up a rational thought of clear universality because they did not succeed in the separation and objectification of self and nature" (p. 28). It is interesting to learn that Japanese people understand time differently. While in the Western world, the social time measured by the clock is linear and goes along a straight line, in Japan, time is nonlinear and goes in circles such that there is no clear hierarchy between past, present, and future. Even their language does not contain specific forms of verbs for the future. The context suggests that the action will take place in the future. That explains why the context Ba plays a central role in understanding the knowledge spiral in the famous model SECI (Socialization, Externalization, Combination, and Internalization) created by Nonaka (1994). Instead of dividing reality continually into its components and then analyzing their attributes and interdependencies, like in the Western tradition, the Japanese philosophy of oneness keeps the world as a whole and tries to reveal the connections that create harmony and organic functionality (Holden & Glisby, 2010; Kaufman, 1994; Nakagawara, 2004). This philosophy integrates *objective knowledge*, represented by rational knowledge, with *subjective knowledge* created by direct experience, represented by tacit knowledge.

Rational knowledge fuels the decision-making process, at least in economics and business. However, our knowledge of the complexity of real life is limited due to the limitations of our thinking models and the available data and information we get from the external environment (Senge, 1999; Stacey et al., 2000). Also, the changing business environment generates uncertainty caused by the absence of knowledge (Spender, 2014). To integrate all these limitations into the rationality and rational decision-making theory, Simon (2000) introduces the concept of "bounded rationality". Thus, decision-makers should seek "good enough" solutions instead of the "best" solutions to their real problems.

The Emotional Knowledge Field

Polanyi introduces the concept of *the tacit dimension* of knowing, showing that the knowing process is much larger and more profound than that focused on explicit knowledge. "I shall reconsider human knowledge by starting from the fact that *we can know more than we can tell*. This fact seems obvious, but it is difficult to say exactly what it means. Take an example. We know a person's face and can recognize it among a thousand and a million. However, we usually cannot tell how we recognize a face we know. So, most of this knowledge cannot be put into words" (Polanyi, 1983, p. 4). Being so close to the Japanese philosophy, there is no wonder that Nonaka (1994) was attracted by the tacit dimension of knowing and developed the theory of tacit knowledge. The root of the word *tacit* comes from the Latin *tacere*, which means to be silent or unspoken (Holden & Glisby, 2010). For Nonaka and Takeuchi (1995), "Tacit knowledge is highly personal and hard to formalize, making it difficult to communicate or to share with others. Subjective insights, intuitions, and hunches fall into this category of knowledge. Furthermore, tacit knowledge is deeply rooted in an individual's action and experience and in the ideals, values, or emotions he or she embraces" (p. 8).

Emotions contribute to the creation of tacit knowledge. However, putting together so many forms of knowledge, it is tough to distinguish their contribution from that of values, insights, hunches and ideals. Changing the iceberg paradigm with that of energy in explaining metaphorically knowledge, we get the opportunity to focus only on emotional knowledge and its impact on decision-making and organizational behavior.

Emotions and feelings generate emotional knowledge, and it is wordless (Damasio, 1999, 2012; Hill, 2008). Emotional knowledge is expressed by body language and facial expressivity. Emotions are reactions of the human body to internal and external stimuli. "The world of emotions is largely one of actions carried out in our bodies, from facial expressions and postures to changes in viscera and internal milieu" (Damasio, 2012, p. 117). Emotional knowledge contributes to the decision-making process with rational and spiritual knowledge and becomes critical in situations of possible danger. A fast body reaction is necessary for protection and survival (Kahneman, 2011).

Emotional knowledge is the raw material for *emotional intelligence* (Goleman, 1995; Mayer et al., 2004) that integrates intrapersonal and interpersonal intelligence (Gardner, 1983). Emotional knowledge and emotional intelligence are critical elements in creating a sustainable system of motivation for employees. Motivation is the main driving force in achieving organizational performance and competitive advantage. Also, motivation is the engine of any knowledge-sharing and innovation processes. Emotional knowledge and emotional intelligence are essential in leading change due to resistance opposed by inertial forces. Organizational change requires a great effort to mobilize people to work hard against all odds and reward those efforts. Even if change design is based mainly on rational knowledge, its realization depends on emotional knowledge and people's motivation (Kotter, 1996; Kotter & Cohen, 2002).

The Spiritual Knowledge Field

If rational knowledge reflects the physical world we live in, and emotional knowledge reflects the emotional states of our body, spiritual knowledge integrates human beings' existential meanings and values. As Maxwell (2007) remarks, "We have to learn to see aspects of the world around us: stones, people, trees, sky. Equally, we must learn to see meanings and value in the world around us, our environment, events, human actions and lives" (p. 274). Seeing and understanding those meanings and values is difficult, but we learn to identify them and use them in all our decisions. Values represent condensed forms of knowledge based on continuous integration of what we learn from our parents in childhood and our professors in schools with what we learn directly from our experience. We learn to distinguish good from bad, right from wrong, responsible from irresponsible and take actions driven by those values and principles reflecting the social web's harmony. Values and ethical principles are the guidelines of any decision-making process in our private or professional life.

With the emergence of the knowledge economy, knowledge workers need to believe in what they are doing, striving for self-actualization. They are driven by the willingness to create knowledge, new products and services, or to innovate in their working procedures. They are looking beyond a simple financial reward for their work. "Knowledge workers cannot be satisfied with work that is only a livelihood. Their aspiration and view of themselves are those of the 'professional' or 'intellectual'. If they respect knowledge, they demand that it becomes the base for accomplishment" (Drucker, 2008, p. 289). Reading this text carefully, we learn a fascinating fact: spiritual knowledge integrates time and the idea of the future. To accomplish something in personal or professional life, one needs to look beyond the present time and define an object to be done. That means vision and strategic thinking. Also, that means dynamics and evolution and a driving purpose. "We know today that human beings are by definition primarily a creature of meaning and value (that is, of 'self-actualization'). We need a sense of meaning and driving purpose in our lives" (Zohar & Marshall, 2004, p. 17).

It is interesting to think metaphorically at the complexity of the micro-world where we find *matter* and *anti-matter*, or *particles* and *anti-particles*. Let us consider two microscopic objects with identical attributes with only one exception. They have opposite values (i.e., plus, minus) for that attribute. For example, an electron and a positron have identical attributes except for the electric charge. The positron has +1 and the electron −1. Because of this characteristic, electrons and positrons will move in opposite directions when put into an electric field. If we consider the positron to represent the matter, the electron will represent the anti-matter. Using metaphorical thinking, we map this feature of opposing attributes to the value system. That means distinguishing between *values* (positive semantic charge) and anti-values (negative semantic charge). We will consider good and right values (with a positive semantic charge) and bad and wrong anti-values (having a negative semantic charge). Then, we will discover that managers who base their decisions on values can contribute to their organization's performance. That is what we call *management*. The organization is doomed to failure when the decisions are based on anti-values. That is *anti-management*. We should understand that anti-management is not bad management, but management focuses on other interests than the organization's. Usually, in this case, the decision-makers focus on their private interests, regardless of the company's decline. Thus, the real difference between performance and failure is not the intelligence of managers but their set of values or anti-values. In other words, the difference is made by their spiritual knowledge and spiritual intelligence (Bratianu, 2015).

In the literature, researchers introduced the concept of Corporate Social Responsibility (CSR) to stress the need for managers to use the positive values of spirituality in making decisions, especially concerning the impact of the business on the natural environment (Basu & Palazzo, 2008; Porter & Kramer, 2011). "The focus on profit being king has caused significant negative, unintended consequences. For over a century and a half, cheap labor, damaged lives, a destroyed planet, and polluted seas were all irrelevant when set against the need for profit. However, this is changing" (Branson, 2011, p. 21).

Lange and Washburn (2012) show that instead of discussing Corporate Social Responsibility, authors should discuss Corporate Social Irresponsibility (CSI), a phenomenon developed on anti-values and negative spirituality. The most known story of CSI is that of Enron, one of the world's largest companies, that filed for bankruptcy in December 2001 (Benston & Hartgraves, 2002; Chatterjee, 2003; Lev, 2002).

Spiritual knowledge is processed by *spiritual intelligence (SQ)*. According to Zohar and Marshall (2004), "This is the intelligence with which we have access to deep meaning, fundamental values, and a sense of abiding purpose in our lives, and the role that this meaning, values, and purpose play in our lives, strategies, and thinking processes" (Zohar & Marshall, 2004, p. 64). Spiritual intelligence defines the same concept that Garner (1983) introduced as existential intelligence in his multiple intelligence model. Spiritual intelligence impacts the value system at individual and organizational levels (Zohar & Marshall, 2000). It is a powerful force capable of acting on a large time scale and of organizational changes when needed. It is a transformative force characterizing transformational leaders (Bass & Riggio, 2006). An excellent example of the transformational leadership of Samsung is based on a new set of values and vision (Song & Lee, 2014). Transformational leaders are also spiritual leaders because they can understand organizational processes' complexity and employees' motivational systems. Leaders cannot accomplish outstanding results without well-defined values and a powerful vision. Spiritual intelligence is an attribute of strategic thinking and visionary leadership (Kotter, 1996; Reeve, 2005; Warren, 2008).

The Theory of Knowledge Dynamics

Knowledge dynamics can be defined in simple terms as being a variation of knowledge in time, a variation of knowledge in space, or a transformation of knowledge from one form into another one (Bratianu & Bejinaru, 2020; Bratianu & Paiuc, 2022). The variety of metaphors used in explaining the concept of knowledge inevitably leads to various interpretations of knowledge dynamics. That situation generates a series of difficulties in knowledge management when applying them to practice. The solution is to reduce the variety of interpretations by creating some semantic clusters based on scientific principles and then analyzing the core meaning of each cluster. Also, we are interested in discovering where and how the dynamics of spiritual knowledge come into play and impact managerial decision-making.

Based on a systematic literature review concerning the knowledge metaphors we presented in the first part of this chapter, we concluded that all metaphors used could be grouped into three semantic clusters: a) knowledge as objects or stocks, b) knowledge as flows, and knowledge as stocks-and-flows; and c) knowledge as energy. Each semantic cluster for *knowledge* creates a semantic cluster for *knowledge dynamics*, as illustrated in Figure 1.1.

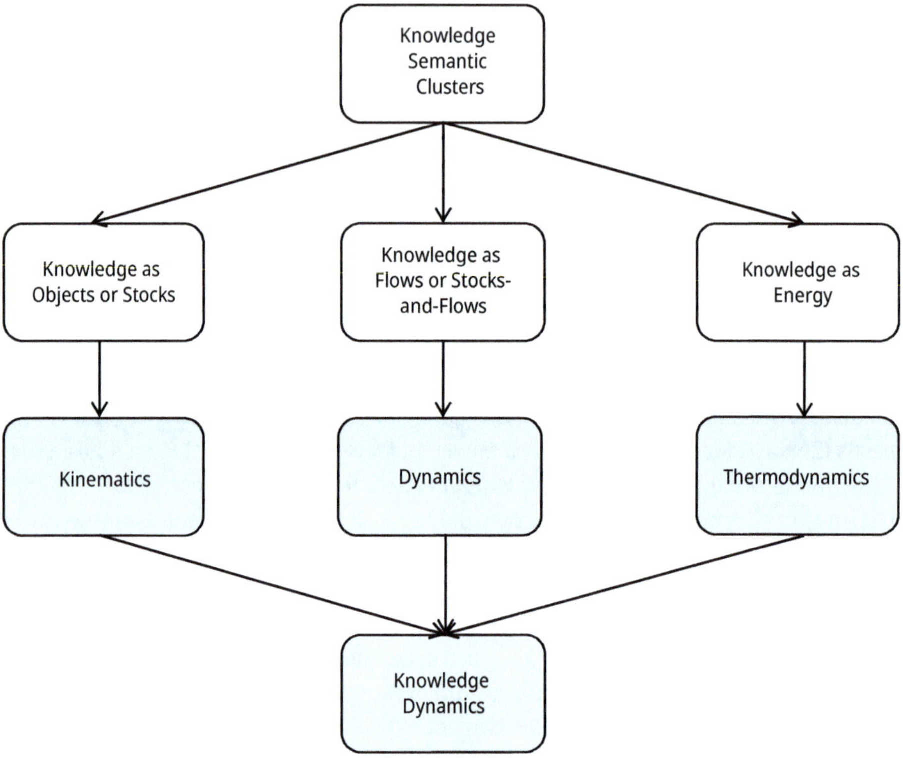

Figure 1.1: Semantic clusters for knowledge dynamics.
Source: Author

Kinematics

Kinematics is a part of Newtonian physics concerned with the motion of objects in space without explaining the forces that generate that motion. Also, we may include here the variation in the time of a particular object. Translating the idea of space motion to knowledge management, we can identify a variation in the space of tacit knowledge due to the motion of individuals through the company space. When walking from one place to another, individuals carry with them their knowledge. It is a Newtonian dynamics of knowledge. When we translate the time variation idea to knowledge management, we consider the knowledge quantity variation in time through accumulation and loss. The quantity of knowledge may increase through learning or decrease due to unlearning, forgetting, or loss (Cegarra-Navarro & Wensley, 2019; Kaiser et al., 2016; Kolb, 2015). However, we remark again that knowledge is nonlinear, and its variation in time should not be a result of summation or subtraction. Knowledge variation is a result of integration and disintegration. Within an organizational context, knowledge results from individuals' interactions and organizational learning (Argote, 2013; Kianto, 2007; Kianto et al., 2017). Also, kinematics reflects the distribution of organizational knowledge and its variation in time, leading to an increase in knowledge entropy (Bratianu, 2019). Managing knowledge entropy becomes important in knowledge creation and innovation.

Dynamics

Dynamics is that part of Newtonian physics concerned with the motion of objects in space and time and the forces that generate that motion. This cluster contains the most significant number of examples of knowledge dynamics. *Knowledge flow* is such an intuitive metaphor that it became almost natural for authors to use it (Leistner,2010; Nissen, 2006; Nonaka et al., 2008). The knowledge flows can be intra-organizational or inter-organizational (Ali et al., 2019; Balle et al., 2019; Keszey, 2018). However, unlike in physics or fluid mechanics, in knowledge management, authors ignore the forces that generate knowledge flow and cannot explain the complexity of knowledge dynamics. For instance, nobody discusses the deficit of knowledge as a driving force or the requested absorptive capacity of the end user of knowledge. Also, there are a series of barriers and perturbations during the flow of knowledge, which are rarely addressed in knowledge dynamics research. The metaphor knowledge flows refers to the explicit or rational knowledge. The knowledge can be transferred from one individual to another or a group using a natural or symbolic language. Thus, spiritual knowledge does not appear in this cluster of knowledge dynamics.

Knowledge flows can be extended from the organizational context to a network structure, where individuals, groups or organizations can represent the nodes. Links between nodes are created when there is a knowledge flow between two nodes (Bedford & Sanchez, 2021). The flow of knowledge is generated by the deficit of knowledge between two adjacent nodes, and it is oriented in the opposite direction of the gradient of that deficit. It is similar to nature when water flows in the opposite direction of the gravity gradient. Researchers use the metaphor stocks-and-flows used for any network process to analyze knowledge dynamics within a network. Knowledge dynamics is changing the distribution of knowledge in nodes and the knowledge entropy of the whole network. The variation of knowledge in nodes requires a continuous re-structuring of the knowledge stock and a process of integrating the new knowledge into the existing one. The knowledge integration process at the node and organization levels is vital to creating the new business model. "The knowledge integration process arising from the formation of business networks, including these cross-industry networks, becomes an important element in the building of horizontal value chains aimed at creating new business models" (Kodama, 2011, p. 25). Knowledge dynamics based on the knowledge flow metaphor are essential and will remain in many research projects. However, it is necessary to reveal the forces that generate knowledge flows intra-organizational and inter-organizational, as well as the changes produced by those flows in organizational knowledge entropy.

Schiuma (2009) attempted to enlarge the semantic spectrum of knowledge by introducing the concept of *knowledge assets* and replacing the concept of knowledge dynamics with that of *knowledge asset dynamics*. It is a method to bridge the intangibility of knowledge with the tangibility of physical objects, which are somehow carriers of knowledge and can be better evaluated in companies' accounting balance sheets. However, there is no clear definition of knowledge assets, no clear differentiation between knowledge and knowledge assets, and between knowledge dynamics and knowledge assets dynamics.

Thermodynamics

Thermodynamics is a science that studies the transformation of one form of energy into another form. It was born in the 19th century when researchers could not explain the transformation of mechanical energy into thermal energy by using Newton's laws of dynamics. Clausius introduced in 1865 the concept of *entropy* as a measure of the irreversibility of the transformation of mechanical energy into thermal energy, and Boltzmann developed in 1870 a statistical formula for computing entropy (Atkins, 2010; Ben-Naim, 2012; Georgescu-Roegen, 1999). Using mechanical statistics, Boltzmann demonstrated that "entropy is a measure of disorder in the system, that a multi-particle system tends to develop to a more probable state, and such a more probable state is a state of higher disorder. This development (toward disorder) continues until a system reaches thermodynamic equilibrium, which is the highest state of disorder for any given system" (Chaldize, 2000, p. 11).

Due to its powerful capacity to express a transformation process and its association with order and disorder in a generic system, the concept of entropy extended rapidly to other domains, enriching its semantic spectrum (Ben-Naim, 2012; Chaldize, 2000). Shannon (1948) used the concept of entropy in his communication theory, defining the concept of *information entropy* with the same mathematical formulation as Boltzmann's. The new concept reflects the distribution of probabilities associated with the information transferred through a communication channel. Bratianu (2019) defines the concept of *knowledge entropy*, showing its utility in measuring the knowledge distribution through the whole organization at a given moment. The purpose of this chapter is not to focus on knowledge distribution and entropy but to have them in mind when discussing spiritual knowledge and knowledge dynamics within an organizational context.

The first attempt to consider knowledge transformation as a manifestation of knowledge dynamics was made by Nonaka (1994) with his dynamic theory of organizational knowledge creation. He was inspired by the works of Ryle (1949) and Polanyi (1983) and based on a solid understanding of Japanese business and culture. The model was further developed and refined by Nonaka and Takeuchi (1995), Nonaka et al. (2008), and Nonaka and Takeuchi (2019). Ryle (1949) explained the difference between *knowing that* and *knowing how*. The result of *knowing that* is knowledge about our reality, the environment, and its concrete objects. The result of *knowing how* valuable knowledge is in performing a specific task. It is one thing to know the recipe for a cheesecake and another to know how to prepare and cook it. Polanyi (1983) introduced the *tacit dimension* of knowing, showing the importance of the knowledge obtained due to direct experience. Nonaka (1994) considered the result of the *tacit dimension of knowing* and called it *tacit knowledge*. Thus, Nonaka (1994) created the paradigm of *tacit knowledge – explicit knowledge* that most researchers shortly adopted. The dynamic theory of organizational knowledge creation transforms tacit knowledge into explicit knowledge, amplifies explicit knowledge through combination within a social context, and transforms the new knowledge into tacit knowledge. This idea is in line with the definition of learning provided by Kolb (2015): "Learning is the process whereby knowledge is created through the transformation of experience" (p. 49).

Nonaka (1994) developed the SECI (Socialization, Externalization, Combination, Internalization) model that explains knowledge creation within an organizational framework. Recently, the model was upgraded to include time as an explicit dimension of knowledge creation (Nonaka & Takeuchi, 2019). *Socialization* is the process of tacit knowledge transfer within a social context, like a project team. Because it is wordless, tacit knowledge can be transferred through observation and imitation. Many authors do not understand the specific meaning given by Nonaka (1994) to socialization and create confusion discussing tacit knowledge transfer by using language and information technologies that use explicit knowledge. *Externalization* is the process of transformation of tacit knowledge into explicit knowledge at the individual level. It is the stage when language comes into play and transforms the learned experience into thoughts that can be expressed verbally. *Combination* is the process of communicating ideas within a social context and developing them through discussions and argumentations. The combination is based on knowledge sharing and depends on the specific organizational culture. Some cultures encourage knowledge-sharing and combination processes; some other cultures may not. *Internalization* is the process of transformation of the new explicit knowledge into tacit knowledge at the individual level. That new tacit knowledge will help to change the individual's behavior. The SECI cycle repeats itself, generating a knowledge spiral that increases over time (Nonaka & Takeuchi, 2019).

Analyzing the SECI model from our perspective, we may say that only two processes (i.e., externalization and internalization) refer to knowledge transformation. In contrast, the other two refer only to knowledge transfer. Even so, it is a transformation between tacit and explicit knowledge such that spiritual knowledge does not appear in that model.

In the knowledge dynamics theory developed by Bratianu (2011, 2015) and refined by Bratianu and Bejinaru (2019, 2020), spiritual knowledge appears in a well-defined field of knowledge and participates directly in knowledge dynamics. Also, by integrating individual spiritual knowledge at the level of a team and then of the whole organization, we get its impact on organizational culture and organizational spirituality (Schein, 2004; Rocha & Pinheiro, 2019, 2021; Yochanan et al., 2022). From a thermodynamics approach, we consider that each form of knowledge (i.e., rational, emotional, and spiritual) can be continuously transformed into another form of knowledge. Managerial decision-making is an excellent example of knowledge dynamics where spiritual knowledge influences the outcome of any decision through values. Thus, decision-making is not based entirely on rational knowledge, but its outcome depends on the transformations between the rational, emotional, and spiritual knowledge fields (Bratianu et al., 2021).

A beautiful psychological experiment described by Kahneman (2011) demonstrates the role of knowledge dynamics based on knowledge fields in decision-making. It was already a tradition in a British university to have a tearoom where students could prepare tea or coffee and buy snacks. There was an "honesty box" where students put their money according to their consumption and price list on the wall. For ten weeks, just above the "honesty box", there were two types of posters without any explanations. One type contained pictures with human eyes looking straight at you, and the other contained flowers. Each type of poster was there for one week. By the end of each day, the researcher who designed the experiment counted the money in the "honesty box". Finally, he made a graph with the sum of money found in the box. The findings showed that each week when the poster contained pictures with human eyes, the sums of money put in by students were significantly higher than when there was a poster with flowers. The psychological processes clearly show the following knowledge transformations: looking at those eyes directed at you creates an emotional state, like being watched by a particular person and how you pay for the consumption. Thus, the direct experience created emotional knowledge that instantaneously transformed into spiritual knowledge – the value system associated with ethical behavior. The result transformed immediately into rational knowledge that led to the decision to pay correctly for consumption. When there was a poster with flowers, there was no connection to ethical behavior, and many students paid less than the value of the purchased items. Thus, knowledge dynamics based on the theory of knowledge fields can explain these knowledge transformations and the dominant role of spiritual knowledge in making decisions.

Wisdom

Wisdom is hard to define and explain because it has dynamic and complex semantics. However, we can find a core of meanings that gave it stability. The *Oxford Advanced Learner's Dictionary* defines wisdom as "the ability to make sensible decisions and give good advice because of the experience and knowledge you have". Thus, wisdom is the competence to make sound judgments based on knowledge, skills, attitudes, and long-term thinking. Rational knowledge is essential in dealing with incomplete knowledge. Emotional knowledge is vital in dealing with uncertainty. Spiritual knowledge is essential in setting critical values in decision-making (Hall, 2010; Maxwell, 2007). The leaders with that competence are called wise leaders, and their companies become wise

(Nonaka & Takeuchi, 2019). "Wisdom includes knowledge and understanding but goes beyond them in also including the desire and active striving for what is of value, the ability to see what is of value, actually and potentially, in the circumstances of life, the ability to experience value, the capacity to help realize what is of value for oneself and others, the capacity to help solve those problems of living that arise in connection with attempts to realize what is of value, the capacity to use and develop knowledge, technology and understanding as needed for realization of value" (Maxwell, 2007, p. 79).

Aristotle (1999) structured his spectrum of knowledge into three large categories: *episteme*, *techne*, and *phronesis*. *Episteme* refers to objective or scientific knowledge. *Techne* refers to the practical knowledge needed to perform a specific task. It is craft knowledge. *Phronesis*, prudence, or practical wisdom, goes beyond knowledge and integrates judgment based on values (i.e., good or bad). "Prudence is a state grasping the truth, involving reason, concerned with action about things that are good or bad for human beings" (Aristotle, 1999, p. 89). *Phronesis* is a critical competence for a company to become wise (Nonaka & Takeuchi, 2019). Reading carefully the definition given by Aristotle, we can identify immediately the presence of all knowledge fields and the dynamics between them directed toward decisions with consequences on the well-being of people.

From a practical perspective, wisdom represents a key ingredient in creating and managing wise companies (Nonaka & Takeuchi, 2019). However, there are many differences in interpreting this concept in knowledge management due to the different cultures, education, and management backgrounds of authors and their understanding of the complexity of knowledge fields and knowledge dynamics (Rocha & Pinheiro, 2019, 2021; Pinheiro & Rocha, 2020). It is essential to understand that wisdom is a meta-concept or a higher-order concept because it integrates spiritual knowledge and decision-making. Decisions and their long-term consequences can make the difference between wise leaders and those interested in their short-term interests. As remarked by Rocha and d'Angelo (2023), "Leadership plays a prominent role in the expression of spirituality in the workplace because the leader is also the main actor in increasing spirituality in the corporate environment" (p. 4). Thus, wisdom should become a dominant topic of further research and corporate training programs for developing competencies and capabilities that integrate spiritual knowledge. It is not so easy to escape the gravitational forces of the profit maximization principle, but it is necessary to create new paradigms for understanding and measuring organizational performance.

Knowledge management should go beyond codification and exploitation of explicit knowledge and contribute to business strategies only with rational knowledge. It is needed to change the whole perspective of knowledge management so that it can explore and use more emotional knowledge, emotional intelligence, spiritual knowledge and spiritual intelligence. Achieving a sustainable advantage requires new thinking methods and designing business strategies incorporating knowledge. Knowledge management should change its focus from what is known to what is not and better manage the balance between known and unknown. That also implies strategic thinking and switching from deterministic to probabilistic thinking to deal with uncertainty and economic crises (Bratianu, 2022; Spender, 2014; Taleb, 2007, 2012).

Future research should focus more on spiritual knowledge, its dynamics and contribution to the creation of wise leaders and organizational spirituality, and on developing new metrics for organizational performance, including knowledge dynamics' contribution to achieving organizational well-being.

References

Ali, A.A., Panner Selvem, D.D.D., Paris, L. & Gunasekaram, A. (2019). Key factors influencing knowledge-sharing practices and its relationship with organizational performance within the oil and gas industry. *Journal of Knowledge Management, 23*(9), 1806–1837. https://doi.org/10.1108/JKM-06-2018-0394. https://www.emerald.com/insight/content/doi/10.1108/JKM-06-2018-0394/full/html

Allee, V. (1997). *The knowledge evolution: Expanding organizational intelligence*. Butterworth-Heinemann, Boston.

Andriessen, D. & Boom, M.d. (2007, May*). Asian and western intellectual capital in encounter*. Paper presented at IC-Congress 2007, Nholland University of Applied Sciences, Haarlem, The Netherlands.

Andriessen, D. (2006). On the metaphorical nature of intellectual capital: A textual analysis. *Journal of Intellectual Capital, 7*(1), 93–110. https://doi.org/10.1108/14691930610639796. https://www.emerald.com/insight/content/doi/10.1108/14691930610639796/full/html

Andriessen, D. (2008). Stuff or love? How metaphors direct our efforts to manage knowledge in organizations. *Knowledge Management Research and Practice, 6*(1), 5–12. https://doi.org/10.1057/palgrave.kmrp.8500169. https://www.tandfonline.com/doi/full/10.1057/palgrave.kmrp.8500169

Argote, L. (2013). *Organizational learning: Creating, retaining and transferring knowledge*. 2nd Edition. Springer, New York.

Aristotle (1999). *Nicomachean ethics*. 2nd Edition. Hackett Publishing Company, Indianapolis.

Atkins, P. (2010). *The laws of thermodynamics. A very short introduction*. Oxford University Press, Oxford.

Audi, R. (2011). *Epistemology: A contemporary introduction to the theory of knowledge*. 3rd Edition. Routledge, New York.

Balle, A.R., Steffan, M.O., Curado, C. & Oliveira, M. (2019). Inter-organizational knowledge sharing in a science and technology park: The use of knowledge sharing mechanisms. *Journal of Knowledge Management, 23*(10), 2016–2038. https://doi.org/10.1108/JKM-05-2018-0328. https://www.emerald.com/insight/content/doi/10.1108/JKM-05-2018-0328/full/html

Bass, B.M. & Riggio, R.E. (2006). *Transformational leadership*. 2nd Edition. Lawrence Erlbaum Associates, Publishers, London.

Basu, K. & Palazzo, G. (2008). Corporate social responsibility: A process model of sensemaking. *Academy of Management Review, 33*(1), 122–136. https://doi.org/10.5465/AMR.2008.27745504. https://journals.aom.org/doi/10.5465/amr.2008.27745504

Bedford, D. & Sanchez, T.W. (2021). *Working methods for knowledge management: Knowledge networks*. Emerald Publishing, Bingley.

Ben-Naim, A. (2012). *Entropy and the second law: Interpretations and misss-interpretationsss*. World Scientific, London.

Benston, G.J. & Hartgraves, A.L. (2002). Enron: What happened and what we can learn from it. *Journal of Accounting and Public Policy, 21*(2), 105–127. https://doi.org/10.101016/S0278-4254(02)00042. https://www.sciencedirect.com/journal/journal-of-accounting-and-public-policy/vol/21/issue/2
Borgo, S. & Pozza, G. (2012). Knowledge objects: A formal construct for material, information and role dependences. *Knowledge Management Research & Practice, 10*(3), 227–236. https://doi.org/10.1057/kmrp.2012.17. https://www.tandfonline.com/toc/tkmr20/10/3?nav=tocList
Branson, R. (2011). *Screw business as usual.* Virgin Books, London.
Bratianu, C. & Bejinaru, R. (2019). The theory of knowledge fields: A thermodynamics approach. *Systems, 7*(2), 20, 1–12. https://doi.org/103390/systems7020020. https://www.mdpi.com/2079-8954/7/2/20
Bratianu, C. & Bejinaru, R. (2020). Knowledge dynamics: A thermodynamics approach. *Kybernetes, 49*(1), 6–21. https://doi.org/10.1108/K-02-2019-0122. https://www.emerald.com/insight/content/doi/10.1108/K-02-2019-0122/full/html
Bratianu, C. & Paiuc, D. (2022). A bibliometric analysis of knowledge dynamics in managerial decision making. *Knowledge, 2,* 702–718. https://doi.org/103390/knowledge2040040. https://www.mdpi.com/2673-9585/2/4/40
Bratianu, C. (2009). The frontier of linearity in the intellectual capital metaphor. *Electronic Journal of Knowledge Management, 7*(4), 415–424. https://academic-publishing.org/index.php/ejkm/article/view/862
Bratianu, C. (2011). Changing paradigm for knowledge metaphors from dynamics to thermodynamics. *System Research and Behavioral Science, 28*(2), 160–169. http://doi.org/10.1002/sres.1080. https://onlinelibrary.wiley.com/doi/10.1002/sres.1080
Bratianu, C. (2015). *Organizational knowledge dynamics: Managing knowledge creation, acquisition, sharing, and transformation*. IGI Global, Hershey.
Bratianu, C. (2018). Intellectual capital research and practice: 7 myths and one golden rule. *Management & Marketing. Challenges for the Knowledge Society, 13*(2), 859–879. https://doi.org/10.2478/mmcks-2019-0010. https://sciendo.com/article/10.2478/mmcks-2018-0010
Bratianu, C. (2019). Exploring knowledge entropy in organizations. *Management Dynamics in the Knowledge Economy, 7*(3), 353–366. https://doi.org/10.25019/MDKE/7.3.05. https://www.managementdynamics.ro/index.php/journal/article/view/325/271
Bratianu, C. (2021). Knowledge dynamics: A semantic approach. In: Garcia-Perez, A. & Simkin, L. (Eds.). *Proceedings of the 22nd European Conference on Knowledge Management (ECKM).* A virtual conference hosted by Coventry University, UK, 2–3 September 2021, pp. 96–103. https://doi.org/10.34190/EKM.21.050
Bratianu, C. (2022). *Knowledge strategies*. Cambridge University Press, Cambridge.
Bratianu, C., Vatamanescu, E.M., Anagnoste, S. & Gandolfo, D. (2021). Untangling knowledge fields and knowledge dynamics within the decision-making process. *Management Decision, 59*(2), 306–323. https://doi.org/10.1108/MD-05-2019-0559. https://www.emerald.com/insight/content/doi/10.1108/MD-05-2019-0559/full/html
Cegarra-Navarro, J.G. & Wensley, A. (2019). Promoting intentional unlearning through an unlearning cycle. *Journal of Organizational Change Management, 32*, 67–79. https://doi.org/10.1108/JOCM-04-018-0107. https://www.emerald.com/insight/content/doi/10.1108/JOCM-04-2018-0107/full/html
Chaldize, V. (2000). *Entropy demystified: Potential order, life and money*. Universal Publishers, New York.
Chatterjee, S. (2003). Enron's incremental descent into bankruptcy: A strategy and organizational analysis. *Long Range Planning, 36*(2), 133–149. https://doi.org/10.1016/S0024-6301(03)00006-2. https://www.sciencedirect.com/science/article/abs/pii/S0024630103000062
Damasio, A. (1999). *The feeling of what happens: Body and emotion in the making of consciousness.* A Harvest Book Harcourt, New York.

Damasio, A. (2012). *Self comes to mind: Constructing the conscious brain*. Vintage Books, New York. Davenport, T.H. & Prusak, L. (2000). *Working knowledge: How organizations manage what they know*. Harvard Business School Press, Boston.
De Geus, A. (1999). *The living company: Growth, learning and longevity in business*. Nicholas Brealey Publishing, London.
Drucker, P.F. (2008). *The age of discontinuities: Guidelines to our changing society*. Transaction Publishers, London.
Dumay, J. (2016). A critical reflection on the future of intellectual capital: from reporting to disclosure. *Journal of Intellectual Capital*, *17*(1), 168–184. https://doi.org/10.1108/JIC-08-2015-0072. https://www.emerald.com/insight/content/doi/10.1108/JIC-08-2015-0072/full/html
Friedenberg, J. & Silverman, G. (2016). *Cognitive science: An introduction to the study of mind*. 3rd Edition. SAGE, Los Angeles.
Gardner, H. (1983). *Frames of the mind: The theory of multiple intelligences*. Basic Books, New York.
Gentner, D., Holyoak, K.J. & Kokinov, B.N. (2001) (Eds.). *The analogical mind: Perspectives from cognitive science*. The MIT Press, Cambridge, Massachusetts.
Georgescu-Roegen, N. (1999). *The entropy law and the economic process*. Harvard University Press, Cambridge, MA.
Goleman, D. (1995). *Emotional intelligence*. Bantam, New York. Hall, S.S. (2010). *Wisdom: From philosophy to neuroscience*. Alfred A. Knopf, New York.
Hill, D. (2008). *Emotionomics: Leveraging emotions for business success*. Revised Edition. Kogan Page, London.
Holden, N. & Glisby, M. (2010). *Creating knowledge advantage: The tacit dimensions of international competition and cooperation*. Copenhagen Business School Press, Copenhagen.
Kahneman, D. (2011). *Thinking, fast and slow*. Strauss, Giroux and Farrar, New York.
Kaiser, A., Kragulj, F., Grisold, T. & Walser, R. (2016). Learning from and envisioned future – An empirical account. *Electronic Journal of Knowledge Management*, *14*, 18–30. https://academic-publishing.org/index.php/ejkm/article/view/1067/1030
Kaufman, S.F. (1994). *The martial artist's book of five rings: The definitive interpretation of Myiamoto Musashi's classic book of strategy*. Tuttle Publishing, Boston.
Keszey, T. (2018). Boundary spanners knowledge sharing for innovation success in turbulent times. *Journal of Knowledge Management*, *22*(5), 1061–1081. https://doi.org/10.1108/JKM-01-2017-0033. https://www.emerald.com/insight/content/doi/10.1108/JKM-01-2017-0033/full/html
Kianto, A. (2007). What do we really mean by the dynamic dimension of intellectual capital? *International Journal of Learning and Intellectual Capital*, *4*(4), 342–356. https://doi.org/IJLIC.2007.016332. https://www.inderscience.com/info/inarticletoc.php?jcode=ijlic&year=2007&vol=4&issue=4
Kianto, A., Inkinen, H., Ritala, P. & Vanhala, M. (2017). A temporal perspective to the intellectual capital in Finnish firms from 2013 to 2017. In: Tsui, E. & Cheung, B. (Eds.). *Proceedings of the 14th ICIKM*, 7–8 December 2017, The Hong Kong Polytechnic University, pp. 134–138, Academic Conferences and Publishing International, Reading. www.academic-conferences.org
Kodama, M. (2011). *Knowledge integration dynamics: Developing strategic innovation capability*. World Scientific, Singapore.
Kolb, D.A. (2015). *Experiential learning: Experience as the source of learning and development*, 2nd Edition, Pearson Education, Upper Saddle River.
Kotter, J. & Cohen, D. (2002). *The heart of change: Real-life stories of how people change their organizations*. Harvard Business School Press, Boston.
Kotter, J. (1996). *Leading change*. Harvard Business School Press, Boston.
Lakoff, G. & Johnson, M. (1980). *Metaphors we live by*. The University of Chicago Press, Chicago.
Lakoff, G. & Johnson, M. (1999). *Philosophy in the flesh: The embodied mind and its challenge to the Western thought*. Basic Books, New York.

Lange, D. & Washburn, N.T. (2012). Understanding attributions of corporate social irresponsibility. *Academy of Management Review, 37*(2), 300–326. https://doi.org/10.5465/amr.2010.0522. https://journals.aom.org/doi/10.5465/amr.2010.0522

Leistner, F. (2010). *Mastering organizational knowledge flow: Building and sustaining the sources of innovation.* Harvard Business School Press, Boston.

Lev, B. (2002). Where have all of Enron's intangible gone? *Journal of Accounting and Public Policy, 21*(2), 131–135. https://doi.org/10.1016/S0278-4254(02)00042-1. https://www.sciencedirect.com/science/article/abs/pii/S0278425402000431

Maxwell, N. (2007). *From knowledge to wisdom: A revolution for science and humanities.* 2nd Edition. Pentire Press, London.

Mayer, J.D., Salovey, C.L. & Caruso, D.R. (2004). Emotional intelligence: Theory, findings, and implications. *Psychology Inquiry, 15*, 197–215.

Nakagawara, C. (2004). The Japanese garden for the mind: The 'bliss' of paradise transcend. *Stanford Journal of East Asian Affair, 49*(2), 83–103. http://www.asia-studies.com/SJEAA.html

Nissen, M.E. (2006). *Harnessing knowledge dynamics: Principled organizational knowing & learning*, IRM Press, Hershey.

Nonaka, I. (1994). A dynamic theory of organizational knowledge creation. *Organization Science, 5*(1), 14–37. https://doi.org/10.1287/orsc.5.1.14. https://pubsonline.informs.org/doi/abs/10.1287/orsc.5.1.14

Nonaka, I. & Takeuchi, H. (1995). *The knowledge creating company: How Japanese Companies create the dynamics of innovation.* Oxford University Press, Oxford.

Nonaka, I. & Takeuchi, H. (2019). *The wise company: How companies create continuous innovation.* Oxford University Press, Oxford.

Nonaka, I., Toyama, R. & Hirotaka, T. (2008). *Managing flow: A process theory of the knowledge-based firm.* Palgrave Macmillan, New York.

O'Dell, C. & Hubert, C. (2011). *The new edge in knowledge: How knowledge management is changing the way we do business.* John Wiley & Sons, New York.

Pinheiro, P. & Rocha, R. (2020). Knowledge sharing: A link between organizational wisdom and organizational spirituality. In: Garcia-Perez, A. & Simkin, L. (Eds.). *Proceedings of the 21st European Conference on Knowledge Management* (pp. 639–647). Coventry University, UK, 2–4 December 2020. https://doi.org/10.34190/EKM.20.131. www.academic-conference.org

Pinker, S. (2008). *The stuff of thought: Language as a window into human nature.* Pinguin Books, New York.

Polanyi, M. (1983). *The tacit dimension.* Peter Smith, Gloucester.

Porter, M.E. & Kramer, M.R. (2011). Creating shared values: How to reinvent capitalism – and unleash a wave of innovation and growth. *Harvard Business Review* (January-February), 63–77. https://hbr.org/2011/01/the-big-idea-creating-shared-value

Reeve, L. (2005). Spiritual values and practices related to leadership effectiveness. *The Leadership Quarterly, 16*(5), 655–687. https://doi.org/10.1016/j.leaqua.2005.07.003. https://www.sciencedirect.com/science/article/abs/pii/S1048984305000718

Rocha, R. & d'Angelo, SM.J. (2023). Samarco's scandal: A perspective of organizational spirituality and corporate social responsibility. *International Journal of Organizational Analysis, 31*(2), 387–411. https://doi.org/10.1108/IJOA-05-2020-2220. https://www.emerald.com/insight/content/doi/10.1108/IJOA-05-2020-2220/full/html

Rocha, R. & Pinheiro, P. (2019). Spirituality in knowledge management: Systematic literature review and future studies suggestions. In: Tome, E., Cesario, F. & Soares, R.R. (Eds.). *Proceedings of the 20th European Conference on Knowledge Management.* Universidade Europeia de Lisboa, Lisbon, Portugal, 5–6 September 2019 (pp. 892–900). https://doi.org/10.34190/KM.19.096. www.academic-conference.org

Rocha, R. & Pinheiro, P. (2021). Can organizational spirituality contribute to knowledge management? *Management Dynamics in the Knowledge Economy*, *9*(1), 107–121. https://doi.org/10.2478/MDKE-2021-0008. https://www.managementdynamics.ro/index.php/journal/article/view/409
Russell, B. (1972). *A history of Western philosophy*. Simon and Schuster, New York.
Ryle, G. (1949). *The concept of mind*. The University of Chicago Press, Chicago.
Schein, E. (2004). *Organizational culture and leadership*. 3rd Edition. Jossey-Bass, San Francisco.
Schiuma, G. (2009). The managerial foundations of knowledge assets dynamics. *Knowledge Management Research and Practice*, *7*(4), 290–299. https://doi.org/10.1057/kmrp.2009.21. https://www.tandfonline.com/doi/full/10.1057/kmrp.2009.21
Senge, P. (1999). *The fifth discipline: The art and practice of the learning organization*. Random House, London;
Shannon, C.E. (1948). A mathematical theory of communication. *Bell System Technical Journal*, *27*(3), 379–423. https://doi.org/10.1002/j.1538-7305.1948.tb01338x. https://ieeexplore.ieee.org/document/6773024
Simon, H.A. (2000). Bounded rationality in social science: Today and tomorrow. *Mind & Society*, *1*(1), 25–39. https://www.mindandsociety.in/index.php/MAS/article/view/400
Song, J. & Lee, K. (2014). *The Samsung way: Transformational management strategies from the world leader in innovation and design*. McGraw-Hill Education, New York.
Spender, J.C. (2014). *Business strategy: Managing uncertainty, opportunity, and enterprise*. Oxford University Press, Oxford.
Stacey, R.D., Griffin, D. & Shaw, P. (2000). *Complexity and management: Fad or radical challenge to systems thinking?* Routledge, London.
Stewart, T.A. (1999). *Intellectual capital: The new wealth of organizations*. Nicholas Brealey Publishing, London.
Sullivan, P.H. (1998). *Profiting from intellectual capital: Extraction value from innovation*. John Wiley & sons, New York.
Taleb, N.N. (2007). *The black swan: The impact of the highly improbable*. Penguin Books, New York.
Taleb, N.N. (2012). *Antifragile: How to live in a world we don't understand*. Penguin Books, New York.
Varela, F.J., Thompson, E. & Rosch, E. (1993). *The embodied mind: Cognitive science and human experience*. The MIT Press, Cambridge, Massachusetts.
Warren, K. (2008). *Strategic management dynamics*. John Wiley & Sons, New York. Yochanan, A., Neal, J. & Mayrhofer, W. (Eds.) (2022). *Workplace spirituality: Making a difference*. De Gruyter, Berlin.
Zohar, D. & Marshall, I. (2000). *SQ: Spiritual intelligence: The ultimate intelligence*. Bloomsbury, London.
Zohar, D. & Marshall, I. (2004). *Spiritual capital: Wealth we can live by*. Berrett-Koehler Publishers, San Francisco.

Alexander Kaiser

Chapter 2
Spiritual Knowledge Management: Managing the Learning Process Towards the Best Version of the Self

Abstract: The field of knowledge management (KM) has undergone significant changes, and it seems time to come up with new ideas to redefine the future role of KM research and practice in a changing and increasingly dynamic world. This chapter outlines one such new idea by proposing the concept of spiritual knowledge management. There is strong empirical evidence that purpose, spirituality and self are more important than ever for individuals and organizations. At the same time, many authors from very different fields come to the same conclusion: the goal of a fulfilling and successful life and work is to move from the current version of yourself to the best version. On this basis, this chapter aims to define and conceptualize the concept of spiritual knowledge management. It will be argued that the basic process of spiritual knowledge management is to enable, guide and organize a process of deep learning to develop the best version of a person (individual) or institution (organization). This chapter is conceptual, and its results will contribute to theory building in this area.

Keywords: Spirituality, Self, Knowledge, Deep Learning

Introduction

In recent years, the arena of spirituality has gained renewed interest in wide-ranging disciplines, including not only disciplines such as health, education, psychology, psychotherapy or personality (Kor et al., 2019) but also management and organizational behavior (Crossman, 2016). In the literature, it is argued that spirituality can be seen with an individual (micro) or organizational (macro) focus or an individual (private) or organizational domain (public) of perceptions and actions and that there are three main perspectives for considering spirituality: personal, in the workplace, and organizational (e.g. (Rocha & Pinheiro, 2021c)). Regarding knowledge management (KM), the connection between spirituality and KM is currently addressed from two perspectives. Bratianu and colleagues have introduced the concept of spiritual knowledge as an additional type of knowledge (Bratianu, 2017), (Bratianu et al., 2020) and argue that

Alexander Kaiser, Vienna University of Economics and Business, Austria, e-mail: alexander.kaiser@wu.ac.at

https://doi.org/10.1515/9783111010410-003

"Spiritual knowledge is about the deep human concerns of our existence, and of our connection with the whole universe" (Bratianu, 2015, p. 72).

This field focuses strongly on the nature of spiritual knowledge as an extraordinary form of knowledge. Rocha and colleagues investigate the relationship between organizational spirituality and KM (Rocha & Pinheiro, 2019; Rocha & Pinheiro, 2021c) and address the question of whether organizational spirituality can contribute to KM (Rocha & Pinheiro, 2021b). So, the main focus of these papers is the impact of organizational spirituality on knowledge management. Although both existing links in the literature between spirituality and KM are interesting, they tackle only relatively small parts of KM (Kaiser, 2023, p. 4911).

However, regarding the overarching subject of this book, "New Perspectives for Knowledge Management and Knowledge Strategies," we are interested in KM as a whole and Spiritual Knowledge Management (SpKM). Therefore, this concept of Spiritual Knowledge Management focuses more on the process perspective and a specific and probably new focus of KM. Surprisingly, a scientific literature review and a Google search for "Spiritual Knowledge Management" returned almost no results. So, the research question of this chapter reads as follows: *How can Spiritual Knowledge Management be defined and conceptualized? What are the main characteristics of Spiritual Knowledge Management, and why should Spiritual Knowledge Management play a role in the future of knowledge management?* (Kaiser, 2023, p. 4912). To answer this research question, this chapter presents the first conceptual work on how the approach of Spiritual Knowledge Management could shape future knowledge management. The purpose of this chapter is not to present a complete and consistently developed solution or model but rather to start the discourse on the topic of Spiritual KM and the future of KM and to provide it with a concept.

What is Spirituality?

To effectively introduce and clarify the concept of spiritual knowledge management, we must first figure out what spirituality means. The subsequent section examines the various definitions of spirituality, followed by a discussion of the central element of spirituality: the self.

Spirituality in the Literature

There is no single, widely agreed definition of spirituality. In a literature review based on around 100 articles and books, Tanyi concludes that spirituality is an inherent component of being human. It is subjective, intangible, and multidimensional and involves humans' search for meaning in life (Tanyi, 2002, p. 500). Here are three definitions of spirituality as examples:

> Spirituality is how a person understands and lives life given her or his ultimate meaning, beliefs, and values. It is the unifying and integrative aspect of the person's life and, when lived intentionally, is experienced as a process of growth and maturity. It integrates, unifies, and vivifies the whole of a person's narrative or story, embeds his or her core identity, establishes the fundamental basis for the individual's relationship with others and with society, includes a sense of the transcendent, and is the interpretive lens through which the person sees the world. It is the basis for community, for it is in spirituality that we experience our co-partnership in the shared human condition. It may or may not be expressed or experienced in religious categories (Fowler & Peterson, 1997, p. 47).

> Spirituality is a belief or value system that permeates all of a person's life, giving life meaning in the context of six fundamental human relationships: 1) to God, or whomever or whatever is considered ultimate reality, 2) to self, 3) to others, 4) to the environment, 5) to the past, and 6) to the future" (Doreen, 2016, p. 6).

> Spirituality is a personal search for meaning and purpose in life, which may or may not be related to religion. It entails connecting to self-chosen and religious beliefs, values, and practices that give meaning to life, inspiring and motivating individuals to achieve their optimal being. This connection brings faith, hope, peace, and empowerment (Tanyi, 2002, p. 506).

Of course, there are many other definitions from different fields and backgrounds. It is far beyond the scope of this chapter to go into all these definitions in more detail and to analyze them. Detailed literature reviews can be found (e.g., see Karakas, 2010; Dyson et al., 1997).

The Self is a Critical Element of Spirituality

One fundamental dimension and critical element of spirituality, which can be found in almost all definitions and approaches of spirituality – even if they are sometimes quite different – is the self (Dyson et al., 1997, p. 1183). A recent Harvard Business Review social media post is below (Harvey, 2022, p. xx). Although this quote comes from a business-oriented context, it perfectly sums up the importance of developing the self.

> To Change Your Behavior Now, Imagine Your Future Self. Many of us think that the person we are today is the person we will always be. We cling to labels like "I am an introvert" or "I am not good with people." However, that type of thinking leaves little room for growth. The reality is that we can and do change. So do not be so wedded to who you are today. Instead, intentionally focus on who you want to be. Start by recognizing how much you have grown and changed from your former self. This will serve as a reminder that growth is possible. Then, imagine who you want to be in the future. Keep that vision of yourself top of mind.

Spirituality is connected inseparably with a continuous evolution of the self towards a fully developed and unfolded self. So, we can also speak of self-development or self-actualization as a key to spirituality. This understanding of spirituality aligns with several authors – from very different fields and backgrounds – who all distinguish between different forms of the self over time.

Richard Boyatzis, who comes from the field of organizational behavior and coaching, differentiates between the authentic self, that is, the self a person currently is, and the ideal self, which is the self a person could be (Boyatzis & Akrivou, 2006), (Boyatzis & Dhar, 2021). Based on this, the Intentional Change Theory is a five-stage model designed to help people achieve and sustain desired changes and reach their goals (Boyatzis, 2006), (Van Oosten, 2006).

Otto Scharmer, whose background is the leadership and change management area as well as the action research field, distinguishes between one's current self and the emerging future Self that represents one's most significant potential (Scharmer & Kaufer, 2013). In his Theory U, Scharmer introduces the phase of presence, in which one connects with the source of the highest future possibility, enabling the presence of one's authentic Self (Scharmer, 2009) and generating self-transcending knowledge (Scharmer, 2001).

Richard Rohr comes from a Catholic clerical background and distinguishes between the true self and the false self (Rohr, 2013), arguing that the true self is the part of yourself that knows who you are and to whom you belong. Like a deeply buried diamond, this authentic self must be discovered and separated from all the ego debris surrounding it. Rohr also points out that the transformation process from false self to true self is primarily linked to forgiveness (Rohr, 2011).

Matthew Kelly, whose background is consulting as well as spirituality, proposes the concept of a 'best version of myself' in comparison to the current self (Kelly, 2004) and suggests that by finding legitimate needs, deepest desires and talents, one may be able to find this 'best-version-of-myself' (Kelly, 2017).

The knowledge management theorist *Ikujiro Nonaka* has a very different background. He describes knowledge creation as a continuous self-transcendental process through which one transcends the boundary of the old self (individually or as an organization) into a new self by acquiring and creating a new context, a new world view and novel knowledge (Nonaka & Konno, 1998). It is a journey "from being to becoming" (Nonaka et al., 2000, p. 8). Furthermore, he argues that "(t)o open oneself means to lose oneself (. . .) 'Losing the self to find the self' is not simply the shedding of preconceptions and biases to perceive reality more clearly. It is about overcoming one's self-centered worldview and seeing oneself in terms of one's relationship with others, mainly clients and customers" (Nonaka, 2012, p. 61).

The psychiatrist and psychotherapist *Viktor E. Frankl* also gave special attention to aspects of the self. He was the first to propose and explain the concept of "self-transcendence" in detail. He argued that human existence is always directed towards something or someone other than oneself and called this constitutive property of human existence self-transcendence (Frankl, 1966). By following the path of transcending the self, we become fully human (Wong, 2016). In this context, Frankl repeatedly emphasizes, referring to a Johann Wolfgang Goethe quote, that if we accept someone as he or she is, we make him or her worse. Conversely, if we take someone as he or she could be, we make him or her better.

Stam et al. (Stam et al., 2014) argue that the self-concept is how we perceive and what we know about ourselves respectively. They differentiate between the self as we currently experience it and the possible self. While the former is connected to the present, considering the current situation, constraints, etc., possible selves are the future-oriented parts of the self. Thus, they do not capture who one is (i.e., the current self). However, one could become (Stam et al., 2014).

Without going into detail, which is beyond the scope of this chapter, it is evident that the categories of these self-concepts are pretty different. Although they come from very different subjects and backgrounds (theology, counseling, leadership, change management, psychology, organizational behavior, coaching), it can be seen that the basic premise is, in fact, very similar: the development of a fulfilling and successful life is closely linked to an unfolded self (Kaiser, 2022). Out of all the terms proposed in the literature (true self, authentic self, Self, etc.), the expression "the best version of myself" is probably the one that works as a generic term. The development towards this future best self is, of course, a process that has to consider various constraints. As discussed below, self-actualization and the transition from the present to the future self-occur at the individual and organizational levels within companies and organizations and, more generally, within any social system (Kaiser, 2023, p. 4913).

Spiritual Knowledge Management on the Individual Level

At first, the concept of Spiritual Knowledge Management will be applied only to persons on an individual level. In doing so, there is also a contribution to personal knowledge management, often considered an under-explored area (Cheong & Tsui, 2010). Knowledge management is often primarily associated with managers and people to be managed and, therefore, only with companies and organizations. At the same time, the same topics at the individual level are more often referred to as self-management. This chapter will use the terms Knowledge Management and Spiritual Knowledge Management regarding the organizational and individual levels.

A Process Perspective on Spiritual KM

Spiritual Knowledge Management focuses on the process from the present self to a future self that is different and somehow "better" (in the sense of more developed and expanded) than the present self (Kaiser, 2023, p. 4913)). Figure 2.1 shows this evolution schematically and in a highly simplified way since it is unlikely to be a straightforward process in practice.

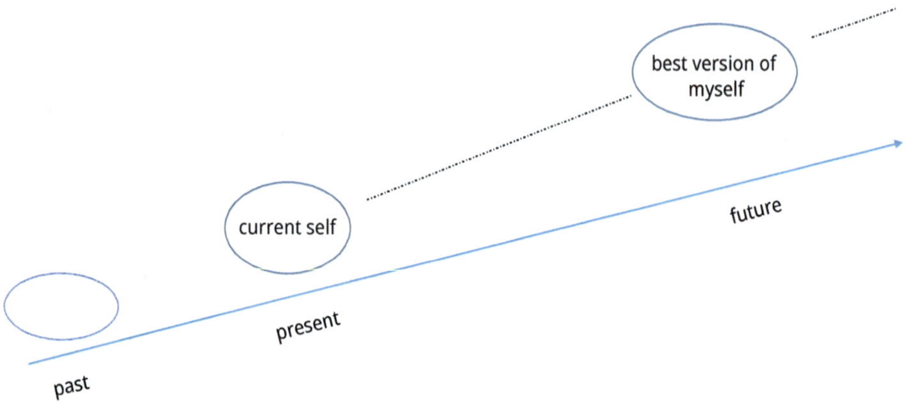

Figure 2.1: Process toward a future self.
Source: Kaiser, 2023

Thus, a stepwise evolution can be understood as a transformation from the current version of the person to his or her best version. Since this future best self is not (entirely) known at the beginning of this journey, this process can be seen as a process of becoming (Clegg et al., 2005) and a process of deep learning. In this learning process, knowledge about the very nature and shape of the best version of oneself is created, and, at the same time, this knowledge shapes and refines not only the best version of oneself but also how to get there (Kaiser, 2023, p. 4914). At the same time, one gets to know and understand one's current self-better. Following Nonaka and other researchers, knowledge can be defined as the capacity to act (Stehr, 2012; Sveiby, 1997; Sveiby, 2001). Therefore, the knowledge created in this deep learning process enables a person to *act* systematically toward becoming the best version of oneself. Therefore, without the creation of this knowledge, a person would be stuck on his or her path and would not be able to develop and grow.

Types of Knowledge

In order to define and conceptualize Spiritual Knowledge Management, it is necessary to explore further the nature and characteristics of the knowledge that is most important in becoming the best version of yourself. First, we can assume that Spiritual Knowledge Management is about creating and processing spiritual knowledge. This is in line with Bratianu's definition that "(s)piritual knowledge is the direct result of the process of thinking about existence, and searching for meaning and purpose in our lives, a process based on deeply held personal values" and ". . . that spiritual knowledge reflects our understanding about the meanings of our existence." (Bratianu, 2017, p. 80). He emphasizes that spiritual knowledge is constantly dynamic with rational and emotional knowledge and is integrated into decision-making. Following this definition and applying it to the learning process for the development of the self, we can argue that

spiritual knowledge consists of different types of knowledge that allow us to make decisions based on our understanding of the meaning of existence:
- Knowledge about the best version of oneself
- Knowledge about the current version of oneself
- Knowledge about previous versions of oneself
- Knowledge about where a person is right now on the way toward the best version of oneself
- Knowledge about whether a person is still on the path toward the best version, or in other words, knowledge about whether the direction of the path is still the right one (Kaiser, 2023, p. 4914)

Spiritual Knowledge Management is about creating these components of spiritual knowledge, transferring existing knowledge from an implicit and perhaps unconscious level to a level where it can be used for action and decision-making and providing enabling factors and processes for creating and transforming knowledge. To create these components of spiritual knowledge requires an enhanced understanding of learning and, thus, an extended theory of learning. It is about combining learning from the past and the future to enable the best possible decision in the present (Kaiser, 2023, p. 4914).

Breaking with the view that learning is strictly and solely connected with our past experiences and giving up the belief that the future is a forward projection of the past, several authors ((Senge et al., 2005), (Jaworski, 1998), (Scharmer, 2009)) propose an alternative source of learning: learning from the future. The idea is to shift attention to the individual's inner world and to sense the very moment by "connecting with the source of one's best future possibility and of bringing this possibility into the now" (Scharmer and Kaeufer, 2010, p. 25f). Thus, it is about learning "from a reality that is not yet embodied in manifest experience" (Scharmer, 2009, p. 138).

Learning from the future has been studied by various researchers in recent years (Peschl, 2022), (Peschl, 2019), (Scharmer, 2009), (Griswold et al., 2017), (Kaiser et al., 2016), (Grisold & Kaiser, 2017), and all these authors have shown that self-transcending knowledge plays an important role. However, what is self-transcending knowledge about explicit and implicit/tacit knowledge? Self-transcending knowledge can be defined as not-yet-embodied knowledge (Scharmer, 2001) and the ability to sense the presence of potential, to see what does not yet exist (intuition and hunches) (Uotila & Melkas, 2008). Self-transcending knowledge can be characterized by a set of criteria (Kaiser & Peschl, 2020):
- Relation and interaction with the world and with something other than it-/oneself;
- Expansion of boundaries (of the self) and the bigger picture;
- Purpose, meaning and final cause;
- Potentiality and tension between what is and what could/should be, what is not yet;
- Pulling and not pushing;
- Future-oriented and yet respecting, cherishing and including past/existing knowledge;
- Self-detachment and forgetting/unlearning;
- The source of novelty is found in an unfolding emerging reality.

Best Version of Myself and Self-Transcendence: Differences and Similarities

The best version of myself can sometimes be understood as an idealized version of one's ego or personality. It may involve setting personal goals and striving to achieve them, improving one's skills and abilities, and enhancing one's self-image. This can be a positive and motivating force, but it can also be limiting if it focuses solely on the individual and their success and well-being. However, our understanding of the best version of oneself is much more focused on the idea of an unfolded self that is in alignment with all of a person's potentials and resources and, of course, with the responsibilities of a person and is based on positive and good values that are helpful not only to the person but also to the broader communities and systems in which the person lives and works. On the other hand, self-transcendence involves moving beyond the limitations of the individual ego and connecting with something greater than oneself. This may involve cultivating a sense of compassion, empathy, and concern for others or exploring spiritual or philosophical traditions that encourage the transcendence of the ego. This way, self-transcendence is less about personal achievement and more about a more profound sense of meaning and purpose. An emphasis on self-transcendence can help individuals move beyond a narrow focus on their personal growth and goals and embrace a broader perspective that includes a concern for others and the world around them. By focusing on self-transcendence, individuals can avoid becoming attached to their ideas and beliefs and remain open to new insights and experiences that can deepen their spiritual understanding. Thus, the concept and idea of the "best version of myself" and the approach of self-transcendence and self-transcending knowledge are not contradictory or identical. Instead, the two approaches are meant to be complementary and mutually influential.

One can conclude that the conception and characteristics of self-transcending knowledge are closely related to the core aspects of Spiritual Knowledge Management. We can even go a step further and argue that learning from the future combined with learning from the past and creating self-transcending knowledge is critical in enabling knowledge about the best version of oneself (Kaiser, 2023). Figure 2.2 illustrates this schematically.

Identifying what needs to be learned in deep learning is necessary to transform from the current to the future self. Various authors (Kelly, 2004; Maureder, 2004; Kelly, 2017; Kaiser, 2017) argue that the fulfilled self, i.e., the best version of oneself, is defined or characterized by (at least) three dimensions, namely, legitimate needs, wishes, and desires, as well as talents, strengths, and resources. If this is true, we must create knowledge about these three dimensions – knowledge about needs, deep desires and wishes, and resources and strengths – as part of the deep learning process (Figure 2.3).

Therefore, Spiritual Knowledge Management should also focus on the factors that enable this deep learning process and the methods for generating these three dimensions of knowledge.

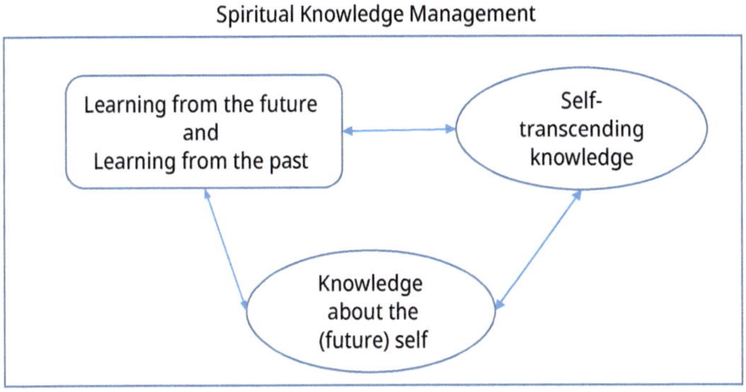

Figure 2.2: Key process for Spiritual KM.
Source: Kaiser, 2023

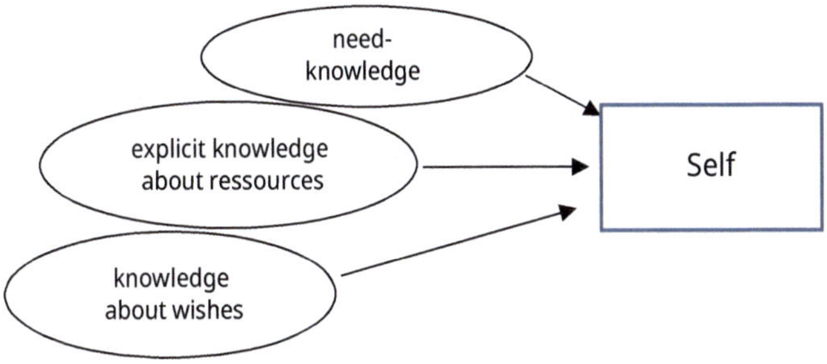

Figure 2.3: Knowledge dimension of the Self.
Source: Kaiser, 2023

Some authors argue that finding the best or ideal version of the self is not only a process of deep learning but also involves getting rid of already existing knowledge. Scharmer calls for 'letting go' (Scharmer, 2009), Boyatzis and Akrivou suggest reducing the influence of the 'ought self' as someone else's interpretation of what a person's ideal self should be (Boyatzis & Akrivou, 2006). Dowrick proposes eliminating familiar aspects when creating a self-model (Dowrick, 2012). Grisold and Kaiser argue that unlearning, as the reduction of the influence of old knowledge, can lead us closer to the best version of ourselves. Underlying this argument is a system-thinking perspective on the concept of unlearning and a knowledge perspective on the self (Grisold & Kaiser, 2017). T The approach to discovering the true self has constantly been recurring in spiritual wisdom and philosophy, requiring periods of detachment and emptiness. Therefore, unlearning should also be recognized as a critical process within spiritual KM.

If all the parts mentioned and discussed are combined, a first general impression of Spiritual KM as a complete system emerges. The following figure 2.4 shows this schematically.

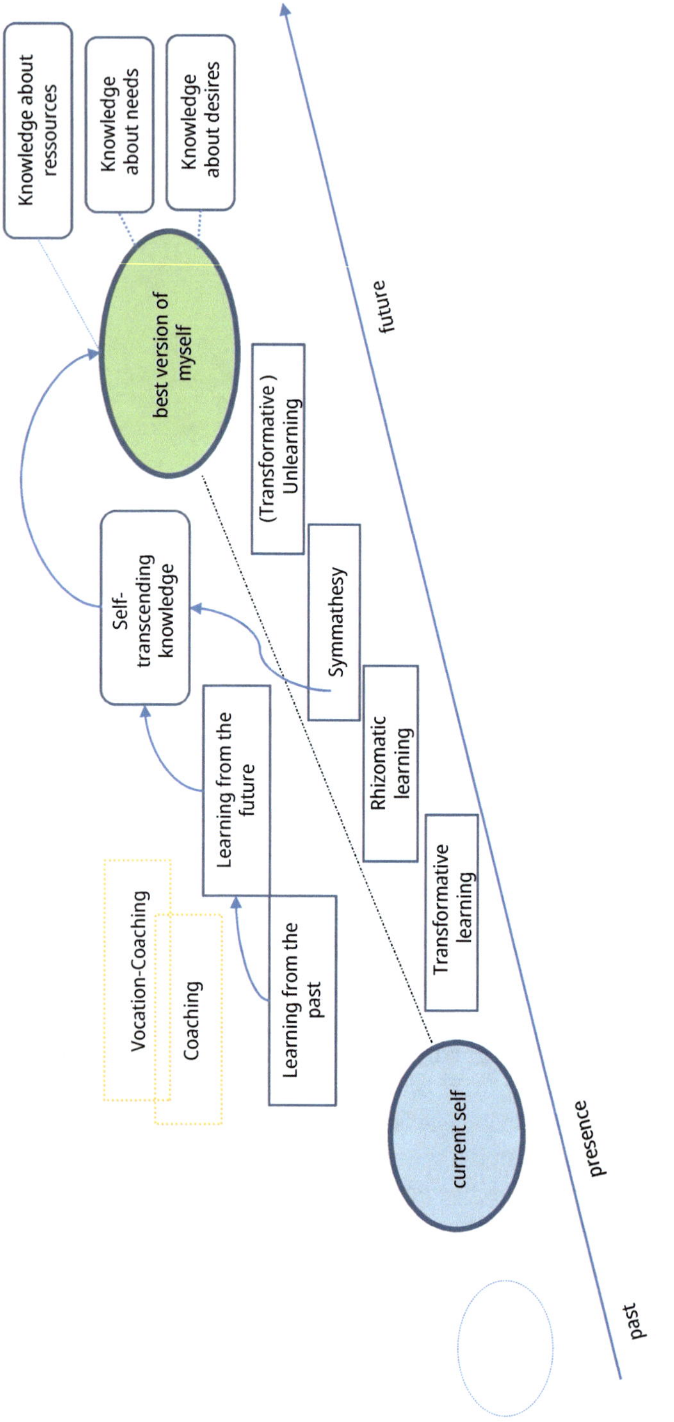

Figure 2.4: Spiritual KM as an entire system.
Source: Kaiser, 2023

Therefore, Spiritual Knowledge Management also has much to do with a vocation (Dik et al., 2012), calling (Duffy & Dik, 2013) and learning about one's vocation.

Characteristics of the Future Self

As mentioned before, the key in the approach of spiritual KM is to achieve the future self, which could be defined as the ideal self or best version of the self, and to learn something about this construct. According to the authors mentioned in section above, the characteristics and qualities of this construct of the best version of myself could be summarized as follows.

The best version of the self is . . .
- highly dynamic and constantly changing and not static or stable over time
- emerging and developing
- a constant process of unfolding and becoming

It is. . .
- authentic
- very good for me and, at the same time, perfect for the world

It has much to do with. . .
- potentiality and enacting and unfolding the full potential
- fulfilling and meaningful life
- taking into account the common good
- enacted purpose

It includes. . .
- knowing about my responsibilities in the world and my place in the world
- knowing about and addressing my substantial needs
- knowing about and addressing my personal why and my deepest desires
- knowing about my strengths, talents and resources and can use them

Which Existing Approaches Could Be Helpful for Spiritual Knowledge Management?

Although the concept of Spiritual Knowledge Management is brand new and quite innovative, it would be quite a challenge to develop everything within this approach starting from zero. Therefore, this section will discuss and highlight whether other scientific fields from which the concept of SpKM could adapt approaches and methods. It is mainly the part of learning within the SpKM approach that has the potential to connect with other scientific fields. The following sections analyze three different streams for their usefulness and suitability in managing the spiritual knowledge process.

Transformative Learning and Spiritual KM

The transformative learning theory was developed by Jack Mezirow around 50 years ago (Mezirow, 1997) and could today be characterized as a complex description of how learners construe, validate, and reformulate the meaning of their experience (Cranton, 1994). According to Mezirow, transformative learning is defined as the transformation of the learners' meaning perspectives, frames of reference, and habits of mind and therefore, learners must engage in critical reflection on their experiences, which in turn leads to a perspective transformation (Mezirow, 2008). The transformative aspect of this learning approach is strongly connected to a kind of "deep" learning that challenges existing, taken-for-granted assumptions, notions, and meanings of what learning is about (Dirkx et al., 2006). The outcomes of transformative learning are a change in worldview, a significant shift in the sense of self, a shift in epistemology and ontology, and a change in behavior and capacity (Mbokota et al., 2022). Three core elements define the process of transformative learning: disorienting dilemma, critical reflection, and rational dialogue (Mbokota et al., 2022).

Early authors in this area see transformative learning as a rational learning process within awareness as a metacognitive application of critical thinking that transforms an acquired frame of reference by assessing its epistemic assumptions (Dirkx et al., 2006). In the last ten to fifteen years, the field of transformative learning shifted to a view that suggests a more integrated and holistic understanding of subjectivity, one that reflects the intellectual, emotional, moral, and spiritual dimensions of our being in the world and associates transformative learning with soul work or inner work (Dirkx et al., 2006) that requires a change in one's sense of self that is, an identity change (Illeris, 2014). It is important to note that the roots of transformative learning are in education, more specifically in adult education. Nevertheless, there are some connection points and possible applications for Spiritual KM. It depends on the form that transforms within transformative learning (West, 2014; Karpen, 2022; Kegan et al., 2000). If the form that transforms is the self, it would be very likely that this understanding of transformative learning could strengthen the learning process within the Spiritual KM model.

There is an apparent connection between transformative learning and spiritual knowledge management, as both imply a process of seeking and gaining new knowledge and understanding of oneself and the world. As described above, transformative learning typically implies a profound and fundamental change in one's beliefs, attitudes and values, which can be seen as spiritual empowerment. Similarly, spiritual knowledge management can be defined as seeking, acquiring and applying spiritual knowledge and insight in one's personal and work life. Both transformative learning and spiritual knowledge management involve a process of self-examination, critical reflection and the search for new knowledge and understanding.

Rhizomatic Learning and Spiritual KM

Rhizomatic learning (RL) is a non-hierarchical and decentralized learning style emphasizing the interconnectedness of different ideas and concepts (Chia, 1999). It is informed by the work of Deleuze and Guatarri (Deleuze et al., 1992) and based on the idea that knowledge is not fixed or hierarchical but is constantly evolving and interconnected. RL is inspired by the rhizome, a plant root system that grows horizontally and can send out new shoots and roots in any direction rather than growing vertically in a traditional root structure. In education, rhizomatic learning involves encouraging learners to explore and connect ideas in a self-directed way rather than following a predetermined curriculum or hierarchy of knowledge (Bissola et al., 2017). It emphasizes the value of personal experience, curiosity, and creativity in learning and often involves the use of collaborative and experiential learning methods as it is characterized by an open-ended, exploratory approach that allows learners to pursue their interests and make connections between different ideas and concepts (Charney, 2017). One of the main benefits of rhizomatic learning is that it allows learners to develop a deeper understanding of complex ideas and concepts as it encourages them to explore and make connections between different subjects and disciplines.

In sum, rhizomatic learning assumes that learning is an ongoing process influenced by one's environment and interaction with others and is not limited to formal (educational) environments.

There are some ways in which rhizomatic learning could be applied to Spiritual Knowledge Management. Some potential ideas might include:

- Encouraging individuals to follow their curiosity and interests and to pursue topics that are personally meaningful to them.
- Encouraging individuals to draw on diverse sources and perspectives in exploring spiritual knowledge rather than limiting themselves to a single tradition or approach.
- Using experiential learning methods to help individuals deepen their understanding of their current and ideal selves and even spiritual concepts and practices. These methods can be particularly effective at helping individuals to integrate spiritual knowledge into their own lives and experiences.

Symmathesy and Spiritual KM

In her work on sympathy, Nora Bateson (Bateson, 2015; Bateson, 2016) describes the process by which different organisms work together to create a functional whole.

She emphasizes the importance of understanding the context and relationships in which different organisms exist rather than just focusing on the individual organisms. Bateson also highlights the role of communication and feedback in sympathy and the idea of emergence, or new properties or patterns emerge from the interaction of different parts. Her work on sympathy offers a unique perspective on the relationships between different organisms and their contribution to the working of complex systems. The concept of sympathy applies to an individual context and can be seen as the process by which different aspects of a person's life come together to create a functional whole. This can include work, relationships, hobbies, and other activities that make up a person's life. By fostering a sense of interdependence and cooperation among the various aspects of life, individuals can create a cohesive whole more significant than the sum of its parts. This can help individuals to lead more fulfilling and balanced lives.

Symmathesy then denotes learning-together or together-learning. From nature, Nora Bateson – who is the daughter of Gregory Batson – uses the example of the tree on the hill:

> A tree is learning to be on a hill; its trunk is at an angle to the hill, its branches reach toward the light away from other trees' shadows, it grows in height according to the nourishment in the soil, and so on. The form of the tree is informed by the contextual and transcontextual mutual learning it is in with the other organisms it shares a hillside with. If you want the trunk to be at a 90-degree angle to the ground instead of the angle the tree has found, the approach will be to manipulate the tree. To do so would upset the precarious balance the tree has found and other organisms living with the tree. It is better to ask, "How is it learning to be in its world?" and immediately notice how the perception moves from the tree to its contextual responsiveness. Is the crookedness in the tree? Alternatively, is it in the context? (Nørlem et al., 2022, p. 11)

Nora Bateson proposed a crucial question in her work about sympathy: "How is it learning to be in its world?" (Nørlem et al., 2022, p. 3). This overarching question suggests that there is probably a potential for a connection between sympathy and Spiritual Knowledge Management. Furthermore, sympathy highlights the topic of mutual learning, defined as "the process of contextual, mutual learning through interaction between multiple variables in a living entity" (Bateson N., 2016, p. 169), which also suggests the applicability to Spiritual KM.

Wisdom Management and Spiritual KM

Recently, *Wisdom Management* was introduced as an extension and further development of knowledge management (Jakubik and Müürsepp, 2021). The authors argue that this approach contributes theoretically to the fifth phase of KM by focusing attention on wisdom and wisdom management as the next potential phase of KM. They explore how wisdom is presented in the KM literature and how understanding wisdom from the philosophy and psychology literature could contribute to KM (Jakubik and Müürsepp, 2021). There is a connection between Spiritual KM and Wisdom Management as it is an aspect of wisdom and a wise person or company to recognize and follow the best version of oneself (Kaiser, 2023). Hylving and Lindberg discuss practical wisdom in the context of ethical dilemmas and big data. (Hylving and Lindberg, 2022).

The concept of practical wisdom, often referred to as phronesis, following an ancient concept of Aristotle, has been gaining popularity in various fields in recent years (Bratianu & Motoc, 2022; Rocha & Pinheiro, 2021a; Rocha et al., 2022; Ames et al., 2020). Phronesis can be seen as an intellectual virtue and is generally understood as the ability to determine and undertake the best action in a specific situation to serve the common good (Nonaka & Toyama, 2007).

The connection to Spiritual KM is evident, as phronesis is one of the multiple aspects of spiritual knowledge, or to put it the other way around, the creation of spiritual knowledge could enable wise decisions and a phronetic attitude (Kaiser, 2023, p. 4916). One could argue that instead of the best version of self, phronetic self would also be a good term for what is central to Spiritual KM (Kaiser, 2023). If Spiritual KM is compared to wisdom management, phronesis, and practical wisdom, the uniqueness of Spiritual KM is in the process perspective of realizing the best version of oneself and creating knowledge about it.

Hunch Mining and Spiritual KM

Even the concept of Hunch mining (Nelson et al., 2018) (Nelson, 2021) could be related to Spiritual KM. Hunches are essential for making time-critical, highly complex decisions in turbulent environments and are strongly related to intuition. While research on hunch mining tends to focus on how to better use and deploy hunches and intuition in the decision-making process and how to lift them "above the surface," so to speak, the relationship to Spiritual KM could be how to use hunches and intuition about the specific form and characteristics of the best version within the learning process. This could also be a topic of future work in further developing the ideas of the Spiritual KM (Kaiser, 2023, p. 4917).

In summary, several concepts exist that have tangents with the proposed spiritual KM and from which spiritual KM could benefit and learn in the future. While the overall concept and critical issues of spiritual KM are relatively new and innovative and may not be substituted by any of the concepts mentioned above, one of the essential topics of future research in the field of spiritual KM will be to investigate and explore these outlined tangents.

Spiritual Knowledge Management in Organizations

Organizations can be viewed as complex living systems constantly (re)producing and sustaining themselves, requiring a continuous lifelong (organizational) learning process. This learning process involves interactions with the external environment and the organization's (internal) self, each influencing the other (Kaiser, 2023). Through these interaction mechanisms, each organization builds itself by shaping its environment and being shaped by it in a constant feedback loop (Kaiser, 2022). On an organizational level, Spiritual Knowledge Management wants to explore these dynamics, discover how an organization can adapt over time, develop a capacity to actively engage with itself, and direct its actions toward realizing its future potential (Kaiser, 2023).

At its core, it is about organizational self-actualization. It can be argued that organizational self-actualization is derived from individual self-actualization. Individual self-actualization is "self-fulfillment, namely the tendency for the individual to become actualized in what he/she is potentially (Kaiser, 2022). It is the desire to become more and more what one is, to become everything that one can become" (Maslow, 1981).

Individual self-actualization is a desire, not a driving force, that could lead to realizing one's capabilities, and it can be interpreted as "the full realization of one's potential" and of one's "true self" (Kaiser, 2023, p. 4916). We hypothesize that an analogy can be made from the individual to the organizational level since the guiding question of every organization is: What is the (unique) (future) value we want to bring into the world? If this holds, it can be defined as organizational Self-Actualization as the "best version" of the organization that becomes actualized in what it is potentially (Kaiser, 2023, p. 4916).

This "best version" lies in the future; thus, it has to be developed in a future-oriented transformation process. It is latent and "not yet". In many cases, it is not fully "visible" and understandable yet and has to be actively developed, i.e., what is hidden has to be brought forth. Organizational Self-Actualization is thought to determine what the organization is about, namely its purpose (Kaiser, 2022). Within this learning process, the organizational self is shaped and oscillates towards the ideal organizational self or the best version of itself.

Given these suggestions about organizational self-actualization, all the claims mentioned for the individual level in the context of Spiritual Knowledge Management are very similarly – or even equally – applicable to organizations. It can be assumed that for the field of Spiritual KM in organizations on existing work of discovering organizational purpose (e.g. (Fontán et al., 2019; Rey & Malbašić, 2019) and vision formation, as well as the development of shared visions (e.g., Hoepfl, 1997; Boyatzis & Dhar, 2021; Kaiser & Fordinal, 2010), can be built on.

Research Agenda

Building on all of the preceding considerations, a research agenda for Spiritual Knowledge Management is defined in the following.

The first block of the research agenda is about the self. In this chapter, a knowledge-based approach to characterize the self has been proposed. However, there are a variety of alternative approaches and concepts about the self that do not consider the self from a knowledge-based perspective. These approaches could also be beneficial and valuable for Spiritual Knowledge Management. An important research aspect must be further elaborating a self-concept (Kaiser & Peschl, 2022).

As mentioned before, an essential point of future research is to investigate how the already existing concepts that have been briefly sketched here – and perhaps others – can be applied or usefully adapted for the Spiritual KM (Kaiser, 2023).

The aspect of Spiritual KM in organizations has only been touched on briefly in this chapter. It is necessary to investigate and research whether Spiritual KM should primarily be established at the individual level or can also be applied to organizations. If this is the case, appropriate methods must be developed (Kaiser, 2022). Especially in the organizational context of Spiritual KM, we need to address the question of whether organizations have a self at all and how this self is characterized and defined (Kaiser & Peschl, 2022). What are the differences to the self on the individual level? To what extent are the individual self of the members of an organization and the self of an organization mutually connected or interacting? (Kaiser and Peschl, 2022)

Furthermore, it can be argued that another essential part of this research agenda is to explore and develop tools and methods to support individuals in deep learning from the current self toward the future best version of self and organizations. There is evidence from research and practice that existing tools from the field of systemic coaching (Boyatzis et al., 2022), (Passmore & Evans-Krimme, 2021) and systemic organizational development (Bond & Seneque, 2013) can be used for this purpose and that these approaches and techniques may be extended and further developed.

Exploring an expanded form of decision support systems is necessary. Both individuals and organizations need support in deciding what kind of change is necessary and appropriate. This includes information about the current position on the path to the best version of self. Consequently, a purpose measurement is required to decide how close a person or organization already comes to its best version, and thus its purpose, and how deeply committed it is to that purpose in its current actions (Kaiser, 2022). For this point, developing sound IT support is also essential. This could be, for example, a dashboard system that presents essential and critical information in a way that allows effective decisions to be made.

Another topic on the research agenda is learning from the future. There are already several research results and evolved methods in this area (Peschl, 2022), (Scharmer & Kaufer, 2013). However, it seems necessary to connect them more and better with the self-aspect and the different types of knowledge along the process of Spiritual KM. The same is true for the entire field of self-transcending knowledge, which needs to be further developed. In particular, this will be about developing enabling factors that foster the generation of self-transcending knowledge (Scharmer, 2001), Kaiser and Peschl, 2020).

Conclusion

Given that meaning and purpose are essential for many people and that the same applies to organizations (and the people acting in them) (Dubois & Saribas, 2020), it is necessary that KM also increasingly addresses and focuses on this topic. This issue is addressed by introducing the concept of Spiritual Knowledge Management, and the discussion and discourse are opened. In order to answer the research question of this chapter, it can be concluded that the field of Spiritual Knowledge Management primarily addresses the essential knowledge of who I can be as a person and who we can be as an organization and explores and develops processes, methods and structures for this purpose (Kaiser, 2023). The umbrella topic for Spiritual Knowledge Management could, therefore, be: *"Enabling the deep learning process towards the best version of myself (individual) or itself (organizational)"* (Kaiser, 2022, p. 12).

The contribution of this chapter is identifying the processes and mechanisms in Spiritual KM and providing a research agenda that identifies areas requiring further research to elaborate Spiritual KM and make it useful for practice methodically. Because this chapter is conceptual, there is a need for empirical research to test whether the elements we have proposed are complete and to examine the structure of the deep learning process on the way to becoming the best version of oneself. Furthermore, concrete techniques and methods along the deep learning process are still missing within this chapter. Although the author has several techniques and methods in mind and has had excellent practical experience with some of them, it is beyond the scope of this chapter to go into detail. It will be the focus of future work to present such methods and evaluate them empirically.[1]

References

Ames, M. C. F. D. C., Serafim, M. C., and Zappellini, M. B. (2020). Phronesis in administration and organizations: A literature review and future research agenda. *Business Ethics: A European Review*, 29:65–83.

Bateson, N. (2015). Symmathesy – A word in progress: Proposing a new word that refers to living systems. In *Proceedings of the 59th annual meeting of the International Society for the Systems Sciences*.

Bateson, N. (2016). *Small arcs of larger circles*. Triarchy Press.

Bissola, R., Imperatori, B., and Biffi, A. (2017). A rhizomatic learning process to create collective knowledge in entrepreneurship education: Open innovation and collaboration beyond boundaries. *Management Learning*, 48(2):206–226.

1 This chapter is mainly based on the paper Kaiser, A. (2023). Spiritual knowledge management: Proposing a new approach and defining a research agenda. In Proceedings of the 56th Hawaii International Conference on System Sciences, pages 4911–4920 where the concept of Spiritual Knowledge Management has been proposed and introduced for the very first time. For this chapter the paper has been expanded (section 3.3. and section 4) and adapted.

Bond, C. and Seneque, M. (2013). Conceptualizing coaching as an approach to management and organizational development. *Journal of Management Development*, 32(1):57–72.
Boyatzis, R. and Dhar, U. (2021). Dynamics of the ideal self. *Journal of Management Development*, 41(1):1–9.
Boyatzis, R. E. (2006). An overview of intentional change from a complexity perspective. *Journal of management development* 25(7):607–623.
Boyatzis, R. E. and Akrivou, K. (2006). The ideal self as the driver of intentional change. *Journal of management development* 25(7):624–642.
Boyatzis, R. E., Hullinger, A., Ehasz, S. F., Harvey, J., Tassarotti, S., Gallotti, A., and Penafort, F. (2022). The grand challenge for research on the future of coaching. *The Journal of Applied Behavioral Science*, 58(2):202–222.
Bratianu, C. (2015). Spiritual knowledge. In C. Andriessen, M. V. A. M. Salerno, & A. Garcia-Zambrana (Eds.), *Organizational Knowledge Dynamics: Managing Knowledge Creation, Acquisition, Sharing, and Transformation* (pp. 72–102).
Bratianu, C. (2017). Emotional and spiritual knowledge. In C. Andriessen, M. V. A. M. Salerno, & A. Garcia-Zambrana (Eds.), *Knowledge and Project Management* (pp. 69–91). Springer.
Bratianu, C., & Motoc, A. (2022). Knowledge dynamics and phronesis in performing family business. In *Proceedings of the European Conference on Knowledge Management* (Vol. 23, pp. 107–114).
Bratianu, C., Vătămănescu, E.-M., Anagnoste, S., and Dominici, G. (2020). Untangling knowledge fields and knowledge dynamics within the decision-making process. *Management Decision*, 59(2):306–323.
Charney, R. L. (2017). *Rhizomatic learning and adapting: A case study exploring an interprofessional team's lived experiences*. PhD thesis, Antioch University.
Cheong, R. K. and Tsui, E. (2010). The roles and values of personal knowledge management: an exploratory study. *Vine*, 40(2):204–227.
Chia, R. (1999). A 'rhizomic'model of organizational change and transformation: Perspective from a metaphysics of change. *British journal of management*, 10(3):209–227.
Clegg, S., Kornberger, M., and Rhodes, C. (2005). Learning/becoming/organizing. *Organization*, 12(2): 147–167.
Cranton, P. (1994). *Understanding and promoting transformative learning: A guide for educators of adults*. Jossey-Bass.
Crossman, J. (2016). Alignment and misalignment in personal and organizational spiritual identities. *Identity*, 16(3):154–168.
Deleuze, G., Guattari, F., Ricke, G., and Rösch, G. (1992). *Tausend plateaus*. Merve Berlin.
Dik, B. J., Eldridge, B. M., Steger, M. F., and Duffy, R. D. (2012). Development and validation of the calling and vocation questionnaire (cvq) and brief calling scale (bcs). *Journal of career assessment*, 20(3):242–263.
Dirkx, J. M., Mezirow, J., and Cranton, P. (2006). Musings and reflections on the meaning, context, and process of transformative learning: A dialogue between John M. Dirkx and Jack Mezirow. *Journal of transformative education*, 4(2):123–139.
Doreen, A. W. (2016). *Spirituality in nursing practice: The basics and beyond*. Springer Publishing Company.
Dowrick, P. W. (2012). Self-modeling: Expanding the theories of learning. *Psychology in the Schools*, 49(1): 30–41.
Dubois, E. and Saribas, A. (2020). Making corporate purpose tangible – a survey of investors. https://corpgov.law.harvard.edu/2020/06/19/making-corporate-purpose-tangible-a-survey-of-investors.
Duffy, R. D. & Dik, B. J. (2013). Research on calling: What have we learned and where are we going? *Journal of Vocational Behavior*, 83(3):428–436.
Dyson, J., Cobb, M., & Forman, D. (1997). The meaning of spirituality: A literature review. *Journal of Advanced Nursing*, 26(6):1183–1188.
Fontán, C., Alloza, A., & Rey, C. (2019). (Re) discovering organizational purpose. In A. R. Chaudhuri, & C. K. Sankaran (Eds.), Purpose-Driven Organizations (pp. 107–118). Springer.

Fowler, M. & Peterson, B. (1997). Spiritual themes in clinical pastoral education. *Journal of Supervision and Training in Ministry*, 18:46–54.
Frankl, V. E. (1966). Self-transcendence as a human phenomenon. *Journal of Humanistic Psychology*, 6(2): 97–106.
Grisold, T. and Kaiser, A. (2017). Leaving behind what we are not: Applying a systems thinking perspective to present unlearning as an enabler for finding the best version of the self. *Journal of Organisational Transformation & Social Change*, 14(1):39–55.
Grisold, T., Kaiser, A., and Hafner, J. (2017). Unlearning before creating new knowledge: A cognitive process. In *Proceedings of the 50th Hawaii International Conference on System Sciences*, pages 4614–4623.
Harvey, N. (2022). To change your behavior now, imagine your future self. https://www.linkedin.com/pulse/change-your-behaviour-now-imagine-future-self-natalie/.
Hoepfl, M. (1997). Choosing qualitative research: a primer for technology education researchers. *Journal of Technology Education*, 9(1):47–63.
Hylving, L. and Lindberg, S. (2022). Ethical dilemmas and big data: The case of the Swedish transport administration. *International Journal of Knowledge Management (IJKM)*, 18(1):1–16.
Illeris, K. (2014). Transformative learning and identity. *Journal of Transformative Education*, 12(2):148–163.
Jakubik, M. and Müürsepp, P. (2021). From knowledge to wisdom: will wisdom management replace knowledge management? *European Journal of Management and Business Economics*, 31(3):367–389.
Jaworski, J. (1998). Destiny and the leader. In L. C. Spears (Ed.), *Insights on Leadership: Service, Stewardship, and Servant Leadership* (pp. 1–11).
Kaiser, A (2022). Spiritual Knowledge Management. Presentation at the 1st virtual symposium on the future of KM (http://wu.ac.at/kbm)
Kaiser, A and Peschl, M. (2022). Spiritual Knowledge Management: some thoughts about the construct of the self within the concept of Spiritual Knowledge. Presentation at the 2nd virtual symposium on the future of KM (http://wu.ac.at/kbm)
Kaiser, A. & Fordinal, B. (2010). Creating a Ba for generating self-transcending knowledge. *Journal of Knowledge Management*, 14(6):928–942.
Kaiser, A. (2017). Towards a knowledge-based theory of developing sustainable visions: The theory wave. In *Proceedings of the 50th Hawaii International Conference on System Science (HICSS)*, pages 4495–4504, Hawaii, USA.
Kaiser, A. (2023). Spiritual knowledge management: Proposing a new approach and defining a research agenda. In *Proceedings of the 56th Hawaii International Conference on System Sciences*, pages 4911–4920.
Kaiser, A. and Peschl, M. F. (2020). The role of self-transcending knowledge in Senge's understanding of learning organizations towards an interdisciplinary taxonomy of self-transcending knowledge. *The Learning Organization*, 27(6):527–539.
Kaiser, A., Kragulj, F., Grisold, T., and Walser, R. (2016). Learning from an envisioned future: An empirical account. *Electronic Journal of Knowledge Management*, 14(1):16–28.
Karakas, F. (2010). Spirituality and performance in organizations: A literature review. *Journal of Business Ethics*, 94(1):89–106.
Karpen, S. C. (2022). The multiple selves framework in transformative learning. *Journal of Transformative Education*, *20*(4):268–280.
Kegan, R., Mezirow, J., & Associates. (2000). What form transforms? A constructive-developmental approach to transformative learning. In J. Mezirow & Associates (Eds.), *Learning as Transformation: Critical Perspectives on a Theory in Progress* (pp. 35–69).
Kelly, M. (2004). *The rhythm of life: Living every day with passion and purpose*. Simon and Schuster.
Kelly, M. (2017). *Perfectly Yourself: Discovering God's Dream for You*. Beacon Publishing.
Kor, A., Pirutinsky, S., Mikulincer, M., Shoshani, A., & Miller, L. (2019). A longitudinal study of spirituality, character strengths, subjective well-being, and prosociality in middle school adolescents. *Frontiers in Psychology*, 10, Article 377. https://doi.org/10.3389/fpsyg.2019.00377

Maslow, A. H. (1981). *Motivation and personality*. Prabhat Prakashan.
Maureder, J. (2004). *Wir kommen, wohin wir schauen: Berufung leben heute*. Tyrolia-Verlag.
Mbokota, D. G., Myres, P. K., and Stout-Rostron, D. S. (2022). Exploring the process of transformative learning in executive coaching. *Advances in Developing Human Resources*, 24(2):117–141.
Mezirow, J. (1997). Transformative learning: Theory to practice. *New directions for adult and continuing education*, 1997(74):5–12.
Mezirow, J. (2008). An overview of transformative learning. *Lifelong Learning*, 40–54.
Nelson, J. (2021). Hunch mining. *International Journal of Knowledge Management (IJKM)*, 17(3):17–30.
Nelson, J., Clark, T., & Stewart, I. (2018). Hunch mining: Intuition augmented with cognitive computing, analytics, and artificial intelligence. In *Proceedings of the 51st Hawaii International Conference on System Sciences*, pages 565–574.
Nonaka, I. (2012). Creating new knowledge the Japanese way. *IESE Insight*, 14:58–65.
Nonaka, I. and Konno, N. (1998). The concept of "ba": building a foundation for knowledge creation. *California Management Review*, 40(3):40–54.
Nonaka, I. and Toyama, R. (2007). Strategic management as distributed practical wisdom (phronesis). *Industrial and corporate change*, 16(3):371–394.
Nonaka, I., Toyama, R., and Konno, N. (2000). Seci, ba and leadership: a unified model of dynamic knowledge creation. *Long range planning*, 33(1):5–34.
Nørlem, J., Klee, N., & Andersen, M. R. F. (2022). A Process Turn in Organizational Learning (OL) Theory to Meet Contemporary Challenges: A Critical Review and New Horizons. *Orgaizational Learning, Knowledge and Capabilities*.
Passmore, J., & Evans-Krimme, R. (2021). The future of coaching: A conceptual framework for the coaching sector from personal craft to scientific process and the implications for practice and research. *Frontiers in Psychology, 12*, Article 715228. https://doi.org/10.3389/fpsyg.2021.715228
Peschl, M. F. (2019). Design and innovation as co-creating and co-becoming with the future. *Design Management Journal*, 14(1):4–14.
Peschl, M. F. (2022). Learning from the future as a novel paradigm for integrating organizational learning and innovation. *The Learning Organization*.
Rey, C., & Malbašić, I. (2019). Harmonization of personal and organizational purpose. In A. R. Chaudhuri & C. K. Sankaran (Eds.), *Purpose-Driven Organizations* (pp. 17–27). Springer.
Rocha, R., & Pinheiro, P. (2019). Spirituality in knowledge management: Systematic literature review and future studies suggestions. In *Proceedings of the European Conference on Knowledge Management* (Vol. 1, pp. 892–XXVI). Academic Conferences and Publishing International.
Rocha, R. and Pinheiro, P. (2021a). Business education: Filling the gaps in the leader's awareness concerning organizational phronesis. *Sustainability*, 13(4):1–17.
Rocha, R. and Pinheiro, P. (2021b). Can organizational spirituality contribute to knowledge management? *Management Dynamics in the Knowledge Economy*, 9(1):107–121.
Rocha, R. G. and Pinheiro, P. G. (2021c). Organizational spirituality: Concept and perspectives. *Journal of Business Ethics*, 171(2):241–252.
Rocha, R. G., Kragulj, F., and Pinheiro, P. (2022). Practical wisdom, the (not so) secret ingredient for responsible knowledge management. *VINE Journal of Information and Knowledge Management Systems*.
Rohr, R. (2011). *Falling upward: A spirituality for the two halves of life*. John Wiley & Sons.
Rohr, R. (2013). *Immortal diamond: The search for our true self*. John Wiley & Sons.
Scharmer, C. O. (2009). *Theory U: Learning from the future as it emerges*. Berrett-Koehler Publishers.
Scharmer, C. (2001). Self-transcending knowledge. Sensing and organizing around emerging pportunities. *Journal of Knowledge Management*, 5(2):137–150.
Scharmer, C. O. and Kaeufer, K. (2010). In front of the blank canvas: sensing emerging futures. *Journal of Business Strategy*, *31*(4), 21–29.

Scharmer, C. O. and Kaufer, K. (2013). *Leading from the emerging future: From ego-system to eco-system economies*. Berrett-Koehler Publishers.
Senge, P. M., Scharmer, C. O., Jaworski, J., and Flowers, B. S. (2005). *Presence: An exploration of profound change in people, organizations, and society*. Currency.
Stam, D., Lord, R. G., Knippenberg, D. v., & Wisse, B. (2014). An image of who we might become: Vision communication, possible selves, and vision pursuit. *Organization Science*, 25(4):1172–1194.
Stehr, N. (2012). Knowledge and non-knowledge. *Science, Technology & Innovation Studies*, 8(1):3–13.
Sveiby, K. E. (1997). *The new organizational wealth: Managing & measuring knowledge-based assets*. Berrett-Koehler Publishers.
Sveiby, K.-E. (2001). A knowledge-based theory of the firm to guide in strategy formulation. *Journal of Intellectual Capital*, 2(4):344–358.
Tanyi, R. A. (2002). Towards clarification of the meaning of spirituality. *Journal of Advanced Nursing*, 39(5): 500–509.
Uotila, T. and Melkas, H. (2008). Complex knowledge conversion processes and information quality in regional innovation networks. *Knowledge and Process Management*, 15(4):224–234.
Van Oosten, E. B. (2006). Intentional change theory at the organizational level: a case study. *Journal of Management Development*, 25(7):707–717.
West, L. (2014). Transformative learning and the form that transforms: Towards a psychosocial theory of recognition using auto/biographical narrative research. *Journal of Transformative Education*, 12(2): 164–179.
Wong, P. T. (2016). Meaning-seeking, self-transcendence, and well-being. In *Logotherapy and Existential Analysis* (pp. 311–321). Springer.

Ludmila Mládková

Chapter 3
Spirituality as a Meta-Story

Abstract: Spirituality is a dynamic phenomenon. It depends on the concrete situation of the human being in the concrete moment. Therefore, it is difficult to capture it. Spirituality can be captured and analyzed via the knowledge we have about it, spiritual knowledge. Storytelling is one of the most important tools for knowledge sharing and creation. We argue that spiritual knowledge is a meta-story built on at least three different types of stories. Stories about the self explain how individuals see themselves and their role in the universe; stories about relationships to others explain how individuals see their role in society; and stories about the relationship to the divine explain how individuals see themselves as a higher power. Together, these stories create the personal meta-story, the spirituality. The paper further explores these ideas and searches for ways to research spirituality from this perspective.

Keywords: Spirituality, Spiritual Knowledge, Story, Meta-Story

Introduction

Spirituality represents one's relationship to the world and how the individual understands self, others and the universe. It is a human phenomenon, and as such, it is imperceptible (Coreth, 1994). It is a term that is difficult to define and fuzzy and develops over time (Bregman, 2012), and we also "sense a certain fluidity, not to say vagueness, in the use of the term" (Principe, 1983, p. 129). Religious spirituality is a specific type connected to a particular religion, religious practices, formal doctrines, and formal church organizations. The decrease of believers in official churches and the development of understanding of spirit as a personal matter caused the redefining the relationship between what is human and what is sacred out of religion (Machů, 2015). Spirituality is a fully integrated approach to life "that seeks to transcend the self and find meaning and purpose through connection with others, nature, and a Supreme Being, which may or may not involve religious structures or traditions" (Buck, 2006, p. 290).

The latest attempts to define spirituality bring even more confusion as various definitions reflect different cultural and religious backgrounds. Spirituality is difficult to research. It is a dynamic element that develops over time and concerns the personal and contextual environment of the individual. It cannot be captured and analyzed

Ludmila Mládková, Prague University of Economics and Business, Czech Republic,
e-mail: ludmila.mladkova@vse.cz

https://doi.org/10.1515/9783111010410-004

because what we can capture is not spirituality itself but the knowledge we have about it, so-called spiritual knowledge.

One of the first who concluded in this way was Emmons (2000, p. 9), who defined spirituality as a "knowledge base" (Emmons, 2000, p. 9). He defined so-called spiritual information as:

> The part of a person's knowledge base that can lead to adaptive problem-solving behavior. For example, spiritual formation is precisely about building an expert knowledge base of information related to the sacred. Spirituality can serve as a source of information to individuals, and as a function of interests and aptitudes, individuals become more or less skilled at processing this information. The depth and breadth of a spiritual knowledge base are developed and refined through the study of sacred texts and the practice of spiritual exercises.

Spiritual knowledge "integrates values and beliefs about life and our existence" (Bratianu, 2013, p. 216). It is "self-knowledge about one's place in the world and connection with everything in the universe, a kind of valuable tacit knowledge that individuals possess and can be shared and transferred among one another" (Samul, 2020, p. 703). Spiritual knowledge is a specific type of knowledge as, for example, moral knowledge, if it exists, is knowledge of propositions which concern moral truth (if they are any)" (Pritchard, 2013, p. 144). Looking at spiritual knowledge from Prichard's perspective (Pritchard, 2013), it is a knowledge of propositions that concern spirituality.

Approaching spirituality by knowing about it allows us to get deeper into its foundations. Spirituality reflects human experience with the world. It is, as Bregman (2012) notes, a bi-polar structure. It develops on personal experience (situations we lived through) and by shared experience (situations somebody else lived through and then shared their knowledge about them with us).

Even though there is a lack of definitions of spiritual knowledge in literature (some authors use the term but do not define it), understanding spiritual knowledge as a piece of knowledge about spirituality allows us to examine spirituality indirectly via tools we have and use to capture, share and examine knowledge, particularly by stories. Stories are the traditional tool for working with knowledge and can also catch the part of knowledge that cannot be formalized and is partly or wholly subconscious. They serve as a virtual environment where we can return to our own experience or live the experience of other people; therefore, we can use them to explore our spiritual knowledge.

People explain and share their experiences in stories. Stories "give events meanings and significance" (Polkinghorne, 1988, p. 18) and are "a basic human strategy for coming to terms with time, process and change" (Herman & Herman, 2007, p. 3). All the stories we developed on our experience, and others shared with us about their experience with the world create a system of stories, a meta-story. From this perspective, spiritual knowledge is the meta-story developed on personal and shared experience.

This essay provides ideas on working with spirituality from the perspective of spiritual knowledge, specifically the stories that create it. The essay aims to introduce this indirect approach that captures the process of spiritual knowledge development and analyses the elements that make a holistic phenomenon, spirituality.

The terminology in the field of spirituality could be more precise. Authors who write about spirituality (except for a few like Bratinanu (2013), Samul (2020), Rocha & Pinheiro (2021a), and Emmons (2000)) do not make the difference between spirituality, spiritual knowledge or spiritual intelligence. We do not make the difference among these terms in our essay either, or we use the term spirituality. As our intention is not to particularise definitions, this approach allows us to capture different constructs of spirituality and the different perspectives they provide.

This essay uses story and narrative, meta-story, meta-narrative, and synonyms. These terms address the same concept in the literature and are often used as synonyms. We also do not differentiate between religious and non-religious spirituality as they are difficult to separate from the perspective we are taking. The leading religion in the region influences spirituality and its stories, and religious spirituality is a type of spirituality as such. Due to the objective of this essay, we work with spirituality regardless of different fields (religion, business, medicine, social work) and environments (individual spirituality, group spirituality, workplace spirituality, global spirituality).

The essay is organized as follows. First, we explain how we understand spirituality and what a meta-story is. A combination of both concepts and the explanation of spirituality from the point of view of a meta-story follows and offers a few approaches to capture the development of spirituality from individual stories. Then, we identify three essential elements of spirituality (relationship to self, relationship to others, relationship to divine – see Table 3.1) that serve as a foundation for classifying different types of stories that create the spirituality meta-story. The final chapter provides even more profound insight. It identifies and creates stories about relationships to self, relationship to others, and relationship to the divine (See Table 3.2).

The essay is based on secondary data. The literature used in this essay was partly collected by the keyword electronic search in scientific (Web of Science, Scopus) and popular journals (Google). Key words were “spirituality”, “spiritual knowledge”, “spirituality concepts”, “spirituality and concept”, “meta-story”, “meta-story development”, and “spirituality and meta-story”. The search did not have the character of the proper detailed literature review. It was not our intention to provide a systemic review of concepts or definitions but to explain how and from which perspective we understand them. We collected up to 20 papers with abstracts most relevant to our keywords for each keyword (if possible, for most of the keywords, the number of documents was smaller) and read them. We identified these papers’ most exciting and relevant citations and ideas, which led us to additional literature (the snowball method). To explore more profound levels of spirituality, we took definitions and concepts of spirituality and psychological scales on spirituality presented in this paper and analyzed them by inductive thematic analysis. The detailed way this was done is explained in the chapter “Looking deeper into spirituality – elements of dimensions of the meta-story”.

Spirituality – A Dynamic Structure

The term spirituality is vague and fuzzy, lacks conceptual clarity (Buck, 2006) and develops in time (Bregman, 2012) or as Principe (1983, p. 129) writes, "we sense a certain fluidity, not to say vagueness, in the use of the term". Therefore, even though this work does not provide a systemic review of concepts or definitions of spirituality, it is necessary to give a few ideas on spirituality to explain how we understand it.

Spirituality concerns what is holistic – it is a multidimensional concept (MacDonald & Friedman, 2002), a fully integrated approach to life.

> Historically, the notion of the spiritual relates to the holy. This translates the Old English word *hālig*, which is "whole" or "complete," which relates to the Greek word *holos* (ὅλος). Thus, spirituality seeks to engage with "life as a whole" rather than its aspects. (Sheldrake, 2013, What is spirituality).

Buck (2006, p. 290) defines spirituality as "The most human of experiences that seek to transcend the self and find meaning and purpose through connection with others, nature, and a Supreme Being, which may or may not involve religious structures or traditions". By Spencer (2012, p. 1):

> Spirituality involves the recognition of a feeling or sense or belief that there is something greater than myself, something more to being human than sensory experience and that the greater whole of which we are part is cosmic or divine.

Principe (1983, p. 136) sees spirituality as:

> How a person understands and lives within their historical context, that aspect of their religion, philosophy or ethic is viewed as the loftiest, the noblest, the most calculated to lead to the fullness of the ideal or perfection being sought.

Říčan (2007) and Kučera (2015) understand spirituality as a dimension of human experience that includes specific values, attitudes, perspectives, beliefs, and emotions. They stress that spirituality is a human phenomenon that exists, at least potentially, in all people (Říčan, 2007; Kučera, 2015). Bregman (2012, p. 5) concludes that thanks to "understanding spirituality as a human phenomenon, one could move from the spirituality of St. Francis' to 'Jewish spirituality' and probably to 'the spirituality of the participants in the traditional Japanese tea ceremony' without stretching things too much" (Bregman, 2012, p. 5).

Spirituality is a bipolar structure with objective and subjective aspects (Bregman, 2012). It is "a generic universal term that considers both aspects of a person's living. A faith or commitment that concerns his or her striving to attain the highest ideal or goal" (Principe, 1983, p. 139) is a subjective aspect and a specific historical context in which it evolved (Bregman, 2012), which is an objective aspect. Alternatively, as van Ness (1996, p. 5) articulates:

> Facing outward, human existence is spiritual insofar as one engages reality as a maximally inclusive whole and makes the cosmos an intentional object of thought and feeling. Facing inward, life

> has a spiritual dimension to the extent that it is apprehended as a project of people's most enduring and vital selves. In other words, the spiritual dimension of life is the embodied task of realizing one's truest self in the context of reality apprehended as a cosmic totality.

Spirituality, then, can mean a convenient focus for one's search for meaning, which all humans strive for but realize in different ways and traditions (Hvidt, 2012).

Even though there are authors who disagree with the separation between religion and spirituality, like Koening (2011), Elkins et al. (1988, p. 8) assume that spirituality is:

> A dimension of human experience – which includes certain values, attitudes, perspectives, beliefs, emotions and so on; exists at least in all persons; it is not the same as religiosity, and a person can be 'spiritual' even though not affiliated with traditional religion and can be described and assessed by theoretical and phenomenological approaches.

Meta-Story

In its broadest sense, a story is "an account of events that are causally connected in some way" (Denning, 2011, p. 13). "A story describes a sequence of actions and experiences done or undergone by a certain number of people, whether real or imaginary" (Ricoeur, 1990, p. 150). Stories "give events meanings and significance" (Polkinghorne, 1988, p. 18) and are "a basic human strategy for coming to terms with time, process and change" (Herman & Herman, 2007, p. 3). "Storytelling is the preferred sense-making currency of human relationships" (Boje, 1991, p. 106), a critical cognitive coping mechanism (Hevern, 2008) as "humans are essentially storytellers" (Fisher, 1984, p. 7), they are "*homo narrans*" (Fisher, 1984, p. 6). People share knowledge and develop their identities in the virtual environment of stories. Stories influence knowledge and beliefs (Gibbons & Prusak, 2020) and directly influence preferences (Akerlof & Kranton, 2005).

Different environments and different cultures expose people to different experiences. "We organize our experience and our memory of human happenings mainly in the form of narrative" (Bruner, 1991, p. 4). Robichaud et al. (2004, p. 619) write:

> Narrative is language's natural provision for making sense of individual experience and social interaction. It establishes the objects and events to which people's attention is directed and provides a complex set of identities and roles that individual actors may enact. Narrative inculcates knowledge of what is accepted as normal within a community and of irregularities regarded as deviant.

Telling a story about oneself describes the actions, choices, and beliefs that transformed the participant's experiences (Hunter, 2010). Stories people tell about their experiences differ about where they are from and which cultural background they belong to, including important narratives that represent the foundations of their spiritual traditions.

A meta-story is "a story embedded within another story or the story about stories themselves" (Yourdictionary, n.d.). For Du Toit (2011, p. 86), it can also be understood as:

> An ideology, paradigm, or system of thought and belief. Such a belief strongly influences what is considered true and just. Furthermore, such truth seems to have an existence independent of that of an individual or society and acts as a measurement against other truths to be judged.

Meta-stories influence the culture and behavior of humans (Somers, 1994), are context-dependent and may turn into myths (Yehoshua, 2004). By Robichaud et al. (2004, p. 618):

> Metanarrative develops through metaconversation or, in other words, a conversation where unitary and pluralistic worlds of talk encounter each other on a single plane of interaction. Narrativity figures both in structuring the text people use to account for events and informing the interaction in which such accounting goes on.

This author argues that:

> Communication mediated by language is recursive, which means that the same conversational procedure operative in constructing a text is also operative in embedding that text within another text (meta-text). A meta-conversation is a conversation that recursively embeds another conversation (Robichaud et al., 2004, p. 621).

The creation of the meta-story is interactive as it depends on changes in conversation among conversation protagonists (Robichaud et al., 2004) where "each conversation narratively frames, implicitly or explicitly, the previous one" (Robichaud et al., 2004, p. 624).

Meta-stories can develop from different sources by different criteria of reasoning; people who use and develop them may give importance to different stories and parts depending on their intentions and previous experience (Izak, 2014). Versions of the individual protagonists might be so different that they may fail to create a meta-story. He also stresses that only some things can be told, and it is necessary to be careful and remember untold stories that also participate in the meta-story creation (Izak, 2014).

Capturing Development of Meta-Story from Individual Stories

The mechanism of meta-story development from separated individual stories and vice versa has yet to be appropriately explained. Only a few authors offer some ideas on how it may work. For example, Montague (2013) describes the creation of the brand story based on five different stories: stories about the participants (customers, employees, partners, the protagonist (the company), the stage (external environment of the company), the quest (ambitions of the company and its contributions to the society) and action map (actions that company is going to take to make the stories reality).

Kolb (2012) did what he calls "an online hypertext narrative demonstration of the interweaving of story and meta-story" (p. 99). He captured this process via nodes and links. He tried to "show how multiple layers, relations, and connections do not nest together in a hierarchy organized around a single core" (p. 99).

To capture separated stories that create a meta-story, Izak (2014) proposes a matrix that visualizes the essential individual stories that generate the meta-story and versions of these stories told by individual participants of meta-story creation. Izak used the matrix to analyze a "story of the collapse of a higher education institution" (Izak, 2014, p. 43). The horizontal level of the matrix comprised different participants of the situation (Ministry of Education, students, teachers, newspapers, etc.), and the vertical class of the matrix was dedicated to their viewpoints (stories) on different aspects of the situation (the problem, who was responsible for it, process of problem evolution). The matrix helped capture other participants' stories about the event and essential aspects of its development, e.g., it showed how the final meta-story was built based on individual levels of individual situation participants.

Another approach that provides an opportunity to examine how separated stories create a meta-story is a meta-narrative review. It is the method used to analyze how different research traditions developed over time and how they developed and shaped research questions and methods (Gough, 2013). The meta-narrative review works with three "overlapping levels (or components). Gough (2013, p. 2) specifies:

> First is an iterative configuring map of the different research traditions in an area. Second, is an iterative configuring and/or aggregative analysis (synthesis) of different traditions within the map. The third is an iterative configuring comparison and contrast of the different meta-narratives to create an overarching synthesis of the whole map.

The method focuses more on "the development of the meta-narrative stories rather than an exhaustive search for all studies from a research tradition" (Gough, 2013, p. 2) and "can be considered a form of multi-level configuring mapping rather than synthesis of research findings. This analysis could involve an interpretative configuring of ideas and the aggregation of data" (Gough, 2013, p. 3).

Creating the meta-story on individual stories and vice versa can also be approached from the perspective of narrative analysis and story restoration used in qualitative research. Restoration is a process of reorganizing and analyzing the key elements of a story and rewriting it within chronological order (Ollerenshaw & Creswell, 2002; Nasheeda et al., 2019). Nasheeda et al. (2019, p. 2) note that:

> Literature suggests a multitude of techniques and approaches to analyzing narrative data; there is no single method to narrative analysis as the story can be told in different forms and retold on different occasions. There is no single procedure that can be claimed as "best" for analyzing narratives.

As Clandinin (2006, p. xv) writes:

> Narrative analysis can be of two types. In the first type, experiential data are collected, and the research aim is to organize the data to create a narrative with a plot that unifies the data. The created story is a narrative explanation of the phenomenon being studied. The second type collects

> data (stories) from research participants or subjects. The narrative data is analyzed for common themes, metaphors, plotlines, and so on to identify general themes and concepts.

All these approaches have their advantages and disadvantages.

Spirituality as a Meta-Story

Spirituality as a meta-story develops through the interaction of independent stories about different aspects of the material and social world. This meta-story is a higher-level construction and provides a holistic understanding of the human, his relation to the world and his roles.

Spirituality is a complex meta-story that combines different types of stories, like stories about the behavior and experience of a specific character, distinct events, and other places. Up to this, stories about the individual's position in these stories are also important.

Spirituality as a meta-story has a character explained by Kolb (2012, p. 99), who writes that meta-story has:

> Multiple layers, relations, and connections do not nest together in a hierarchy organized around a single core. There are gaps, slidings, and self-reflections even in what seems solid identity, especially as those identities endure through time by reproducing and reinterpreting themselves.

Spirituality is an "overarching story or storyline that gives context, meaning, and purpose to all of life. It is the "big picture" or all-encompassing theme that unites all smaller themes and individual stories" (Gotquestions, n.d.).

Robichaud et al. (2004, p. 618) explain how such a meta-story is developed:

> The recursive property of language is instrumental in producing what we call a "meta-conversation," that is, the conversation in which a collective identity is constituted. The role of narrativity is central in such a constitution. Different spiritual traditions understand and organize their narratives in their distinct way via "the dispersed network of local conversations as being, by analogy with computer programming, hyperlinked, with the "links" being activated by the people who migrate between and participate in various conversations.

They may stress different elements of spirituality and express them in other stories. "How narrative elements are combined may deliberately discourage alternative combinations" (Izak, 2014, p. 42). As Churchill (2009, p. 11) notes, "spirituality, like politics, is a local phenomenon. Nobody practices religion or spirituality in general".

Izak's matrix and the meta-narrative review can potentially analyze how spirituality as a meta-story develops and which elements create it. Still, it is necessary to remember that the mechanism of meta-story development from separated individual stories and vice versa represents a research gap and needs more exploration and explanation. Mapping stories and their interrelations may be complex due to the intangibility of subjective and objective aspects of spirituality (Bregman, 2012) and difficulties with its externalizations. People may also, as Izak (2014, p. 42) notes:

> Favor 'meaningful' readings of stories by assembling them into neatly structured narratives, for instance, those of success, collapse, struggle, betrayal, and others. From the definition, such readings emphasize (and deemphasize) matching elements. Others may go unnoticed or be deleted for the benefit of 'the story'. The predilection to 'tell the story', to immobilize its elements into the final (for us) or official (if the external agency is involved) version, renders more stories silent than it gives voice to.

Looking into Basic Elements of Spirituality – Dimensions of the Meta-Story

We are aware of the fact that some authors (Wach, 1957; Skalický, 2005; Kučera, 2012) think that it is not possible to explain spirituality by materialization, e.g., to break it down to something that is not spiritual and examine it with methods of Aristotelean science that work well with measurable elements but may not provide tools to explore what evolves in a non-logic and nonlinear way. Or, as Belzen (2009) writes, a standard definition of spirituality may lead to confusion because some types of human behavior may be understood as spiritual, even as an act of spiritual heroism, and simultaneously be positive for one group of people and negative for another. Still, we think that looking deeper, identifying, collecting and examining stories on the separated elements of spirituality and their relationships may provide deeper insight into what spirituality is and how it develops. We also know that any such attempt will capture aspects of spirituality and spirituality in the given moment, as spirituality develops constantly, and its dynamic evolvement may be too fast to be captured.

Differences in worldview, self-definition, personal beliefs and experiences influence how people in different parts of the world understand and explain spirituality. We can learn more about spirituality, spiritual concepts and their differences and commonalities with the help of stories they are based on. Before examining stories that create spirituality, we must organize them logically. Or differently, if we want to explore spirituality and its development from the point of view of meta-story, we must first identify which types of stories spirituality is based on. The classification of stories will then guide us to concrete kinds of stories, their relation and their role in meta-story development.

Definitions, concepts and scales presented below are used as a guideline that helps us to identify different stories creating spiritual meta-story. MacGillivray et al. (2006) see spirituality built of an intangible part of self, transcendence and connectedness with the universe or other people, emotions, occupation, one's dreams and their pursuit, one's beliefs and values, the search for the meaning of life, relationship with God/many Gods or a higher power, and religion as essential elements of spirituality.

Buck (2006, p. 289) proposed five elements of spirituality:

1. Spirituality is an internal human experience not limited by cognitive adaptability;
2. It incorporates the metaphysical components of ontology (the nature of being of the individual) and teleology (the ultimate purpose or end of the individual);
3. Self is transcended;
4. Connection to others, nature, and/or a Supreme Being is experienced;
5. It may or may not involve religious structures and traditions.

Buck (2006, p. 289) notes that:

> Spirituality can also be expressed within the context of individual belief systems, inner life experiences, and in a general sense of being, and the definition of spirituality often encapsulates concepts of meaning (or purpose), value (or beliefs), transcendence (beyond the self), connecting (with others), and becoming (the life journey).

Reed (1992) sees three factors that create spirituality: a factor based on the individual connection to self (personal integration, values), a relationship between individuals (friendship, trust) and a connection of the individual to transcendent dimensions (mystical or religious experiences). Delaney (2005) proposed four elements of spirituality: self-discovery (intrapersonal), relationships (interpersonal), higher power/universal intelligence and eco-awareness (transpersonal). His research showed that one factor is higher power/versatile intelligence and eco-awareness (Buck, 2006).

Kučera (2012) proposes, based on the works of Skalický (2005), the matrix-based model of spirituality. The part of spirituality that concerns supernatural, superhuman, mysterious, absolute and the highest creates the vertical dimension; the role of spirituality that reflects the practical manifestation of the vertical dimension (values, relationship to others, practices) is the horizontal dimension (Kučera, 2012). "As such, spirituality interconnects question of why (causal tasking) and what (descriptive tasking) with questions on the sense and meaning (tasking on value)" (Kučera, 2012, p. 77). He sees spirituality as values, belongings, internal desires and quests (Kučera, 2012).

Rocha and Pinheiro (2021b, p. 248) see the spirituality of an individual as "a personal identity, a way of life that represents habits, the pursuit of meaning and purpose, search for transcendence, connection with the others, and the divine in all aspects and areas (personal and work)" and "a phenomenon that brings the connection between individuals, enlightening the purpose of their lives, it also connects individuals with other communities and generations". Giacalone (2003, p. 13) writes that spirituality can be defined as "a framework of organizational values evidenced in the culture that promotes employees' experience of transcendence through the work progress, facilitating their sense of being connected to others in a way that provides feelings of completeness and joy". Ashmos and Duchon (2000, p. 134) understand "the spiritual dimension of human beings" as the "dimension concerned with finding and expressing meaning and purpose and living about others and to something bigger than oneself".

Emmons (2000, p. 10) understands spirituality as a form of intelligence created of five components. They are:

> (a) the capacity for transcendence; (b) the ability to enter into heightened spiritual states of consciousness; (c) the ability to invest everyday activities, events, and relationships with a sense of the sacred; (d) the ability to utilize spiritual resources to solve problems in living; and (e) the capacity to engage in virtuous behavior or to be virtuous (to show forgiveness, to express gratitude, be humble, display compassion).

Piedmont (1999, 2001) proposes spiritual transcendence theory, one of the most complex theories of spirituality. Piotrowsky et al. (2013, p. 471) explain that the Piedmont's spiritual transcendence theory:

> Identifies seven aspects (or facets) of spiritual transcendence: prayer fulfilment (feelings of joy and contentment that result from personal encounters with a transcendent reality, fulfilment in prayer or meditation), universality (a belief in the unitive nature of life), connectedness (a belief that one is part of a larger human orchestra whose contribution is indispensable in creating life's continuing harmony), tolerance for paradoxes (the ability to live with inconsistencies and contradictions in one's own life, to think of things in terms of "both-and" rather than "either-or," tolerance for inconsistency and incoherence), nonjudgmentally (an ability to accept life and others on their own terms and to avoid making value judgments; a sensitivity to the needs and pains of others), existentialism (a desire to live in the moment and to embrace the experiences that life confronts us with as opportunities for growth and joy), gratefulness (an innate sense of wonder and thankfulness for all the many shared and unique features of one's life).

They add one more aspect to this concept, concretely "the feeling of being part of a cause or idea more important than oneself" (Piotrowsky et al., 2013, p. 472), which they called ideologicality.

Detailed insight into elements of spirituality is also provided by psychological scales developed to measure it. Again, the scales below are just examples, not a definitive list.

Elkins et al. (1988) developed 85 items Spiritual Orientation Inventory. This measure comprises eighty-five items in nine categories: transcendent dimension, meaning and purpose in life, mission in life, sacredness in life, material values, altruism, idealism, awareness of the tragedy and fruits of spirituality. The transcendent dimension captures the belief of the individual that there is a transcendent dimension of life. Regardless of "whatever is the content, typology, metaphors or models to describe the transcendent dimension, a spiritual person believes in an 'unseen world', and that harmonious contact with and adjustment to this unseen dimension is beneficial "(Elkins et al., 1988, p. 10) and he experienced it. Meaning and purpose in life represent every person's experience and its meaning. "The actual ground and content of this meaning vary from person to person, but the common factor is that each person has filled the 'existential vacuum' with an authentic sense that life has meaning and purpose" (Elkins et al., 1988, p. 11). Mission in life represents "a sense of responsibility to life, a calling to answer, a mission to accomplish, or in some cases, even a destiny to fulfill" (Elkins et al., 1988, p. 11).

The sacredness of life means that life is 'holy' and that the sacred is in the ordinary" (Elkins et al., 1988, p. 11). The spiritual person appreciates material values but "knows that 'ontological thirst' can only be quenched by the spiritual and that ultimate satisfaction is found not in material, but spiritual things" (Elkins et al., 1988, p. 11). Altruism then plays a significant role in a spiritual person's life, representing a sense of social justice and love for others. Altruistic people accept responsibility for others. Meaning of idealism is that the person is committed to the "betterment of the world" (Elkins et al., 1988, p. 11) and has a deep belief in humanity but at the same time is aware of "the tragic realities of human existence" (Elkins et al., 1988, p. 11). Fruits of spirituality mean that "true spirituality affects one's relationship to self, others, nature, life and whatever one considers to be the Ultimate" (Elkins et al., 1988, p. 12)

Howden (1992) developed a spirituality assessment scale (SAS). It comprises twenty-eight questions organized into four categories – interconnectedness, purpose and meaning in life, innerness and transcendence. Interconnectedness covers a general sense of belonging, forgiveness, kindness to others, connection to all life, service to others, and community participation. Purpose and meaning in life cover life's fulfillment and goals and aims. Innerness covers topics of the ability to cope with bad events, inner strengths in hard times, the ability to go beyond the loss, and internal resources that help people cope with uncertainty and balance in life. Transcendence concerns relationships to a Higher Purpose or Supreme Being and the planet.

When improving the Quality of Life measure (WHOQOL), WHO decided to upgrade it to a specific module on spirituality, religiousness and personal beliefs (SRPB), resulting in four sections: transcendence, personal relationships, code to live by and specific religious beliefs, Transcendence is represented by connectedness to the spiritual being or force, the meaning of life, awe, wholeness/integration, divine love, inner peace/serenity/harmony, inner strength, death and dying, detachment/attachment, hope/optimism, and control over life. Personal relationships focus on kindness to others, acceptance of others, and forgiveness. Code to live by is about code to live by freedom to practice rituals and faith. Specific religious beliefs are issues that are important for practicing religion.

McDonnald (2000) introduces the Expressions of Spirituality Inventory (ESI). The tool has ninety-eight questions that create a five-dimensional measure model of spirituality. The dimensions are cognitive orientation towards spirituality, experiential/phenomenological dimension, existential well-being, paranormal beliefs and religiousness. Cognitive orientation towards spirituality "embodies beliefs, attitudes, and perceptions about the relevance of spirituality to one's daily functioning" (McDonnald et al., 2002, p. 117), e.g., an individual's spiritual beliefs and perceptions. The experiential/phenomenological dimension is focused on spiritual and mystical experiences. Existential well-being "involves three general components: purpose and meaning in life, a sense of inner strength and perception of self as able to cope with the basic issues of life, and a relaxed orientation towards self and day-to-day matters" (McDonnald et al., 2002, p. 118). Paranormal beliefs are unusual thoughts and behavioral patterns. Researches show that such belief may be related to health problems and disorders (McDonnald et al., 2002). According to McDonnald et al. (2002, p. 118), religiousness is an:

> Intrinsic religious orientation or engaging in religious practice for its own sake. Extrinsic religious orientation (i.e., using religion to accomplish another end, such as acquiring social status in one's community) and formal aspects of institutional religion are explicitly excluded. Both nondenominational beliefs about the existence of a higher power and religious practice (including prayer, meditation, and attendance at religious services) comprise the two critical components of this dimension.

Říčan (2006) created the scale for spirituality measurement based on five factors – mystical experience, eco-spirituality, communality, moral interest and transcendental-monotheistic experience. Mystical experience is feeling unified with something beyond the individual, inner peace, and ecstatic fascination with the art. Eco-spirituality is the feeling of unity with nature and sacred responsibility for it. It understands the Earth as a mother and the tree as a brother and cares respect for the living and nonliving nature. Communality presents the pleasure from the human sense of belonging and closeness and amazement from the unity in diversity. Moral interest represents the desire to start again and better, fear of making mistakes that ruin one's life, admiration of the exceptional good of others, sympathy with those who suffer, and disgust with the bad. Transcendental-monotheistic experience captures the fascination with the "higher truth" and "the highest reality" and death as "the return to home" (Kučera, 2012).

The ideas of upper authors can be classified into three essential elements of spirituality (Table 3.1).

Table 3.1: Three essential elements of spirituality – dimensions of meta-story.

References	Relationship to self	Relationship to others	Relationship to divine
MacGillivray et al. (2006)	The intangible part of self, emotions, occupation, dreams and pursuits, beliefs and values, search for meaning.	Connectedness with other people	Relationship with higher power, religion
Buck (2006)	Meaning (or purpose), value (or beliefs), becoming (the life journey)	Connecting (with others)	Transcendence (beyond the self)
Reed (1992)	Factor-based on the individual connection to self (personal integration, values)	The connection between individuals (friendship, trust)	Connection of the individual to transcendent dimensions (mystical or religious experiences)
Delaney (2005)	Self-discovery (intrapersonal)	Relationships (interpersonal)	Higher power/universal intelligence and eco-awareness (transpersonal)
Kučera (2012)	Values, practices	Relationship to others	Supernatural, superhuman, mysterious, absolute and the highest

Table 3.1 (continued)

References	Relationship to self	Relationship to others	Relationship to divine
Rocha & Pinheiro (2021b, p. 248)	A personal identity, a way of life that represents habits, the pursuit of meaning and purpose, Enlightening the purpose of their lives	Connection with the others, The connection between individuals connects individuals with other communities and generations.	Search for transcendence, the divine in all aspects and areas.
Giacalone (2003)	A framework of organizational values, Feelings of completeness and joy	Sense of being connected to others	Employees' experience of transcendence
Ashmos and Duchon (2000)	Dimension concerned with finding and expressing meaning and purpose	Living about others	Something bigger than oneself
Emmons (2000)	The ability to enter into heightened spiritual states of consciousness, the ability to utilize spiritual resources to solve problems in living	The capacity to engage in virtuous behavior	The capacity for transcendence, the ability to invest everyday activities, events, and relationships with a sense of the sacred
Piedmont (1999, 2001)	Existentiality	Connectedness, nonjudgmentality	Prayer fulfilment, universality, tolerance for paradoxes
Piotrowsky et al. (2019)	Existentiality	Connectedness, nonjudgmentality, ideologicality	Prayer fulfilment, universality, tolerance for paradoxes
Elkins et al. (1988)	Meaning and purpose in life, mission in life, material values, awareness of the tragic, fruits of spirituality	Altruism, idealism, awareness of the tragic, fruits of spirituality	Transcendent dimension, sacredness in life, fruits of spirituality
Howden (1992)	Innerness, purpose and meaning in life	Interconnectedness	Transcendence
WHO (1998)	Inner peace/serenity/harmony, death and dying, inner strength, hope/optimism, control over life, code to live by freedom to practice rituals, faith	Detachment/ attachment, kindness to others, acceptance of others, forgiveness, code to live by	Spiritual being or force, the meaning of life, awe, wholeness/integration, divine love, Issues that are important for practicing concrete religion.

Table 3.1 (continued)

References	Relationship to self	Relationship to others	Relationship to divine
McDonnald et al., 2002	Cognitive orientation towards spirituality, experiential/ phenomenological dimension, existential well-being,	–	Paranormal beliefs and religiousness.
Říčan (2006)	Moral interest	Moral interest, eco-spirituality, communality	Mystical experience, transcendental-monotheistic experience

Source: Author

Concepts, definitions and scales presented in Table 3.1 create three fundamental elements of spirituality: the relationship to self, the relationship to others and the relationship to the divine. Relationship to self represents stories about tangible and intangible parts of self, emotions, dreams, beliefs, values, search for meaning, self-discovery, habits and purpose. Relationship to others reflects stories about connectedness with others and with previous generations. The relationship to the divine are stories about the relationship to a higher power, religion, transcendence dimensions, and what is mysterious and of higher order.

Technically, stories about elements of spirituality are also meta-stories as they can be broken down into simpler stories. As such, they may provide the springboard for research on spirituality and allow it to capture its elements and follow its development over time.

Looking Deeper into Spirituality: Elements of Dimensions of the Meta-Story

The development of spirituality as a meta-story is demonstrated in Table 3.2. Spirituality as a meta-story is at the top of the hierarchy of stories. Three primary groups of stories create it: relationship to the divine, relationship to others and relationship to self. These basic elements are also made by specific stories (we call them detailed elements, and we identified 11 such stories), e.g., they also have a character of a meta-story.

To explore more profound levels of spirituality, e.g., to find out based on which stories spirituality and its three essential elements are built, we took all definitions, concepts and psychological scales (presented in this paper) and analyzed them by inductive thematic analysis. We analyzed accurate expressions of definitions and concepts as provided in the literature; as for psychological scales, we understand and approach them as distinct concepts of spirituality; therefore, we focused on categories in which the questions are organized, not on the questions themselves.

The coding was thematic; we collected relevant data from the definitions, concepts and scales and generated initial codes, then we searched for themes that led to the identification of lower-level categories (detailed elements of spirituality). Finally, these categories were organized into higher-level categories (essential elements of spirituality). Lower-level categories represent the topics of stories that serve as the foundation of three basic types of stories creating spirituality. The results are provided in Table 3.2.

Table 3.2: What spirituality is based on.

Initial codes	Detailed elements of spirituality (lower level category)	Basic elements of spirituality (Higher level category)
Fruits of spirituality; true spirituality; spiritual being or force; awe; wholeness/integration; cognitive orientation towards spirituality; beliefs, attitudes and perceptions about the relevance of spirituality to one's daily functioning; experiential/phenomenological dimension; spiritual experience	Spirituality	Spirituality
Connectedness with the universe; connection with nature; relationship to the planet; eco-spirituality; feeling of unity with nature; sacred responsibility for nature; Earth as a mother; tree as a brother; respect to living and nonliving nature.	Nature	Relationship to divine
Transcendence (4); internal human experience not limited by cognitive adaptability; self is transcended; concepts of transcendence; connection to transcendent dimension; employees' understanding of transcendence; mysterious; search for transcendence; the capacity for transcendence; encounters with a transcendent reality; personal encounters with a transcendent reality; transcendent dimension; there is a transcendent dimension of the life; belief that person experienced contact with transcendent dimension; transcendental-monotheistic; view of the individual that belief of that harmonious contact with and adjustment to this unseen dimension is beneficial; mystical experience; the sacred is in the ordinary; mystical experience; paranormal beliefs; unusual thoughts; unusual behavioural patterns; mystical experience; being unified with something that goes beyond the individual; the highest reality'; death as 'the return to home'; divine in all aspects and areas; relationships with a sense of the sacred; divine love.	Transcendence	

Table 3.2 (continued)

Initial codes	Detailed elements of spirituality (lower level category)	Basic elements of spirituality (Higher level category)
Relationship with God/many Gods; relationship with a higher power; connection to Supreme Being; higher power/universal intelligence; superhuman; absolute; the highest; Supreme Being.	Good/Higher Being	
Religion; religious structures; religious traditions; religious experience; religiousness; intrinsic religious orientation; engaging in the religious practice for its own sake; beliefs about the existence of a higher power; religious practice; prayer; meditation; attendance at religious services; fulfillment in prayer or meditation; freedom to practice rituals; faith; specific religion; practicing concrete religion; prayer fulfillment; deep belief in humanity.	Religion; concepts of belief; religious practice	
The person is committed to "betterment of the world" – has effect on one's relationship to self, nature, life, whatever one considers to be the Ultimate; connection to all life; the search for the meaning of life; a general sense of being; becoming – life journey; the ultimate purpose or end of the individual; the top end of the individual; the pursuit of meaning and purpose; enlightening the purpose of their lives; finding and expressing meaning; finding and expressing purpose; living to something bigger than oneself; a belief in the unitive nature of life; meaning life; purpose in life; mission in life; sacredness in life; meaning and purpose in life; "existential vacuum" with an authentic sense that life has meaning and purpose; mission in life represent; a sense of responsibility to life; a calling to answer; a mission to accomplish; a destiny to fulfil; sacredness of life; life is "holy"; control over life; code to live by; purpose in life; meaning in life; meaning of life; life fulfilment; life meaning; goals and aims for life; balance in life; death and dying; aware of "the tragic realities of human existence".	Relationship to life	
Connectedness with other people; connection with others; connecting with others; the connection between individuals; relationships (interpersonal); relationship to others; belongings; connection with the others; the connection between individuals; connects individuals with other communities;	Belonging and connectedness to other people	Relationship to others

Table 3.2 (continued)

Initial codes	Detailed elements of spirituality (lower level category)	Basic elements of spirituality (Higher level category)
connects generations; a sense of being connected to others; living about others; the belief that one is part of a larger human orchestra whose contribution is indispensable in creating life's continuing harmony; others; general sense of belonging; being part of the community; connectedness; personal relationships; the pleasure from human sense of belonging and closeness; friendship; connectedness; interconnectedness; communality; detachment/attachment.		
Trust; to show forgiveness; to display compassion; tolerance for inconsistency and incoherence; nonjudgmentality; ability to accept others on their terms; avoid making value judgments; a sensitivity to the needs of others; sensitivity to pains of others; altruism; altruism; a sense of social justice; love to others; accept responsibility for others; forgiveness; kindness to other people; service to others; kindness to others; acceptance of others; forgiveness; sympathy with those who suffer; fear to make mistakes that ruin one's life; admiration of the exceptional good of others; the capacity to engage in virtuous behavior or to be virtuous; express gratitude; be humble; tolerance for paradoxes; appreciates material values but ultimate satisfaction is found not in material but spiritual things.	Desired behavior toward other people	
Appreciates material values – ultimate satisfaction is found not in material; but spiritual things; one's dreams and their pursuit; the ability to invest everyday activities; events; the ability to utilise spiritual resources to solve problems in living; the ability to live with inconsistencies and contradictions in one's own life; ability to think of things in terms of "both-and" rather than "either-or; existentiality; gratefulness; an innate sense of wonder and thankfulness for all the many shared and unique features of one's life; ideologicality; feelings of joy; universality; purpose and meaning; ; innerness; ability to cope with bad events; inner strengths in hard times; ability to go beyond the loss; internal resources that help people to cope with uncertainty; ; inner peace; serenity; harmony; inner strength;	Abilities	Relationship to self

Table 3.2 (continued)

Initial codes	**Detailed elements of spirituality (lower level category)**	**Basic elements of spirituality (Higher level category)**
hope/optimism; sense of inner strength; sense of perception of self as able to cope with the fundamental issues of life; relaxed orientation towards self; relax direction to day-to-day matters; the feeling of inner peace; moral interest; disgust with the bad; Idealism; existential well-being; ecstatic fascination by the art; amazement of unity in diversity; the ability to enter into heightened spiritual states of consciousness; material values; idealism; feeling of contentment.		
Individual connection to self; personal integration; self-discovery (intrapersonal); practices; the nature of being of the individual; a personal identity; feelings of completeness and joy; ability to accept life on their terms; emotions; occupation; inner life experiences; quests; intangible part of self.	Personal identity	
Internal desires: a desire to live in the moment, a willingness to embrace the experiences that life confronts us with as opportunities for growth and joy; The desire to start again and better.	Desires	
One's beliefs, values, individual belief systems, concepts of meaning, concepts of value, images of beliefs, personal values, values; a way of life representing habits, framework or organizational values.	Values	

Table 3.2 shows that we identified twelve distinct lower-level categories. One of them is the category of spirituality. This category stays separated from other types because it does not provides additional information on spiritual elements.

Out of the remaining eleven, five lower-level categories (nature, transcendence, God/Higher Being; Religion, concepts of belief, religious practice and life relationship) create higher-level category relationships to the divine. Two lower-level categories (belonging and connectedness to other people; desired behavior to others) build higher-level category relationships with others. Four lower-level categories (abilities, personal identity, desires, values) create higher-level category relationships to self.

Table 3.3 summarises findings and lists stories that create the meta-story spirituality.

To conclude, spirituality as a meta-story is built on three lower-level stories about the individual's relationship to self, others, and the divine. These three stories are also

Table 3.3: Stories that create meta-story spirituality.

	Spirituality – Meta-Story		
1st level stories on	Relationship to self	Relationship to others	Relationship to divine
2nd level stories on	abilities personal identity desires values	belonging and connectedness to other people desired behavior to other people	Nature transcendence God/ Higher Being Religion concepts of belief, religious practice relationship to life

meta-stories. The relationship to self is created from stories about an individual's abilities, identity, desires and values. The story about the relationship to others is developed on stories about belonging and connectedness to other people and the story about desired behavior to other people. The story about the relationship to the divine is built on stories about nature, transcendence, God/Higher Being, religion/religious practices/ concepts of belief and the story about their life relationship.

When doing the empiric research, lower-level stories can be examined deeper, which may identify more detailed reports that create them. The psychological scales for spirituality measurement offer concrete questions that can be adjusted to the needs of such thorough research.

Stories can also be examined from different points of view than the topic, for example, from their origin. Table 3.3 indicates the bipolar structure of stories (Bregman, 2012). Some lower-level stories suggest that they develop more based on personal experience (personal identity), and some develop more on shared experience (for example, desired abilities or behavior toward others).

Conclusions

For (Elkins et al., 1988, p. 8), "religion has been the mother of the world's greatest spiritual giants, the 'best of the species' in the area of spirituality and is the incubator and reservoir of the world's most vital spiritual values". Hochheimer (2012, p. 22) explains:

> Humankind is a meaning-making species. Throughout our lives, we build our abilities to exist within the world we both experience and create. We may evolve in our spiritual comprehension, or we may stagnate. Or, we may have been taught to believe we have no right to ask such questions. But we live following the meanings we perceive and express.

This author adds: "Our efforts to do so (i.e., build the meaning) have always been incomplete because our perceptions of it (i.e., meaning) are grounded in the historical, cultural, societal, biological and/or developmental contexts within which meaning is incompletely, imperfectly and provisionally constructed" (Hochheimer, 2012, p. 25).

Spirituality is a dynamic phenomenon. It is a phenomenon that depends on the concrete situation of the human being in the concrete moment. Therefore, it is difficult to capture and analyze it. Spirituality can be captured and explored via the knowledge we have about it, spiritual knowledge. Storytelling is one of the most important tools for knowledge sharing and creation. We argue that spiritual knowledge is a meta-story built on at least three different types of stories. Stories about the self that explain how the individuals see themselves and their role in the universe, stories about relationships to others that explain how individuals see their role in society, and stories about the relationship to the divine that describe how individuals see themselves about higher power create the personal meta-story, spirituality.

We recommend researching the foundations and development of spirituality indirectly from spiritual knowledge. Spiritual knowledge is the knowledge people have about their spirituality. From the perspective of spiritual knowledge, spirituality is a meta-story created by stories about different parts of one's spiritual life. Capturing these stories helps us to learn more about what makes spirituality and how it develops.

The proper method of researching these stories has yet to be developed. Our paper recommends using a meta-narrative review methodology, thematic narrative analysis, or Izak's story matrix (Izak, 2014).

As for future research, though not all elements of spirituality discussed in this paper apply to workplace spirituality, the workplace or organization may serve as an experimental plot for research on spirituality. They have clear borders and develop in a shorter period, and spirituality related to the workplace or organization may be easier to research than religious or general spirituality.

Even though it looks attractive, the approach to spirituality as a meta-story has disadvantages. The creation of a meta-stories from individual stories or breaking down the meta-story into personal stories may be a challenging problem because even though the central theme of each meta-story may be the same, the actual content of stories that create a meta-story can differ (Gordevicius et al., 2010, p. 1909). Said differently, similar or identical meta-stories may be based on different stories, and one meta-story can be broken down into other ones. Another problem may develop from so-called untold stories (Izak, 2014). Untold stories the individual subconsciously or consciously does not share may bias the research results. Or it may be challenging to capture individual stories as respondents of the research may resist fragmenting their experience into thematic categories and tell so-called "long story" with diversions to stories that are not relevant (Riessman, 2020).

References

Akerlof, G. A., & Kranton, R. E. (2005). Identity and the Economics of Organizations. *Journal of Economic Perspectives*, *19*(1), 9–32. https://doi.org.10.1257/0895330053147930.

Ashmos, D. P., & Duchon, D. (2000). Spirituality at work: A conceptualization and measure. *Journal of Management Inquiry*, *9*(2), 134–145. https://doi.org/10.1177/105649260092008.

Belzen, J. A. (2009). Některé podmínky, možnosti a hranice psychologických studií spirituality [Some conditions, posiblities and borders of psychological studies on spirituality]. *Ceskoslovenska Psychologie*, *53*(4), 396–407.

Boje, D. M. (1991). The storytelling organisation: A study of story performance in an office-supply firm. *Administrative Science Quarterly*, 36, 106–126.

Bratianu, C. (2013). The triple helix of the organisational knowledge. *Management Dynamics in the Knowledge Economy*, *1*(2), 207–220.

Bregman, L. (2012). Spirituality definitions: A moving target. In *Spirituality: Theory, praxis and pedagogy*, Brill, 3, 1–10. https://doi.org/10.1163/9781848880917_002.

Bruner, J. (1991). The narrative construction of reality. *Critical Inquiry*, *18*(1), 1–21.

Buck, H. G. (2006). Spirituality: concept analysis and model development. *Holistic Nursing Practice*, *20*(6), 288–292.

Churchill, L. R. (2009, February). Religion, spirituality, and genetics: Mapping the terrain for research purposes. In *American Journal of Medical Genetics Part C: Seminars in Medical Genetics*, Hoboken: Wiley Subscription Services, Inc., A Wiley Company. 151 (1), 6–12. https://doi.org/10.1002/ajmg.c.30195.

Clandinin, D. J. (2006). Narrative inquiry: A methodology for studying lived experience. *Research Studies in Music Education*, *27*(1), 44–54. https://doi.org/10.1177/1321103X060270010301.

Coreth, E. (1994). Philisophische Grundlagen der Theologie Karl Rahners. *Stimmen der Zeit (Freiburg)*, *212*(8), 525–536.

Delaney, C. (2005). The spirituality scale: Development and psychometric testing of a holistic instrument to assess the human spiritual dimension. *Journal of Holistic Nursing*, *23*(2), 145–167. https://doi.org/10.1177/0898010105276180.

Denning, S. (2011). *The leader's guide to storytelling: Mastering the art and discipline of business narrative*. John Wiley & Sons.

Du Toit A., (2011). *Lyotard dictionary. Grand Narrative, Metanarrative.* (S. Sim, Ed.). Edinburgh University Press.

Elkins, David N., Hedstrom L. J., Hughes L. L., Leaf J. A., &Saunders C. (1988). Toward a humanistic-phenomenological spirituality: Definition, description, and measurement. *Journal of Humanistic Psychology*, *28 (4)*, 5–18. https://doi.org/10.1177/0022167888284002.

Emmons, R. A. (2000). Is spirituality an intelligence? Motivation, cognition, and the psychology of ultimate concern. *The International Journal for the Psychology of Religion*, 10(1), 3–26. https://doi.org/10.1207/S15327582IJPR1001_2.

Fisher, W. R. (1984). Narration as a human communication paradigm: The case of public moral argument. *Communications Monographs*, *51*(1), 1–22.

Giacalone, R. A. (2003). Toward a science of workplace spirituality, in Giacalone, RA and Jurkiewicz, CL (Eds), *Handbook of Workplace Spirituality and Organizational Performance*, ME Sharpe, Armonk, NY.

Gibbons, R., & Prusak, L. (2020, May). Knowledge, stories, and culture in organisations. In *AEA Papers and Proceedings* (Vol. 110, p. 187–92).

Gordevicius, J., Estrada, F. J., Lee, H. C., Andritsos, P., & Gamper, J. (2010, October). Ranking of evolving stories through meta-aggregation. In *Proceedings of the 19th ACM International Conference on Information and Knowledge Management.* 1909–1912. https://doi.org/10.1145/1871437.1871761.

GotQuestions (n.d.) What is a metanarrative. Retrieved November 30, 2022, https://www.gotquestions.org/metanarrative.html.

Gough, D. (2013). Meta-narrative and realist reviews: guidance, rules, publication standards and quality appraisal. *BMC medicine*, 11(1), 1–4.
Herman, D., & Herman, R. D. (Eds.). (2007). *The Cambridge companion to narrative*. Cambridge University Press.
Hevern, V. W. (2008). Why narrative psychology can't afford to ignore the body. *Journal of Social, Evolutionary, and Cultural Psychology*, *2*(4), 217. https://doi.org/10.1037/h0099343.
Hochheimer, J. L. (2012). Communication, Spirituality and the Sharing of Meaning. In Fowler, M., Martin, J. D. I., & Hochheimer, J. L. (2020), *Spirituality: Theory, praxis and pedagogy* (p. 21–30). Brill. https://doi.org/10.1163/9781848880917_004.
Howden, J. W. (1992). *Development and psychometric characteristics of the Spirituality Assessment Scale*. Texas Woman's University.
Hunter, S. V. (2010). Analysing and representing narrative data: The long and winding road. *Current Narratives*, *1*(2), 44–54.
Hvidt N. C. (2012) Making Meaning of Meaning-Making Research: The Background of Key Dimensions. In Fowler, M., Martin, J. D. I., & Hochheimer, J. L. (2020), *Spirituality: Theory, praxis and pedagogy*. Brill, 11–20. https://doi.org/10.1163/9781848880917_003.
Izak, M. (2014). A story-in-the-making: an intertextual exploration of a multivoiced narrative. *Tamara Journal for Critical Organization Inquiry*, *12*(1), 41–57.
Koenig, H. G. (2011). *Spirituality and health research: Methods, measurements, statistics, and resources*. Templeton Press.
Kolb, D. A. (2012, June). Story/story. In *Proceedings of the 23rd ACM conference on Hypertext and social media* (p. 99–102). https://doi.org/10.1145/2309996.2310013.
Kučera, D. (2012). Weberova teze „ducha kapitalismu "jako podnět pro hledání spirituálních potenciálů v podnikatelském a manažerském prostředí [Weber's thesis "spirit of capitalism" as an impulse for search of spiritual potential in entrepreneurial and managerial environment]. [Doctoral thesis. Prague University of Economics and Business]. Prague.
MacDonald, D. A. (2000). Spirituality: Description, measurement, and relation to the five factor model of personality. *Journal of Personality*, *68*(1), 153–197. https://doi.org/10.1111/1467-6494.t01-1-00094.
MacDonald, D. A., & Friedman, H. L. (2002). Assessment of humanistic, transpersonal, and spiritual constructs: State of the science. *Journal of Humanistic Psychology*, *42*(4), 102–125. https://doi.org/10.1177/002216702237126.
MacGillivray, P. S., Sumsion, T., & Wicks-Nicholls, J. (2006). Critical elements of spirituality as identified by adolescent mental health clients. *Canadian Journal of Occupational Therapy*, *73*(5), 295–302. https://doi.org/10.2182/cjot.06.006
Machů, K. (2015). Dotazník Expressions of spirituality inventory (ESI) jako metoda měření spirituality [Questionnaire Expressions of spirituality inventory (ESI) as a method of spirituality measurement]. *E-psychologie*, *9*(3), 1–9.
Montague, T. (2013). *True story: How to combine story and action to transform your business*. Harvard Business Press.
Nasheeda, A., Abdullah, H. B., Krauss, S. E., & Ahmed, N. B. (2019). Transforming transcripts into stories: A multimethod approach to narrative analysis. *International Journal of Qualitative Methods*, *18*, https://journals.sagepub.com/doi/pdf/10.1177/1609406919856797.
Ollerenshaw, J. A., & Creswell, J. W. (2002). Narrative research: A comparison of two restorying data analysis approaches. *Qualitative inquiry*, *8*(3), 329–347. https://doi.org/10.1177/1077800400800300.
Piedmont, R. L. (1999). Does spirituality represent the sixth factor of personality? Spiritual transcendence and the five-factor model. *Journal of Personality*, *67*(6), 985–1013. https://doi.org/10.1111/1467-6494.00080
Piedmont, R. L. (2001). Spiritual transcendence and the scientific study of spirituality. *Journal of Rehabilitation*, *67*(1), 4–14.

Piotrowski, J., Skrzypińska, K., & Żemojtel-Piotrowska, M. (2013). The scale of spiritual transcendence: Construction and validation. *Roczniki Psychologiczne, 16*(3), 469–485.
Polkinghorne, D. E. (1988). *Narrative knowing and the human sciences*. Suny Press.
Principe, W. (1983). Toward defining spirituality. *Studies in religion/sciences religieuses, 12*(2), 127–141.
Pritchard, D. (2013). *What is this thing called knowledge?* Routledge.
Reed, P. G. (1992). An emerging paradigm for the investigation of spirituality in nursing. *Research in nursing & health, 15*(5), 349–357. https://doi.org/10.1002/nur.4770150505
Říčan, P. (2006). Spiritualita jako klíč k osobnosti a lidským vztahům [Spirituality as a key to personality and human relationships]. *Československá psychologie, 50 (*2), 119–137.
Říčan, P. (2007). *Psychologie náboženství a spirituality [Psychology of religion and spirituality]*. PORTÁL sro.
Ricœur, P. (1990). *Time and narrative*, University of Chicago Press.
Riessman, C. (2012). In Gubrium J. F., Holstein J. A., Marvasti A. B. and McKinney K. D. (Eds.), Analysis of personal narratives. SAGE Publications, Incorporated. https://doi.org/10.4135/9781452218403.n26
Robichaud, D., Giroux, H., & Taylor, J. R. (2004). The Metaconversation: The Recursive Property of Language as a Key to Organizing. *Academy of Management Review, 29*(4), 617–634. https://doi.org/10.5465/amr.2004.14497614.
Rocha, R. G., & Pinheiro, P. (2021a). Can organisational spirituality contribute to knowledge management? *Management dynamics in the knowledge economy*. 9(1), 107–121. https://doi.org/10.2478/mdke-2021-0008.
Rocha, R. G., & Pinheiro, P. G. (2021b). Organisational spirituality: Concept and perspectives. *Journal of Business Ethics*, 171(2), 241–252.
Samul, J. (2020, December). Spiritual knowledge at work: Linkages between managers' spiritual intelligence and workplace perspective. In European Conference on Knowledge Management (p. 702–XXII). Academic Conferences International Limited.
Sheldrake, P. (2016). Christian spirituality and social transformation. Oxford Research Encyklopedia of Religion. https://doi.org/10.1093/acrefore/9780199340378.013.231.
Skalický, K. (2005). *V zápase s posvátnem: náboženství v religionistickém bádání [In the fight with sacred: religion in religious research]*. Centrum pro studium demokracie a kultury.
Somers, M. R. (1994). The narrative constitution of identity: A relational and network approach. Theory and Society, 23 (5), 605–649.
Spencer, M. (2012). What is spirituality? A personal exploration. *Retrieved March 16*, 2020. https://www.rcpsych.ac.uk/docs/default-source/members/sigs/spirituality-spsig/what-is-spirituality-maya-spencer-x.pdf
Van Ness, P. H. (1996). *Spirituality and the secular quest,* World spirituality, 22. New York Crossroad.
Wach, J. (1957). Types of religious experience Christan and non-Christian. University of Chicago Press.
World Health Organization. (1998). *WHOQOL and spirituality, religiousness and personal beliefs (SRPB)* (No. WHO/MSA/MHP/98.2). World Health Organization.
Yehoshua, A. B. (2004). From myth to history. *AJS Review*, 28 (1), 205–211. https://doi.org/10.1017/S0364009404000121
Yourdictionary. (n.d.) Metastory definition. In yourdictionary.com. https://www.yourdictionary.com/metastory

II Exploring Spirituality in Knowledge Dynamics Across Contexts: Communities, Workplace, Higher Education, and Entrepreneurship

Vanessa C. M. Englert and Welmoed van Hoogen

Chapter 4
A Human-Centered Perspective on Knowledge Management: The Management, Spirituality and Religion Group and Knowledge

Abstract: In this chapter, we apply relevant knowledge management (KM) literature to an opinion piece we previously wrote about the Management, Spirituality and Religion (MSR) group. The MSR group is an Interest Group of the Annual Academy of Management Conference, of which both authors are members. The chapter centers around three themes: values in research, diversification of ways of knowing and research topics, and skill building. We take a human-centered approach to these topics, centering the individual human and its well-being as the core point of interest. By applying KM literature to MSR research and the MSR group and using a human-centered approach, we aim to show opportunities to expand KM's knowledge. Secondly, we hope to provide an impetus for further MSR group – seen as a knowledge system – development and diversification. Ultimately, insights gained from this chapter can be applied to other knowledge systems akin to the MSR group.

Keywords: Epistemic Change, Knowledge Management, Ways of Knowing, Ontology, Epistemology, Wisdom

Introduction

This chapter combines knowledge management theory with a previously written opinion piece about the Management, Spirituality and Religion group, an academic Interest Group of the Academy of Management. Applying knowledge management (KM) theory to our observations shows how this academic discipline contributes to our understanding of the organization. Furthermore, we present how current and future demands of MSR research – as we perceive it now and its development – invite to expand KM's body of knowledge to include a human-centered approach and different ways of knowing.

Acknowledgements: The authors would like to express their gratitude to Harald Gaski and Charles Tackney for sharing their insights.

Vanessa C. M. Englert, Vrije Universiteit, Netherlands, e-mail: mail@vanessaenglert.de
Welmoed van Hoogen, e-mail: wvhoogen@hotmail.com

https://doi.org/10.1515/9783111010410-005

Ultimately, based on literature insights, we aim to help develop the community the organization represents. Individual engagement with this text may offer an opportunity for self-reflection due to both its content and the way it is written, including dialogical learning, narrative development, and contextualization of our thoughts.

MSR and Knowledge Management

The Management, Spirituality and Religion Interest Group (MSR) is one of 26 Interest Groups and Divisions of the Academy of Management (AOM). The AOM is an international academic and practitioner management studies association founded in 1936 in the United States of America (AOM, n.d.). The Interest Group has been operational since 2000 (Tackney et al., 2017) and has roughly 630 members across the globe. The group is part of the annual Academy of Management conference and has, among other scholarly activities, monthly meetings, an annual retreat, and a research colloquium. MSR envisions promoting "[h]uman flourishing and global consciousness that illuminates – and are illuminated by – spiritual and religious dimensions of life in management research, teaching, and practice" by bettering "the world through a transdisciplinary network of management academics and practitioners exploring the role of the significant and sacred" (MSR, n.d.).

We view the MSR group as a knowledge-based, not-for-profit organization and community. A knowledge-based organization, or knowledge system, is viewed as an ensemble of resources and people that, through interaction, create knowledge whereby the organizational boundaries are dynamic and malleable (Zack, 2003). As a research group, MSR exists to generate and disseminate knowledge for scholars and practitioners through papers, symposia, teaching, and general idea creation.

The group is concerned with knowledge about spirituality and religion about management. Because of the personal appreciation of spirituality and religion members, the group uses multiple forms of knowledge-sharing dynamics (Rocha & Pinheiro, 2019). Emotional, spiritual, and rational knowledge about spirituality and religion is shared. This knowledge-sharing is done through in-person activities and – especially since the start of the pandemic – through online activities like presentations and meetings. As such, we see the MSR group also as a 'virtual community of practice' whereby the community's individuals use an online platform to come together and share knowledge (Shaw et al., 2022).

About the Researchers

Both authors recognize that the researcher influences the research. Hence, we think it necessary to introduce ourselves to share the lenses through which we process information, as well as our relation to MSR, to contextualize the discussed ideas.

By the time of writing, we have been a part of the MSR Interest Group for two years. We also met in a virtual MSR Monthly get-together and connected for peer-spirit offline. Our relationship is based on trust and respect and complemented by humor while we explore and bridge contrasts between us and the topics we focus on. As relatively new MSR members, we noticed specific group and organizational tendencies. Based on our observations, we wrote a short opinion piece that centers around the following three themes: values and value guidelines, diversification of research, continued self-reflection and skill-building, which structure this contribution.

Regarding ontology, we explicate our two voices to be specific about our stances. We use the pronoun "I" to acknowledge the role the subjective researcher plays in research (Storberg-Walker, 2021) and to add a personal narrative to de-center us as researchers (see, e.g., Olsen, 2017). I, the alphabetical first author (actively try to) engage in co-creative research with my environment and participants from an integrative worldview in which one is aware of life's web-like, de-centralized and context-dependent nature and its underlying commonality at the same time (Nandram & Bindlish, 2022; Nandram et al., 2017). My understanding of spirituality in research is "one's ability to connect to existence beyond one's perceived existence" (Nandram et al., 2022, p. 238). I believe in something that underlies my shape-shifting and context-dependent identities and which is constant. I reach for and sense this "something" in day-to-day interactions and my spiritual practice. Through this practice, I have also received access to various ways of knowing, which I apply in both work and research. I was born into a middle-class, small-town environment and a family of craftspeople and entrepreneurs. I am the first in my immediate family to attend college and – in my extended family – to pursue a doctoral degree. My education has been mainly in the Westernized, patriarchal system, as has my professional trajectory.

I, the second alphabetical author, am a white, non-Indigenous, European woman from a middle-class socio-economic background. I have studied and currently study in Northwest Europe, meaning that I am the educational product of Western academia. I understand spirituality as "the capacity of the human consciousness to apprehend ultimate meaning and ultimate value symbolically" (Tackney et al., 2017, p. 246).

On Knowledge, Wisdom, and Spirituality

In an organizational and knowledge system (henceforth KS) context, knowledge can be defined as "a clear understanding of information and their associated patterns and learning about knowledge [. . .] as the process of analysis and synthesis of information" (Bierly et al., 2000, p. 600). Knowledge is about understanding data and information, know-how, and know-how of processes and things. Wisdom entails both holding justified beliefs – being knowledgeable – and being able to enact fitting judgment in living and decision-making. Wisdom is the result of experience, passion, and spirituality. Spirituality is connected primarily to wisdom as a two-folded enabler. First, creating a core set of beliefs and understanding life's purpose articulates an individual's goals and objectives. Second, it provides a context of hope, courage, and faith in complex environments, which drives wise actions and decision-making (Bierly et al., 2000).

We approach knowledge management concerning promoting wisdom and spirituality in the organization as being human-centered. Rather than regarding wisdom and knowledge as instruments for organizational performance improvements, we focus on what these two concepts can mean for the well-being of employees in the organization, the organization itself, and its context. When using the term organization, we refer to any organized knowledge system (KS). From our point of view, knowledge management can potentially ameliorate the lived experience of individuals as spiritual beings in the organization. So, ideally, KM is a springboard that serves human development in an organizational setting. The human-centered approach to KM has implications for values in research (theme one) and research approaches and areas (theme two).

In what follows, we share the three themes which formed our opinion piece. We discuss the themes based on relevant KM theories and explain how these notions can improve the topics at hand: expanding on the KM literature and taking up MSR as an object of study. We conclude with a discussion of this web of our main ideas, practical implications for the MSR interest group, and similar knowledge-based organizations and avenues for future research.

A Human-Centered Approach and Themes

A Human-Centered Approach

Before turning to the themes, we discuss why we take a human-centered approach. First, this view of KM relates to the values the KS, or organization, holds: What is essential to promote in the organization and in what way? Are values motivators for change? Does the organization, through KM, wish to promote wisdom and spirituality because it will improve the lived realities for those who are part of the system or because it will lead to improved system performance? This difference is illuminated by a parallel discussion about values as motivators in diversity, equity, and inclusion management in the literature and practice. In broad strokes, two organizational value approaches, or motivators, to implementing diversity, equity, and inclusion management (DEI) can be taken: a business case and a social justice case. Whereas the former advocates for DEI on the grounds of organizational performance and market logic, the latter does so as it is the right thing to do based on societal logic (Bleijenbergh et al., 2010; Fine & Sojo, 2019; Norbash & Kadom, 2020).

In a capitalist society, we are aware of the necessity of market logic entering the organizational decision-making process and regarding approaches to internal policies for future organizational well-being. However, suppose the organization is treated as an actor of positive change. In that case, today's climate of increasingly turbulent, fast-evolving, uncertain organizational environments gives way to a values-as-motivators approach based on societal logic rather than market logic. Even if one would like, in this day and age, pure market logic does not suffice in driving "business and society toward genuine, substantive sustainable development" (Stubbs, 2018, p. 63). Suppose the organization aims to protect its contributors' current and future well-being, the enterprise itself, its contexts, and the rest of the world. In that case, societal logic should form the core 'value as motivator'.

In answering the question posed at the beginning of this section, we would argue that MSR wishes to promote wisdom and spirituality through knowledge management. It might not lead to improved system performance, but it will improve the lived realities for those who are part of the system and those whom the organization serves. Arguments for this are found in the group's mission of promoting human flourishing and global consciousness, which showcases a human, individual approach to a global phenomenon or improving a global state of being (MSR, n.d.).

Second, in a human-centered approach, we intend to include a variety of forms of knowing, knowledge, and wisdom. This is particularly relevant for MSR, as it is originally a United States of America-based KS. At the same time, MSR consists of scholars and practitioners with different worldviews – ontologies and epistemologies – with most of them working and performing in and with a Western(ized) higher educational setting. Through the history of European colonizers and Western ethnocentrism, legitimate knowledge is Western, understood as universal and objective knowledge (Akena, 2012). Concurrently, other forms of knowledge – like Indigenous knowledge – have been delegitimized as "savage, superstitious, and primitive" (Akena, 2012, p. 600) and, therefore, unfit to be used in the sciences. Considering the variety of worldviews coming together when creating or sharing knowledge, acknowledging varied ways of knowing necessarily becomes a part of KM. Therefore, reducing ways of knowing to one dominant form limits KM's scope while limiting human self-expression.

Western(ized) academia and its subsequent education are considered a profoundly colonial, institutionalized knowledge system (e.g., Kuokkanen, 2000; Nakata et al., 2012; Simpson, 2014; Smith, 2012). Per MSR's place of belonging – being a part of the Academy of Management – it functions in this colonial system. Although MSR has a history of initiating and backing diverse ways of knowing and researching topics and having an international membership base, as a Western knowledge system, it moves naturally in the 'space' of legitimate knowledge. As a group, the majority (we) not only work with a system that values one sort of knowledge over others, but we also reinforce it by working with the system in terms of what we research, what we publish, what we teach, and where we do this all[1].

The implications of this are beyond the scope of this chapter. However, what should be noted is that the MSR KS, knowledge creation, working with knowledge, and

1 For ideas about indigenizing business schools, see Woods, C., Dell, K., & Carroll, B. (2022).

knowledge dissemination are shaped by institutional, colonial, and Western standards. Knowledge and getting to know are not per se neutral, value-free, a-political activities but are shaped by the context in which they occur.

Themes: Values, Diversification of Research, and Skill Development

Now, we turn to our three themes: values, diversification of research, and continued self-reflection and criticism. The parts of the text in italics show the opinion piece text; text with a regular font is our discussion of these themes for this chapter.

Theme One: Values

Values are pivotal in KS, encapsulating what is jointly valued as organizationally meaningful (Bratianu & Bejinaru, 2019). In the shape of an organizational statement, organizational core values expand on how the organization's vision will become a reality (Gurley et al., 2015), for example, by guiding decision-making (Bratianu & Bejinaru, 2019). They "shape much of the work processes and, as such, influence how an institution moves forward positively" (Calder, 2011, p. 24). As the core values provide behavioral guidelines, they bridge the theoretical and the practical. They are critical in practically translating what the organization stands for and what it desires to engender. In our opinion piece, we wrote the following regarding MSR's vision, mission, and value statements, whereby an articulation of the latter was missing at the time of writing. We wrote the following about the absence of a value statement:

> While the group's mission and vision are well developed and articulated in a conceptual sense, the mission and vision have not necessarily been translated into practice. This is because current pointers or guidelines concerning values and ethics' role in conducting, assessing, and understanding research remain underdeveloped.
>
> Such a (non-)-articulation of pointers affects research based on specific values and with a particular intent. On an interactive group level, it influences the research and, as a result, the knowledge accumulation and dissemination that MSR represents. This is especially relevant when research takes an instrumental approach to religion, spirituality or philosophy in management, organizations, and organizations to improve functioning in the capitalist sense. We propose that MSR take up a written statement that informs about what is understood as ethical and unethical research.
>
> Such a written statement could come as a value statement, including guidelines for ethical research. A statement would still guarantee freedom of academic research choices but would also provide clear preferences regarding the valuation of one's own and others' epistemological and ontological choices. Such as, e.g., "we value research that openly puts the own approach into perspective over studies that reduce research to one 'right version'".

In a way, we see these guidelines as promoting wisdom in the MSR KS as well: to be knowledgeable as a group and to develop the ability to enact fitting judgment in living and decision-making, inside and outside a research and organizational setting (Bierly et al., 2000). By doing so, the group can also realize its spiritual knowledge potential as this relates to "[. . .] shared values and moral judgments which emerge in any social context as a reference system in making judgments and decisions" (Bratianu & Bejinaru, 2019, p. 5).

The value-based promotion of wisdom in the organization showcases that it is a developmental process. Wisdom is understood here as "a function of deep, accurate insight and understanding of the central existential issues of life, plus practical skill in responding effectively and benevolently" (Walsh, 2012, p. 16). In such a process, individual members of the group or KS "hone their capabilities of self-knowledge, self-integration, nonattachment, self-transcendence, compassion and understanding of life, mainly through improved self-regulation and ethical choices" (Ferreira Vasconcelos, 2021, p. 375). By doing so, through the individual's application of wisdom, the greater good for both others and the self can be achieved in the organization. Applying wisdom as a developmental process in the hope that it improves the greater good befits the MSR KS, as it aims to be a driver for positive change.

Provided with a clear mission, vision, and value statement(s), MSR group members would have a point of reference, informed by which they could undertake research. Such a reference point would safeguard core values – like how ontologies and epistemologies are valued – while pushing for academic diversity. This brings us to our second theme: diversification of research, holding two subthemes: broadening how and what to research.

Theme Two: Diversification of Research

We noted that the MSR group shows a tendency towards carrying out a specific type of research:

> Our understanding is that the group's research centers around improving realities and the theoretical understanding, examination, and conceptualization of already "semi-positive" situations and contexts. For example, the amelioration of the human experience – which may or may not relate to improved organizational performance as a direct or indirect consequence – by including space for spiritual, religious, and, to a lesser extent, philosophical practices. This focus on "semi-positive" realities surprises us, given the mission of creating human flourishing and the group's serious commitment to generating positive change. As such, we would argue that too little research is done at the fringes of, or about less palatable issues in, our societies [. . .].
>
> We define "broadening work" as research into work, management, and organizing that is contended, variedly viewed and known, or little understood by researchers and their respective academic fields. This refers to the domination of Western research/ways of knowing, the marginalized voices this creates, and the space given to research topics that differ in their cultural, societal, historical, legal, and religious acceptance and understanding.

We understand the promotion of human flourishing to be a ground-up, inclusive, and broad undertaking. To help humans flourish means to understand societies in the broadest sense, from well-developed research areas and topics to emerging ones. Shying away from research into various topics, varying in their cultural, spiritual, and religious acceptance or understanding, means that the MSR group overlooks knowledge areas. It is those research and knowledge areas that are to become a necessary part of MSR's research repertoire.

Given the group's mission and vision, a research focus on the "semi-positive" – detailed in the text above – could be understood as either a form of organizational and mission drift or a result of something akin to groupthink. We use the former two terms to highlight the discrepancy that can arise between centrally designed practices and local modifications to these practices in the organization or system. Alternatively, in an MSR context, there is a discrepancy between the vision and mission of the group and the type of research being carried out.

Organizational drift results from actors and sub-systems adapting to local pressures and structural issues affecting information flows (Reiman et al., 2015). In the MSR context, local pressures can be understood as an individual's primary educational affiliation and publication norms. Perhaps "home" institutes are not necessarily open to conducting broadening research and the publication thereof, even if an individual group member is. Mission drift denotes the process in which organizations and those who are part of them lose "sight of their purpose and values in the quest for organizational survival and efficiency" (Ebrahim et al., 2014, p. 82).

Even if no organizational or mission drift occurs, the concept emphasizes that the MSR group is part of a larger organization, which impacts MSR to a certain degree. Moreover, MSR members are part of multiple KS, like other research groups, educational institutes, and organizations, all presenting local pressures and structures that potentially inform and shape individual MSR members' interests and behavior in a research setting. For MSR, this poses a balancing question: How far is uniformity in values of individual members desired to create a space that pushes for an inclusive mission-building research space? An anchoring value statement suffices to designate an MSR-specific research space while pushing for broadening work.

Too much uniformity could lead to groupthink, "a mode of thinking that people engage in when they are deeply involved in a cohesive in-group when the members' strivings for unanimity override their motivation to realistically appraise alternative courses of action" (Janis, 2006, p. 237). This would bar broadening work to be done, as differing views about what and how to research would be suppressed as to adhere to the "semi-positive" norm. Alternatively, too much uniformity in ways of thinking and too little constructive discussion about how we can include broadening research and ways of knowing can lead to 'false reflection'.

On an individual level, false reflection would mean a person takes an altogether soloist approach to reflecting. A person is in dialogue only with their selves, without the input of others, when aiming to come to a moment of insight about specific ideas and notions. Such an approach can have unwanted consequences: "The self-reflection of a lone subject [. . .] requires a quite paradoxical achievement: one part of the self must be split off from the other in such a manner that the subject can be in a position to render aid to itself. [. . .] [Furthermore], in the act of self-reflection, the subject can deceive itself (Habermas, 1974, p. 29 in Kemmis, 2008). Taken to a group level, too much uniformity and conformity in discussion will lead to false reflection, resulting in an empty dialogue. The continuous agreement will not create enough friction to engender change or new ideas in a group, barring impetus for broadening work.

To overcome this fallacy on an individual level, Habermas suggests incorporating others in the work of reflecting, making it a social, collective process. Here, the group and its individuals provide a critical capacity to arrive at insights regarding the understanding of practices, settings, and circumstances of practices (Kemmis, 2008). On a group level, such a view would mean that a culture of non-conformity or appreciation of valuing differing ideas is fostered, whereby group members bring critical thoughts, ideas, and insight to the group discussions. MSR is an open group anyone can join, and its scholarship program that brings in interested young scholars provides enough space for critical, meaningful discussion and reflection. We suggest that MSR actively works on setting up discussion sessions for the group and potentially subgroups, during which we reflect on what research has been and is carried out and which topics we would like to invest in.

The Broadening of How to Research

A facet of the human-centered approach to KM explicitly acknowledges different ways of knowing as equally legitimate and combining the notion that group- and self-reflection are social processes that can aid in avoiding too much uniformity, we are led to the discussion of ontology (what is reality, what is knowledge) and epistemology (how do we come to know) within our field. Our understanding of ontology and epistemology acts as a filter for data selection (Freeburg, 2017) and as a sense-making blueprint for how information is related to each other and how one relates to the data (Bracken, 2010). Concurrently, knowing and knowledge are often viewed in narrowing, limiting ways, which reduces learning and new thinking opportunities (Fazey et al., 2020). What we see as knowledge and legitimate ways of knowing is thus directly related to KS, knowledge sharing and KM. We discuss different ways of knowing in this sub-theme to overcome narrow focus.

> The difference in understanding the spiritual landscape[2] between European and American scholars would be worth looking into. A mere example of culture and historicity shaping one's understanding of the to-be-researched concept and how this translates to potentially differing approaches to such a concept within the Western-oriented research scope is found in the work of Nolan et al. (2011).

2 A term that arose in the MSR Monthly and was gifted by Mark Argent.

> Concurrently, as a group, MSR could lead the way to equally value all local, emically understood contexts and research methods. To sharpen: let us be conscious of the different lenses through which research is done and which we accept as quality research. Are we genuinely welcoming in worldviews other than the American-European one? How can we say that we do? [. . .]. Nandram & Bindlish (2022), Storberg-Walker (2021), and Wilson (2008) give instructive accounts of doing research from a different worldview and the consequence this change of "how" has on the choice of "what" is being researched.

The differences in understanding a sole concept – spirituality – draw attention to the urgency of creating a broad palette of ontologies and epistemologies in the group when we research many topics. This allows for a more holistic understanding of the world, necessary to match knowledge with the actual lived realities and experiences of people around the globe. Different or differing ways of knowing, extend validation of knowledge beyond an intellectual-Western, positivist approach to 'reality', or what Heron (1996, pp. 33–34) calls propositional knowing. We see a propositional approach to knowing to be widespread in the Academy of Management. This becomes clear in the annual Academy of Management conference and the (lack of) diversity of ways of conducting research that is presented.

The discussion concerning ontology and epistemology, e.g., what defines and separates them, the philosophical base of an ontological understanding, and the role they play in academia, is complex, in which we are no experts.

Multiple authors have developed and passed on philosophical understandings and practical approaches to applying multiple ways of knowing in a research context. We want to honor (some of) those pursuing other ways of researching, knowing and being in the academic profession. We add our own synthesis in theme two. In theme three, we operationalize the idea of using various ways of knowing within MSR research by introducing observable behavior as researcher skills needed to apply the mentioned ways.

In brief, we envision MSR scholars as experts in applying different ways of knowing within mixed-ontological contexts, creating academic rigor and improving our research's social impact. This is due to the nature of MSR research, which includes and goes beyond the secular and therefore demands the application of propositional – or intellectual, linear – and various ways of knowing to do the phenomena and the audience justice.

We start with a voice encouraging MSR researchers to expand the current understanding of what knowledge is (ontology) and what legitimate ways of knowing (epistemology) are. The author does so by relating ontological understandings to the task that MSR researchers dare to tackle: We choose to engage with the elusive yet impactful nature of spirituality and religion in and for a world that does not necessarily speak the language of the subtle[3] – be it Western(ized) academia or management. The following quote is long, as the power of the statements develops within the narrative. Neal (2013) shares a vision for MSR's role as a field that has not lost its topicality:

3 By which we mean that what potentially can be sensed to exist within and between entities.

> Many of the authors in this volume have pointed to the need to do research that fits the social science standards of the mainstream. This is a valuable strategy for making a difference and influencing a system from within, and we must continue pursuing this path. At the same time, we have a huge potential for exploring noetic ways of knowing (Mitchell, 2008). If any field of study is likely to expand human ways of knowing, it is our field. We have much to learn from the methodologies utilized in studying consciousness and spirituality in such places at [sic] the Institute for Noetic Sciences, [. . .], and the Fetzer Institute.
>
> What if there is a way of inner knowing or spiritual guidance that can be used to further our research? The hard sciences are replete with stories of scientific discoveries made by scientists with dreams or altered states of consciousness (Neal, 2006). Many business leaders create new strategies, find new markets, and develop new products using intuition or nonlinear thinking (Robinson, 2006). I sincerely hope we do not get so caught up in being accepted by the mainstream that we lose our creativity and spiritual gifts. We are scholars, leaders, and practitioners but human beings (p. 738).

The quote reminds us of what is at stake when we talk about what MSR knowledge is and how we come about knowing as individuals and as a group. Taking a position regarding ontology and epistemology – in our case, acknowledging that all ways of knowing are equally legitimate – is not only an academic discourse. It also stands for the felt experience of having a space where what one does is acknowledged as legitimate and respected without having to defend "one's place at the table". Further, the cited work reflects what academic and social impact potential lies in MSR research because it has the mission and mandate to capture a more holistic part of human existence than, e.g., purely positivist research is called to explore and, owing to this potential, what responsibility may be implied when engaging with it. In the following section, we celebrate voices that researched or applied multiple ways of knowing in their research.

Anderson and Braud point out the necessity of engaging with different types of knowing because the nature and topic of the research necessitates this (2013; Braud & Anderson, 1998):

> [. . .] in the course of the investigation, the integral inquirer practices many complementary forms of knowing, being, and doing, including conventional, tacit, intuitive, body-based, feelings-based, and "direct" forms of knowing; ordinary and non-ordinary states of consciousness; analytical/linear and nonanalytical/nonlinear ways of working with data; and alternative ways of expressing findings (themes, narratives, metaphors, similes, symbols, and nonverbal creative expressions) (Anderson & Braud, 2013, pp. 249–250).

As the authors highlight, there is no need to choose either-or, but instead, there is a need to integrate different epistemologies along the research process. Similarly, Nandram et al.'s work on objectivizing subtle cues in entrepreneurial decision-making shows how intuitive and rational processes are commensurate and often intertwined in the same activity (Nandram et al., 2019; Nandram et al., 2018). Heron also invites us to understand different ways of knowing as enabling and building on each other, rather than prioritizing one type, as is done, e.g., with the intellect or propositional knowledge, in positivist-minded academia (1996, pp. 33–34). Similarly to Anderson and Braud's understanding that different types of knowledge enable each other (2013), Scharmer states that one draws upon explicit, embodied-tacit and not-yet-embodied knowledge simultaneously (2001).

In their extension of the cooperative inquiry epistemology, Heron and Reason (2008) describe that humans intuitively use different types of knowledge and naturally weave them into their actions. We deduce it is a human birthright and natural skill to access and apply different ways of knowing. Heron and Reason differentiate between four types of knowing that build on each other. The first, and the base of knowing, is experiential knowing through sharing presence with something or someone. "It is knowing through the immediacy of perceiving, through empathy and resonance" (2008, p. 367). The outcome is found in how the perceiver relates to this something or someone and how all involved experience this relation. From this relation, the knower is then "intuiting significant form and process in that which is met.", termed presentational knowing as the second form (Heron & Reason, 2008, p. 367). The significant form can be understood as a perceived meaningful connection between sensations, like a focused spotlight on connecting sensations or, metaphorically, as something knocking on the door wanting to be expressed.

The process stands for the way this expression unfolds. In presentational knowing, the person directs what was previously a fuzzy felt sense into a directional aesthetic expression. This is "nondiscursive through the visual arts, music, dance and movement, and discursively in poetry, drama and the continuously creative capacity of the human individual and social mind to tell stories" (Heron & Reason, 2008, p. 372). This presentation is valuable research and an essential foundation for propositional knowing (Heron & Reason, 2008). This third type of knowledge is best known in academia as the "intellectual knowing of ideas and theories. Its product is the informative spoken or written statement." (Heron & Reason, 2008, p. 367). There is a distinction between the knowledge and the knower; the knower is no longer part of the experience as there is a distance between the idea and the thinker. Lastly, when propositional knowing can be applied, practical knowing comes into play, which is the fourth type of knowledge. Its outcome is a skill or competence (Heron & Reason, 2008, p. 367). In research, Heron and Reason argue that applying the different knowledge modes becomes an intentional act to improve its rigor (Heron & Reason, 2008, pp. 367–368).

Bindlish et al. (2018) support giving experiential knowing a prominent place in research. From the background of Hindu Spirituality, the authors mention indigenous ways of learning by example of "embodied knowing through experience, intuition, and contemplation" (Bindlish et al., 2018, p. 224) and remind us of their academic validity and of the respect they deserve from the mainstream research community Wilson introduces us to relationality as a "shared aspect of an Indigenous ontology and epistemology" (2008, p. 8). From this view, "relationships do not merely shape reality; they are reality" (2008, pp. 8–9). For example, the researcher's relationship to the idea or between the reader and the author (Wilson, 2008).

Ripeka Mercier, Stevens and Toia (2012) offer another way to see the importance of relating within KM from a mātauranga Māori (Māori knowledge) perspective. They apply mātauranga Māori to the Western-based Data- Information- Knowledge- Wisdom (DIKW) hierarchy, as also used by Bierly et al. (2000), turning it into a prism. In doing so, the authors introduce a mātauranga Māori understanding of how data, information, knowledge and wisdom define each other (Ripeka Mercier et al., 2012). In this view, data "has no significance beyond its existence," and information comes from the "systematization of pieces of data according to identified relationships" (Ripeka Mercier et al., 2012, p. 105). In other words, knowledge does not stem from data points but from how the setting providing the data relates to the data, how data amongst itself is related, how the researcher refers to the research (e.g., data, concepts, people and environment involved), how the reader relates to the data and finally how the reader relates to the researcher/author. Data and knowledge are always relative and relational (Deloria Jr., 1999; Simpson, 2014).

Storberg-Walker explains relational ontology as a term to: "describe various philosophies or ways of knowing that blur the distinction between subject and object; between researcher and the researched; and between human and nature. These philosophies/ways of knowing offer diverse ways to critically reflect on researcher subjectivity, competencies, and skills needed for meaningful MSR research" (2022, p. 261).

Following Heron's types of knowing, a focus on experiential knowing seems to be in service of living relational ontology as "Its product is the quality of the relationship in which it participates, including the quality of being of those in the relationship." (Heron & Reason, 2008, p. 368). Dissolving the separation of the researcher, the research and what is to be researched (Bindlish et al., 2018) can also be connected to Scharmer's understanding of presencing: "The terms 'action-intuition' and 'presenting' signify a state of mind that transcends the distinctions between 'inside' and 'outside', between 'I' and 'thou', and between knowing and acting" (Scharmer, 2001, p. 141). Scharmer opens up a possibility of locating the knower, by enriching the dichotomy of explicit-tacit knowledge with the layer of not-yet embodied tacit knowledge, a "capacity for 'pre-cognition', the ability to sense and actualize emerging potentials", or self-transcending knowledge (Scharmer, 2001, p. 137).

The knower, or where the knowledge comes from in the case of self-transcending expertise, is a space or field rather than the individual mind. From this field, knowledge emerges (Scharmer, 2001, p. 142). This notion aligns with Bratianu and Bejinaru's thermodynamics-based theory of knowledge as a field (2019) and with quantum ontology. This ontology is based on the insights of quantum physics and sees information coming from an existing area of consciousness, which is the source of information and connects us all and with all of existence (Laszlo, 2020; Tsao & Laszlo, 2019).

In conclusion, we share a part of an inner monologue reaction that arose during the writing of this presentation of voices. It can serve as a synthesis or illustration of the previously described. It occurred to me that this inner-monologue style is alphabetical first author inspired by Storberg-Walker's paper (2021). We later added the author dialogue that followed our feedback process. We hope the reader takes away their impression of the narration and continues the conversation elsewhere.

> The knowledge dynamics that move through an MSR researcher seem to resemble a dynamic flow between (inter)active-outwards and receptive-inwards inquiry. [W: Do knowledge dynamics move through the researcher, or is it the reverse? V: That is the necessary change of view, in my opinion. That knowledge happens to us and is not done by us. We get to have the thought or sensation, but we do not produce it.].
>
> The picture of a horizontal lying eight comes to mind, with one loop going inside a person and the other reaching outwards. The outward journey leads the researcher to interact with their environment for data, experiences, impressions, and learnings gained by being reflected on other people or circumstances. The researcher is engaged with and is defined by their context. Heading inward, they are becoming the instrument for the research in silent inquiry. [W: No idea what this means, but maybe the average reader of this book will. V: I am convinced that "silent inquiry" is quite average, if not like this. It is the innate human capacity to be without doing (including not thinking or feeling). Moreover, now being in this way while in a research process and seeing what happens (yes, without actively doing anything) is what I understand as silent inquiry. Your only job is to become, stay calm, and let go of that. It is what meditation is for, for me. I also like Marshall and Reason (2007)].
>
> What if an idea, as a vibration, has its independent shape and what if we (mainly as researchers) are akin to receivers that catch their signals? As instruments for knowledge, we should sharpen our perceiving, including our inner listening, to be an adequate instrument in service of what we ought to pick up; maybe Bindlish thought something similar when writing the research preparation piece (Bindlish et al., 2018). Every researcher is a unique instrument; you and I receive different things, which is good – it is needed to complement each other for the whole picture!

The Broadening of What to Research

In the previous section, we discussed how to research by presenting different ways of knowing, using various ontologies and epistemologies. This subsection is concerned with the broadening of what to research. It includes science's role in modernity, different science paradigms, contemporary challenges to KS, and practical knowledge's role in solving these challenges. We originally wrote the following:

> We think broadening work is essential for at least two reasons. Firstly, research should shed light on all societal, institutional, cultural, and practical realities to generate inclusive, unbiased, positive change. Only when societies are examined in full or topically broad range can a claim to aim for positive change be made. Even when specific organizations or working methods are institutionalized as "unaccepted" by existing, they are still worth looking into. [. . .]. Secondly, we believe it is time for MSR to diversify its researched topics, something broadening research can help with. Whereas in her initial growth phase, the group focused on 'clear' MSR topical research to create an in and outgroup and legitimize the Interest Group, we believe the group is now at a stage of growth that allows for more diverse analysis [. . .].

Science and technology are two essential tools of Western-based late-modernity, which as a societal process and way of thinking is understood as a "characteristic mode of civilization" expanding into all domains of society (Baudrillard, 1987, p. 63; Hanlon et al., 2012). Regarding knowledge production and KM in modernity, Western systems have assumed knowledge to be a commodity in a growth-based economy, whereby speed, profit, achievement, and competition have been emphasized over quality, well-being, fulfillment, and collaboration (Fazey et al., 2020). Science – our interest in the chapter – enabled modernity by researching and establishing 'the truth' through finding and examining evidence, de-coupling science from the domains of aesthetics and ethics (Hanlon et al., 2012). We want to add that a decoupling of a fourth domain, spirituality, also took place.

This decoupling meant two things. Firstly, on a meta-level, the three domains had significant autonomy in their development. Secondly, it allowed an "imperialistic form of science to develop and dominate the other spheres by claiming that it alone had access to 'reality', through the objectivity and value-neutrality of the scientific method (an ideology best described as scientism)" (Hanlon et al., 2012, p. 314). It is the 'true' (science) that has been and is valued the most in modern institutions, with the 'good' (ethics) and 'beautiful' (aesthetics) mostly left to the private spheres. The heavy emphasis on the 'true', or a segregated view of these domains, leads to a cultural narrowness of institutions (Hanlon et al., 2012).

Roughly, scientific development and insight aims fall under two normative frameworks (Kläy et al., 2015). The current dominant framework is that of competitiveness, befitting modernity, in which science's role as a value-free, objective vessel is to benefit a nation-state's institutions and economy. A second framework is sustainability-based, whereby science, as value-imbued and based on accountability, serves the transition towards (more) sustainable development (Kläy et al., 2015). The latter framework promises the most potential for solving modern challenges and ingraining values and ethics into science and research. For the domain of KS and knowledge creation, this is echoed by the call for a paradigm shift relating to the second framework. This call urges KS to engage "in knowledge creation with identity, purpose, values, beliefs, expectations and goals" (Fazey et al., 2020; Jakubik, 2011, p. 372; Jakubik & Müürsepp, 2021). Here, KS, as representative of science, has the potential to become a driver for positive change.

Current KS faces multiple challenges that hamper their ability to aid in navigating global, sustainable transformation (Fazey et al., 2020), of which two have been touched on above. Firstly, knowing and knowledge are viewed in narrowing, limiting ways – see also our discussion about ontologies and epistemologies – which reduces learning and new thinking opportunities (Fazey et al., 2020). As part of any KS, a researcher is influenced by factors (systems, structures, norms, cultures) determining which questions are asked and which research receives funding. Secondly, academic disciplines tend to be disconnected to a large extent, making them unable to mirror the connectedness of environmental and social issues, thus leading to an inability to bring forth holistic solutions. Lastly, KS often produces knowledge decoupled from practice, meaning the action following insight is more challenging (Fazey et al., 2020).

In conclusion, as KS are closely related to culture, economy, and society, they risk reinforcing the same limited thinking and action patterns already in existence, diminishing creative solution capacity development regarding societal challenges (Fazey et al., 2020). Paradigm shifts, methodological pluralism, and promoting wisdom rather than knowledge in KS are all components that will enable science to mirror its interconnected, dynamic environments better[4] (Fazey et al., 2020; Jakubik & Müürsepp, 2021; Kläy et al., 2015). Ingraining the 'good' and the 'beauty' in research allows KS to transform society responsibly and sustainably. Indeed, in the domain of business, due to the need for a shift "from exclusively rational, calculative, profit-oriented and financial goals in business to moral and ethical values," the relevance of wisdom in organizations, efficient wisdom or phronesis, has become more apparent (Jakubik, 2020, p. 4).

Wisdom knows three conceptualizations: the wisdom of knowledge (episteme), the wisdom of life (Sophia), and the wisdom of practice (phronesis) (Jakubik, 2020; Jakubik, 2021). Practical wisdom (PW) in management has multiple characteristics: action-oriented, integrative, normative, social, pluralistic, personal, limited in nature, and acknowledges cultural heritage (Bachmann et al., 2018). For this chapter, we highlight two PW characteristics: it is action-oriented and personality-related. For the former, PW "always targets realization in practice as it transforms every manifestation of knowledge, beliefs, and decisions into action" (Bachmann et al., 2018, p. 155; Bierly et al., 2000). The latter characteristic means that practical wisdom "is inseparably connected with a particular person/persons and is expressed as acting appropriately and authentically in a self-disciplined and self-aware manner in order to aspire after right, credible, inspiring, and convincing goals" (Bachmann et al., 2018, p. 157).

Combining these characteristics means that PW is a driver for change that takes into account the personal, allowing the individual to act authentically[5]. It fits the framework of science and research as value-imbued and knowledge creation based on values, beliefs, and identity (Jakubik, 2011; Kläy et al., 2015). PW is so acutely relevant for KS that aim to change their internal and external environments, like MSR. Additionally, KS and KS members' coupling to respective cultures, economies, and societies necessitates group and individual reflection about values and motivators. As a group, we should inquire into why we research what we research and by which ideas, structures, and values this is informed. What would it mean for the group, its mission, and our collective abilities to develop more holistic, creative research, solutions and thinking?

4 Nora Bateson and "warm data" come to mind.

5 For a discussion about cognitive structures and authenticity in living and decision-making, see the works of Bernard Lonergan.

Theme Three: Skill Building

The last theme revolves around discussing implementable suggestions that play into MSR's future goal of becoming a Division at the Academy of Management. We wrote the following:

> We understand the starting point of MSR as one that aims to fortify the group's unique characteristics to create a designated and demarcated research space and space for belonging. The Interest Group now has set out to gain Division status, thereby further integrating into the American Academy of Management; any change in the organizational context will naturally lead to a change within the organization. Creating a self-critical reflection stream could be valuable to accompany this change. This stream would evaluate what is researched in the group, how it relates to its vision, and what needs to be done to grow and maintain an MSR uniqueness.
>
> Questions that come to mind are: A) How can we live up to the international character of our group and ensure that diverse ways of doing and knowing find their way into MSR community work? B) Focus on the practicality: How will we bring forward flourishing? What are indicators of progress? Moving away from a culture that stays solely in the abstract. C) Internal focus: How can we establish critical thinking about what is and is not done? D) What is the shared meaning behind often-used concepts such as "human flourishing" or "oneness"? Current efforts by two MSR teams in documenting the trajectory of the MSR field and defining the social impact of MSR research are critical elements of this self-critical reflection.

MSR's goal of attaining a division status brings further professionalization and development to the group. Combined with the perceived need for broadening ways of knowing and researching topics, this goal calls for skill building and development in the group. We suggest that MSR pays attention to both self-reflection and knowing application skills to build MSR-related academic rigor and social relevance.

Role of Self-Reflection in Knowledge Management

Self-reflection plays an essential role in different forms of KM. For example, drawing from the field of information science, a lack of self-reflection can lead to selective knowledge creation, as the unawareness of one's mental models can hinder the absorption of information: "Information is not inherently powerful, and it is only through an honest and reflexive uncovering of beliefs and assumptions that individuals can allow information to impact them" (Freeburg, 2017, p. 974). We define reflexivity as one's ability to adjust their sense-making of their social world and self-identity based on the constant influx of new information and knowledge (Giddens, 1991). It enables people to adapt to unknown social conditions, such as cross-cultural encounters (London & Siva, 2011) and dialogue across spiritual traditions (Watson, 2009).

Although reflexivity is an individual skill, its application includes teams (e.g., Barry et al., 1999 for academic research team) and macro structures such as societal reflexivity through political discourse (Giddens, 1991). With the group's intention to develop into a domain within the AOM organization, a practice of group or organizational self-reflection can serve as a tool for a community-led change process.

Skills for Applying Various Ways of Knowing

We discuss skills to generate a practical portfolio of acquirable capabilities that help engage in rigorous MSR research, moving from the abstract presentation of multiple ways of knowing to introducing an employable skill set. It is also a presentation of capabilities beneficial for KM when it integrates various ways of knowing. This way, we contribute to what we envision MSR scholars to be: experts in applying different ways of knowing within cross-ontological contexts for academic rigor and social impact. These skills are suggestions offered as an impulse for self-reflection and an invitation to broaden one's view of what it means to be an MSR researcher. Whether these capabilities apply depends on the researcher's professional and personal context. Hence, not all skills are relevant or accessible to everyone. However, we would like to highlight that without the appreciation of the associated mindset and underlying ontology (what is knowledge) of the skill, one will not be able to acquire the capability, nor will it have the wished-for outcome.

Before one starts with research, becoming aware of one's worldview and intentionally engaging with it seems vital for rigorous research in a paradigm that recognizes the researcher as part of the research, in contrast to an objective observer. For the bhārati indigenous context, Bindlish et al. give an account of this intentional engagement with one's worldview, which calls for several skills throughout the process. The four phases of research preparation are "Reverse social engineering", "Self-deglobalisation and contextualization", "Developing Iintegral [sic] perspective", and "Immersion in indigenous culture" (2018, p. 226).

As shown in theme two, it is necessary to intentionally apply different ways of knowing depending on the specific research context and phase and to acknowledge the interaction between and relation among different types of knowing. Hence, rather than choosing one way of knowing and unthinkingly sticking to it, rigorous research means having the knowledge and skills of various modes of knowing and knowing when each is most applicable. We understand this as a need to master different types of knowing and integrate them into one adaptive research journey when applicable. There needs to be a response-ability for the research design and conduct, such as in a live research design, which adapts to the needed type of knowing as the situation demands it. This response-ability is yet another form of practical wisdom for the field of MSR. Further, a researcher's skill of consciously interacting with the environment simultaneously with one's inner world – or the researcher's "quality of being" – is an overarching enabler for applying various ways of knowing – (Marshall & Reason, 2007, p. 370).

Laszlo, Waddock, Maheshwari, Nigri and Storberg-Walker connect other ways of knowing with engaging in direct-intuitive practices as a skill to connect to the underlying Quantum field that connects all of existence (2021). Having access to experiential knowledge is a common enabler for using most of the previously mentioned ways of knowing (e.g., Bindlish et al., 2018; Heron, 1996; Heron & Reason, 2008; Nandram et al., 2018; Scharmer, 2001; Storberg-Walker, 2021, 2022). These direct-intuitive practices speak of the ability to be present for the experience and to work with it – in other words allowing for emergence (e.g., of images, thoughts, feelings, physical sensations, etc.) to happen while being observant of patterns that seem meaningful to the question or context at hand; this way of allowing for and engaging with experiential knowledge is, for instance, known from presentational knowledge (Heron, 1996) or presencing (Scharmer, 2001). For the former, any verbal and non-verbal form of expression by the researcher that allows for communicating an inner experience to the outside, such as drawing/painting, poetry, storytelling, dance, music, or sculpture, is relevant.

We learn from Scharmer that the researcher wanting to access self-transcending knowledge, or the place from which this precognition emerges needs the skill of presenting as well as creating and holding the thinking-and-being space from which this not-yet-embodied knowledge forms. Presenting requires the capability to blur the lines between one's existence and beyond the perceived self (Scharmer, 2001, p. 141), which many meditation and mind-body practices can teach us, while the space holding can be connected to the practice of dialogue (Banathy & Jenlink, 2005; Bohm & Nichol, 1996; Isaacs, 1999).

A high ambiguity tolerance and an appreciation of what cannot be seen or measured serve to integrate non-positivist ways of knowing. Further, an acuteness or sensibility of perception of the sense organs and access to one's felt sense (Purton, 2021; Siegrist, 2021) leads to the translation of inner feeling and enables communication with others. Especially in the relational way of knowing, the researcher needs to have the ability to appreciate the spaces in-between, e.g., in-between people or in-between ideas. For that, re-wiring a linear, definition-prone brain to see and make sense of a research phenomenon's context and the multi-layered relationships within a research phenomenon is an essential task. As detailed in theme two, we refer to Bindlish et al.'s (2018) and Wilson's (2008) work.

Having presented the three themes of values and value guidelines, diversification of research, and continued self-reflection and skill-building from a KM perspective, we summarize and conclude with calls to action and inspiration for future research.

Discussion

In this chapter, we have expanded on our previously written opinion piece by embedding our thoughts in relevant KM literature. Three main themes were discussed: values, the broadening of research, and continuing self-reflection and skill development. In doing so, we showed why we think it is essential for the MSR group to include a value statement, why applying different ways of knowing and researching, as well as a broadening of research topics, is relevant for the group, and what skills, such as self-reflection, are essential in this. The chapter reflects a broadening form of presenting knowledge by including dialogical learning, narrative development, and contextualization of our thoughts.

Based on the discussed ideas, we present two calls for action for all of us as MSR group members as well as for participants of similar groups and (academic) organizations: to apply to academia what is already offered in the industry and to continuously reflect on the phenomenon of spirituality in KS and KM. Firstly, of the MSR authors mentioned in this chapter, multiple people consult and train in the industry, such as the u-school (Theory U), OMRISE Research Group and the Global Consciousness Institute (Quantum leadership). These and similar institutes translate knowledge into social impact by co-transforming, for example, ways of working, organizational structures, and leadership approaches, touching the lives of individuals, groups and organizations. Our invitation is to apply what is being trained, consulted and published in practice as a scholar within one's research team and scholarly community. In this way, academia as a social system can be shaped to be a place where various paradigms are welcomed and accepted. While this may demand to go against dominant paradigm currents, we argue that this current is less intense within MSR and other KS, where the 'non-dominant' is welcomed to be explored and lived. Hence, MSR lends itself to be and research differently together; we argue it has the responsibility to do so.

Secondly, we encourage other researchers to take a human-centered approach to academia, re-centering and valuing the human. We adhere to the idea that as a researcher, a human is permanently embedded in different networks and brings worldviews – and so values – to knowing, being, and decision-making. We agree with the contestation of research as a non-political, neutral activity. Combining this with our human-centered approach, we see it as the responsibility of researchers to live up to personal and group values, acknowledging the notion that research has a goal and should serve the promotion of good in society. Broadening ways of knowing and topics to know will lead to more creative and holistic answers to challenges currently faced by people worldwide. To enable this, by enacting values in research, we urge the group to commit to continued self-reflection on a personal and group level and to embrace learning from others.

We selectively presented the KM and KS literature and identified additional research avenues. Firstly, the role of knowledge environment or ba/basho (e.g., Bratianu, 2015; Nonaka & Takeuchi, 2019) for all forms of knowing, especially regarding virtual groups, would be interesting. Due to the COVID-19 pandemic and subsequent online KS activity, how different ways of knowing can be promoted in virtual groups is therefore relevant for contemporary research. When it comes to know-how, how tacit knowledge is dispersed in virtual groups could also be of great interest for MSR (Erden et al., 2008; Olaisen & Revang, 2018).

Secondly, we could look at how the organizational structure of a virtual community of practice (Mckellar et al., 2014; Shaw et al., 2022) influences our collective knowing which is an intersubjective form of knowing: "The intersubjective exists in the communicative space in which speakers and hearers encounter one another – in speech and writing." (Kemmis, 2008, p. 128). This place of encounter can be linked, once again, to the concept of knowledge environments or ba. Linking quantum understanding (e.g., Laszlo, 2020), the thermodynamic approach to knowledge (Bratianu & Bejinaru, 2019) or presencing (Scharmer, 2001) with the concept of ba (e.g., Bratianu, 2015; Nonaka & Takeuchi, 2019) we need to consider how we can engage with the field from which the knowledge comes; including the intersubjective, outer and intersubjective, inner field. Lastly, we see aesthetics as sensual knowledge (Goldman, 2001) as a deep dive into experiential and especially presentational knowledge as a valuable addition to our narration of non-positivist ways of knowing.

References

Akena, F. A. (2012). Critical Analysis of the Production of Western Knowledge and its Implications for Indigenous Knowledge and Decolonization. *Journal of Black Studies*, *43*(6), 599–619.

Anderson, R., & Braud, W. (2013). Transpersonal Research and Future Directions. In *The Wiley-Blackwell Handbook of Transpersonal Psychology* (pp. 239–260). John Wiley & Sons, Ltd: Chichester, UK. https://doi.org/10.1002/9781118591277.ch13

AOM. (n.d.). *The History of the Academy of Management*. Retrieved 22-12-2022 from https://aom.org/about-aom/history

Bratianu, C., & Bejinaru, R. (2019). The Theory of Knowledge Fields: A Thermodynamics Approach. *Systems*, *7*(2), 20. https://doi.org/10.3390/systems7020020

Bachmann, C., Habisch, A., & Dierksmeier, C. (2018). Practical Wisdom: Management's No Longer Forgotten Virtue. *Journal of Business Ethics*, *153*(1), 147–165.

Banathy, B. H., & Jenlink, P. M. (Eds.). (2005). *Dialogue as a Means of Collective Communication*. Springer.

Barry, C. A., Britten, N., Barber, N., Bradley, C., & Stevenson, F. (1999). Using Reflexivity to Optimize Teamwork in Qualitative Research. *Qualitative Health Research*, *9*(1), 26–44. https://doi.org/10.1177/104973299129121677

Baudrillard, J. (1987). Modernity. *CTheory*, *11*(3), 63–72.

Bierly, E. P., Kessler, H. E., & Christensen, W. E. (2000). Organizational Learning, Knowledge and Wisdom. *Journal of Organizational Change Management*, *13*(6), 595–618.

Bindlish, P. K., Nandram, S. S., Gupta, R., & Joshi, A. (2018). How to Prepare the Researcher for Indigenous Context: An Integrative Approach. *International Journal of Indian Culture and Business Management*, *17*(2), 221–237.

Bleijenbergh, I., Peters, P., & Poutsma, E. (2010). Diversity Management Beyond the Business Case. *Equality, Diversity and Inclusion: An International Journal*, 413–421.

Bohm, D., & Nichol, L. (1996). *On Dialogue*. Routledge. https://doi.org/10.4324/9780203180372

Bracken, S. (2010). Discussing the Importance of Ontology and Epistemology Awareness in Practitioner Research. *Worcester Journal of learning and teaching* (4). https://eprints.worc.ac.uk/843/

Bratianu, C. (2015). Knowledge Dynamics. In *Organizational Knowledge Dynamics: Managing Knowledge Creation, Acquisition, Sharing, and Transformation* (pp. 103–126). IGI Global. https://doi.org/10.4018/978-1-4666-8318-1.ch005

Bratianu, C., & Bejinaru, R. (2019). The Theory of Knowledge Fields: A Thermodynamics

Braud, W., & Anderson, R. (1998). *Transpersonal Research Methods for the Social Sciences: Honoring Human Experience*. Sage Publications.

Calder, W. B. (2011). Institutional VVM Statements on Websites. *Community College Enterprise*, *17*(2), 19–27.

Deloria Jr., V. (1992). Relativity, Relatedness and Reality. In Deloria, Jr., V, Scinta, S., Foehner, K., & B. Deloria (Eds.), *Spirit & Reason: The Vine Deloria, Jr., reader* (pp. 32–39). Fulcrum.

Ebrahim, A., Battilana, J., & Mair, J. (2014). The Governance of Social Enterprises: Mission Drift and Accountability Challenges in Hybrid Organizations. *Research in organizational behavior*, *34*, 81–100.

Erden, Z., von Krogh, G., & Nonaka, I. (2008). The Quality of Group Tacit Knowledge. *Journal of Strategic Information Systems*, *17*(1), 4–18. https://doi.org/10.1016/j.jsis.2008.02.002

Fazey, I., Schäpke, N., Caniglia, G., Hodgson, A., Kendrick, I., Lyon, C., Page, G., Patterson, J., Riedy, C., & Strasser, T. (2020). Transforming Knowledge Systems for Life on Earth: Visions of Future Systems and How to Get There. *Energy Research & Social Science*, *70*, 1–18.

Ferreira Vasconcelos, A. (2021). Wisdom Capital: Definitions, Meaning and a Two-Level Model. *International Journal of Organizational Analysis*, 365–388.

Fine, C., & Sojo, V. (2019). Women's Value: Beyond the Business Case for Diversity and Inclusion. *The Lancet*, *393*(10171), 515–516.

Freeburg, D. (2017). A Knowledge Lens for Information Literacy: Conceptual Framework and Case Study. *Journal of Documentation*, *73*(5), 974–991. https://doi.org/https://doi.org/10.1108/JD-04-2017-0058

Giddens, A. (1991). *Modernity and Self-identity: Self and Society in the Late Modern Age*. Polity Press.

Goldman, A. (2001). The Aesthetic. In The Routledge Companion to Aesthetics (pp. 255–266). Taylor & Francis: Abingdon, UK. https://doi.org/10.4324/9780203390795_chapter_20

Gurley, D. K., Peters, G. B., Collins, L., & Fifolt, M. (2015). Mission, Vision, Values, and Goals: An Exploration of Key Organizational Statements and Daily Practice in Schools. *Journal of Educational Change*, *16*(2), 217–242. https://doi.org/10.1007/s10833-014-9229-x

Hanlon, P., Carlisle, S., Hannah, M., Lyon, A., & Reilly, D. (2012). A Perspective on the Future Public health: An Integrative and Ecological Framework. *Perspectives in Public Health*, *132*(6), 313–319.

Heron, J. (1996). *Co-operative Inquiry: Research into the Human Condition*. SAGE.

Heron, J., & Reason, P. (2008). Extending Epistemology within a Co-operative Inquiry. In *The SAGE Handbook of Action Research* (2nd ed.). SAGE Publications Ltd. https://doi.org/10.4135/9781848607934

Isaacs, W. (1999). *Dialogue and the Art of Thinking Together*. Doubleday.

Jakubik, M. (2011). Becoming to Know. Shifting the Knowledge Creation Paradigm. *Journal of Knowledge Management*, *15*(3), 374–402.

Jakubik, M. (2020). How Can Practical Wisdom Manifest Itself in Five Fundamental Management and Leadership Practices? *Vilakshan-XIMB Journal of Management*, 3–25.

Jakubik, M., & Müürsepp, P. (2021). From Knowledge to Wisdom: Will Wisdom Management Replace Knowledge Management? *European Journal of Management and Business Economics*, 367–389.

Janis, I. (2006). Groupthink. In E. M. Griffin (Ed.), *A First Look at Communication Theory* (pp. 235–246). McGraw-Hill.

Kemmis, S. (2008). Critical Theory and Participatory Action Research. In *The SAGE Handbook of Action Research* (pp. 121–138). SAGE Publications Ltd: 1 Oliver's Yard, 55 City Road, London England EC1Y 1SP United Kingdom https://doi.org/10.4135/9781848607934.n14

Kläy, A., Zimmermann, A. B., & Schneider, F. (2015). Rethinking Science for Sustainable Development: Reflexive Interaction for a Paradigm Transformation. *Futures*, *65*, 72–85.

Kuokkanen, R. (2000). Towards an "Indigenous Paradigm" From a Sami Perspective. *The Canadian Journal of Native Studies*, *20*(2), 411–436.

Laszlo, C. (2020). Quantum Management: The Practices and Science of Flourishing Enterprise. *Journal of Management, Spirituality & Religion*, *17*(4), 301–315. https://doi.org/10.1080/14766086.2020.1734063

Laszlo, C., Waddock, S., Maheshwari, A., Nigri, G., & Storberg-Walker, J. (2021). Quantum Worldviews: How Science and Spirituality are Converging to Transform Consciousness for Meaningful Solutions to Wicked Problems. *Humanistic Management Journal*, *6*(3), 293–311. https://doi.org/10.1007/s41463-021-00114-0

London, K., & Siva, J. P. S. (2011). The Role of Reflexive Capability in Relation to Intellectual Capital on Multi International Partnerships. *International Journal of Project Management*, *29*(7), 846–855. https://doi.org/https://doi.org/10.1016/j.ijproman.2011.05.007

Marshall, J., & Reason, P. (2007). Quality in Research as "Taking an Attitude of Inquiry". *Management Research News*, *30*(5), 368–380. https://doi.org/10.1108/01409170710746364

Mckellar, K. A., Pitzul, K. B., Yi, J. Y., & Cole, D. C. (2014). Evaluating Communities of Practice and Knowledge Networks: A Systematic Scoping Review of Evaluation Frameworks. *EcoHealth*, *11*(3), 383–399. https://doi.org/10.1007/s10393-014-0958-3

MSR. (n.d.). *Vision – Mission*. Retrieved 12-12-2022 from https://msr.aom.org/about-us/vision

Nakata, M., Nakata, V., Keech, S., & Bolt, R. (2012). Decolonial Goals and Pedagogies for Indigenous Studies. *Decolonization: Indigeneity, Education & Society*, *1*(1), 120–140.

Nandram, S. S., & Bindlish, P. (2022). Indigenous Studies with an Integrative Research Approach. In Y. Altman, J. Neal, & W. Mayrhofer (Eds.), *Workplace Spirituality: Making a difference*. DeGruyter.

Nandram, S. S., Bindlish, P. K., & Keizer, W. A. J. (2017). *Understanding Integrative Intelligence: Embodied in S-model*. Praan Uitgeverij.

Nandram, S. S., Bindlish, P. K., Sukhada, & Shrestha, A. K. (2022). Spirituality Led Ethical Decision Making with Yogic Yamas and Niyamas. *Journal of Management, Spirituality & Religion*, *19*(3), 237–257. https://doi.org/10.51327/EHZW1674

Nandram, S. S., Mourmant, G., Bindlish, P. K., & Sandra, D. (2019). Integrating Reason and Intuition: An Integrative Approach to Objectivizing Subtle Cues. In *Developing Informed Intuition for Decision-Making* (pp. 115–136). Taylor & Francis. https://doi.org/10.1201/9780429298097-7

Nandram, S. S., Mourmont, G. T., Norlyk Smith, E., Heaton, D. P., & Bindlish, P. K. (2018). Understanding Entrepreneurial Decision-making by Objectivizing Subtle Cues. *Journal of Management, Spirituality & Religion*, *15*(5), 398–423. https://doi.org/10.1080/14766086.2018.1503088

Neal, J. (2013). Epilogue: Where Do We Go from Here? In *Handbook of Faith and Spirituality in the Workplace: Emerging Research and Practice* (pp. 733–739). New York, NY: Springer https://doi.org/10.1007/978-1-4614-5233-1_44

Nolan, S., Leget, C., & Saltmarsh, P. (2011). Spiritual Care in Palliative Care: Working Towards an EAPC Task Force. *European Journal of Palliative Care*, *18*, 86–89.

Nonaka, I., & Takeuchi, H. (2019). *The Wise Company: How Companies Create Continuous Innovation*. Oxford University Press.

Norbash, A., & Kadom, N. (2020). The Business Case for Diversity and Inclusion. *Journal of the American College of Radiology*, *17*(5), 676–680.

Olaisen, J., & Revang, O. (2018). Exploring the Performance of Tacit Knowledge: How to Make Ordinary People Deliver Extraordinary Results in Teams. *International Journal of Information Management*, *43*, 295–304. https://doi.org/10.1016/j.ijinfomgt.2018.08.016

Olsen, T. A. (2017). Privilege, Decentring and the Challenge of Being (Non-) Indigenous in the Study of Indigenous Issues. *The Australian Journal of Indigenous Education*, *47*(2), 206–215. https://doi.org/10.1017/jie.2017.16

Purton, C. (2021). *The Focusing-Oriented Counselling Primer (second Edition)* (2nd ed.). PCCS Books. https://public.ebookcentral.proquest.com/choice/PublicFullRecord.aspx?p=6957431

Reiman, T., Rollenhagen, C., Pietikäinen, E., & Heikkilä, J. (2015). Principles of Adaptive Management in Complex Safety–critical Organizations. *Safety Science*, *71*, 80–92.

Ripeka Mercier, O., Stevens, N., & Toia, A. (2012). Mātauranga Māori and the Data–Information–Knowledge–Wisdom Hierarchy: A Conversation on Interfacing Knowledge Systems. *MAI*, *1*(2), 103–166.

Rocha, R., & Pinheiro, P. (2019). Spirituality in Knowledge Management: Systematic Literature Review and Future Studies Suggestions. European Conference on Knowledge Management. https://doi.org/10.34190/KM.19.096

Scharmer, C. O. (2001). Self-transcending Knowledge: Sensing and Organizing around Emerging Opportunities. *Journal of Knowledge Management*, *5*(2), 137–151. https://doi.org/10.1108/13673270110393185

Shaw, L., Jazayeri, D., Kiegaldie, D., & Morris, M. E. (2022). Implementation of Virtual Communities of Practice in Healthcare to Improve Capability and Capacity: A 10-Year Scoping Review. *International Journal of Environmental Research and Public Health*, *19*(13), 7994. https://doi.org/10.3390/ijerph19137994
Siegrist, U. (2021). Die Rolle des Felt Sense im Coaching: Veränderung im Kontext Körperlich-emotionalen Erlebens. *Organisationsberatung, Supervision, Coaching*, *28*(1), 59–72. https://doi.org/10.1007/s11613-021-00689-5
Simpson, L. B. (2014). Land as Pedagogy: Nishnaabeg Intelligence and Rebellious Transformation. *Decolonization: Indigeneity, Education & Society*, *3*(3), 1–25.
Smith, L. T. (2012). *Decolonizing Methodologies: Research and Indigenous Peoples*. Zed Books.
Storberg-Walker, J. (2021). A Window of Our Own: Towards a Quantum Research Ontology. *Journal of Management, Spirituality & Religion*, *18*(6), 92–129. https://doi.org/10.51327/BQLC1209
Storberg-Walker, J. (2022). Relating Differently: Exploring How a Relational Ontology Might Catalyze Transformative and Emancipatory Action- Oriented MSR Research. In *Workplace Spirituality: Making a Difference* (pp. 261–276). De Gruyter: Berlin, Boston. https://doi.org/10.1515/9783110711349-018
Stubbs, W. (2018). Examining the Interplay of Social and Market Logics in Hybrid Business Models: A Case Study of Australian B Corps. In *Sustainable business models* (pp. 63–84). Springer.
Tackney, C. T., Chappell, S., Harris, D., Pavlovich, K., Egel, E., Major, R., Finney, M., & Stoner, J. (2017). Management, Spirituality, and Religion (MSR) Ways and Means: A Paper to Encourage Quality Research. *Journal of Management, Spirituality & Religion*, *14*(3), 245–254.
Tsao, F. C., & Laszlo, C. (2019). *Quantum Leadership: New Consciousness in Business*. Stanford Business Books, an imprint of Stanford University Press. https://doi.org/10.1515/9781503609167
Walsh, R. (2012). Wisdom: An Integral View. *Journal of Integral Theory and Practice*, *7*(1), 1–21.
Watson, J. (2009). Responding to Difference: Spiritual Development and the Search for Truth. In *International Handbook of Education for Spirituality, Care and Wellbeing* (pp. 821–838). Springer Netherlands: Dordrecht. https://doi.org/10.1007/978-1-4020-9018-9_44
Wilson, S. (2008). *Research is Ceremony: Indigenous Research Methods*. Fernwood Publishing. http://catdir.loc.gov/catdir/toc/fy1002/2008431436.html
Woods, C., Dell, K., & Carroll, B. (2022). Decolonizing the Business School: Reconstructing the Entrepreneurship Classroom through Indigenizing Pedagogy and Learning. *Academy of Management Learning & Education*, *21*(1), 82–100.
Zack, M. H. (2003). Rethinking the Knowledge-based Organization. *MIT Sloan Management Review*, *44*(4), 67–72.

Edwina Pio and Duncan Cryle

Chapter 5
Clear Sky: A Petri Dish for Heart-Based Organizational Practices

Abstract: A fruitful source of insights into workplace spirituality is spiritual-based organizations and how they integrate their wisdom traditions and contemplative practices for effective and compassionate action in the world. We focus on Clear Sky, a Buddhist-based meditation center in Canada. Clear Sky serves as a petri dish for heart-based organizational practices, and the chapter highlights a key triumvirate: Karma Yoga, Dāna and Shadow Integration. Their radical reframing for organizations enhances accountable flourishing, incorporating spirituality and management learning. We explore how, at Clear Sky, Karma Yoga – often translated as compassionate service or meditation-in-action – is enacted. We unpack how it bridges the inner work of a wisdom tradition and outer action and fosters a dynamic learning environment. Dāna – Sanskrit for "generosity" – the second dimension, highlights mutually generative exchanges and energy flows. This resonates with sacred economics, donut economics and the gift economy. We explore how these energies are unleashed and manifested through a quadruple bottom-line financial, environmental, social, and spiritual generativity approach. The third dimension is Shadow Integration. Vital energies tied up in money, sex, and power are often bypassed or misused by leaders. We explore how Clear Sky surfaces and integrates shadow aspects to remove blocks and free up energy for doing good. Our contribution is to provide a sky map for spirituality and management learning through charting how Clear Sky incorporates the triumvirate of Karma Yoga, Dāna and Shadow Integration. We offer a template for organizations to experiment with heart-based dynamic organizational practices.

Keywords: Clear Sky, Dāna, Heart-based Organizational Practices, Karma Yoga, Shadow Integration, Wisdom Traditions

Edwina Pio, Emeritus Professor of Diversity and Independent diversity specialist, Aotearoa New Zealand, e-mail: edwina.pio@aut.ac.nz
Duncan Cryle, Clear Sky Learning and Study Foundation; SS&C Technologies, e-mail: duncan@clearskycenter.org

https://doi.org/10.1515/9783111010410-006

Introduction

New perspectives on how organizations flourish and how knowledge is managed well in those organizations can be gained from a growing body of work on workplace spirituality (Altman et al., 2022; Marques, 2019; Neal, 2013). In her numerous writings, Pio stresses the need to integrate faith, spirituality and knowledge for an organization and individuals to function holistically. She underscores the fact that spirituality is integral to individuals as human beings, irrespective of their gender, ethnicity and religious orientation, and this awareness can lead to enhanced functioning on our planet, including heart-based organizational practices (Pio, 2005, 2015, 2018; Pio & Merelo, 2022; Jayawardene-Willis et al., 2020; Pio & McGhee, 2019).

Our research question explores what insights can be gained from spiritual-based organizations that have integrated their wisdom traditions and contemplative practices into how the organization functions and how this affects how knowledge is managed and shared. Our contribution is to provide a sky map for how heart-based organizational practices can integrate spirituality, knowledge management and management learning to support organizational flourishing. To explore this, we focus on a case study of Clear Sky (www.clearskycenter.org), a Buddhist-based meditation center in Canada. For the case study, we have selected a key triumvirate of practices used at Clear Sky. Two of these – Karma Yoga and Dāna – are wisdom tradition-based, drawing from Hinduism and Buddhism. The third – Shadow Integration – is an addition to modern psychology. Our contribution is to provide a sky map for how heart-based organizational practices can integrate spirituality, knowledge management and management learning.

There are several reasons for selecting Clear Sky as a case study. One of this chapter's co-writers was a founding member of Clear Sky and has been intimately involved in its evolution, giving us extensive access to its practices and perspectives. The other co-author recognized the value of the journey of Clear Sky for enhancing knowledge management and spirituality and suggested that this could be an exemplar for this book chapter. Spirituality is the organization's foundation as a Buddhist-based center, enabling Clear Sky to draw on a rich set of contemplative and spiritual practices such as Karma Yoga and Dāna. Clear Sky provides concrete examples of how these ancient practices can be applied in a modern organization. In addition, Clear Sky members have made a concerted effort to integrate modern management learning. They have evolved organizational practices by combining wisdom traditions and management learning. Lastly, Clear Sky has piloted non-denominational forms of these practices in various organizational settings. For example, one of this chapter's co-writers was a pioneer of IBM's mindfulness movement that grew to over 10,000 members, and since 2020, has led a mindfulness program at SS&C, a financial software company with 25000 employees. Clear Sky provides an interesting case study of how these practices may be operationalized in organizational settings.

Clear Sky Center

Clear Sky (www.clearskycenter.org) is a Buddhist-based meditation center and community-based in British Columbia, Canada. It is located on the unceded territory of the K'tunaxa (pronounced 'k-too-nah-ha') First Nation, whose people have occupied lands adjacent to the Kootenay and Columbia Rivers and the Arrow Lakes of British Columbia, Canada, for more than 10,000 years. The center rests on 310 acres in a region known as the "Serengeti" of the north for its rich biodiversity.

Founded in 2004, Clear Sky focuses on transformative growth by offering meditation retreats, residential training programs and online courses. Clear Sky is a registered Canadian charity. Clear Sky is primarily rooted in a Buddhist lineage. Clear Sky's founding and resident teachers are Acharya Doug "Qapel" Duncan (hereafter referred to as "Qapel") and Catherine Pawasarat Sensei (hereafter referred to as "Sensei"). They both studied with Namgyal Rinpoche (né "George Dawson"), a Canadian-born teacher. Dawson was ordained as an Ananda Bodhi monk in the Burmese Theravadin tradition, studying with the respected Sayadaw U Thila Wanta (Matthews, 2006, p. 50). He was later recognized by His Holiness the 16th Karmapa in the Karma Kagyu school of Tibetan Buddhism (Matthews, 2006, p. 22). His teaching approach was grounded in the Burmese Theravadin tradition and the Vajrayana approach of the Karma Kagyu school. He also taught using Western approaches such as Kabbalah and Tarot, science, psychology, art, music, and travel. This eclectic and exploratory approach continues with Qapel and Sensei at Clear Sky today and influences Clear Sky's approach of fusing Karma Yoga and Dāna with modern management learning.

Clear Sky was created as a center for hosting meditation retreats. The founding group (all long-term meditators) quickly found that running a 310-acre retreat center meant running a complex business and referring to the next ten years as a crash course "inner MBA". Clear Sky operates to a quadruple bottom line of financial, social, environmental, and spiritual sustainability. Decisions at the center consider these four aspects. Recognizing that in the damaged state of our world, sustainability of what remains is not enough, Clear Sky now focuses on "generativity" – solutions that actively build back capacity, resilience, and health.

Each community member offers Karma Yoga and has set responsibilities and portfolios. In addition, some community members have parallel paid careers outside of Clear Sky as coaches, counselors, tradespeople, and managers. Transparent Sky's community is diverse, international, and multi-generational. It is composed of long-term residents (18 months+), extended-stay visitors (3–18 months), shorter-stay residential program participants (2 weeks to 3 months), day visitors, and an international virtual community. The onsite community is an experiment in the form of a modern monastery or nunnery, which Clear Sky playfully refers to as a "Monvent" (combining "monastery" and "convent") and its residents as "Nunks" (combining "nuns" and "monks").

Clear Sky aims to embody the concept of a "spiritual container". This means the supportive environment and conditions people need to be able to go through depth transformation, like a caterpillar in a chrysalis. The Centre unpacks the spiritual container into five principles: honor your space; structure and routine are your friends; conversations shape the space where we meet; cleaning up significant areas of your life frees up energy; and it is easier with others (see https://www.clearskycenter.org/our-five-principles). Clear Sky uses These principles extensively to shape the physical environment and daily rhythm of community life, cultivate generative conversations, support working through complex blocks, and facilitate a strong team and community. These principles are an essential part of a conscious organization: "One of the ways to increase organizational energy is by creating sacred space at work . . . an environment full of life-giving energy, passion, delight, and awe. I am talking about the kind of environment that nurtures people who see work as a spiritual path" (Neal, 2013, p. 35)

In summary, Clear Sky is a petri dish for heart-based organizational practices or a petri dish "living lab" for practicing the teachings of awakening. Alongside this inner work, the Centre aims to facilitate and co-create cutting-edge approaches to society, money, and the environment. It provides a specific context of a solid spiritual container, a conscious community with spiritual teachers, a shared vision for learning, communication, and accountability, and members with meditative solid practices promoting resilience and insight.

Karma Yoga

Karma Yoga has been well studied in the academic and practitioner literature. It can be defined as compassionate/selfless service or awakening through action. It is a central law to the philosophy of yoga (Singh, 2022) and is the yoga of action (Shruthi et al, 2022). Karma Yoga is one of the four pathways of yoga. These pathways include Raja, Bhakti, and Jnana Yoga (Jijina & Biswas, 2021).

Krishnan and Mulla (2014) define Karma Yoga as the intelligent method of performing motivation-based actions that are purely selfless. "Intelligent" here is a way to mean that if we understand that clinging is the cause of suffering, then the intelligent choice to act in a way that supports (liberation). This way is Karma Yoga, which involves training the mind and working without selfish desire or expecting an outcome of success or rewards.

Navarre and Pandey (2022) divide Karma Yoga into five dimensions. Manonigraha relates to control over the mind and refraining from negative thoughts. Samabuddhi maintains an evenness of intellect throughout grief and happiness, loss and gain, pleasure and pain, and comfort and discomfort. Phalasa Tyaga is letting go of ego-centric attachment to outcomes. Svadharma represents the 'Dharma' of an individual self, the individual role we play in the universe, which brings us meaning and intrinsic joy to fulfill. Finally, Lokasamgraha is responsible for nurturing and protecting society or a group of people existing in a more extensive cosmic system and being concerned for the well-being of all the people, society, and the social and natural environment.

These five dimensions of Karma Yoga transform the frame of reference behind each action. The first three nurture and develop the balanced inner self; the latter two manifest in a social context through responsible action. These aspects work together. For example, as we train the mind and loosen our self-centered attitude of interconnection and care: "Karma Yoga transforms the self-centered attitude behind any action and makes it dharma centric. It facilitates transcendence from narrow self-interest to dharma, the intrinsic and extrinsic harmony principle. The notion of Lokasaṃgraha in Karma Yoga is the manifestation of transcended self-interest. When the self-centric approach to the work fades away, the attachments to the outcome weaken. A sense of interconnectedness and interdependence arises between the self and the larger social and natural environment. It creates awareness and a sense of responsibility for maintaining the system, which is the essence of Lokasaṃgraha" (Navare & Pandey, 2002, p. 282)

The practice of Karma Yoga in the workplace has numerous benefits. Navare and Pandey (2022) write that Karma Yoga positively impacts mindfulness and self-transcendence. Drawing on concepts from positive psychology, they present evidence that Karma Yoga supports psychological capital (a sense of efficacy, optimism, hope, and resilience), thriving (a state in which individuals experience a sense of vitality and learning), and flourishing (experiencing positive emotions and functioning well psychologically and socially).

Krishnan and Mulla (2022) review various research studies that showed Karma Yoga can enhance the positive effect of transformational leadership, support life satisfaction, and provide a holistic model for moral development. Umashankar and Charitra (2021) relate Karma Yoga to positive psychology via the PERMA Model (Positive Emotions, Engagement, Positive Relationships, Meaning and Purpose, and Accomplishment) and find many parallels.

A related concept from Buddhism is samu from Zen: "In sitting meditation practice, we concentrate on our breath or a loan. In samu or work practice, we concentrate on our work. If we are cutting the grass, we just cut the grass." (Glassman & Fields, 1996, p. 72). Another parallel is the Mahayana teachings of compassion and the path of the Bodhisattva. While these are distinct methodologies, there are interesting similarities with Karma Yoga. Harvey (2000) describes the Bodhisattva as "one on the path to perfect Buddhahood, whose task is to help beings compassionately while maturing his or her wisdom (p. 123). This is like the goal of Karma Yoga: to reach moksha (liberation) through unselfish action. Chi Vu and Gill (2019a) note that Buddhism considers the pursuit and attachment to expectations as the cause of suffering and add, "Buddhist principles of impermanence and emptiness highlight the importance of acknowledging the present moment without attachment" (p. 365). This parallels the non-attachment aspect of Karma Yoga. Williams (1989) notes that compassion is the basis and motivating force of the Bodhisattva. He describes the thorough mind training necessary to be a Bodhisattva (pp. 197–204), which can relate to the Manonigraha, Samabuddhi, and Phalasa Tyaga aspects of the inner development of Karma Yoga. Shantideva beautifully expresses the Bodhisattva's commitment to selfless service (Karma Yoga): "May I be the doctor and the medicine, and may I be the nurse for all sick beings in the world until everyone is healed" (Williams, 1989, p. 203).

Another relevant concept from the Buddhist wisdom traditions is skillful means (Chi et al., 2019a). Skillful means relate to how we act and communicate in the world based on compassion and in a state of non-attachment. The non-attachment provides a framework for flexibly applying the most skillful approach for each specific context without being attached to fixed views, theories, or acting methods. Chi Vu and Gill (2019b) further introduce a concept of fusion leadership based on the conc means. Fusion leadership is a flexible approach of weaving together elements from East and West according to the context and cultural situation we emphasize in this chapter.

Dāna

Dāna, a Sanskrit and Pali word meaning "generosity" or "giving", is a central part of Buddhist life and practice (Findly, 2003). Bhikkhu Bodhi (1990) explains that the Buddha invariably gave Dāna as a first practice in his graduated exposition of the Dharma (duty, way of life), and it serves "as a basis and a preparation which underlies and quietly supports the entire endeavor to free from the mind from the defilements" (p. 7). He adds that Dāna is the first of the pāramis (perfections) to be developed by a Bodhisattva on the path to Buddhahood. Harvey (2000) describes Dāna as the primary ethical activity a Buddhist learns to develop and the basis for further moral and spiritual development. The Venerable Namgyal Rinpoche (2002) similarly describes Dāna as the starting point and links it to interest and involvement: "Where do you begin? With the practice of Dāna, giving. However, what do you have to give? Your greatest gift is interest; it increases the depth of your involvement and energy . . . Dāna is the direct way to loosen the stagnation of ego-clinging" (p. 2). The Venerable Saddhatissa (1971) describes Dāna as an outward manifestation of concern for the welfare of others, going beyond habitual giving to developing a will to give whenever and however is needed. He suggests the closest equivalent Western concept to Dāna is the Caritas (love of humankind, charity) of the New Testament.

Asih et al. (2021) notes that the practice of Dāna is one of the foundations of practicing Buddhism. It concludes from a study of a Buddhist association in Java that its practice had positive organizational benefits of breaking down divisions between social class and rich and poor.

Along with its function as a spiritual practice, Dāna – generosity – also applies to business practices. Wing and Gera (2020) examined how family businesses create a culture of generosity and communication. Glickman (2011) explored how generosity can be a crucial business and career success driver. Crocker, Canevello and Brown (2017) found that otherness (wanting and striving to benefit others) benefits psychological well-being, physical health, and relationships.

Dāna practice aims to develop a state of openness, interest, and curiosity. This suggests exciting linkages to management learning tools. For example, Dethmer et al. (2014) distinguish between working “above the line” (open, curious, and committed to learning) and “below the line” (closed, defensive, committed to being right). They expand on this to discuss ways of leading across different dimensions, such as money and time. For the money dimension, low levels of leadership start from a scarcity mentality, then progress to a more empowered approach, then to a sense of abundance, and finally, at the highest level of leadership, to a sense of the vibrant mutual flow of energy. This is the same journey that Dāna practice encourages; we infer that Dāna supports working from “above the line” at a high leadership level.

There is also a relationship between Dāna and economic systems. For example, sacred economics (Eisenstein, 2021) and donut economics (Raworth, 2012) apply Dāna-like principles of generosity and mutually sustainable energy flow. This is important because Dāna is a heart-based practice within an organization and potentially a basis for how an organization interacts with other organizations and the broader economic system.

Shadow Integration

While Karma Yoga and Dāna have evolved from ancient practices, the psychological concept of shadow – and the related work of Shadow Integration – is a more modern innovation. It is an essential complement to Karma Yoga and Dāna as they are practiced in a modern organization. Carl Jung, the famous Swiss psychiatrist and psychoanalyst who founded Analytical Psychology, wrote: “By shadow, I mean the ‘negative side’ of the personality, the sum of all those unpleasant qualities we like to hide, together with insufficiently developed functions and the content of the personal unconscious” (Abrams & Zweig, 1991, p. 29). Psychologist Edward Whitmont wrote that “the term shadow refers to that part of the personality which has been repressed for the sake of the ego ideal” (Abrams & Zweig, 1991, p. 38). Poet Robert Bly refers to it as the “long bag we drag behind us” – we put any aspects and energies that are not acceptable in our families or societies and stuff them in a bag behind us (Abrams and Zweig, 1991, p. 32), and he further notes that there are both personal shadows and collective shadows. Considerable energy is tied up in the shadow. Continuing his metaphor, Bly states, “We can think of our bag as containing energy now unavailable to us”.

Shadow Integration means becoming aware of and integrating the shadow elements into the personal. Abrams and Zweig (1991) note that for Jung: “psychotherapy offers a ritual for renewal in which shadow personality can be brought to awareness and assimilated, thus reducing its inhibiting or destructive potentials and releasing trapped, positive life energy” (p. 29).

Abrams and Zweig (1991, p. 18), drawing from psychoanalyst Molly Tuby, list ways the shadow can appear in everyday interactions, such as exaggerated feelings and anger about others, impulsive and inadvertent acts, and consistently having the same troubling effect on several people. Abrams and Zweig (1991, pp. 22–23) link –shadow drives to a variety of social issues, such as uncontrolled drives for power, self-righteous compulsion to help, fast-paced and dehumanized workplaces, and maximization of business growth at the expense of unethical and unsustainable choices. Shackleton (Abrams & Zweig, 1991, pp. 131–133) outlines examples of the destructive effect of the shadow at work, such as quashed creativity and enthusiasm, embezzlement, passive-aggression, and workaholism. Although there appears to be a lack of evidential studies on the impact of the shadow in an organizational context, we can hypothesize from these examples that there are high personal and organizational costs.

Another example of the high organizational costs can be seen in the idealized design for an organization of the future proposed by Mitroff et al. (1994). Their design consists of four main centers. One of these is the Recovery/Development Center, which looks at the healthy development of employees and the company. Mitroff et al. (1994) note that many organizations have deep institutional sickness, which forms a fundamental part of the culture and are seen as "normal" rather than "sick". People lauded as role models in many organizations often have serious psychological problems such as lust for power, feelings of grandiosity, destructiveness, or intense cravings and addictions (LaBier, 1986). A vital essential function of the Recovery/Development Center is to study, name and find remedies for these dysfunctions. We may infer that many of these dysfunctions have shadow elements and significant negative organizational impacts.

The Key Triumvirate

For this case study, we have selected three critical organizational practices used at Clear Sky: Karma Yoga, Dāna and Shadow Integration.

The first is Karma Yoga. After its founding, Clear Sky members realized they needed a spiritual practice appropriate for running a thriving center. Krishnan and Mulla (2014) describe a negative approach to the spiritual life ("neti, neti", not this, not this) and a positive approach ("iti", this). While the negative approach is focused on renunciation, they explain, "The other way is to plunge into the world and learn the secret of work, and that is the way of karma-yoga" (p. 4). They continue that Karma Yoga is "suited for people with an active temperament who have chosen to remain in the world and aspire for liberation" (p. 4). Clear Sky's teachers express it like this: "With Karma Yoga, we harness ourselves to the path of work, our vocation, and dedicate the effects or results of our work to the benefit of all beings" (Duncan & Pawasarat, 2018, p. 72). Therefore, Karma Yoga became a central organizational practice to turn every activity of running a meditation center into a spiritual practice. As a Buddhist center, Clear Sky's approach to Karma Yoga also draws on the Mahayana teachings of compassion, the path of the Bodhisattva, and the concept of skillful means.

The second practice is Dāna. Like many Buddhist teachers, Clear Sky's teachers offer teaching without fixed cost and depend upon Dāna offerings from students for material support. Clear Sky was purchased and built by the generosity of many people. Therefore, the Dāna practice has been part of the culture at Clear Sky from its inception.

With the challenges of running a financially sustainable organization, Dāna took on a new relevance. Like many spiritual practitioners, Clear Sky members tended to see money as evil or corrupt. Some members felt that having a financial plan or budget was not quite spiritual. Others felt money was someone else's job to take a few generous donors). Another pattern was a scarcity mindset, which led to undercharging for services. A consultant advising on financials calculated that even with full occupancy, pricing for accommodation was too low for Clear Sky to break even. It became essential to Clear Sky's survival to make a significant reframe around money. Dāna provided an alternative framework for an abundant mindset that was not extractive or consumerist and includes – but is not overly focused on – financials. It gave a way of embracing abundance and flowed around money based on a spiritual worldview. Clear Sky started to see abundance and financial accountability as part of the flow of generosity. Thus, through sustainable revenue, Clear Sky could be more generous to grow the Center and serve more people.

Clear Sky members also discovered that Dāna helped strengthen the team. How members listened, shared, supported each other, and worked together were all positively changed by applying Dāna in the form of listening, offering mutual support, and giving appreciation. Dāna becomes an organizational linchpin, in line with the Buddhist teachings: "Giving, kind words, beneficial help, and consistency in the face of events, in line with what is appropriate, in each case. These bonds of fellowship (function) in the world like the linchpin in a moving cart" (Thānissaro, 2017, pp. 17; 135–136).

Author of Sacred Economics, Charles Eisenstein (2021), links community renewal explicitly with giving and receiving: "We are starving for spiritual nourishment. We are starving for a personal, connected, and meaningful life. By choice, that is where we will direct our energy. When we do so, the community will arise anew because this spiritual nourishment can only come to us as a gift, as part of a web of gifts in which we participate as giver and receiver" (p. 368). In line with this, Clear Sky members found that Dāna helped build community.

The third dimension is Shadow Integration. Considerable energy is tied up in the shadow. Clear Sky's teachers said, "The shadow consists of those aspects of our being hidden from us. They act like cement, holding the ego's unacknowledged fears in place, constricting our freedom. By undertaking the arduous but growth-filled process of bringing the shadow out of the closet and into the light of the conscious mind, a humongous amount of energy becomes available to us . . . we can then use this energy towards more wholesome pursuits, such as integrating our spiritual practice with our daily life and getting creative about ways to benefit all beings" (Duncan & Pawasarat, 2018, p. 215).

Clear Sky realized much energy tied up in shadow elements around money, hierarchy, power, control, and identity. These shadow elements caused conflict and log jams in the organization. Further impetus to embrace Shadow Integration came from the Integral Spirituality approach of Wilber (2006), who makes a compelling case that Shadow Integration is essential for anyone on a spiritual path. Wilber argues that the calm of meditation can allow spiritual practitioners to bypass dealing with essential dysfunctions. Wilber's injunction was taken seriously by Clear Sky members. Along with the energy loss and organizational logjams, Clear Sky adopted Shadow Integration as a critical practice.

Next, we explore each practice and how they are operationalized at Clear Sky.

The Practice of Karma Yoga

We focus on five organizational practices based on Karma Yoga used at Clear Sky. These are framing each activity as a meditation, a four-quadrant Integral Spirituality practice, the space-holder practice, the holistic clearing review, and skillful means in adopting management learning.

Sitting meditations traditionally start with an aspiration that the meditation will benefit all beings. During meditation, practitioners train the mind to be fully present, calm, concentrated, balanced, curious, energized, and joyful. At the end, practitioners do a review, noting patterns and insights. Lastly p, practitioners "share the merit" – offering benefits from the meditation to all beings.

Similarly, for each Karma Yoga activity (whether a meeting or preparing a retreat cabin), Clear Sky members set an intention to benefit beings. Members aim to use the activity to train the mind to be present, calm and engaged. Before closing a meeting or activity, members reflect on what went well, what did not, and what was learned. Finally, there is a short prayer to offer up benefits from the work.

As well as training the mind – the Manonigraha, Samabuddhi and Phalasa Tyaga aspects of Karma Yoga – links every activity to a bigger vision and context. Rather than just cooking a meal, members are nurturing and supporting the growth of residents and students. Rather than just cleaning a cabin, members are creating a supportive space for retreatants to recharge and gain insights. This develops Lokasaṃgraha, acting for the welfare of humanity and the natural environment.

The four-quadrant practice aims to bring awareness during Karma Yoga to Wilber's Integral Spirituality quadrants (Wilber, 2006). Wilber proposes experience can be categorized into four quadrants: the "I" (or inner-individual), the "It" (or outer-individual), the "We" (or inner-communal), and the "Its" (or outer-communal). Clear Sky combines this approach with traditional Karma Yoga practices to integrate each action across the four quadrants. A simple example is shown in Figure 5.1 of making the bed for a visitor coming to make a retreat:

I	It
Training the mind to be fully present while making the bed Overcoming preference Letting go attachment to outcome	The outer physical action – in this example, the physical action of making the bed well and neatly
We	**Its**
Sense of team and belonging (making the bed well is part of my contribution to the team) Accountable and supportive community of practitioners	Awareness of the wider context - making the bed well gives the visitor a more conducive space to gain insights that help them contribute more to the world

Figure 5.1: An integral spirituality four quadrant view of Karma Yoga: Making a bed.

To create a daily environment of accountability and learning, Clear Sky developed the "space-holder" practice. Each day, a different "space-holder" is responsible for ensuring that daily tasks are completed and that teachers and visitors are provided with meals and any other needs. Their role is to maintain a space where everyone is focused, mindful and engaged in learning. The space-holder role rotates daily, allowing every resident to cultivate attentiveness and leadership abilities. The space-holder typically leads a morning group meditation, including opening prayers of compassion for all beings, followed by a daily contemplation and discussion circle. Themes range from Buddhist or Karma Yoga teachings to management learning tools. This focuses the rest of the day's activities, and at meals, frequently, the group discusses questions sparked by the contemplation.

Another practice is called the "holistic clearing review". The practice is based on a meditation methodology called Holistic Clearing (Namygal Rinpoche, 1989). Using the template in Table 5.1, a group process is facilitated for each person, with the person going through the process also participating.

The team first reviews the person's strengths, weaknesses, and lack (areas not yet developed). Next, they review areas of learning for the person's spiritual unfoldment and growth. They review the person's Karma Yoga role and whether it helps build their strengths, overcome weaknesses, and develop lacks. The group brainstormed how the person's career and Karma Yoga learning can support each other. Lastly, the group summarizes this in a pithy summation statement the person can use to work with – each person creates a small card with the summation statement they can put on their deck or keep in their wallet/purse. This develops the Svadharma aspect of Karma Yoga – an individual's innate nature and purpose, the activity that fits them best.

Table 5.1: Clear Sky Center – holistic clearing review.

Name
Strengths
Weaknesses
Lacks
Training – significant learnings and shifts to make
Karma Yoga
Career integration
Summation statement

Source: Authors

Another organizational practice employed at the Centre is skillful means to adapt and integrate management learning. The bulk of research around management learning is around for-profit businesses. Initially, Clear Sky members had some resistance to embracing corporate-style business practices and management learning systems. Clear Sky's teachers comment: "Standard business frameworks of selling to consumers and maximizing profit margins clashed dramatically with our culture of generosity and enlightenment. We could not get our minds around considering awakening meditators as customers buying a retreat unit" (Duncan & Pawasarat, 2018, p. 83).

However, it became apparent that to indeed be of compassionate service, this was unavoidable. Applying the concept of skillful means, members had the flexibility to embrace business practices. Using the concept of fusion leadership, members could blend the best of both worlds – finding ways to apply modern management learning within a framework of Buddhist practice, Karma Yoga, and Dāna. The practices which were incorporated encompassed a range of management research, from principles for learning organizations (Senge, 2006) (Scharmer & Kaeufer, 2013), conscious business (Kofman, 2006), building teams (Lencioni, 2002) (Arbinger Institute, 2000), improving communication (Kahane, 2017), and conscious leadership (Dethmer et al, 2014), to working with educators bridging business and spiritual practices such as the InnerMBA program (https://innermba.soundstrue.com/) created by Sounds True, Wisdom 2.0 and Linked In.

In summary, organizational practices at Clear Sky for Karma Yoga include framing each activity as a meditation, a four-quadrant Integral Spirituality practice, the space-holder practice, the holistic clearing review, and applying the skillful means to adapt management learning.

The Practice of Dāna

Three practices that operationalize Dāna at Clear Sky are the quadruple bottom line, mutual support, and mutual appreciation.

The quadruple bottom line used at Clear Sky is to be generative – socially, environmentally, financially, and spiritually. This is an evolution of the triple bottom line of people, planet and profit coined by John Elkington (1997) and now increasingly used by companies (Correia, 2019). A fourth bottom line was added for the spiritual dimension.

The quadruple bottom line is used as a Dāna practice, asking continually, "How can we be generous and engaged financially, environmentally, socially, and spiritually?" Much of our modern economy has an attitude of extraction with management thinking based on neoliberalism with individual responsibility, self-interest, free markets, and never-ending growth in ascendance (Pio & Waddock, 2021). When we reframe from what we can get to what we can give, there is often a focus on sustainability instead of extraction: ". . . coming from a place of ego or self-centeredness is tiring and unpleasant – and ultimately, unprofitable – both for ourselves and others. Unawakening or unwholesome mind-states could be pollution of the mind's natural, radiant awakening state. Conversely, an awakening mind-state naturally leads to sustainable actions" (Duncan & Pawasarat, 2018, pp. 86–87). Clear Sky members consider that the center is flourishing across all four bottom lines, as indicated in Table 5.2.

A Dāna-based practice used to strengthen the team is giving mutual support. For example, Clear Sky members would go to the Clear Sky marketing manager with requests for web pages, social media campaigns, etc. She became overloaded without any support and resentful that no one seemed aware of her workload. Applying the Dāna principle, members trained themselves to think, "What can I contribute to ease the load?" and quickly found generative solutions. For example, the three-month residential program manager realized he could support marketing by asking participants to write blogs about their experiences and post reflections and photos on social media. This provided the marketing manager social media support and blog material she could share in the monthly newsletter. It also gave three-month participants a forum to distill their learning and share their voices.

Another Dāna practice is ending meetings with mutual appreciation. Each participant shares a few sentences about something they appreciated about another person's contribution. This simple practice shifted the team dynamic to where everyone noticed and celebrated others' contributions. It is a simple form of Dāna: bringing attention to the generosity of each person's contribution and having the generosity of spirit to acknowledge and celebrate it. Wing and Gera (2020) note that acknowledging someone's generosity towards us creates an atmosphere of positivity and a positive spiral.

Clear Sky uses a tool from Chapman (2015) that outlines five ways to express and receive love called "love languages" to refine this practice. These are gifts, quality time, words of affirmation, acts of service, and physical touch. Clear Sky members learn each other's love languages and show appreciation in a way that resonates most with an individual's perception of being appreciated. Clear Sky's teachers explain: "We had been trying desperately to communicate that we cared about one another but in ways that the other did not find meaningful – or even register as congenial. One person glowed when commended on a well-done job, while another felt awkwardly singled out.

Table 5.2: The quadruple bottom line.

BOTTOM LINE	EXAMPLES
Financial	Cultivating the financial maturity of team members Consistent budget surplus and resources to embark on ambitious new building projects. Using pay-from-the-heart pricing models
Environmental	Restoring the native grasslands ecosystem Practicing permaculture and holistic land management Eco-friendly energy efficient buildings
Social	Building local community connections Working with local ranchers/farmers for food supplies Teaching mindfulness at the local colleges and Chamber of Commerce
Spiritual	Providing a rich calendar of retreats and courses Providing a nurturing space for individual retreats Encouraging residents to do a minimum two-week retreat per year

Source: Authors

Someone else wished their colleague would stop touching their shoulder, while the next person received it as a heartwarming gesture . . . We asked one another what our love languages were. We expressed friendliness in their preferred modalities" (Duncan & Pawasarat, 2018, p. 92). Awareness of different styles of giving and receiving love helped build trust and rapport.

In summary, Dāna practices at Clear Sky include the quadruple bottom line, mutual support, and mutual appreciation. Dāna practice creates a framework for a healthy relationship with money, serves as the foundation of a quadruple bottom line of being generative financially, socially, environmentally, and spiritually, and forms the basis for trust and collaboration.

The Practice of Shadow Integration

The Shadow is considered the negative side of an individual's personality, and considerable energy is tied up in it. Four practices of Shadow Integration at Clear Sky are discussed: community feedback, playing a role as someone you have difficulty with psychological money coaching and the exercise of the challenge. An individual's shadow aspects are frequently visible to others who know them well. Clergyman and therapist William Miller lists requesting feedback as one of five effective ways of gaining insight into shadow aspects (Abrams & Zweig, 1991, pp. 64–69): "When two or more people independently tell me they perceive in me a common shadow trait, I would do well to believe them and explore more deeply their observations" (p. 65). At Clear Sky, teachers and team members aim to communicate where they feel shadow elements exist for someone proactively. The team member who hears this feedback aims to listen, reflect, and seek feedback from more community members. Members have found that having consistent feedback from several trusted colleagues is a powerful way of making a shadow element more conscious.

A second approach Miller proposes is listing all the qualities we do not like in other people, particularly qualities that trigger us. He suggests the resulting shortlist will be a reasonably accurate picture of our shadow. Clear Sky operationalizes this by playing another person for a day, particularly someone in the community who has a different personality or seems challenging. The practice is enacted during a regular day of activities at Clear Sky. The person tries to act and talk the same way as the different/challenging person does, express their opinions, and embrace their mannerisms. The intent is to build empathy and gain insight into one's shadow aspects by embodying qualities seen as "not me". Wilber puts it like this: "Through playing our opposites, through giving the Shadow equal time, eventually we extend our identity . . . the split between persona and Shadow is 'wholed and healed'" (Abrams & Zweig, 1991, p. 305).

A practice at Clear Sky is psychological money coaching to address the money shadow. In 2012, Clear Sky underwent organizational money coaching using Jungian-style archetypes outlined in Price, 2000. Price uses archetypes such as the innocent, martyr, creator-artist, warrior, and tyrant to label and surface unconscious patterns and mental models around money. For example, the innocent archetype expects someone else to care for money matters. The martyr tends to over-give and self-sacrifice. The creator-artist works for pure art or love and feels it would sully things to charge money. Today, Clear Sky requires all members in a position of responsibility to have undergone personal money coaching. As well as freeing up energy for individuals, this helps the group collectively to spot whenever money shadow elements are causing blocks and tension in meetings.

Final practice is the challenges exercise (Duncan, 2013, pp. 22–23). Once each week, members do a small challenge. This is doing something different, perhaps brushing their teeth with a different hand or eating something different and unusual. Once each month, members do an enormous challenge. Examples would be being louder or speaking first at a meal if they usually speak quietly or last. Alternatively, they wear something very different from what they would usually wear. Finally, members do something "impossible" once a year – a big challenge that is hard for them to imagine doing. For example, someone who is nervous about heights going parachute jumping! The guideline is that the challenges should not be harmful to anyone. Challenges are self-chosen since what one person would categorize as a monthly challenge might be a weekly – or even yearly – challenge to another person. The challenges are one way to do Shadow Integration through embracing actions outside an individual's 'normal' range, and where there is some resistance, often unearths shadow elements within the individual.

In summary, Shadow Integration practices include leveraging community feedback, playing a role as someone you have difficulty with, psychological money coaching, and the exercise of the challenge. Shadow Integration frees up vast amounts of energy, deepens team trust, and opens the door to a new level of maturity and functionality.

Karma Yoga, Dāna and Shadow Integration as Heart-Based Organizational Practices

Mitroff and Denton (1999) define various forms of spiritual organizations: religion-based, evolutionary, recovering, socially responsible and values-based, and pointing to features of a best-practice model. They note that "the challenge today is to learn how to evolve from the Values-Based to the Spiritually Based Organization. For organizations to become more spiritual, they must learn to incorporate a deeper set of texts and practices from both Eastern and Western traditions" (Mitroff & Denton, 1999).

Similarly, Senge (2006) notes the importance of wisdom traditions: "Personal mastery is the discipline of continually clarifying and deepening our vision, of focusing our energies, of developing patience, and of seeing reality objectively. It is an essential cornerstone of the learning organization – its spiritual foundation. An organization's commitment to and capacity for learning can be no greater than its members. The roots of this discipline lie in both Eastern and Western spiritual and secular traditions" (Senge, 2006, p. 19).

We propose that Karma Yoga, Dāna, and Shadow Integration provide just such a set of practices from Eastern and Western traditions. They provide a crucial bridge between inner-individual spirituality and effective collaborative action worldwide. By inner-individual spirituality, we mean the sense of wisdom, faith, and the inner experiences of meditation or prayer of an individual. One of the great strengths of Eastern wisdom traditions is the thoroughness and detail devoted to practice methodologies. Karma Yoga comes with a profound and established body of practices. Dāna similarly has an ancient and well-defined body of practices. If we are to act from "source" – from inner wisdom, compassion and love, and a sense of something greater than ourselves – it helps to have a set of tried and tested practices for how to do this. The key word is *practice* – applying a set of practices to operationalize spirituality in the workplace.

For these approaches to be generally applicable, it is essential to find a non-denominational expression. While Karma Yoga and Dāna are rich bodies of practice that cannot, with justice, be swapped out with alternative concepts such as compassionate service or generosity, nevertheless, we believe many of the core principles can be applied in a non-denominational way, i.e., not requiring a practitioner to be a Hindu or a Buddhist. The Fetzer community of change is an inspiring example that attempts to embrace many different traditions under a standard shared narrative of Spirit: "By "Spirit" we mean that "something more" within and beyond physical reality that binds us together with each other and with all things in a deeply interconnected, meaningful, and sacred reality, and that calls us to a life of love. Some traditions conceptualize this "something more" as God; others conceptualize it in nontheistic terms . . . The shared experience of Spirit is the spiritual common ground for our Fetzer community, and we believe it can be the spiritual common ground for the global community" (Fetzer Theory of Change v. 1.14.19, p. 8).

We hypothesize that this sense of Spirit is a common feature of heart-based organizations. Individuals in a heart-based organization are moved by "something more". It can be hard to reconcile or integrate this with traditional profit-focused business practices. Perhaps non-denominational forms of Karma Yoga and Dāna can be developed based on this concept of a sense of Spirit that could be applied more generally at various organizations. Table 5.3 gives examples of generalized forms in which these practices could be used.

Table 5.3: Non-denominational forms of Karma Yoga and Dāna.

PRACTICE	EXAMPLE GENERALIZED HEART-BASED PRACTICES
Karma Yoga	Compassionate service + Mindfulness/training the mind + Commitment to deep learning and transformation through action
Dāna	Generosity + Culture of mutual sharing, support and appreciation + Quadruple bottom line
Shadow Integration	Uncompromising integrity to wholeness and truth + Uncovering and integrating hidden blocks and dysfunctions

Source: Authors

Clear Sky members have piloted aspects of these practices with various organizations. One Clear Sky member offers organizational money coaching to nonprofits and small businesses. This approach combines principles of Dāna practice (generosity, abundance, overcoming scarcity mentality, quadruple bottom line) with Shadow Integration work (surfacing unconscious or hidden tension and mental models around money, both collective and individual). The work aims to help organizations reorient to a sense of sufficiency and free up shadow energies and tensions. Another approach Clear Sky piloted based on Karma Yoga is integrated mindfulness. This applies mindfulness to all aspects of the environment, routines, habits, communication, tensions around productivity, time management, health, stress, and team relationships. Here, mindfulness trains the mind and builds resilience and calm (Manonigraha and Sambuddhi). Applying the power of mindfulness to communication and empathy is a step towards a broader sense of interconnection and service (Lokasaṃgraha).

Linkages to Knowledge Management

Rocha and Pinheiro (2020) explore links between organizational spirituality, knowledge management, and practical wisdom. Dividing knowledge management into knowledge creation/sharing, shared contexts, and organizational learning, they argue that organizational spirituality fosters knowledge management. A genuine organizational spirituality implies belonging, shared purpose, and motivation for inner improvement, which will support knowledge management. Drawing on Rowley and Gibbs (2008) they propose that learning depends on a sense of being and practice and on a workplace that provides a culture of climate and peace where members feel at home. They suggest spirituality is the bridge between knowledge and learning because of the deeper reflection and sense of purpose it provides.

We propose that the triumvirate practices provide a powerful medium for organizational spirituality to support knowledge management. In Karma Yoga, setting an aspiration for each activity supports a robust shared purpose and context. There is a central focus on learning – both personal and organizational. Significant activities are reviewed individually and as a group to find practical and spiritual learnings. The learning reviews and exercises, such as the holistic clearing group review, are designed to create and share knowledge and practical wisdom. Lastly, the shared purpose of compassionate service and the conscious training to go beyond the ego support culture and climate of peace, where the individual and group commitment to learning and knowledge outweighs ego protection and defensiveness.

Dāna practice, as we have seen, focuses on mutual sharing, support and appreciation. In addition, we have seen that it creates a culture of trust and belonging. In an organization practicing Dāna well, we can infer there is a free and open sharing of knowledge and resources. Finally, considering Shadow Integration, we mentioned previously some destructive effects of the shadow at work, such as quashed creativity and enthusiasm, embezzlement, passive-aggression, and workaholism. Such traits are unlikely to lead to free knowledge creation and sharing or members feeling at home. We can, therefore, infer that Shadow Integration helps remove obstacles to developing knowledge management and organizational practical wisdom.

Therefore, we propose that Karma Yoga, Dāna and Shadow Integration practices illustrate specific ways organizational spirituality supports knowledge management and practical wisdom.

A Sky Map – Bringing It All Together

The triumvirate practices work together, though each has a different focus. Karma Yoga provides a set of practices for transforming busy activity into a spiritual path. According to Navare and Pandey (2022), Karma Yoga answers three existential questions: how to work – Manonigraha, Samabuddhi, and Phalasa Tyaga; what to work – Svadharma; and why to work – Lokasaṃgraha" (p. 290).

"How to work" is the mind and heart training necessary to act with entire presence, without ego-identification or over-attachment to results, and with a spirit of service and selflessness. In a secular context, mindfulness is one vehicle that provides training in how to work. Svadharma – "what to work" – provides a spiritual framework for linking many modern approaches to help develop vision, mission, and values organizationally and personally. Lokasamgraha – "Why to work" – provides an overarching vision of compassion and interconnectedness. Work is seen as a calling and an act of service to society and the planet.

Where Karma Yoga focuses on activity, Dāna emphasizes relationship, providing a set of practices to support heart-centered relating to oneself, others, and the world. Do we relate in an extractive way to what we can get, rooted in a scarcity mentality? Or do we relate in a free-flowing, open state of generosity and connection? At the personal level, Dāna practice develops a state of abundance, openness, and flow. In relationship to others, Dāna brings mutual support, appreciation, and trust. About the world, Dāna provides an orientation of generativity and interconnection. We might see Dāna as the warm, heart-centered lubrication for the engine of Karma Yoga.

The practice of Shadow Integration complements Karma Yoga and Dāna by providing integrity. As Gill writes, "Spirituality, organizational spirituality has a dark side. There are examples of its distortion and exploitation for instrument purposes, such as cynical impression management, control, and domination; and the hope and expectation of making more money" (Altman et al., 2022, p. 34). Potential shadows of Karma Yoga are overwork and burnout, over-humility, and (ironically) taking an identity in being "selfless". Potential shadows of Dāna are over-giving and martyr mindsets or taking an identity in being generous. Shadow Integration protects the integrity of these practices by digging into these potential distortions and making them conscious.

In summary, Karma Yoga provides practices for compassionate action. Dāna provides practices for building generative and caring relationships. Shadow Integration provides practices for creating integrity. It is important to recall that the practices are most effective within an accountable and supportive community of practitioners. Together, these practices mediate between inner-individual spirituality and effective collaborative action in the world.

We propose these practices support a complete integration of workplace spirituality, as well as supporting knowledge management and organizational practical wisdom. We have also seen in the discussion of Karma Yoga how this practice supports embracing the best management learning. There is ample evidence that workplace spirituality supports personal and organizational flourishing (see Pio et al., 2021), and management learning is intended to support organizational flourishing. We can, therefore, infer that good knowledge management, organizational practical wisdom, and management learning on a firm foundation of workplace spirituality will support personal and organizational flourishing. Summarizing this, we can propose a "sky map" in Figure 5.2.

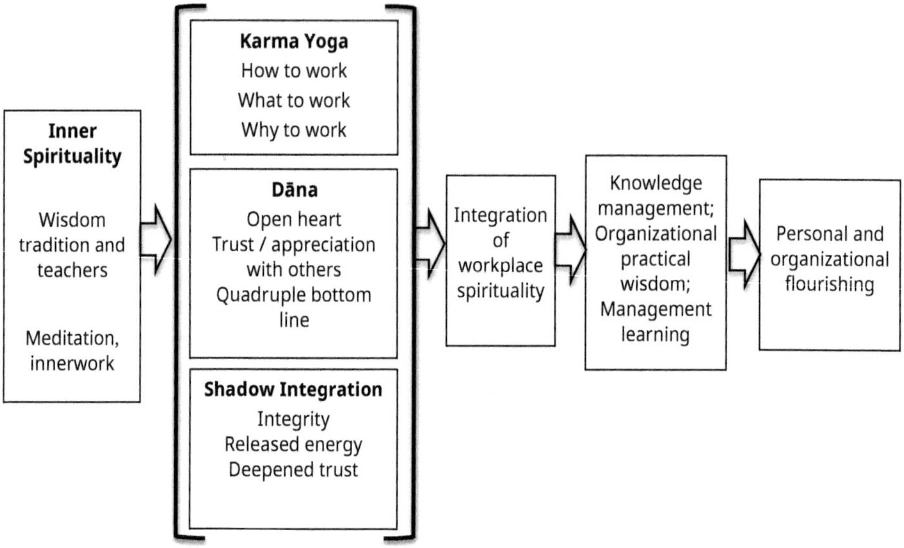

Figure 5.2: Sky map for integrating spirituality and management learning.
Source: Authors

We offer this as a template for organizations to better integrate spirituality and heart-based practices, with the full acknowledgment that this sky map is partial and may change over time.

References

Abrams, J. & Zweig, C. (1991). Meeting the Shadow: The Hidden Power of the Dark Side of Human Nature. Tarcher Perigee. https://www.amazon.com/Meeting-Shadow-Hidden-Power-Nature/dp/087477618X

Altman, Y., Neal, J., Mayrhofer, W. (2022). Workplace Spirituality: Making a Difference. Vienna, Austria: De Gruyter. https://doi.org/10.1515/9783110711349

Arbinger Institute. (2000). Leadership and self-deception: getting out of the box. San Francisco, Berrett-Koehler.

Asih, S., Umanailo, M.C.B., & Sudardi, B. (2021). Dana paramita as a social movement. Psychology and Education, 58(2), 6419–6422. https://doi.org/10.17762/pae.v58i2.3170

Bhikkhu Bodhi. (1990). Dāna: The Practice of Giving. Kandy, Sir Lanka: Buddhist Publication Society.

Chapman, G. (2015). The 5 Love Languages: The Secret to Love that Lasts. Chicago, Illinois: Northfield Publishing.

Chi Vu, M., & Gill, R. (2019a). "Letting go of the raft" – The art of spiritual leadership in contemporary organizations from a Buddhist perspective using skillful means. Leadership, 15(3), 360–380. https://doi.org/10.1177/1742715018761931

Chi Vu, M., & Gill, R. (2019b). Fusion leadership: A transcultural interpretation and application. International Journal of Cross-Cultural Management, 19(2), 140–159 https://doi.org/10.1177/1470595819847229

Correia, M.S. (2019). Sustainability: An Overview of the Triple Bottom Line and Sustainability Implementation. International Journal of Strategic Engineering, 2 (1),29–38 https://doi.org/10.4018/IJoSE.2019010103
Crocker, J., Canevello A., Brown, A.A. (2017). Social Motivation: Costs and Benefits of Selfishness and Otherishness. Annual Review of Psychology, 68, 299–325. https://doi.org/10.1146/annurev-psych-010416-044145
Dethmer, J., Chapman, D., Klemp, K.W. (2014). The 15 Commitments of Conscious Leadership. Conscious Leadership Group. 2014. https://www.amazon.com/15-Commitments-Conscious-Leadership-Sustainable/dp/0990976904
Duncan, D. (2013). Dhama If You Dare: Living Life With Abandon. Printed by the author. https://www.planetdharma.com/book-dharma-if-you-dare/
Duncan, D., Pawasarat, C. (2018). Wasteland to Pureland: Reflections on the Path to Awakening. Printed by the author. https://www.planetdharma.com/pureland/
Eisenstein, C. (2021). Sacred Economics: Money, Gift, and Society in the Age of Transition. Berkeley, California: North Atlantic Books.
Elkington, J. (1997). Cannibals with forks: the triple bottom line of 21st century business. Oxford, United Kingdom: Capstone. https://doi.org/10.1023/A:1006129603978
Fetzer Institute. (2004). Fetzer Theory of Change v. 1.14.19. Retrieved November 1st, 2023 from https://backend.fetzer.org/sites/default/files/2019-01/Fetzer%20Theory%20of%20Change%201.14.19.pdf
Findly, E.B. (2003). Dana: Giving and Getting in Pali Buddhism (Buddhist Tradition, Vol. 52). Motilal Banarsidass. https://www.amazon.com/Dana-Getting-Buddhism-Buddhist-Tradition/dp/812081956X
Glassman, B. & Fields, R. (1996). Instructions to the cook: A Zen master's lessons in living a life that matters. Harmony. https://www.amazon.ca/Instructions-Cook-Masters-Lessons-Matters-ebook/dp/B003FCVFYK
Glickman, J. (2011, June 8). Be Generous At Work. Harvard Business Review. Retrieved November 1st, 2023 from https://hbr.org/2011/06/be-generous-at-work
Harvey, P. (2000). An Introduction to Buddhist Ethics. Cambridge, United Kingdom: Cambridge University Press. http://dx.doi.org/10.1017/CBO9780511800801
Jayawardena-Willis, T., Pio, E., & McGhee, P. (2020). Why manage with insight? A Buddhist view that goes beyond mindfulness (pp. 280–292). In S. Dhiman (Ed). Routledge Companion to Mindfulness at Work. New York, NY: Routledge http://dx.doi.org/10.4324/9780429244667
Jijina, P., & Biswas, U.N. (2021). Various pathways for cultivation of equanimity: An exploratory study. Psychology Studies, 67(1), 1–14 https://doi.org/10.1007/s12646-021-00634-7
Kahane, A. (2017). Collaborating with the enemy: how to work with people you don't agree with or like or trust. Oakland, California: Berrett-Koehler Publishers.
Kofman, F. (2006). Conscious Business: How to Build Value Through Values. Boulder, Colorado: Sounds True.
Krishnan, V.R., & Mulla, Z.R. (2022). Karma-Yoga: Philosophy of moral development and work motivation. In A. Pandey, P. Budhwar, & D. P. S. Bhawuk (Eds.), (2022), Indigenous Indian management: Conceptualization, practical applications and pedagogical initiatives, Chapter 5, pages 127–156 http://dx.doi.org/10.1007/978-3-030-87906-8
Krishnan, V.R., & Mulla, Z.R. (2014). Karma Yoga: The Indian model of moral development. Journal of Business Ethics, 123(2), 339–351 https://doi.org/10.1007/s10551-013-1842-8
LaBier, D. (1986). *Modern Madness: The Emotional Fallout of Success*. Reading, MA: Addison-Wesley.
Lencioni, P. (2002). The Five Dysfunctions of a Team. San Francisco, California: Jossey-Bass.
Marques, J. (Ed.). (2019). Routledge Companion to management and workplace spirituality. New York: Routledge. http://dx.doi.org/10.4324/9781351015110
Matthews, B. (2006). Buddhism In Canada. New York, New York: Routledge
Mitroff, I, I., Denton, E.A. (1999). A Spiritual Audit of Corporate America: Multiple Designs for Fostering Spirituality in the Workplace. San Francisco, California: Jossey-Bass.

Mitroff, I., Mason, R., and Pearson, C. (1994) Radical surgery: What will tomorrow's organizations look like? Academy of Management Perspectives, 8(2), 11–21 https://doi.org/10.5465/AME.1994.9503101062
Namgyal Rinpoche. (2002). The Path of Victory: Discourses on the Pāramita. Kinmount, Ontario: Bodhi Publishing.
Namygal Rinpoche. (1989). Holistic Clearing Meditation: An Anti-Paralytic Practice for Human Liberation. Kinmount, Ontario: Bodhi Publishing.
Navare, A., & Pandey, A. (2022). Karma Yoga: Scale development and studies of the impact on positive psychological outcomes at the workplace. International Journal of Cross-Cultural Management, 22(2), 271–299. https://doi.org/10.1177/14705958221111239
Neal, J. (2013a). Creating Enlightened Organizations: Four Gateways to Spirit at Work. New York, New York: Palgrave MacMillan. http://dx.doi.org/10.1057/9781137327673
Neal, J. (Ed.) (2013b). Handbook of Faith and Spirituality in the Workplace: Emerging Research and Practice. Arkansas, USA: Tyson Centre for Faith and Spirituality in the Workplace, University of Arkansas. http://dx.doi.org/10.1007/978-1-4614-5233-1
Pio, E. (2005). A Change process imbued with an Eastern ethos revitalizes an Indian Business. Journal of Organizational Excellence, 24 (3), 3–9. https://doi.org/10.1002/joe.20057
Pio, E. (2018). Buddhist Brahmaviharas and Religious Diversity at work. In J. Syed, C. Hartel, Klarsfield, and F. Ngunjiri. (Eds.) Religious Diversity in the Workplace: Conflict, Harmony and Performance. (pp. 198–220). Cambridge University Press. https://doi.org/10.1017/9781316477106
Pio, E. (2015). Karma makers? Organisations and Indigenous people in India. In C. Spiller and Wolfgramm, R. (Eds.). Indigenous spiritualties at work: Transforming the spirit of business enterprise. Charlotte, NC: Information Age Publishing.
Pio, E. & McGhee, P. (2019). Spirituality and religion at work: Christian traditions in action. In J. Marques (Ed.). Routledge Companion to management and workplace spirituality (pp. 88–100). New York: Routledge. https://doi.org/10.4324/9781351015110-10
Pio, E., & Merelo, G. (2022). Gender & Diversity in Management, Spirituality & Religion. (pp. 155–167). In Y. Altman, J. Neal, & W. Mayrhofer (Eds). Workplace Spirituality: Making a Difference. Vienna, Austria: De Gruyter.
Pio, E., Kilpatrick, R. & Pratt, T. (Eds.). (2021). Reimagining Faith and Management: Implications for the workplace. UK: Routledge. https://doi.org/10.4324/9781003041733
Pio, E. & Waddock, S. (2021). Invoking Indigenous Wisdom for Management Learning. Management Learning 52(3), 328–346. https://doi.org/10.1177/1350507620963956
Price, D. (2000). Money Magic: Unleashing your true potential for prosperity and fulfilment. Novato, California: New World Library.
Raworth, K, (2012). A safe and just space for humanity: Can we live within the doughnut. Oxfam Policy Pract. Clim. Change Resil. 8.
Rocha, R.G., & Pinheiro, P.C. (2020). Organizational spirituality and knowledge management supporting organizational practical wisdom. Spiritual Studies, 7(1), 68 – 83. https://www.spirituality-studies.org/dp-volume7-issue1-spring2021/files/assets/common/downloads/files/7-1-raysa-geaquinto-rocha.pdf
Rowley, J., & Gibbs, P. (2008). From Learning Organization to Practically Wise Organization. The Learning Organization 15 (5): 356–72 https://doi.org/10.1108/09696470810898357
Saddhatissa, H. 1971. The Buddha's Way. London, United Kingdom: George Allen & Unwin Ltd.
Senge, Peter. (2006). The Fifth Discipline: The Art and Practice of the Learning Organization. New York, New York: Doubleday.
Singh, A. (2022). Importance of yoga in Indian philosophy. Central Asian Journal of Literature, Philosophy and Culture, 3(8), 19–24.
Sruthi, M., Mishra, A.K., Harti, S.S. (2022). Yoga and its path to spirituality – a review article. International Journal of Alternative and Complementary Medicine, 3(2), 26–29 https://doi.org/10.46797/ijacm.v3i2.347

Thānissaro, B. (2017). Handful of Leaves. Volume Four: An Anthology from the Anguttara Nikāya. Metta Forest Monastery. Retrieved November 1st, 2023 from https://www.dhammatalks.org/Archive/Writings/Ebooks/AnguttaraNikaya210

Umashankar, K. & Charitra, H.G. (2021). Swami Vivekananda's Karma Yoga and Seligman's PERMA model: A conceptual study. Metamorphosis, 20(2), 90–98. https://doi.org/10.1177/09726225211049017

Wilber, K. (2006). Integral Spirituality. Boston, Massachusetts: Shambhala Publications.

Williams, P. (1989). Mahāyana Buddhism: The Doctrinal Foundations. London, United Kingdom: Routledge. http://dx.doi.org/10.4324/9780203428474

Wing, C. & Gera, R.K. (2020, May 18). Create a Culture of Generosity and Communication in Your Family Business. Harvard Business Review. Retrieved November 1st, 2023 from https://hbr.org/2020/05/create-a-culture-of-generosity-and-communication-in-your-family-business

Raysa Geaquinto Rocha, Paulo Pinheiro and Nitika Sharma

Chapter 6
Underlying Why Leaders Cultivate Organizational Spirituality

Abstract: Our purpose is to answer the following research questions: (1) why do leaders support the development of organizational spirituality? Moreover, (2) what is the correlation between organizational spirituality and its theory-driven elements? We conducted a mixed-method study, collecting data through interviews with twenty-three leaders. Accordingly, we followed a qualitatively driven mixed-method research approach. To answer the first research question, we conducted a thematic analysis. In addition, we conducted quantitative content analyses (i.e., frequency and Pearson correlations) to answer the second research question. Overall, the thematic analysis indicates that leaders support the development of organizational spirituality to improve performance and well-being and enhance stakeholder connectedness. Moreover, they emphasized the crucial role of knowledge management and organizational learning in disseminating spirituality. On the other hand, bureaucracy, legislation, and technology hinder corporate spirituality from unfolding. Additionally, we outline decision-making supported by spirituality, considering the qualitative aspect, which is a shortage in the literature. Likewise, the correlation analysis identified significant positive correlations between organizational spirituality construct elements and influencers (e.g., knowledge management and macro-environment), supporting its theoretical conceptualization. This article pioneered empirically analyzing organizational spirituality and its theory-derived conceptualization, constituent elements, and influencers. Furthermore, it challenges assumptions about why leaders cultivate corporate spirituality while offering a fresh perspective and generating synergies with other academic domains.

Keywords: Organizational Spirituality, Leadership, Performance, Knowledge Management, Organizational Learning, Well-being, Decision-making, Mixed Methods

Acknowledgements: This work was supported by the NECE – Research Center in Business Sciences funded by the Multiannual Funding Program of R&D Centres of FCT – Fundação para a Ciência e Tecnologia, Portugal, under Grant UIDB/04630/2020. This research is also being supported by a Research Grant sponsored by Santander Totta.

Raysa Geaquinto Rocha, University of Essex, United Kingdom; NECE – Research Center in Business Sciences, University of Beira Interior, Portugal, e-mail: raysa.rocha@essex.ac.uk
Paulo Pinheiro, NECE – Research Center in Business Sciences, University of Beira Interior, Portugal, e-mail: pgp@ubi.pt
Nitika Sharma, International Management Institute New Delhi, India, e-mail: nitika.sharma@imi.edu

https://doi.org/10.1515/9783111010410-007

Introduction

Spirituality influences our way of being and experiencing life, directly and indirectly impacting companies (Hart & Brady, 2005; Lynn et al., 2011; Rocha & d'Angelo, 2021). Overall, organizational spirituality (OS) is a relevant aspect of business that regulates all corporate domains, i.e., micro, meso, and macro elements (Chan-Serafin et al., 2013; Wagner-Marsh & Conley, 1999). Moreover, its academic relevance has been increasingly recognized over the last decades (Crossman, 2016; Rocha & Pinheiro, 2021c).

The movement toward a spiritually-based corporate culture is essential to cognize (Krishnakumar & Neck, 2002; Rocha & Fry, ahead of print). Economic crises reflect organizations' lack of transcendent vision (Nonaka & Takeuchi, 2021; Porter & Kramer, 2011). In addition, technological development and all the information available require a sense of purpose greater than material goods for companies to be successfully longevous (Goede, 2011; Nonaka & Takeuchi, 2021; Rowley, 2006). Accordingly, researchers and practitioners can no longer ignore spirituality in management (Bass & Bass, 2008), either by the excess of positivism seen in research over the last few years or by its rhetorical and functionalist use in leadership (Rocha & d'Angelo, 2021; Ul-Haq, 2020).

The emphasis on the leader's spirituality is rife in the literature (Fry & Cohen, 2009; Geh, 2014). Moreover, they are crucial to enabling, enforcing, and stimulating OS (Karakas, 2010a; Tourish & Pinnington, 2002). Nevertheless, research on their insights about OS is not prevalent. Therefore, to address the literature gap, and since leaders are primarily responsible for embedding spirituality in the company, this research aims to understand why leaders support organizational spirituality development. Therefore, we aim to answer two research questions: (1) why do leaders support the development of organizational spirituality? Moreover, (2) what is the correlation between organizational spirituality and its theory-driven elements?

Moreover, this study focuses on OS perceptions by leaders from distinct cultural backgrounds, respondents with religion and no religion, and considering the current global crisis to build a framework for the OS journey from individual to collective level. Furthermore, we outline decision-making supported by spirituality, considering the qualitative aspect, a dearth in the literature. Accordingly, this study provides valuable contributions addressing a gap in the management literature with theoretical and practical implications.

Theoretical Background

This section presents the theoretical background of the main concepts we relied on in developing the analysis of the results. Hence, we address the dimensions of spirituality in business, and we outline the role of leadership and knowledge dynamics.

Spirituality in Business

Research has shown that OS is an essential facet in current times and requires attention; it has strategic value to organizations, as it affects performance (Karakas, 2010b), interpersonal relationships (Gotsis & Kortezi, 2008), and organizational commitment (Rego & Pina e Cunha, 2008). Thus, the rhetorical use of spiritual discourse is a helpful tool for capitalism and the thirsty search for power and improved performance without considering people (Rocha & d'Angelo, 2021; Ul-Haq, 2020). Additionally, there is significant mysticism around spirituality in business (Friedman et al., 2005).

Moreover, spirituality in organizations has three dimensions: individual, workplace, and organizational (Salajegheh et al., 2016). The concept of spirituality used in this article is philosophy-based, acknowledging the intangible and imperishable realm beyond the material (Hunt, 1998; Huxley, 1965; Plato, 1961/ca. 370 B.C.E., trans-R G Bury). In a non-religious theory (Houtman & Aupers, 2007), it is a way of being and experiencing life that comes about through an awareness of a transcendent dimension. Identifiable values characterize the self, others, nature, life, and whatever one considers the ultimate (Elkins et al., 1988, p. 10). Thus, it is concerned with those traits of the human spirit, such as love and compassion, forgiveness, patience, tolerance, a sense of wholeness and harmony, contentment, and a sense of responsibility, which brings one and others happiness (Yang & Fry, 2018). Other perspectives also echo personal growth (Driver, 2005).

Following the next dimension, workplace spirituality (WS) is a spiritual experience at work (Pawar, 2017). Furthermore, WS is the workplace's individual and collective spiritual expression, which can cause conflicts when spiritual and religious pluralism is not respected (Hicks, 2002; Quatro, 2004). Its features are a sense of meaning and purpose, employee well-being, community, and interconnectedness (Karakas, 2010b). Additionally, virtue ethics and Kantian deontological basis in the workplace support several spiritual values, like integrity, honesty, humility, gratitude, hope, forgiveness, and compassion (Gotsis & Kortezi, 2008).

Given the emerging state of theory concerning OS, there are still many sparse and few empirically explored definitions (Lynn et al., 2011; Poole, 2009; Rocha & Pinheiro, 2021c). Rocha and Pinheiro (2021c, p. 248) positioned OS as "an organizational identity that results from its values, practices, and discourse, composed of the workplace and individual spirituality, including that of the leader and other members. OS is influenced by the environment, organizational culture, and knowledge management, and it generates value and social good visible in the image, mission, vision, and stated organizational values". We selected it because their research explored several identified conceptualizations and proposed a comprehensive definition encompassing the literature's most relevant elements (Rocha & Pinheiro, 2021c). This definition was an effort to integrate the understanding of the construct.

The development of OS leads toward a spirituality-based corporate culture (Krishnakumar & Neck, 2002). Organizational culture manifests in employees' sensemaking processes and structures (Harris, 1994). The interactive sensemaking process contributes to meaning in the workplace (Wrzesniewski et al., 2003). There are six significant practices and attitudes towards a thriving spiritually-based corporate culture, i.e., honesty with self, articulation of the corporation's spiritually-based philosophy, mutual trust and honesty with others, commitment to quality and service, commitment to employees, and hiring employees to match the corporation's spiritually-based philosophy (Wagner-Marsh & Conley, 1999, p. 299). A spirituality-based corporate culture will ultimately enhance corporate performance and many common advantages to people and businesses (Krishnakumar & Neck, 2002).

Leadership

Leadership is an ongoing process constructed on social interactions that produce meanings, where they are both receptors and transmitters (Fairhurst & Grant, 2010). Leaders are responsible for the company to capture this sense of integration with society in pursuing doing good and creating economic value (Fry & Egel, 2021; Tourish & Pinnington, 2002). Likewise, their motivating language supports workplace spirituality (Daniel et al., 2022). Leadership is the main path to embodying organizational spirituality (Fry & Cohen, 2009).

Notably, in current times, only leaders' motivational and influential roles are not enough. They are central in dealing with external change (Bezemer et al., 2002) and implementing, feasibility, and fostering OS (Rocha & Pinheiro, 2021c; Tourish & Pinnington, 2002). Their vision of social good is in their spiritual values. Then, leaders can bond all members around spiritual values (Hicks, 2002) and influence employee voice (Detert & Treviño, 2010). Conversely, some leaders use the spiritual discourse to dominate and tyrantize (Tourish & Tourish, 2010). Therefore, leaders' perspectives on cultivating OS are relevant for academia and practitioners.

Knowledge Dynamics

Knowledge Management (KM) is any deliberate effort to manage companies' workforce knowledge. It can be achieved through an extensive range of approaches, including directly, through technology, or more indirectly through managing social processes, configuring organizations in specific ways, or using cultural and people management practices (Hislop et al., 2013).

Efficient KM is crucial to disseminate the organizations' beliefs, values, and behavior patterns (Nonaka & Takeuchi, 2019). Organizational knowledge creation occurs from a continual knowledge dynamic, a dialogue between members' knowledge, which leads to new insights and concepts (Nonaka & Takeuchi, 1995, 2019). These occur in the shared context named *ba*. It can be physical, virtual, mental, or blended (Nonaka &

Takeuchi, 2019). Additionally, KM has mechanisms that foster members' feelings of belonging and appreciation (Nonaka & Takeuchi, 2019). Furthermore, KM is an enabler of organizational learning (Senge, 1990).

Method

This research seeks to critically analyze leaders' understanding of OS through primary qualitative data (Flick, 2005; Macnaghten & Myers, 2007). Accordingly, we carried out a "qualitatively driven mixed method research approach" (Hesse-Biber, 2022, p. 619) to answer the research questions: 1) why do leaders support the development of organizational spirituality? Moreover, (2) What is the correlation between organizational spirituality and its theory-driven elements?

A construct's perception is a 'knowledge' about the construct, as the confidence that the phenomena are natural and hold specific characteristics (Berger & Luckmann, 1991, p. 13); one rises, shares, and maintains it in a social context. Hence, specific historical socio-cultural elements form common sense. Moreover, it is relative to a group's concrete social environment in a concrete historical situation (Berger and Luckmann, 1991, p. 28). Similarly, with the lack of theoretical agreement on OS (Poole, 2009; Rocha & Pinheiro, 2021c), leaders' broad and diverse understanding of OS should be investigated. Comparably, OS is still a construct unknown to some leaders.

Moreover, the script is suitable because it grants interviewees freedom of expression and the option of obtaining more in-depth and complex answers to the phenomenon studied (Flick, 2005). Initially, we developed the semi-structured script based on Rocha and Pinheiro's (2021c) OS definition, characteristics, dimensions, and influences for empirically exploring how leaders perceive OS development. Appropriately, we provide the OS conceptualization during the interviews. Then, we conducted two pretests. After this, we refined some questions to ensure the comprehensibility of the questions (Ezzy, 2002).

The sampling was done by gradual selection with maximum variation and convenience (Flick, 2005, pp. 70–71). Being a convenience sample, the first author's network was used to recruit the leaders. Their recruitment was done by direct invitation from the first author, where the interview scope was explained, and the consent to use their answers. The theoretical sampling saturation occurred when the constructs were sufficiently explained (Ezzy, 2002). Then, the unit of analysis is the leaders. Also, the respondents belong to organizations from different sectors and countries (cultures), with varied sizes, the number of members, and income (Table 6.1).

The sample consists of twenty-three managers (top and middle) who were interviewed electronically between June 2019 and May 2020, with CATI – computer-assisted telephone interviewing (Couper & Hansen, 2001). The interviews were done by audio recording on WhatsApp and e-mail to reduce the interviewer's role (Couper &

Hansen, 2001). CATI's advantages are bringing better interviewer uniformity in delivery, reducing interviewer effects, offering a greater standardization of questions, promoting researcher safety, and spurring greater cost-efficiency (Shuy, 2001). Thus, CATI lessens factors influencing respondents, like the interviewer's characteristics, such as gender, age, race, nationality, social class, and appearance (Johnson, 2001; Warren, 2001). The interviewer conducted the interviews in English, Portuguese, and Spanish. The qualitative cross-language data collection is inclusive and provides cultural competence to the investigation (Resch & Enzenhofer, 2018).

Analysis of the Results

We conducted a hybrid analysis (qualitative and quantitative) with the qualitative as the main component and the quantitative part being secondary, assisting the qualitative analysis (Hesse-Biber, 2022, p. 619). This approach was selected because OS is a highly subjective phenomenon that cannot be fully quantified (Fassinger & Morrow, 2013; Günther, 2006). Edmondson and McManus (2007, p. 1157) also explain that hybrid methods increase validity and create a "greater understanding of the mechanisms underlying quantitative results in at least partially new territory". Furthermore, the authors recommend hybrid methods for research in a field within an intermediate state of development.

Coding Procedure

The interviewer transcribed the interviews, coded raw data manually, and wrote memos, and the researchers did several team meetings to codify the data – naming and categorizing by a close examination (Ezzy, 2002; Jenks, 2018). The interviews' preliminary reading and coding were necessary to evaluate and adjust, if necessary, the script. For example, we transcribed without indicating speech changes of the participants; we ignored repeated words and sounds (mm, uh-huh); we indicated uncertain and inaudible passages; we reported only the conventional score, without pauses, volumes, intonations, or stress (Macnaghten & Myers, 2007).

Excerptions were categorized and coded based on the codebook we built before the interviews and finalized after analyzing all data (Bazeley & Jackson, 2013; Macnaghten & Myers, 2007). The inductive-deductive codification began with OS conceptualization; hence, it was rooted in literature and refined in analyzing the results. First, we categorized relevant interventions for the discussion according to the literature. Once we used deduction and induction in coding, the following step was searching for codes that emerged from the answers (Macnaghten & Myers, 2007). For example, the code 'organizational learning' emerged in analyzing the results. We did a *micro-anal-*

ysis in the first interviews because there were no contradictions to solve (Bazeley & Jackson, 2013). Some passages of the interviews had to be *sliced* since they shared more than one code. It provides a stratified view of the selection and its meaning. The simultaneous multiple-coding captures what is happening in a quote (Bazeley & Jackson, 2013).

Table 6.1: Characterization of interviewees.

ID	Age (Years)	Sex	Time in the Organization	Country	Number of Employees	Industry
1	38	Female	20 years	Brazil	420	Brand representation with carrier
2	29	Female	9 years	Serbia	10	Tourism Agency
3	40	Male	4 years	Bulgaria	40	Business Development Outsourcing Solutions
4	65	Male	31 years	Argentina	360	Claims settlement company
5	40	Female	19 years	Brazil	80,000	State Bank
6	41	Female	20 years	Brazil	150	Family group with radio, soccer team, and college
7	33	Male	10 years	Brazil	1,600	Hospital
8	41	Male	9 years	Brazil	300	Oil Extraction
9	23	Female	1 year	Portugal	29	Nursing home
10	40	Male	2 years	Angola	10	Commerce, Health Services, and Services.
11	31	Male	13 years	Brazil	65	Automation, Energy, Telecommunications, Information, and Technology
12	58	Male	28 years	Portugal	10	Public Autarchy
13	37	Male	1 year	Australia	3	Sports School
14	54	Male	20 years	China	10	Pharmacy
15	44	Male	9 years	Indonesia	46	Fishing Industry
16	36	Male	5 years	USA	8	Civil Construction
17	29	Male	9 years	Pakistan	450	Public Autarchy
18	52	Male	4 years	Spain	8	Food imports
19	46	Female	1 year	France	150	Textile sector
20	51	Female	24 years	South Africa	3,000	Academic Institution
21	55	Female	20 years	Brazil	8	Physical therapy clinic
22	31	Female	6 years	Brazil	8	Food retail
23	49	Female	27 years	USA	10	Insurance Broker

We used NVivo 12 software to increase efficiency and effectiveness in qualitative and quantitative analyses (Bazeley & Jackson, 2013; O'Kane et al., 2019). The software supported the codification for both analyses. Therefore, after the manual coding, we meticulously checked it with the *Compound Query* tool (Bazeley & Jackson, 2013, p. 120). In addition, we provided code retrieval (coding stripes) to support and clarify the codebook (O'Kane et al., 2019). Nevertheless, there are synonymous words and expressions that the software cannot discover. Consequently, a *line-by-line reading* was done before and after the coding process to ensure the analysis's depth and robustness (O'Kane et al., 2019).

Thematic Analysis

Then, to scrutinize the results and answer the first research question, we conducted a thematic analysis (qualitative) (Corbin & Strauss, 2008). We used analytics tools to explore the interviews, such as questioning, comparisons, and thinking about a word with several meanings (Corbin & Strauss, 2008, p. 65). The interviews' mimetic analysis was done through the symbolic interactionism theory and interpreted by thematic analysis (Ezzy, 2002). Early reflection on the collected data in the thematic analysis was necessary, so we took notes and reviewed the literature during transcription and interview analysis (Macnaghten & Myers, 2007). Table 6.2 displays excerpts of their answers concerning OS and how they see it in their organizations. Additionally, Appendix A presents excerpts concerning the other codes.

Leaders' Perspectives

In describing the leader's role in developing OS, the interviewees perceive leaders as the prominent actors in fostering OS. "The leader's role is fundamental in developing the organization's spirituality, developing and motivating the best of everyone. The leader must 'orchestrate', serve, and develop the organizational values before the whole team" (#11). Moreover, they portrayed leaders as role models and highlighted their communication skills and personality traits, like charisma. "Leaders are role models; if leaders lead us to spirituality, most employees will follow them. However, spirituality belongs to a very private area. However, leaders also have their charisma, which makes it an example" (#15). Likewise, "the role of the leader in OS is that they bring meaning and purpose to their surrounds. They must desire to connect to other people and be part of a community" (#20).

The tensions between stakeholders' and leaders' spirituality and religion are latent in their answers. "We have not practiced [OS] because the only spiritual practice is the reverence we give to the Buddha" (#14). Additionally, the importance of aligning OS with external stakeholders is present in the responses. "We have, I feel, great obstacles sometimes in my work for this reason [different religions] because they are of another religion [. . .] Imagine me as a technical director who orders products to cook at a nursing home, meat, fish, everything, within my institution is not allowed. Mine. In the institution I run, the administration is not allowed to buy pork for the users. However, the users are not to blame for any of the religion of the administration" (#9).

Members and Workplace Spirituality

The interviewees know that belief in the sacred may come from religion (#14) or not (#7 and #10). In developing WS, members pursue reciprocal relationships in the company, where all learn, cooperate, and grow together (#1 and #17). Respect and empathy for beliefs are fundamental to unfolding them. "It is indispensable certain qualities, those types of qualities in a person, that sometimes can also be defects. I would not say qualities that would be indispensable: respect, empathy, and listening capacity. I think it relates to empathy" (#9).

Table 6.2: Interviewers' (Id) understanding concerning organizational spirituality.

Id	Excerpts
1	"Organizational Spirituality is working for the common good and working positively; is to see sense and make the team perceive the sense of what it does, what it generates; is to achieve values at the individual and collective levels, work in a socially responsible way, internal and external social well-being within the organization, work its values. It is a way of seeing that its employees can see the problems that happen internally and externally is to do leadership in an effective way where all this can be disseminated".
2	"I considerate it (OS) is the key to success".
3	"Business is a machine. It has no feeling and no regard for personal matters, and the only thing that makes it work is eating money. However, the spirit of business only exists when it has the element of giving back, whether helping a crashing business or making money for clients' life goals".
4	"What we mean by organizational spirituality is that there is a connection between body and soul to carry out your task or your project work properly".
5	"I think that Organizational Spirituality is the recognition by organizations that their employees, as human beings, need connection and inner life. It is necessary to have an alignment between personal values and the purpose of the organization (mission) so that its members identify themselves with this purpose and can have a more satisfactory quality of life in their work".
6	"The organization has a soul that aligns with that of its employees, creating a connectivity, which motivates them to seek to adapt to organizational values and interests".
7	"For me, it is the respectful interaction between people without a focus on religion, but rather an empathic relationship with others".
8	"From my point of view, Organizational Spirituality is the well-being as a whole of the whole workforce. So, it encompasses both spirituality and religion as well as the good quality of the activity of the workplace as a whole".

Table 6.2 (continued)

Id	Excerpts
9	"I think Organizational Spirituality is very much about what we feel and what we want others to feel".
10	"I believe that it will be that quality of the beings belonging to that organization, in which they provide meaningful work, therefore expressed through individual values within the organization, the interior life of the collaborators. In this case, that is expressed by the possibility of reflecting and connecting with the interior life and, nevertheless, to realize a self-reflection to be concerned with the dimensions of transcendence and full attention of the members belonging to the organization".
11	"I understand it that (OS) as the "meaning" of work, which is why I do my job. Motivation for a common purpose, where we unify the values of the corporation with the expectations of each member".
12	"I understand the Organizational Spirituality as the existence of opportunities within the organization to produce meaningful work, in the context of a community, with a sense of joy and respect for the inner life. I understand such a definition as a process that encompasses dimensions such as a sense of community, alignment of the individual with the organization's values, a sense of service to the community (work with meaning); joy at work; opportunities for the inner life".
13	"I believe it (OS) is the way the company is conducted, the way you pass the knowledge . . . it would basically be the core, the principles the values the mission of the company".
14	"I understand that it that (OS) is the company to be guided or managed with much love and faith and with moral, mental transformation".
15	"In my opinion, organizational spirituality is the spiritual values that the company adheres to in carrying out its main duties and functions of the company. Spirituality values are important things that become the basic rules for companies in carrying out daily activities such as honesty, commitment, transparency, accountability, responsibility, including humanity, mutual respect, and togetherness".
16	"It is the spirituality and knowledge of those who are working for this organization".
17	"I think that organizational spirituality is something that recognizes people are inherent spiritual that they are compelled to sic meaning and purpose in all aspects of life that naturally includes the meaning of one's work. So, a strong commitment to social responsibility, CSR, spiritual managing in terms, of marketing, in public relations activates involvement in spirituality in the workplace moment, helps the other, and cooperates with everyone. I think something that may define spirituality correctly (. . .) The spiritual organization, all people relate with spirituality, individual spirituality, especially organizational spirituality, is concerned; we have a democratic organization. So, I did not think so that such spirituality exists in such organizational spirituality exists in my organization".
19	"I would interpret that (OS) as the company's own culture, its values, its DNA. This culture allows you to gain in time, explanations, communication".
20	"When the organization performs in line with spiritual values. When they work together and provide meaning to an individual. When they show that they care about their employees and help them develop behavior which demonstrates values, such as integrity, courage, honesty, kindness, confidence, and self-discipline".
21	"The whole organization. An element that guides behaviors and enables the growth of the perception of managers, members, and clients about the company".

Table 6.2 (continued)

Id	Excerpts
22	"I have never actually heard the term Organizational Spirituality. To what we hear, the joining of words makes much sense in a world where our work has become our religion. Somewhere I read a definition of inner peace as the harmony between what we do and what we think".
23	"I understand that Organizational Spirituality is the company's ability to maintain a good relationship with the community and its employees. The company generates pride and pleasure for its employees (. . .) Organizational Spirituality cannot be taught in training. It will exist as a consequence the good environment provided by the organization".

Source: Authors

Interviewees emphasized respect and appreciation in the workplace as the basis of WS. "All must respect the foundations and personal beliefs of all" (#18); likewise, "it is important for each person to make others feel understood and appreciated and must show empathy and appreciation" (#20); also, "work in a humanized way, in a continuous search for dialogue and relationship" (#12). Furthermore, they remarked that cooperation in the workplace is a reflection of spirituality (#17).

The interviewees mentioned members' opportunities to conduct meaningful work, e.g., "spirituality is represented in the occasions to do meaningful work in the context of a group with a sense of joy and respect for the inner life" (#6). Likewise, it "is a way to give meaning to the person within your assignment of task, within your assignments, is to give meaning even within your scale of work" (#1). Additionally, "members should feel like spiritual beings whose 'souls' need to be nurtured at work, and who experience a sense of purpose and meaning in their work" (#12).

They also mentioned a sense of belongingness, "the organization grows when its members feel they belong to this organization, each one individually fulfills its objective, and, in the end, it is only to make the sum of these objectives" (#10). Similarly, "spirituality is based on an emotional bond within the organization" (#6). In addition, "members should feel part of a team community. They should be aligned with the organization's values" (#12). "The spiritual harmony of each member is fundamental so that, as a whole, the results are optimal" (#4). Moreover, "when employees feel respected in their beliefs and values, and if there is correspondence with the organization's values, the development occurs more satisfactorily" (#5).

Leaders also pointed out internal bureaucracy hindering OS development: "If the members are spiritual enough, the organization may be spiritual. However, it is not in my case because it is a bureaucratic type of administration; the organizational structure is bureaucratic, so I do not think so" (#17).

Organizational Spirituality Outputs

Interviewees (#4, #5, #6, and #17) perceived social good rising. Others (#2 and #3) stressed success and money in their insights about OS outcomes. For example, "I consider it (OS) to be the key to success" (#2). The alignment of values and the employees' well-being were linked to improved workplace performance, not the organization. On the other hand, interviewees (#2, #7, #8, #9, #10, and #21) perceive the organization's existence, purpose, organizational learning, the creation of direct and indirect jobs, community care programs, and donations to the most vulnerable as the generation of social good. Also, avoiding conflicts with the community where the organization is based demonstrates respect for society and maintains social good (#15). For example, "spirituality is represented in the occasions to do meaningful work in a group with a sense of joy and respect for the interior life. Therefore, spirituality is based on an emotional bond within the company. Commitment." Concluding with "the most affectionate and committed people are likely to be more motivated to contribute to the organization's performance" (#6).

Additionally, the common good similarly appears in practical terms, "through actions in the community that we have involved, the gains are intangible and are moments experienced uniquely, and that has no way to calculate why these gains are not materialized" (#1). Likewise, "via innovation, new technologies and systems are developed for the common good" (#11). Moreover, employees commit and engage in actions generating social good (#1) and feeling helpful in the community (#12).

Knowledge Dynamics and Organizational Learning

The interviewees demonstrated awareness of the OS dependency on knowledge dynamics. "KM is fundamental to encourage employees to train and evolve, which generates a feeling of appreciation and belonging" (#5). Also, "KM must become part of the organizational culture and always focus on some objective so that the information presented is relevant and leads the human capital to a permanent evolution of its intellect. Leadership should permeate all organizational levels and foster knowledge management actions" (#12).

They stressed how knowledge creation and sharing affect the workplace (#2). "Without knowledge creation/sharing, [OS] will not be something that lives in the daily implementation of corporate tasks. It will only have a value that may be known but not implemented, and does not become a reference in the daily lives of the company" (#15). Additionally, "sharing knowledge within the organization, we inevitably practice, acting for the good of each involved in favor of the established goals" (#11). Likewise, "the creation/exchange of knowledge results from a conscious" (#19). Also, they talked about decision-making, "spirituality brings calmness and facilitates rational decisions" (#9) and "spiritual orientation assists in decision-making" (#3).

In analyzing the results, the code ‘organizational learning’ emerged while coding knowledge dynamics. “A comfortable and pleasant workplace, in my view, provides better learning and greater absorption” (#7). Additionally, “it is a reciprocal relationship [between KM and OS], a learning relationship of wanting to grow and wanting the other to grow together” (#1). Furthermore, “you learn all the time, and you can be in the development of your activity, and someone come and show you an easier way to develop that activity, so I think the place for the dissemination of knowledge is all the space of the company” (#8). Similarly, “organizations, which face situations of uncertainty, changing environments and intense competition, must be able to learn and, in doing so, develop new management practices in order to survive” (#12).

Figure 6.1: A word cloud of most frequent words.
Source: provided by NVivo

Macro-Environment

The interviewees also mentioned the macro-environment (e.g., environment, economics, legislation, technology, and national culture). For example, “The environment interferes directly with employees and consequently affects OS” (#11). Also, they pointed out that legislative changes may obstruct innovation (#2) and technological development (#12) because they usually do not accompany society’s rapid changes. Nevertheless, conversely, “the norms were born by tradition, by the religion following, so that will positively affect” (#17).

Additionally, it states that technology can make people insensitive to spiritual values. "The use of technology that is too advanced makes us less sensitive to the values of spirituality. Technological and environmental changes should not change our spiritual values. Spirituality must be an integrated basic value of ourselves and organizational behavior" (#15).

Content Analysis

We conducted quantitative content analyses of the data to answer the second research question. Word Frequency Query was first analyzed (Bazeley & Jackson, 2013; O'Kane et al., 2019). It used the following selection criteria: a) with stemmed words, b) one hundred most frequent words, and c) with 'three' minimum length by default. In addition, we withdrew words like *organization* and *company* because there was a significant presence and an absence of its utility in the analysis. Figure 6.1 illustrates the result.

The third analysis we did refers to linking the interviews to the codes. The software provided a matrix – *Matrix Coding Query* – MCQ (Figure 6.3) – displaying how much each code is present in each interview. It helps explore patterns across the unity of analysis (O'Kane et al., 2019). For example, interviewee six had more coding in *members* than interviewee 13, who had no quote coded in it. Interviewee 17 excelled in having a large codification in *organizational culture*. In contrast, interviewees 1, 2, 4, 6, 7, 14, and 23 presented no *organizational culture* codification. The responses covered KM, leadership, outputs, and WS in varying degrees.

The word cloud center reveals the importance that interviewed leaders attach to employees' singularities. Moving from the center towards the edge of the cloud, we infer the relationship between those actors, be they members, teams, or the organization's leaders. The receiver should be cognizant of the transmitter's spirituality and values to embrace the whole shared because they share much more than just their knowledge. These processes' development and results appear on the edges of the word clouds.

After, we explored the existence or absence of correlation between the concept and its constructs through the word similarity. We made the second analysis of the coding clustered *by-word similarity* using the Pearson correlation coefficient (NVivo 12). Except for the outputs (moderate correlation), the constructs listed as components (leaders, members, and workplace) present a strong correlation with OS. In contrast, the influencers (organizational culture, environment, and KM) present a moderate correlation (Appendix B). This positive correlation indicates that the variables move in the same direction. Figure 6.2 shows the correlations between ≥ 0.5 and ≤ 1 (Appendix B). Therefore, there is a significant and positive correlation between the elements and influencers of the OS construct from leaders' perceptions.

The frequency and correlation analysis presented the most present words and how they relate. For example, the word cloud presented the most frequent words. Also, the

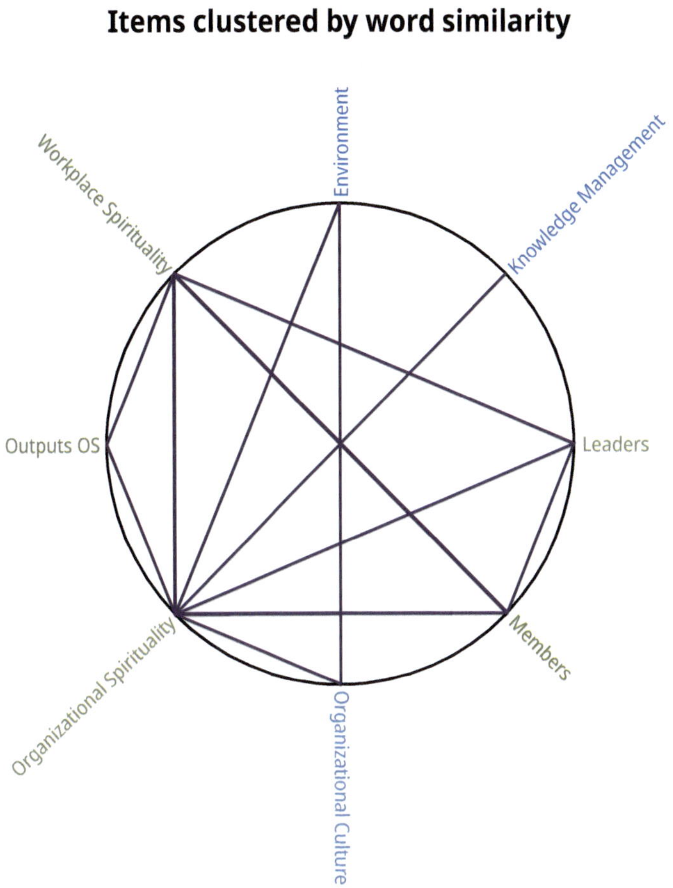

Figure 6.2: Diagram of codes cluster analysis by word similarity using the Pearson correlation coefficient.
Source: provided by NVivo

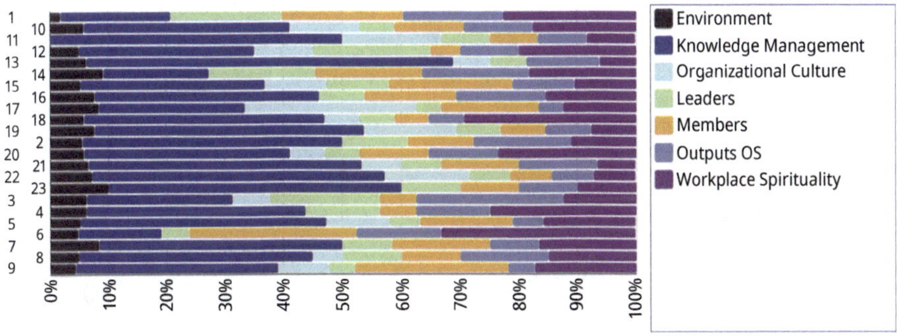

Figure 6.3: Matrix coding query chart.
Source: provided by NVivo

MCQ identified the patterns linking the interviews' answers and the codes. Furthermore, the correlation analysis identified significant positive correlations between OS construct elements and influencers supporting the theoretical conceptualization of OS.

Discussion

This section discusses the findings and addresses the impact on decision-making.

Leadership

Leaders acknowledged that they are significant in developing OS toward a spirituality-based organizational culture. They understand their role as change agents (Bass & Bass, 2008, p. 52), a model to be followed by the members (Geh, 2014). Likewise, they should touch on members' core values and communicate them through examples (Bass & Bass, 2008). Also, a leader's altruism towards the members strongly affects the company's actions (Chen & Yang, 2012).

Furthermore, leaders are aware that they affect the motivation and other capabilities of the other group members (Bass & Bass, 2008). Therefore, they acknowledge their responsibility to raise the members' values and the organization (Fry & Egel, 2021). Additionally, leaders should drive organizations toward shared value and economic profit (Fry & Egel, 2021; Nonaka & Takeuchi, 2021).

Concerning leaders' religious practices and spirituality in the workplace (Chan-Serafin et al., 2013), they acknowledge that religion can be both a guide and an obstacle to the development of OS. The barrier will occur in misalignment between the religious and spiritual values of owners, members, and clients, as sometimes rigid religious ideologization may hamper spirituality. Additionally, the importance of aligning with external stakeholders (Tourish & Pinnington, 2002), such as suppliers and clients, was highlighted in the responses. Hence, as an encouragement, leadership with spiritual orientation contributes to an organization's committed and spiritual workplace (Biberman, 2009).

Spirituality in the workplace

Employee spirituality is an element of OS (Pawar, 2017; Rocha & Pinheiro, 2021c). People in the process of spiritual fulfillment believe that life has a transcendental dimension beyond what is achieved by the senses (Elkins et al., 1988). They are responsible for responding to a call to fulfill their vocation. They revere and wonder about the sacredness of life; all of life is holy. They also appreciate material goods, knowing that non-material, spiritual things will quench their 'ontological thirst' (Elkins et al., 1988, p. 11). They articulate mutual trust, integrity, and honesty with themselves and others to maintain organizational spirituality, and their values can be aligned with corporate values to set goals.

The necessity to find meaning and purpose in one's life reflects the belief that one's existence has a purpose (Elkins et al., 1988). The transcendent dimension of spirituality in the workplace is related to the spiritual development of members in the workplace, and the feeling that their work has a meaning and purpose greater than themselves (Gotsis & Kortezi, 2008; Karakas, 2010b) was also addressed by them.

The sense of belonging and positive social relations bring more satisfactory results to the teams because they win together. The organization develops when its members nurture and facilitate WS. Bonding activities are necessary to develop a connection among members (Erden et al., 2008, Nonaka & Takeuchi, 2019). It is also helpful in restoring values and improving interpersonal ties. Spirituality has grounds for an emotional connection within the company. The members behave as a family when there is a sense of community and interconnection. The feeling of belonging and the alignment of values go sideways. It facilitates relationship building and business. Therefore, OS develops in alignment between organizational and personal values.

Well-being in the workplace was the most present construct within the WS. It is reflected in the experience of well-being, joy, completeness, transcendence, and a feeling of interconnection between members (Gotsis & Kortezi, 2008). There is no possibility of well-being and spiritual development without satisfying the member's basic needs (Tischler, 1999). Leaders also consider the financial aspect, providing bonuses and financial rewards. Respect, quality of life at work, and promotion of members' development are also integrated. Likewise, emotions such as love (Barsade & O'Neill, 2014) and empathy are essential in the workplace to celebrate an inclusive organizational identity (Gorbatai et al., 2021). Moreover, leaders perceive WS as a factor that generates positivity and cooperation in the workplace. One of the tools to understand members' perceptions of their well-being in the workplace is the climate survey.

Hence, several aspects of employee well-being and the relationship with WS exist. However, in operational terms, how it happens daily and how members' spiritual aspects are fostered were not addressed. Again, an empty speech seems to raise the belief that spirituality's positive power is visible without deep explanations on how this is achieved and how the organizational actions foster such behaviors (Driver, 2005).

Moreover, interviewees perceive bureaucracy as a rigid structure that inhibits spiritual expression and freedom. At the personal and workplace level, bureaucracy appeared as a barrier. Bureaucratic structures based on rationality try to eliminate or control external influences that affect their members' behavior (Aldrich, 1979). This closure to unwanted influences hinders OS development. Nevertheless, recognizing the social good in the organizational purpose. Thus, we highlight the need for other studies on spirituality in bureaucratic organizations.

Knowledge and Learning in the Organization

The interviewees mentioned how KM is related to OS and stated that leadership must foster it for KM to be successful as it attempts to understand the knowledge in organizations. They perceive the leader as responsible for creating a pleasant environment, mediating the differences between the members, and bringing commitment with a common purpose that generates the desire to connect. Additionally, they understand their role in providing an ambiance and nourishment for learning (Fry, 2003, Fry et al., 2005) and spirituality at all levels, which nourishes and flourishes knowledge sharing.

The interviewees recognized that knowledge sharing improves the understanding of spiritual values, and its application will be part of everyday life. The reassurance of knowledge sharing and tutoring members about when and how to use the knowledge acquired is part of the KM process (Nonaka & Takeuchi, 2019). Due to the accelerated changes, members must update their knowledge frequently (Bolisani & Bratianu, 2018) and facilitate practical wisdom.

Leaders mentioned meeting rooms, auditoriums, face-to-face and online training, social media, phone calls, notebooks, dialogs, intranet, and e-mail as sharing contexts. They also mentioned the organization's external ambiance, such as cafeterias, yachts, parks, beaches, and restaurants. On the other hand, some interviewees answered that he has no place to create or share knowledge in their organization.

Each type of dialogue has a corresponding type of shared context (Nonaka & Konno, 1998; Nonaka et al., 2000). Leaders understood the need for a context for sharing, often more explicitly, as rooms for meetings and training. Leaders with specialized qualifications mention the contexts for sharing knowledge at the tacit level a few times. Additionally, leaders mentioned the *original sharing context*, where emotions and feelings are generated, facilitating knowledge sharing at the most diverse levels and stages of the SECI model (Nonaka, 1994; Nonaka & Takeuchi, 2019) and, ultimately, enhancing learning.

Leadership engagement influences employees' and clients' knowledge and performance by establishing a pleasant and open environment (Khan et al., 2022), which balances organizational knowledge and learning (Rocha & Pinheiro, 2021). Moreover, the journey affects society (Sharma et al., 2020).

Organizational Spirituality Outcomes

The interviewees saw spirituality in business and talked about its benefits, including economic ones; they could not explain which habits, behaviors, or organizational policies are responsible for these results. Hence, consistent with previous research (e.g., Rocha and D'Angelo, 2021), the discourse of spirituality proved to be more present than conscious organizational actions considering spiritual values. It reflects Ul-Haq's (2020) warning about managers using spirituality as a tool for capitalistic goals. Their point of view regarding the organization shapes this perception of social good. We expected economic motivation and social and spiritual worries (Schudt, 2000). However, in contrast to our expectations, there is additional empty speech (Driver, 2005). Some answers focused on the material aspects, distancing themselves from the spiritual and virtuous aspects of spirituality in business and setting OS as a means to commitment, motivation, well-being, and organizational performance.

External Environment

Interviewees understood the macroenvironment's importance for OS. Besides, the relevance of the environment lies in its variation. Interviewees repeatedly mentioned the macro-environment negatively fluctuating OS. The more significant variation, the greater the need for companies to anticipate or adapt to external changes (Aldrich, 1979). Companies need to monitor the macroenvironment (economy, politics, and technological changes) because opportunities and threats can arise from its changes (Kotler & Keller, 2016). Unstable environments hinder learning and increase the need for responses and adjustment (Aldrich, 1979). Moreover, in Pakistan, for example, the state is not secular. It is different from other countries where there is a separation between religious institutions and the state.

Organizational Spirituality and Decision-Making

Spirituality facilitates the management of knowledge and skills as participants stated that leaders assist with the sharing of context, emotions, and learning, which nurture the organizations (Bratianu, 2015). Previous studies discoursed the links between spirituality, knowledge sharing, and organizational learning (Rahman et al., 2015; Sorakraikitikul & Siengthai, 2014). Leadership establishes WS, which stimulates inner consciousness as stated by the respondents and manifested by past studies (Widodo & Suryosukmono, 2021; Gotsis & Kortezi, 2008; Pawar, 2009). Individual spirituality influences performance enhancement, as respondents indicated that a cohesive and open environment enhances productivity. Also, past studies supported that spirituality holistically improves performance at work by understanding self-transcendence and organizational capabilities (Mir et al., 2019; Driver et al., 2005).

OS leads to effective and ethical decision-making as it manifests mindfulness and integrity. However, autocratic and bureaucratic workplaces restrict spirituality as sometimes capitalistic emplacement is too strong, which might subdue the adobe of organizational spirituality as broached by respondents and supported by past studies (Casey, 2004; Sass, 2000). Not only that but in the current context, working affairs are onerous for individuals and organizations. Therefore, the Macro-environment limits the functioning of spirituality and restricts OS (Kumar & Modi, 2022). These might cause ineffective decision-making as the present situation is dynamic and requires urgent actions (Thorén & Vendel, 2018), leading to ineffective decision-making. Also, OS barriers hinder innovation, an open environment, and smooth functioning. High-level OS can stimulate effective decision-making, whereas low-level OS obstruct decision-making.

Implications for Research and Practice

This article delves into the investigation of spirituality in business. Although management researchers have made promising theoretical and qualitative advances on spirituality in the workplace (e.g., Karakas & Sarigollu, 2019; Rocha & Pinheiro, 2021b), the organizational dimension still needs qualitative studies as the concept of spirituality is abstract and notional (Rocha & D'Angelo, 2021). Therefore, we provide novel knowledge to further the understanding and discussion of the concept subjectively. Furthermore, by addressing the leaders' perspective on OS development, our research fills a gap in other areas, such as knowledge management and organizational culture.

Our outcomes challenge assumptions about why leaders have chosen to implement a spirituality-based organizational culture, especially assuming it is for mystical and esoteric reasons (Friedman et al., 2005). Not only did we reveal the importance of performance improvement and well-being as significant incentives for leaders to see advantages, but the absence of mystical motivations. Our findings also contribute to broadening a critical perspective on spirituality in business. The discourse about finding meaning in the workplace and having transcendental purpose is presented simultaneously with the quest for increased economic performance. It makes explicit the need to decrease the romanticization of research on spirituality in business.

Furthermore, our outputs extend the literature on organizational spirituality by showing the presence and relevance of knowledge management practices to developing OS toward a spirituality-based organizational culture. Earlier research theoretically introduced the idea of spiritual knowledge (e.g., Bratianu, 2015) and the importance of knowledge management for developing organizational spirituality (e.g., Rocha & Pinheiro, 2021a). Nonetheless, the current study provides empirical findings on leaders' perceptions and their organization's frequent KM practices.

Likewise, by portraying the tensions between the customers' religiosity and the leaders' religiosity, it expands previous research that majorly dealt with religious tensions within the workplace (e.g., Chan-Serafin et al., 2013). In sum, it offers a fresh perspective on OS and generates novel areas for research in this domain.

The outcomes also provide practical implications. The tensions between the customers' and managers' religiosities can represent the main obstacle, for example, in internationalization scenarios. We recommend considering this factor when choosing target countries in this process. In the case of immigrant managers and owners, we suggest market analysis to target customers at the intersection of compatible religious and spiritual practices. In the public sector and bureaucratic organizations, the leader's creativity will be further enhanced by the commitment to embody a spirituality-based organizational culture while meeting the stringent requirements of administrative law.

On the other hand, leaders may be even more likely to pursue this goal in public organizations with a social orientation. In addition, the importance of educating leaders is supported by the resultas as mentioned in the literature (Phipps, 2023). We recommend that in such cases, OS should be pursued along the path of ethical values, altruistic actions, and compassion toward citizens. Likewise, we suggest frequent organizational climate surveys, evaluating spiritual practices, and developing a spirituality-based organizational culture.

Conclusions

This article is a pioneer in empirically analyzing organizational spirituality and its theory-derived conceptualization, constituent elements, and influencers. It paves the way for leaders and researchers to rethink OS at all company levels. Furthermore, it challenges assumptions about why leaders cultivate organizational spirituality while simultaneously introducing a novel angle and generating synergies with other academic domains.

Overall, the thematic analysis indicates that leaders support the development of organizational spirituality to improve performance and well-being and enhance stakeholder connectedness. Moreover, they emphasized the crucial role of knowledge management and organizational learning in spreading spirituality. On the other hand, bureaucracy, legislation, and technology were pointed out as factors hindering organizational spirituality unfolding. Additionally, decision-making supported by spirituality is outlined considering the qualitative aspect, which is a dearth in the literature. Likewise, the correlation analysis identified significant positive correlations between organizational spirituality construct elements and influencers (e.g., knowledge management and macro-environment), supporting its theoretical conceptualization.

Furthermore, it contributes to spirituality's research in management by empirically exploring OS since researchers have addressed it mainly theoretically. We emphasize that our critic refers to myopia caused by the empty speech and rhetorical use of spirituality in business. This distortion by over-positivity and functionalist application of spirituality harms employees and leads spirituality to become a control instrument and tool of savage capitalism. To change perspective, the need for concern with the virtuous transcendent aspect of people and organizations must be analyzed and understood. People need to be protected and respected despite a profit drive (Schudt, 2000). More than a spiritual discourse, virtuous action is needed to develop virtuous companies. Therefore, one must be careful with the discourse of spirituality's miraculous power in management.

Nevertheless, there were limitations. One of the data-collection challenges is using the *lingua franca* (English) to communicate (Resch and Enzenhofer, 2018). Another limitation is the sample since cultural, industrial, gender, political, financial, religious, and environmental diversity interferes with the results, making it impossible to generalize. Finally, we only explored the discourse and values of OS through leaders' speech, without source triangulation, setting aside organizational practice analysis in this investigation. These limitations are the orientation for future empirical research involving case studies with observation, action research, and experiments. Then, we suggest further investigation using other lenses and research considering the limitations above.

Researchers still have a long path ahead of them. Consequently, there are additional suggestions for future investigations. First, researchers should use other qualitative methods, such as case studies, ethnographic, document analysis, focus groups, and observation. Second, scrutinize internal and external stakeholders' perceptions concerning OS. Third, conducting longitudinal studies would facilitate an understanding of spiritual evolution within organizations toward a spirituality-based organizational culture. Fourth, study the motivations and impacts of spirituality's rhetorical use. It would also be enriching to investigate leaders' behavior toward the members when they are highly aware of OS and related constructs. Finally, research how transformational leadership rhetoric is used in fostering OS.

Appendix A

Excerpts of the interviews concerning organizational spirituality components and influencers categorized by thematic codes

Thematic codes		Excerpts
Workplace Spirituality	Employee well-being	"To work with spirituality is to work in a humanized way, in a continuous search for dialogue and relationship" (i12). "The foundations and personal beliefs of all must be respected by all" (i18). "Although it is important to make profits, student and staff well-being are very important to my organization" (i20).
	Meaning and purpose	"Then is a way to give meaning to the person within your assignment of task, within your assignments, is to give meaning even within your scale of work" (i1). "Spirituality is represented in the opportunities to do meaningful work in the context of a community with a sense of joy and respect for the interior life" (i6). "Members should feel like spiritual beings whose "souls" need to be nurtured at work, and who experience a sense of purpose and meaning in their work" (12).

(continued)

Thematic codes		Excerpts
	Sense of community and Interconnectedness	"The organization grows when its members feel they belong to this organization, each one individually fulfills its objective, and, in the end, it is only to make the sum of these objectives" (i10). "Members should feel part of a team community. They should be aligned with the values of the organization" (i12).
	Values alignment	"In the organization, the spiritual harmony of each member is fundamental so that as a whole, the results are optimal." (i4). "When employees feel respected in their beliefs and values, and if there is a correspondence with the values of the organization, the development of organizational spirituality occurs more satisfactorily" (i5). "Spirituality is based on an emotional bond within the organization" (i6).
Members	Individual spirituality	"We have not practiced, because the only spiritual practice is the reverence we give to the Buddha" (i14). "Spirituality actually belongs to a very private area" (i15). "Regarding Individual spirituality, yes, there is a culture of cooperativeness; in my organization, the people help one another by going to ask their daily issues, for some routine discussion, related with any problem they direct guide and help their fellows. It is a minor level of spirituality, individual spirituality, not the organizational one" (i17).
	Induvial perspective	"I think it is indispensable certain types of qualities, those types of qualities in a person, qualities that sometimes can also be defects. I would not say qualities that would say indispensable characteristics, respect, empathy, and listening capacity. Basically, I think it is very much related to empathy" (i9). "It is important for each person to make others feel understood and appreciated and must show empathy and appreciation" (i20).
	Altruism	"There are several social actions with the community and also with the employees" (i7). "We usually make donations" (i14).
	Outcomes	"Sharing the knowledge and spirit and everything we affect one to each other" (i2).
Leadership		"Spirituality is present in organizations, regardless of whether the organization has a spiritualized management or not" (i6). "The leader's role is fundamental in developing the organization's spirituality, developing and motivating the best of each individual. The leader must "orchestrate", serve and develop the organizational values before the whole team" (i11).

(continued)

Thematic codes		Excerpts
		"For us, leaders are role models; if leaders lead us to spirituality, then most employees will follow them. Although spirituality actually belongs to a very private area. But leaders also have their own charisma, which makes it an example" (15). "The role of the leader in organizational spirituality is that they bring meaning and purpose to their surrounds. They must have the desire to connect to other people and to be part of a community" (20).
Knowledge Management	Knowledge Management	"Knowledge management is fundamental to encourage employees to train and evolve, which generates a feeling of appreciation and belonging" (i5). "Knowledge management must become part of the organizational culture and always focus on some objective so that the information presented is relevant and leads the human capital to a continuous evolution of its intellect. Leadership should permeate all organizational levels and foster knowledge management actions" (i12). "If the Organizational Spirituality exists in an organization that knowledge management process that you already mentioned knowledge creation or knowledge sharing it may also be including knowledge utilization or knowledge acquisition, then the people will create, share, or utilize their knowledge, according to with the situation." (17).
	Knowledge creation/sharing	"Our company we have like short meetings of sharing the knowledge about anything" (2). "Sharing knowledge within the corporation, we automatically practice organizational spirituality, acting for the good of all involved in favor of the established goals" (11). "Without knowledge creation/sharing, organizational spirituality will not be something that lives in the daily implementation of corporate tasks. It will only be a value that may be known but not implemented and does not become a reference in the daily lives of the company" (15). "The creation/exchange of knowledge results from a conscious organizational spirituality" (i19).
	Shared context (*ba*)	"A comfortable and pleasant environment, in my view, provides better learning and greater absorption" (i7). "I believe that there is no place for sharing because you learn all the time and you can be in the development of your activity and someone come and show you an easier way to develop that activity, so I think the place for the dissemination of knowledge is all the space of the company" (i8). "Necessary for the well-being of the team and the professionalism of the actions" (21).

(continued)

Thematic codes		Excerpts
	Organizational learning	"It is a reciprocal relationship (between Knowledge Management and OS), a learning relationship of wanting to grow and wanting the other to grow together" (i1). "Therefore, the company must become a place of production, of profits, but also becomes a place of learning, of sharing experience, of wisdom, making it possible to achieve the MBO, that is the Management By Objectives, both within the MBO the organizational spirituality plays a crucial role" (i10). "Organizations, which face situations of uncertainty, changing environments and intense competition, must be able to learn and, in doing so, develop new management practices in order to survive" (i12).
Outputs	Social good	"Through actions in the community that we have involved, the gains are intangible and are moments experienced uniquely, and that has no way to calculate why these gains are not materialized." (i1). "There are several social actions with the community and also with the employees" (i7). "Through innovation, developing new technologies and systems for the common good" (i11). "We usually make donations" (i14).
	Economic value	"The most affectionate and committed people are likely to be more motivated to contribute to the organization's performance" (i6). "It generates economic values through much work that we have. Values are created through the work we do" (i16). "We encourage the team to provide personalized customer service, meet deadlines for delivery of goods and supply of first-class products" (i18).
Macro-environment	Environment	"The environment interferes directly with employees and consequently affects organizational spirituality" (i11).
	Economic	"From the point of view of legislation, I see a huge backlog that harms mainly the small ones" (i22).
	Legislation	"That is so many borders because of economic legislation" (i2). "The Labor Legislation in Brazil, which a priori and would be the mediator of labor relations, is extremely complex, which generates conflicts and engages processes that could be easily resolved" (i21).

(continued)

Thematic codes		Excerpts
	Technology	"The use of technology that is too advanced makes us less sensitive to the values of spirituality. In fact, technological and environmental changes should not change our spiritual values. Spirituality must be an integrated basic value of ourselves and organizational behavior" (i15). "I see technology as the superpowers necessary to achieve collective survival. Especially for the leader" (i23).
	National culture	"It is Australia and Sydney; it is very multicultural, so we work with people of various nationalities so, in order for you to understand and be able to transmit this knowledge and the final project of our work, you need to understand a little of their culture" (i13). "In my opinion, the norms were born by tradition, by the religion following, so that will positively affect organizational spirituality" (i17).
Organizational Culture		"I would interpret that (OS) as the company's own culture, its values, its DNA. This culture allows you to gain in time, explanations, communication (. . .) Listening to each other, understanding each other, and maturing their own ideas to create a true corporate culture" (i19).

Appendix B

Codes clusters by word similarity using the Pearson correlation coefficient (NVivo 12)

Code A	Code B	Pearson correlation coefficient
Codes\\OS	Codes\\OS\Members	0.870205***
Codes\\OS\WS	Codes\\OS	0.82616***
Codes\\OS\WS	Codes\\OS\Members	0.755862***
Codes\\OS	Codes\\OS\Leaders	0.694084**
Codes\\OS\Outputs OS	Codes\\OS	0.607018**
Codes\\Organizational Culture	Codes\\Environment	0.587239**
Codes\\OS	Codes\\Environment	0.553336**
Codes\\OS	Codes\\KM	0.545825**
Codes\\OS\WS	Codes\\OS\Outputs OS	0.543599**
Codes\\OS	Codes\\Organizational Culture	0.524939**
Codes\\OS\WS	Codes\\OS\Leaders	0.50923**
Codes\\OS\Members	Codes\\OS\Leaders	0.504692**

Note: (***) strong correlation; (**) moderate correlation

References

Aldrich HE (1979) *Organizations and Environments* Prentice-Hall, ed. (New Jersey).
Aftab, J., Sarwar, H., Kiran, A., Qureshi, M. I., Ishaq, M. I., Ambreen, S., & Kayani, A. J. (2022). Ethical leadership, workplace spirituality, and job satisfaction: the moderating role of self-efficacy. *International Journal of Emerging Markets*, (ahead-of-print).
Barsade SG, O'Neill OA (2014) What's Love Got to Do with It? A Longitudinal Study of the Culture of Companionate Love and Employee and Client Outcomes in a Long-term Care Setting. *Adm. Sci. Q.* 59(4):551–598.
Bass BM, Bass R (2008) *The Bass Handbook of leadership: Theory, Research, and Managerial Applications* Fourth. (Free Press, New York).
Bazeley P, Jackson K (2013) *Qualitative Data Analysis with NVIVO* 2ª. (SAGE Publications Inc., Thousand Oaks).
Benefiel M (2005) The second half of the journey: Spiritual leadership for organizational transformation. *Leadersh. Q.* 16(5):723–747.
Berger P, Luckmann T (1991) *The Social Construction of Reality: A Treatise in Sociology of Knowledge* (London).
Bezemer, P.-J., Langmann, S., & Vlaar, P. W. L. (2022). Death or Resurrection? Christian Church Leader Responses to External Change. *Journal of Management, Spirituality & Religion*, 19(1), 1–20. https://doi.org/10.51327/wblt3098
Bolisani E, Bratianu C (2018) *Emergent Knowledge Strategies* Bolisani E, Handzic M, eds. (Springer International Publishing, Cham).
Biberman, J. (2009). What makes an organization spiritual? Applied spirituality in organizational structure, design, processes, and practices. The Workplace and Spirituality: New Perspectives on Research and Practice. Woodstock: Skylight Paths Publishing, 111–118.
Bratianu, C. (Ed.). (2015). *Organizational knowledge dynamics: Managing knowledge creation, acquisition, sharing, and transformation: Managing knowledge creation, acquisition, sharing, and transformation*. IGI Global.
Casey, C. (2004). Bureaucracy re-enchanted? Spirit, experts and authority in organizations. *Organization, 11*(1), 59–79.
Bratianu C (2015) Spiritual Knowledge. *Organ. Knowl. Dyn. Manag. Knowl. Creat. Acquis. Sharing, Transform.* (IGI Global, Hershey), 72–102.
Chan-Serafin S, Brief AP, George JM (2013) How Does Religion Matter and Why? Religion and the Organizational Sciences. *Organ. Sci.* 24(5):1585–1600.
Chen CY, Yang CF (2012) The Impact of Spiritual Leadership on Organizational Citizenship Behavior: A Multi-Sample Analysis. *J. Bus. Ethics* 105(1):107–114.
Corbin J, Strauss A (2008) *Basics of Qualitative Research: Techniques and procedures for developing grounded theory* 3rd ed. (SAGE Publications Inc., Los Angeles, CA).
Couper MP, Hansen SE (2001) Computer-Assisted Interviewing. Grubrium JF, Holstein JA, eds. *Handb. Interview Res. Context Method.* (Sage Publications Inc, Thousand Oaks), 557–601.
Crossman J (2016) Alignment and Misalignment in Personal and Organizational Spiritual Identities. *Identity* 16(3):154–168.
Daniel, J. L., Chatelain-Jardon, R., Mayfield, J., & Mayfield, M. (2022). The Influence of Leader Motivating Language on Workplace Spirituality. *Journal of Management, Spirituality & Religion*, 19(2), 215–233. https://doi.org/10.51327/uqmh2278
Detert JR, Treviño LK (2010) Speaking Up to Higher-Ups: How Supervisors and Skip-Level Leaders Influence Employee Voice. *Organ. Sci.* 21(1):249–270.
Driver M (2005) From empty speech to full speech? Reconceptualizing spirituality in organizations based on a psychoanalytically-grounded understanding of the self. *Hum. Relations* 58(9):1091–1110.
Edmondson AC, Mcmanus SE (2007) Methodological fit in management field research. *Acad. Manag. Rev.* 32(4):1246–1264.

Elkins DN, Hedstrom LJ, Hughes LL, Leaf JA, Saunders C (1988) Toward a Humanistic-Phenomenological Spirituality. *J. Humanist. Psychol.* 28(4):5–18.
Erden Z, von Krogh G, Nonaka I (2008) The quality of group tacit knowledge. *J. Strateg. Inf. Syst.* 17(1):4–18.
Ezzy D (2002) *Qualitative Analysis: Practice and Innovation* 1°. Group T& F, ed. (Routledge, London).
Fairhurst GT, Grant D (2010) The Social Construction of Leadership: A Sailing Guide. *Manag. Commun. Q.* 24(2):171–210.
Fassinger R, Morrow SL (2013) Toward best practices in quantitative, qualitative, and mixed-method research: A social justice perspective. *J. Soc. Action Couns. Psychol.* 5(2):69–83.
Flick U (2005) *Métodos Qualitativos na Investigação Científica* 1st ed. Monitor – Projectos e Edições L, ed. (Lisboa).
Friedman VJ, Lipshitz R, Popper M (2005) The mystification of organizational learning. *J. Manag. Inq.* 14(1):19–30.
Fry L, Egel E (2021) Global Leadership for Sustainability. *Sustainability* 13(11):6360.
Fry LW (2003) Toward a theory of spiritual leadership. *Leadersh. Q.* 14(6):693–727.
Fry LW, Cohen MP (2009) Spiritual Leadership as a Paradigm for Organizational Transformation and Recovery from Extended Work Hours Cultures. *J. Bus. Ethics* 84(S2):265–278.
Fry LW, Vitucci S, Cedillo M (2005) Spiritual leadership and army transformation: Theory, measurement, and establishing a baseline. *Leadersh. Q.* 16(5):835–862.
Geh EZ (2014) Organizational spiritual leadership of worlds "made" and "found": An experiential learning model for "feel." *Leadersh. Organ. Dev. J.* 35(2):137–151.
Goede M (2011) The wise society: Beyond the knowledge economy. *Foresight* 13(1):36–45.
Gorbatai A, Dioun C, Lashley K (2021) Making Space for Emotions: Empathy, Contagion, and Legitimacy's Double-Edged Sword. *Organ. Sci.* 32(1):42–63.
Gotsis G, Kortezi Z (2008) Philosophical Foundations of Workplace Spirituality: A Critical Approach. *J. Bus. Ethics* 78(4):575–600.
Günther H (2006) Pesquisa qualitativa versus pesquisa quantitativa: esta é a questão? *Psicol. Teor. e Pesqui.* 22(2):201–209.
Harris SG (1994) Organizational Culture and Individual Sensemaking: A Schema-Based Perspective. *Organ. Sci.* 5(3):309–321.
Hart DW, Brady FN (2005) Spirituality and Archetype in Organizational Life. *Bus. Ethics Q.* 15(3):409–428.
Hesse-Biber S (2022) Mixed Methods Research Designs in Qualitatively Driven Research. Flick U, ed. *SAGE Handb. Qual. Res. Des.* (SAGE Publications ltd, Los Angeles), 618–635.
Hicks DA (2002) Spiritual and religious diversity in the workplace. Implications for leadership. *Leadersh. Q.* 13(4):379–396.
Houtman D, Aupers S (2007) The Spiritual Turn and the Decline of Tradition: The Spread of Post-Christian Spirituality. *J. Sci. Study Relig.* 46(3):305–320.
Hunt C (1998) An Adventure: from reflective practice to spirituality. *Teach. High. Educ.* 3(3):325–337.
Huxley G (1965) Aldous Huxley. *J. Humanist. Psychol.* 5(2):117–121.
Jenks CJ (2018) Recording and Transcribing Social Interaction. Flick U, ed. *SAGE Handb. Qual. Data Collect.* (SAGE Publications Ltd, London), 118–130.
Johnson JM (2001) In-Depth Interviewing. Gubrium JF, Holstein JA, eds. *Handb. Interview Res. Context Method.* (Sage Publications Inc., Thousand Oaks), 103–119.
Karakas F (2010a) Exploring Value Compasses of Leaders in Organizations: Introducing Nine Spiritual Anchors. *J. Bus. Ethics* 93(S1):73–92.
Karakas F (2010b) Spirituality and Performance in Organizations: A Literature Review. *J. Bus. Ethics* 94(1):89–106.
Karakas F, Sarigollu E (2019) Spirals of Spirituality: A Qualitative Study Exploring Dynamic Patterns of Spirituality in Turkish Organizations. *J. Bus. Ethics* 156(3):799–821.

Khan, I. U., Amin, R. U., & Saif, N. (2022). Individualized consideration and idealized influence of transformational leadership: Mediating role of inspirational motivation and intellectual stimulation. *International Journal of Leadership in Education*, 1–11. Kotler P, Keller KL (2016) *Marketing Management* 15th ed. (Pearson Education, Essex).
Krishnakumar S, Neck CP (2002) The "what", "why" and "how" of spirituality in the workplace. *J. Manag. Psychol.* 17(3):153–164.
Kumar, V., & Modi, S. (2022). Leading in New VUCA Environment: Role of Positive Leadership Through Spiritual and Ethical Values. In *Leadership after COVID-19* (pp. 561–573). Springer, Cham.
Lynn ML, Naughton MJ, VanderVeen S (2011) Connecting religion and work: Patterns and influences of work-faith integration. *Hum. Relations* 64(5):675–701.
Macnaghten P, Myers G (2007) *Qualitative Research Practice* Paperback. Seale C, Gobo G, Gubrium JF, Silverman D, eds. (SAGE, London).
Mir, U. R., Hassan, S. S., Egel, E., & Murad, H. S. (2019). An integrated framework for organizational performance enhancement through spirituality. *Journal of the Research Society of Pakistan*, *56*(2), 233.
Neal JA, Bergmann Lichtenstein BM, Banner D (1999) Spiritual perspectives on individual, organizational and societal transformation. *J. Organ. Chang. Manag.* 12(3):175–186.
Nonaka I, Konno N (1998) The Concept of "Ba": Building a Foundation for Knowledge Creation. *Calif. Manage. Rev.* 40(3):40–54.
Nonaka I, Takeuchi H (2019) *The Wise Company: How Companies Create Continuous Innovation* (Oxford University Press, New York).
Nonaka I, Takeuchi H (2021) Humanizing strategy. *Long Range Plann.* 54(4):1–11.
Nonaka I, Toyama R, Konno N (2000) SECI, Ba and Leadership: a Unified Model of Dynamic Knowledge Creation. *Long Range Plann.* 33(1):5–34.
O'Kane P, Smith A, Lerman MP (2019) Building Transparency and Trustworthiness in Inductive Research Through Computer-Aided Qualitative Data Analysis Software. *Organ. Res. Methods*:109442811986501.
Pawar, B. S. (2009). Individual spirituality, workplace spirituality and work attitudes: An empirical test of direct and interaction effects. *Leadership & Organization Development Journal.*
Pawar BS (2017) The relationship of individual spirituality and organizational spirituality with meaning and community at work. *Leadersh. Organ. Dev. J.* 38(7):986–1003.
Phipps, K. A. (2023). Leading Spiritually Diverse Organizations: A Graduate Course to Prepare Leaders. *Journal of Management, Spirituality & Religion*. https://doi.org/10.51327/jpws4207
Plato (1961) *Laws (translation by R G Bury)* LITTD TEPC, ed. (Havard University Press, Cambridge).
Poole E (2009) Organisational spirituality – A literature review. *J. Bus. Ethics* 84(4):577–588.
Porter ME, Kramer MR (2011) Creating Shared Value: How to reinvent capitalism-and unleash a wave of innovation and growth. *Harv. Bus. Rev.* 89(January-February):63–77.
Quatro SA (2004) New Age or Age Old: Classical Management Theory and Traditional Organized Religion as Underpinnings of the Contemporary Organizational Spirituality Movement. *Hum. Resour. Dev. Rev.* 3(3):228–249.
Rahman, M. S., Osmangani, A. M., Daud, N. M., Chowdhury, A. H., & Hassan, H. (2015). Trust and workplace spirituality on knowledge sharing behaviour: Perspective from non-academic staff of higher learning institutions. *The learning organization*.
Rego A, Pina e Cunha M (2008) Workplace spirituality and organizational commitment: an empirical study. *J. Organ. Chang. Manag.* 21(1):53–75.
Resch K, Enzenhofer E (2018) Collecting Data in Other Languages – Strategies for Cross-Language Research in Multilingual Societies. Flick U, ed. *SAGE Handb. Qual. Data Collect.* (SAGE Publications Ltd, London), 131–147.
Rocha RG, D'Angelo MJ (2021) Samarco's scandal: a perspective of organizational spirituality and corporate social responsibility. *Int. J. Organ. Anal.* ahead-of-p(ahead-of-print).

Rocha RG, Fry LW Mapping the research on spirituality and culture: A bibliometric analysis. *J. Manag. Spiritual. Relig.*
Rocha RG, Pinheiro PG (2021a) Organizational spirituality and knowledge management supporting organizational practical wisdom. *Spiritual. Stud.* 7(1):68–83.
Rocha RG, Pinheiro PG (2021b) Phronetic workplace: A step forward into a practically wise company. *Open Insights* 12(26):130–166.
Rocha RG, Pinheiro PG (2021c) Organizational Spirituality: Concept and Perspectives. *J. Bus. Ethics* 171(2):241–252.
Rowley J (2006) Where is the wisdom that we have lost in knowledge? *J. Doc.* 62(2):251–270.
Salajegheh S, Abdoli H, Oskouei SKM (2016) Investigation of the relationship between workplace spirituality and organizational commitment (Case study: The employees of National Iranian oil distribution company). *Res. J. Appl. Sci.* 11(4):110–115.
Sass, J. S. (2000). Characterizing organizational spirituality: An organizational communication culture approach. *Communication Studies*, *51*(3), 195–217.
Schudt K (2000) Taming the Corporate Monster: An Aristotelian Approach to Corporate Virtue. *Bus. Ethics Q.* 10(3):711–723.
Sharma, N., Lal, M., & Deshwal, P. (2020). Being spiritually green: Investigating the impact of spiritually motivated environmentalism on green purchasing intentions. *International Journal of Service Science, Management, Engineering, and Technology (IJSSMET)*, *11*(4), 101–121.
Shuy RW (2001) In-Person versus Telephone Interviewing. Gubrim JF, Holstein JA, eds. *Handb. Interview Res. Context Method*. (Sage Publications Inc., Thousand Oaks), 537–555.
Sorakraikitikul, M., & Siengthai, S. (2014). Organizational learning culture and workplace spirituality: Is knowledge-sharing behaviour a missing link? *The Learning Organization.*
Strack, G., Fottler, M. D., Wheatley, M. J., & Sodomka, P. (2002). Spirituality and effective leadership in healthcare: Is there a connection?/commentaries/replies. *Frontiers of health services management*, *18*(4), 3.
Thorén, K., & Vendel, M. (2018). Backcasting as a strategic management tool for meeting VUCA challenges. *Journal of Strategy and Management.*
Tischler L (1999) The growing interest in spirituality in business. *J. Organ. Chang. Manag.* 12(4):273–280.
Tourish D, Pinnington A (2002) Transformational Leadership, Corporate Cultism and the Spirituality Paradigm: An Unholy Trinity in the Workplace? *Hum. Relations* 55(2):147–172.
Tourish D, Tourish N (2010) Spirituality at work, and its implications for leadership and followership: A post-structuralist perspective. *Leadership* 6(2):207–224.
Ul-Haq S (2020) Spiritual development and meaningful work: a Habermasian critique. *Hum. Resour. Dev. Int.* 23(2):125–145.
Wagner-Marsh F, Conley J (1999) The fourth wave: the spiritually-based firm. *J. Organ. Chang. Manag.* 12(4):292–302.
Warren CAB (2001) Qualitative Interviewing. Gubrium JF, Holstein JA, eds. *Handb. Interview Res. Context Method*. (Sage Publications Inc., Thousand Oaks), 83–101.
Widodo, S., & Suryosukmono, G. (2021). Spiritual leadership, workplace spirituality and their effects on meaningful work: Self-transcendence as mediator role. *Management Science Letters*, *11*(7), 2115–2126.
Wrzesniewski A, Dutton JE, Debebe G (2003) Interpersonal sensemaking and the meaning of work. *Res. Organ. Behav.* 25(03):93–135.
Yang M, Fry LW (2018) The role of spiritual leadership in reducing healthcare worker burnout. *J. Manag. Spiritual. Relig.* 15(4):305–324.

Elaine C. Long

Chapter 7 Spiritual Knowledge Management Through Faith at Work: People, Places, Practices, and Tools

Abstract: Employee flourishing involves rational, emotional, and spiritual knowledge in knowledge management. The spiritual dimension can seem like an indistinct philosophical abstraction; however, Long's (2022) empirical study of Faith at Work: People, Places, Practices, and Tools (FAW: PPPT) transects the knowledge management domain with the management, spirituality, and religion domain bringing real-world examples to life. Relevant to practitioners and interesting for the knowledge management academic community, these practical faith-at-work explanations enact spiritual knowledge (SK) and spiritual intelligence (SQ) *in motion*. Through the lens of employees and managers – the people, their places or organizational environments, their spiritual practices, and tools illustrate specific ways that individual SQ unleashes individual SK at work, which can build organizational SK. From a deeper understanding of spiritual knowledge management within the FAW context comes operationalized definitions of SQ and SK and their development processes, proposing a human flourishing (HF) organizational model that revises traditional human resources development for intrinsic value creation.

Keywords: Knowledge Management, Spiritual Knowledge, Spiritual Intelligence, Faith-At-Work, Human Flourishing, Workplace Spirituality

Purpose and Premise

Knowledge management literature enumerates how modern organizations access, control, modify and keep knowledge to improve performance, explain the dynamic nature of implicit and explicit knowledge creation, and how they use logical, empirical, and rational knowledge toward work's objective and material aspects. However, knowledge management is a triple helix involving spiritual, emotional, and rational elements.

Acknowledgements: We acknowledge that this chapter draws from doctoral dissertation research, which is original research, and we intentionally maintain the integrity of that work by not changing the wording.

I thank Dr. G. W. Hay and D. Moore for their insightful and valuable comments on earlier versions of this chapter.

Elaine C. Long, The Chicago School of Professional Psychology, e-mail: elong1@thechicagoschool.edu

https://doi.org/10.1515/9783111010410-008

Omitting or minimizing the spiritual orientation causes us to believe that only the external parts of work are essential and lack depth and meaning for individuals and organizations (Bratianu, 2015; Bolisani & Bratianu, 2018; Farnese et al., 2019; Gull & Doh, 2004). Individuals demand that the self – rational, emotional, and spiritual – be acknowledged and look to satisfy higher-level needs at work today. At the same time, workplace spirituality in organizational and management literature often neglects or is inconsistent with how organizations can identify, support, and manage a spiritual orientation (Ashforth & Pratt, 2003; Dehler & Welsh, 2015; Fry et al., 2010; Gull & Doh, 2004; Lips-Wiersma & Mills, 2014; Miller & Ewest, 2015; Mitroff & Denton, 1999a, 1999b; Ouimet, 2005; Ouimet & Semen, 2013) including spiritual knowledge and intelligence. Mitroff and Denton (1999b) recognized that "we have gone too far in separating the key elements. . . . No organization can survive for long without spirituality and soul. We must examine ways of managing spirituality without separating it from the other elements of management" again, including spiritual knowledge (SK) and spiritual intelligence (SQ) management (see *Terms* for definitions).

Concurring that modern organizations could improve archaic management approaches to embrace higher-level needs with practical applications, an initial step would be to gain a deeper understanding of the higher-level needs in the spiritual domain through some of Long's (2022) Faith at Work: People, Places, Practices, and Tools (FAW: PPPT) empirical and practical workplace spirituality research findings. This chapter uses the real-life, empirical study of faith-at-work (FAW) experience elements to explain SK and SQ *in motion* as they are lived and enacted and clear examples of how these are implemented.

In addition, because "usefulness is the key metric for new knowledge in the organizational context" (Bolisani & Bratianu, 2018. p 4), a human flourishing (HF) model that reaches beyond a traditional human resource department is proposed and emanates from the spiritual knowledge, spiritual intelligence, and faith-at-work relationships in the modern organization context. "If spirituality infusions in modern organizations are to be successful, they must be introduced effectively, and they must be well managed" (Hoover, 2007, p. 324) and so this chapter provides details for effective spiritual knowledge management (SKM) with a non-materialistic, intrinsically-valuable, human flourishing perspective. However, they note that the proposed, implementable strategy, structure, policies, roles, and processes are part of a larger, complex shared frame of reference. It provides an essential contribution to the management literature for scholars and practitioners, enlightening organizations to move beyond their current grasp of the SKM domain and conjuring similar successful strategies to achieve intrinsic value creation and perhaps competitive advantages (Bolisani & Bratianu, 2018).

The chapter's fundamental premise is that some of Long's (2022) empirical research findings, including 24 experience elements and 14 frameworks (see *Background* for study details), are akin to SK and SQ *in motion* in the workplace. This chapter will provide details, from the knowledge management perspective, that FAW consists of four dimensions (people, places, practices, and tools) where tools and practices are more apparent and less noticeable are the nuances of the places and the people, individually and collectively, contributing to spiritual knowledge management. These real-life shifts in employees' SQ and organizational SK and the upside potential of a FAW human flourishing (HF) model as a new mental model for spiritual knowledge management addresses the research gap "to reveal how to design the working place such that to transform a physical environment into a full spiritual one, in which people can find meaning and purpose for their work and existence" (Bratianu, 2015, p. 21).

The three sections of this chapter build upon one another to support the purpose of understanding more deeply and apply the relationships between SK, SQ, and FAW to enhance organizational value creation. The three sections advance the premise that faith-at-work is like SQ and SK *in motion* at work, and people use various spiritual tools, practices, and places such that SK can trigger SQ responses, and SQ development can attain SK. A brief description of each section follows.

Section 1 presents employees' and managers' SQ *in motion*, beginning with one of several basic FAW practices called spiritual discernment, a sub-element noted as faithful emotional intelligence, and one of the many wholistic spiritual exercises noted as a respectful pluralism dialogue (RPD) technique or tool derived from Long's (2022) FAW: PPPT research. This section also demonstrates the dynamic nature of how people develop spiritually (intelligence) at work.

Section 2 presents employees' and managers' SK *in motion* in the faith-at-work dimension of the workplace environment. FAW: PPPT study participants use their SQ to shift their own and the organizations' SK by reducing FAW barriers or increasing FAW potential within their physical locations. These demonstrations translate to 14 actual FAW frameworks conceived by the participants, which become conceptual and practical applications for scholar-practitioners and employers.

Section 3 looks at the upside potential of a human flourishing organizational model, which promotes people using their SQ to attain SK and creating, on a standard level, an organizational change from one level of SK to another. The model aligns with Barrett's (2015) applied workplace spirituality model of developing personal and organizational consciousness – from the ego to the soul's hierarchical needs for workplace spirituality. The proposed human flourishing model creates an even better workplace and a "dynamic context in which people express themselves and strive for their fulfillment" (Bratianu, 2015, p. 14), embracing spirituality. "Since managers are interested in the practical implications of the deployment and exploitation of knowledge, they need conceptual tools to handle the notion of knowledge" (Bolisani & Bratianu, 2018, p. vi), which this chapter intends to provide.

In summary, the entire chapter supports the argument that FAW as SQ and SK *in motion* in the knowledge management domain generates valuable solutions for companies so that spiritual knowledge management is an organizational value creator in "the knowledge-based nature of today's economy and of organizations such that knowledge workers and knowledge processes are at the basis of organizations' competitiveness, and knowledge management is a necessary dimension connecting operations and strategy in order to translate knowledge into organizational performance, value outputs, and impacts" (Bolisani & Bratianu, 2018, p. vi). An employee's flourishing intrinsic value also rests on integrating rational, emotional, and spiritual knowledge. This integration into a working HF model could alter current human resources development processes as they intentionally cultivate the enactment of SQ while igniting the respectful integration of faith at work.

Terms and Background

Interpretations of concepts may vary. Thus, clarity of terms and concepts from key sources is essential to aligning faith-at-work with knowledge management and the proposed practical applications. Definitions of terms like "spirituality" or "religion" depend on the context and sources and require explanation (Koenig, 2011), and the starting axioms must be clear to enhance the scholarship and reduce potential confusion (Dent, 2019). The following clarification of terms and background from key sources reflect the viewpoints of this chapter.

First, this chapter relies on critical components of Bolisani and Bratianu's (2018) knowledge management scholarship, such as knowledge is the result of knowing and a specific human process "in organizations, it [knowledge] often becomes embedded not only in document or repositories but also in organizational routines, processes, practices, and norms" (p. 9). Additionally, "usefulness is the key metric for new knowledge in the organizational context" (p. 4), and "knowledge is created by the human brain, and then it is amplified and integrated into organizational knowledge by social interaction" (p. 19). The term "spiritual knowledge" integrates values and beliefs about life" (Bolisani & Bratianu, 2018, p. 18) and "reflects our understanding about the meaning of our existence" (p. 19). Spiritual knowledge is the third component, in addition to rational and emotional knowledge, of the triple helix of knowledge, an intangible asset encompassing possible answers to more profound questions about what is of value in this life, aspirations, motivations, and ethical principles, including one's working life. SK has a spectrum of manifestations with a scale of 16 motivations, integrating emotional knowledge with spiritual knowledge, and is also the foundation for the spiritual capital of any organization (Bratianu, 2015). The motivation scales for SK are paradigms of thinking and decision-making and resemble personal hierarchical needs, including spirituality, developing from the ego to the soul, as well as the stages of organizational consciousness growth from survival to unity where, with awareness, one can shift on the scales (Barrett, 2015).

Secondly, several sources explain the meaning of spiritual intelligence (SQ) in this chapter. Intelligence is "a bio-psychological potential. . . evolved diverse information-processing capacities. . .to solve problems or to fashion products" (Garner, 2006, p. 29, as cited in Bolisani & Bratianu, 2018, p. 16) integrates with "the spiritual in human beings makes us ask *why* we are doing what we are doing" (Bratianu, 2015, p. 4) and how to do it better coming from a non-physical, non-material perspective. Adding more depth, Zohar and Marshall's (2000) definition of SQ is "the intelligence with which we address and solve problems of meaning and value" (p. 3) because humans "have a longing to see our lives in some larger, meaning-given context" (p. 4), along with the understanding that SQ "plugs us into meaning and value. . . . causes us to strive, gives us a sense of purpose, a sense of context" (p. 292). Finally, "SQ is a framework for identifying and organizing skills and abilities needed for adaptive use of spirituality" (Emmons, 1999, p. 163, as cited in Bratianu, 2015, p. 8), and "SQ is the ability to be peaceful, wise, and compassionate in the face of chaos" (Wigglesworth, 2013, p. 442).

Furthermore, for individuals and organizations, SQ is expandable and a powerful transformation force (Zohar & Marshall, 2000). SQ can expand from the individual to an organizational level to conceive organizational spirituality (Bratianu, 2015). "SQ is a dynamic force [that can dissolve old motives and create new ones] that processes the spiritual knowledge we create" (Bratianu, 2015, p. 8). SQ has 21 measurable and changeable competencies or behaviors to meet SQ goals (Wigglesworth, 2013). Ultimately, we develop and use SQ to create and process spiritual knowledge efficiently, building organizational consciousness, or spiritual capital, to create societal value.

Thirdly, the term "faith-at-work (FAW)," rather than spirituality or religion, in this chapter is based on "faith," including all forms of belief and filters through which one constructs meaning and purpose in the world (Miller, 2007, p. 18) and the entwinement of faith and spirituality, as Neal (2017) said, such that a Faith relationship is trust in and loyalty to centers of value that are of ultimate concern to a human being and to the images of power with which an individual aligns himself or herself and upon which he or she acts to survive in an uncertain world. Spirituality is a faith relationship with the Transcendent where the Transcendent is beyond and independent of the material universe. (Long, 2022, p. 23–24)

Noting there are many ways to describe spirituality, this chapter recognizes that, "Spirituality is the ongoing transformation of a human being in an engaged and responsible relationship with oneself, the other, the world, and God" (Dienberg &Warode, 2018, p. 815). Interestingly, Giacalone and Jurkiewicz (2003; 2015) provide a representative sampling of 14 definitions of spirituality and ten definitions of the dimension of spirituality from workplace spirituality literature between 1975 and 2000. Fifty percent of these 14 definitions include transcendence, and another 50 percent include God, divine, higher power, ultimate, or beyond oneself. (Long, 2022, p. 25)

The axiom regarding religion stems from The American Heritage Dictionary of the English Language and "nothing in the definition of religion necessitates membership in an organized religion. One's religion, then, is one's 'set of beliefs concerning the cause, nature, and purpose of the universe'" (Dent, 2019, p. 76). As some social science research supports multi and interdimensional connections of spirituality and religion (Ewest & Miller, 2019), this chapter maintains that,

> In this study, faith at work (FAW) combines workplace religion, spirituality, and the spirit at and of work (Lynn et al., 2009, 2013; Miller & Ewest, 2013b) . . . . Bell and Taylor's (2001) view that spirituality at work is not bounded by formal religious practice, but because the spirit is a sacred power, it is drawn *from* religions. . . and that, "All work had a potential spiritual meaning" (p. A–4) may contribute to the meaning of FAW (Long, 2022, p. 47–48).

Thus, faith accommodates formal and defined expressions of belief as found in religious constructs, plus informal and less-defined expressions of belief as found in spirituality (Miller & Ewest, 2015). Additionally, the author concurs that "while the workplace spirituality literature has been important to bringing one's whole self to work, it needs to take more seriously that religious belief is part of the whole for many individuals" (Lynn et al., 2009) and "addresses the debate whether workplace spirituality scholarship should include religion or not (Peterson & Seligman, 2004), ... supporting researchers Syed et al.'s (2018) focus on integrating faith and making sense of religious beliefs or practices in the workplace" (Long, 2022, p. 173). The key takeaway for this chapter is about living one's experience of faith at or in the workplace. [See Long's (2022) research pages 42–49 for further detail on the Unity of Spirituality, Religion, and Faith in the WPS Construct and the Specialties of Spirit (SAW) and Faith at Work (FAW).]

Lastly, the term "human flourishing" draws upon the definition from a research brief by The International Science and Evidence-Based Education Assessment and is,

> Both the optimal continuing development of human beings' potentials and living well as a human being, which means being engaged in relationships and activities that are meaningful, i.e., aligned with both their own values and humanistic values, in a way that is satisfying to them. Flourishing is conditional on the contribution of individuals and requires an enabling environment. (De Ruyter et al., 2020, p. 2)

A brief background on Long's (2022) Faith at Work: People, Places, Practices, and Tools (FAW: PPPT) empirical research follows to set the stage for how the spiritual knowledge management domain complements and expands with integrating some of the findings. This phenomenological study provides a theoretical and practical understanding of workplace spirituality (WPS) as faith-at-work (FAW) with the aim of a deeper awareness of the experience in the lives of employees and managers considering various faith-at-work organizational frameworks (Miller & Ewest, 2015) and individual practices and tools. The research questions are: (1) How do people experience work in relation to their spiritual and faith beliefs, and (2) How are the respondents' environment, practices, tools, and characteristics part of their experience? The coding, analysis, and findings resulted in a series of six mega-experience elements or themes of (1) tri-identity, (2) spiritual discernment, (3) wholistic spiritual exercises, (4) dynamic processes, (5) creating the right FAW environment, and (6) Faith in the Work (FitW) and W(holy)-ness, these were further clarified into 24 sub and micro-experience elements or categories. Summaries of the findings by each question gave context to the themes where some of the FAW experience elements and sub or micro-elements are common to all the respondents, some represent similarities among a few, and others are unique to one yet have a powerful impact on a deeper understanding of the spiritual phenomenon.

In addition to the semi-structured interviews, the manager and employee participants completed a 5-day journal to enhance research triangulation and richness. They took photographs of their FAW tools or practices in their workspaces. These prompted and captured real-time perspectives of their lived spiritual phenomenon. The enhanced methodology also incorporated the management spirituality religion scholar's inner work of deep reflection and reflexivity via a researcher's journal and analytical memos throughout the study for transparency (Delbecq, 2009). The interpretation and analysis processes of the participants' experiences acknowledged the researcher's epoch as influenced by familial and professional exposure to multiple faiths and worldviews. In this study, the researcher's lens did not dissolve into the background, nor was a claim made for a bias-free interpretation of the data. The researcher is both a collector and teller of these stories and is part of the story itself (Alvesson & Gabriel, 2013).

Three phases of coding and analysis based on Moustakas' (1994) structures assembled the more significant phenomenological meanings and made sense of the parts in a hermeneutical approach. A brief overview of the process is that the first phase was pre-coding, the second phase was first-cycle open coding and member-checking, and the third phase was second-cycle coding, bottom-up theme analysis, and learning about the author to bracket but not reduce the researcher's heuristic, perspectives, judgments, and everyday understanding. During the third phase, second-cycle coding themes emerged from bottom-up coding, resulting in 20 preliminary analyses Excel tables. Pseudonyms protected the confidentiality of the eleven coded participants.

The analysis of 3450 codes from multiple sources was not based solely on description codes (14%) but delved deeper into personal values (32%), processes (23%), and felt emotions (13%). The InVivo (11%) and Themeing-the-data (7%) codes were invaluable for the member-checking narrative summaries (Phipps & Matkin, 2014) – eight code types captured deeply personal hermeneutical understandings and theoretical and practical organizational design and development considerations. The intense level of interrogation used throughout the coding and analysis processes ensured research rigor, fidelity, and trustworthiness.

Manager and employee beliefs, values, and practices from both theistic and humanistic spheres revealed the 24 faith-at-work experience elements. They identified 14 potential organizational environmental frameworks and new workplace possibilities for spiritual knowledge management. Understanding the concrete ways managers and employees fused workspace environmental dimensions, reduced barriers, or expanded the faith-at-work potential to address dualism when employees who have religious world views and spiritual orientations must compartmentalize their life at work and leave a portion of themselves behind (Miller & Ewest, 2015), leads to a significant contribution to the spiritual knowledge management domain as explained in the following sections.

Section 1: Faith at Work (FAW) as Spiritual Intelligence (SQ) *in Motion*

Organizational scholar-practitioners can take seriously the spiritual dimension of humanity as a fundamental nature of reality at work by seeing SQ *in motion* using the Long (2022) study because "studying the complex wholeness of society requires attention to the sociology of the supernatural. . .studied through observation and analysis of indicators and variables presumed to reflect spirituality" (Moberg, 2002, pp. 135–136). Practitioners and scholars know spiritual knowledge is essential in decision-making because it contains values and ethical principles, and values influence rational arguments (Bolisani & Bratianu, 2018). Also, creating this knowledge requires spiritual intelligence or a framework that identifies and organizes skills and abilities needed for adaptation, such as solving problems and attaining goals (Ahmed et al., 2016), and involves heightened states of consciousness that infuse a sense of sacred in every day relationships and activities transcending the physical (Bratianu, 2015, p. 8).

However, what does this look like? Employees and managers in the FAW: PPPT study provided examples of spiritual intelligence, or SQ, *in motion*, accessing spiritual knowledge to make successful decisions. Among the six mega-experience elements in the study, the second was spiritual discernment, a matter of faith put into practice, and contains a sub-element called "faithful emotional intelligence". In the study, spiritual discernment is like "not only distinguishing the right from the wrong; it means distinguishing the primary from the secondary, the essential from the indifferent, and the permanent from the transient. It means distinguishing between the good and the better, and even between the better and the best" (Ferguson, 2020).

The managers and employees in the study recognized a tri-identity of mind, body, and spirit at work, as well, that is involved with the third mega experience element of wholistic (all-inclusive) spiritual exercises intending to develop relationships with self, God, and others and be free from anything that disrupts their ability to experience faith-at-work. Among the many holistic spiritual exercises was a sub-element referred to as a "respectful pluralism dialogue" and an example of SQ *in motion.*

The fourth mega-experience element was the dynamic nature of the faith-at-work processes, which appears similar to the continuous process of SQ accessing spiritual knowledge to deal with ever-changing problems. Explanations of each of these follows.

FAW Practice: Spiritual Discernments' Faithful Emotional Intelligence

Some faith-at-work experience elements are lived and enacted examples of spiritual intelligence, and each FAW: PPPT employee or manager regularly implemented an average of eight faith-at-work practices – thoughts, behaviors, and feelings. [See Long (2022) Appendix L: *FAW Practices (Thoughts, Behaviors, Feelings) by Respondent Quotes* for details]. Among these practices were mega-element 2.0 spiritual discernment and sub-element 2.5 faithful emotional intelligence, types of SQ *in motion*. To explain, first note that SQ and emotional intelligence (EQ) are related; SQ is a step up from EQ, and successful spiritual growth may require some basics of EQ (Wigglesworth, 2011; 2013). Emotional intelligence consists of awareness of one's and others' emotions and successful management techniques.

Some employees and managers exhibited faithful emotional intelligence when they applied spiritual discernment to their own and others' emotional awareness and management, helping them make decisions they considered proper behavior. Specific incidents from FAW: PPPT Long (2022) include when Joyce, a finance employee, was trying to be tolerant and patient at work with others; she explained how she dealt with them by saying, "My faith is emotional control, and my faith is behavioral control. I feel like I had an excellent attitude of life because of, again, my Creator, and I want that" (p. 126). Another example was Kia, a consultant and manager, who stated, "When things are callous at work, praying is just focusing on emotional control. It is just a way to try to stay detached and, um, calm to aspire to be a better person in all things" (p. 126).

Sometimes, the SQ *in motion*, or faithful emotional management of oneself, deliberately helps others and is an intentional SQ goal. For example, Joyce explained, "I know that if I have this attitude, hopefully, it rubs off on people, and they are in a better place. They are happier. . .I want to ensure that people are comfortable, happy. . . my faith is caring for and helping others" (p. 126). Similarly, Eve concurs that SQ *in motion* or faithful emotional intelligence is a way to help others, as she said:

> I value others' emotional comfort; I practice emotional awareness and management and use Cognitive Behavioral Therapy techniques with my faith. The steps are: be aware, acknowledge, envision, and then respond. . .again, how you treat others shows the most of what you believe. So, I process events and choose not to react negatively; I reflect on negative emotions later (p. 126).

In the Long (2022) study, Jacob, a military employee, demonstrated SQ *in motion* with deliberate discernment and faithful emotional intelligence practices, stating: "I need to be able to pull myself out of [anxiety]. . . faith is also mental health support. . . . I follow my beliefs during challenges. . .behaving consistently with my beliefs is peaceful" (p. 127). Eve adds, "Faith is useful at work when you need balance or emotional strength, especially in stressful situations" (p. 127). In these FAW examples, their SQ *in motion* accesses spiritual knowledge as a powerful transformational force that extends the realities of daily routines to existential limits and changes old motives and behaviors (Bratianu, 2015).

FAW Tool: Wholistic Spiritual Exercises' Respectful Pluralism Dialogue (RPD)

According to Long (2022), one of the many faith-at-work tools, also considered SQ *in motion,* is the micro-element 3.3.b. of the mega-element 3.0, wholistic spiritual exercises, called a respectful pluralism dialogue (RPD). The finding was that for more than half of the participants, a critical aspect of creating proper (proper is according to their discernment) relationships with God, self, and others for the participants is having a respectful pluralism dialogue at work. Respectful pluralism is when one can still express spiritual, religious, political, cultural, and other commitments with either cooperation or conflicts at play (Hicks, 2002, 2003). These managers and employees often used SQ to access spiritual knowledge to serve others, not themselves. The RPD is like a spiritual intelligence conversation where SQ conversations "offer people a way to get at a deeper motivation" (Wigglesworth, 2013, p. 445). For many, RPD is a specific faith-at-work experience that entails giving and getting mutual respect without necessarily agreeing with various viewpoints, thus applying intelligence for spiritual knowledge. In Long (2022), Theodore, an IT financial manager, explained,

> I practice my faith without expecting others to practice a faith. . .if asked, I tell them facts and do not proselytize. In turn, they proffer their faith experiences as a way to relate. You want the Holy Spirit to work like flowers. You cannot force a flower to open; it has to open at its proper time and season (p. 136).

Another example of this type of SQ *in motion* is Griffin, a semi-retired sole proprietor consultant, who explained that the RPD process is:

> Being a good witness is being obedient to serving all. Serving Christ through sharing the gospel and serving Christ is following the Great Commission. The Great Commission refers to several passages in the Gospel of Matthew, where Jesus Christ urges his apostles to make "disciples of all the nations" and "baptize" them. I know better now how to do this from when I was a new believer. I learned it is not about me driving others; it is honing, in the sense of trying to draw people out and allowing the wooing of the Holy Spirit to be the driver, not your personality (Long, 2022, p. 137).

Also noted by Long (2022) was the motivation of positive reciprocation in spiritual intelligence interactions. For example, Joyce said, "I would like them to be helpful back to me and not be rude and you know shut me down," and "In my life as a Christian, I always want to treat others as I would like them to treat me" (p. 137). Amrit, a management professor, said: "I believe in reciprocation with colleagues, when I am good to them, and in return, they also exchange back to me" (p. 137). Furthermore, Eve, a new manager, expressed her SQ *in motion* in the RPD process, stating, "trying to be able to understand where people are coming from, maybe seeing it from their perspective. But ultimately, just trying to connect with them and handle differences with respect" (p. 137). The respectful, pluralistic attitude and an RPD can also promote SQ freedom, as Theodore said:

> If someone had a question or people asked what I did over the weekend, I mean, church comes up. . .being a Cantor is a big part of my life outside of work. Your attitude promotes freedom with faith at work. . . you respond when asked; you do not initiate the conversation. . .people prefer when they can lead the conversation about faith. Again, you want the Holy Spirit at work (p. 137).

A unique type of SQ conversation or RPD as SQ *in motion*, occurred when Miriam, a Senior VP Wealth Advisor, used the greeting, "Shabbat Shalom" at work, meaning "What is [the state of] your peace?" (which she learned from the Mussar study of character traits and intentional soul-work) to address others' SQ in motion respectfully.

These multiple examples inform scholar-practitioners and enlightened organizations about how employees and managers attain spiritual knowledge to have proper relationships with God, self, and others and to serve others using SQ *in motion* practices and tools. Miriam best summarized it as, "Sitting in front of my computer and taking yet another phone call will not change my life, but taking care of myself [via soul-work] might change someone else's life if I can handle them better" (Long, 2022, p. 138). Respectful pluralism dialogue, or an SQ conversation, is one of many possible faith-at-work tools to access spiritual knowledge. [For further details on all the tools, refer to Table 24 *FAW Tool Types, an Example, and a Reason* and Appendix M *FAW Tools by Type – Quotes, Examples, and Reasons* in Long, 2022].

Dynamic Process and SQ Development

The faith-at-work experiences and SQ *in motion*, such as spiritual discernment and spiritual exercises, may not necessarily occur in a single instance but as part of a continuous process like knowledge management. In Long (2022), the faith-at-work mega-element 4.0 dynamic processes included real-life examples of developing spiritually (including spiritual intelligence) at work, reaping "fruits" from how people treat others, and using theological and moral virtues as well as character strengths. Focusing on how employees and managers develop spiritually, some regarded it as a personal commitment and a responsibility to others. For example, to continuously develop SQ, and thus SK, sole-proprietor, Griffin keeps a daily Day-Timer journal and uses Post-It notes for his weekly prayer lists because he stated, "everyone needs nourishment through the Word and through prayer time and other things. . .what I am referring to is spiritual development," and "it is kind of a command not just to be served, and be the caterpillar," referring to a spiritual lesson not to let yourself conform to the world but to be transformed by seeing the world from God's perspective. His reasoning for this continuous spiritual development was:

> I grew up with my, my dad. . . he is, it was a teacher. My mom's side of the family was all teachers. . .that was kind of in my blood, you know, you teach somebody how to fish, not throw them a fish (p. 139)

Spiritual intelligence development occurs in other ways; for example, Jacob, who is in military ministry and a psych/health technician, said:

> God uses small moments, maybe 20 to 30 minutes. . . of prayer and meditation, and I find I have what I need to endure the responsibilities that come along. . . which ensures I can complete the business and give everything else to my family (p. 139).

Miriam, Senior VP, realized how her spiritual intelligence development can unintentionally affect others at work:

> Well, people watch what you do. . .sometimes, I feel guilty. I prioritize [she leaves the office at 3 PM on Fridays for Shabbat]. Those things are essential to me. . .I did not realize that it inspires others. . . [my assistant] sees that a working mom, uh, is a mom who works [and develops a strong faith] (p. 139).

On the other hand, Amrit is intentional about his SQ development by keeping a faith-at-work tool, a world globe, on his desk because he believes that "the world is a family" and the globe is a constant reminder of developing his faithfulness. The reason, he stated:

> Not just for oneself but to be good to others. Being Indian, we have a collectivist approach to spirituality. . .beliefs are molded by parents, society, or community teaching religious values. Faith is a part of the culture. . . That is the most challenging thing in India to manage. . .people's faith at work. . .but being a professional, you try to break away from some workplace rules (p. 140).

We are developing SQ, whether deliberately or instantaneously for oneself, intentionally or unintentionally, to impact others is a dynamic nature of SQ *in motion*. In summary, this section recognized examples of faith-at-work practices, tools, and the dynamic nature of SQ *in motion*, and the next section moves from developing SQ for individual spiritual knowledge (SK) to the relationship between individual and organizational SK.

Section 2: Employees' Spiritual Knowledge (SK) *in Motion* Shifting Organizational SK

The second central understanding in this chapter is that in addition to dynamic spiritual intelligence as noted by people's faith-at-work practices and tools, the place of work, or the environment, supports and potentially shifts spiritual knowledge (SK) to develop spiritual intelligence. Recall that SK is the third component of the triple helix of knowledge. This intangible asset provides possible answers to life values, aspirations, motivations, and ethical principles even while at work – one naturally shifts and moves along a spectrum of SK manifestations (Bratianu, 2015). In the Long (2022) study, a shared experience to access spiritual intelligence was activating individuals' and the organizations' SK *in motion* through consciously integrating environmental factors and creating the "right" environment for oneself or others' faith at work. "All people in the FAW: PPPT study recognized, to various degrees, their need for and the effort to create the right FAW environment for themselves or others" (Long, 2022, p. 144).

In the study, the employees and managers took photographs of their faith-at-work workplaces and wrote a five-day journal. During the semi-structured interviews, they shared these, divulging their practices, tools, and working environments in visual, written, and verbal detail. Additionally, they were asked to read and reflect on a one-page summary of Miller and Ewest's (2015) four FAW frameworks – Faith-Avoiding, Faith-Safe, Faith-Based, and Faith-Friendly. The descriptions of the four frameworks were by the organizations' levels of religious accommodations, formal policies, and fatal dualism parameters [see Long, 2022, pp. 231–232, for the details]. Participants described their work environment experiences compared with Miller and Ewest's (2015) four frameworks and indicated the most accurate depiction of their workplace. Monty, an interim CFO for a synagogue, pointed out that:

> I have been on every end of the spectrum there. I have been where you can, you know, practice your faith freely, and I have been at the end of the spectrum where once you tell them what your faith is, nobody wants to, and you become the pariah (Long, 2022, p. 144).

The experiences varied by location, resulting in 14 different FAW frameworks, as presented and expanded upon below.

In the study, the fifth faith-at-work mega-element was "Creating the right FAW environment for oneself," and the corresponding first sub-element was "Dualism" due to the employees' and managers' restrictions for compartmentalization of their tri-identity (mind, body, spirit) at work. Employees and managers explained ways personal and organizational cultural consciousness levels were shifted. They addressed dualism by various methods, identified in the study as additional sub-elements, including adapting one's FAW to the workplace, changing the workplace to adapt to one's FAW, reducing FAW barriers or expanding the potential for FAW at the work location, and fusing multi-dimensions into a single FAW framework (Long, 2022). They accessed individual spiritual knowledge and even shifted organizational spiritual knowledge, as demonstrated in the following real-life examples of SK *in motion*.

Dualism

Sometimes deliberate or coincidental dualism requires people to compartmentalize their tri-identity at work. For some people in Long's (2022) FAW: PPPT, their work environment requires a "professional image," separating or diminishing a part of their whole self. For example, all the higher education professors in the study deliberately omitted any faith-at-work artifacts at the work office, and some purposefully were indirect about their spiritual knowledge due to fears of being atypical, discriminated against, or excluded from opportunities or relationships. Eve, a new manager, deliberately lacked *any* personal items in her work environment because of the teasing and sarcasm, such as, "Oh, do not say anything around the Christian girl." She, therefore, decided: "I accept the teasing and sarcasm to avoid problems, and I have to separate some parts of my faith from work. I am younger and female among mostly male older managers, so I also do not want to look for other excuses to lose credibility. . . feels safer and less vulnerable by not sharing my whole self at work" (p. 145).

Not all dualism is from the immediate work environment; as Adeline mentioned, "The country of France is secular, and therefore, we are not to make our faith known" (p. 145). Even as a Spiritualist-Minister-Medium and a professor in higher education, Adeline's academic professional environment prohibits any inclinations of spirituality or faith. Another difference in how dualism can impact spiritual knowledge is whether there is a corporate versus a sole-proprietor work environment, as Griffin stated:

> Spirituality at work was much more limited and restricted when I worked for a major pharma company in the Chicagoland area. People want to be open about their faith at work, but the subjects never get brought up because of not good reasons, fear, not wanting to offend somebody or all different reasons (p. 145).

However, not all people accept dualism or compartmentalizing their faith-at-work by using spiritual intelligence to create SK *in motion* for their whole self at work, such as adapting their faith-at-work to the location, changing the work environment to adapt to their faith-at-work, reducing barriers or expanding potentials for faith-at-work, and fusing the environmental dimensions within their faith-at-work framework as explained below.

Adapting One's FAW to the Location

Some people choose to adapt their faith-at-work to the work location or a real-life example of SK *in motion* to access spiritual intelligence (identifying and organizing skills needed for the adaptive use of spirituality). From Long (2022), Monty explained that when he:

> works in the synagogue's administrative offices, you will not notice that you are in the building of faith. What separates us from a downtown office is that we have that sanctuary. I work in a very spiritual place. . .; you are rising into a place of holiness. . . . You walk into a religious setting; you follow the rules. You still feel that way [in the administrative office], although the finance department does not require it, "I do not want to bring anything that's not considered holy into a holy building, so I am making sure that everything I bring in has a hechsher on it (p. 146).

Another example of adapting faith-at-work to the work location, or a real-life example of SK *in motion*, was when Griffin worked in a corporate setting and organized a voluntary "faith experience" lunch discussion group to give his staff time to talk safely about stressful issues using their SK. However, the company required "positive dualism" where the name of the discussion group had to be "very general so, it was ecumenical. . ., non-denominational, but also it did not necessarily have to be Christian," said Griffin, "we did not want to be imposing or think that there was any gain whatsoever in attending something like that. Obviously. . .you do not want to show any partiality, and you do not want to make people uncomfortable." (p. 146)

Adapting faith-at-work to the environment, as in these examples, made SQ accessible to create the SK *in motion* and to flourish in the workplace.

Changing the Work Environment to Adapt to One's FAW

On the other hand, sometimes changing the work environment to adapt to one's faith at work is another way to access SK *in motion*. As Amrit, a management professor, explained, workers in India are more apt to change their workplace to fit their faith-at-work needs. Otherwise, the employers must adapt to the workers (Long, 2022). Specifically, Amrit stated:

> People will be motivated primarily to stick with their faith system rather than be very loyal to organizations. . .if it [the organization] is crisscrossing in their faith system. They [the employees] would probably prefer to be with their faith rather than the organization. Essentially, faith drives them [team members], what they do, and how they do it; in India, the organizations cannot afford to have Faith-Avoiding FAW frameworks, right? Because it will not work. Faith affects productivity, but workers do not care; people prefer to leave organizations if it conflicts with their value system or faith (p. 147).

Within a "faith culture" such as this, Amrit explained how he changed his physical office environment to access SK to increase SQ. He said:

> I propose that why can't we have a meeting outside? Let us not sit in a room. Let us go outside. We have a beautiful campus here, and it is very spacious. Let us sit somewhere and then do it. I prefer to be with it [spiritual elements] and see nature and spirituality connect (p. 147).

Pushing the boundaries of the work environment to shift SK *in motion* is possible, as seen in Amrit's situation. A spontaneous example of shifting SK *in motion* was during our semi-structured interview when Kia, a Human Resources consultant, realized that her current job's faith-at-work framework was ultimately "faithless." She exclaimed, "That is sort of shocking, surprising to me to read these [Miller & Ewest's (2015) frameworks] and, go, oh, boy, it [faith] is just not important, it is not, not part of the framework [at this current job]," and decided at that moment, "I should pray for another job," (p. 147) and discussed how she could change to a new job. On the other hand, some people plan faith-at-work environments to access a desired level of SK, to grow SQ and shift their consciousness levels from ego to soul. In Long (2022), Monty displayed his faith-at-work pictures of Jerusalem on his work desk because, he said:

> Jewish people longed for their capital for so long, and one of my dreams growing up was to work at a synagogue. Jewish people's prayers were answered about the return. However, my prayer about returning to the temple and religious life was also restored. . .working for a temple fulfilled his [grandfather's] goal of me being part of the Jewish world and that I would continue to grow in my Jewish identity (p. 148).

Reducing Barriers or Expanding Environmental Potentials for FAW

Deliberately planning or spontaneously changing the work environment can deepen faith-at-work experiences and opportunities for SQ and SK *in motion*. Most employees and managers in Long (2022) choose to either reduce barriers or expand the environmental potential for faith-at-work with various methods. Examples include Pat, a professor in higher education, who realized that:

> Learning about [my] coworker's religious views and practices made me feel closer; when I opened up, he opened up too. . .including aspects of atheism into the assignment allowed my worldview to be a part of my workday. I just felt like it was more inclusive, and I think that not only did it make me feel more included in the work I was doing, but I also hoped that it might feel more inclusive to students who do not practice a religion (p. 148).

For Griffin, incorporating online meetings reduced his faith-at-work barriers by increasing access to SK *in motion* as well as the potential for SQ, as he stated:

> In the previous corporate setting, we had that separation dualism, which does not exist now [using virtual meetings]; we can talk freely about Bible study. There were natural barriers in the workplace, but the Holy Spirit is working on this (p. 148).

Changes in the financial industry expanded the potential for individual SK *in motion*, and perhaps organizational SK *in motion* itself, according to Miriam, by providing Wellness Rooms for prayer, meditation, or rest, employees can access SK and develop greater SQ. She compares this to a time when, "in the heyday of the financial industry, they brought strippers into the office for people's birthdays! . . . We now have a Wellness Room at the office, and anybody [non-denominational] who wants to use it can [for faith-at-work]" (Long, 2022, p. 149). Miriam's journal described how the right faith-at-work environment evolved slowly over time, impacting both her and others' SK, thus leading to organizational SK shifts. She wrote:

> The weekend is here, and so are all the positive thoughts that come with nearing the end of the workweek. However, I have an additional layer that veils my Friday thinking. . .my assistant knows to look at my calendar on Friday and not to schedule anything after, like, two. It did not use to be this way. It was like, "Where is she going?" and I was like, "It is Shabbat!" However, now, they, over the years, just turned the other way where they are like, "Hey, it is three o'clock; why are you still here?" She would like to shoo me out the door (p. 149).

Miriam's assistant and others, including the organization, now know, acknowledge, and support specific efforts to access SK and increase SQ by respecting her needs. The changes occurred over time to reduce barriers and increase the potential for faith-at-work, SQ, and SK *in motion*. Reflecting on these efforts, Miriam shared:

> Twenty years ago, I do not think I would have done the work on myself that I do now. . . I certainly would have cared more about what other people think. It took me 10 to 15 years; I have been doing it for 30 years. It took 10–15 years or more to create this [FAW] work environment (p. 149).

In comparison, Theodore worked with other IT managers to directly expand the potential for the right faith-at-work environment to include opportunities for SK *in motion* because he said, "We wanted to help reduce the horrible compartmentalization at work. . .so we can talk about work problems and non-work-related stuff. . .and get time off to do personal [spiritual development] research projects" (Long, 2022, p. 149).

Lastly, Griffin's call to action for organizational leadership highlights the importance of making timely environmental barrier reductions or enhancements for SK *in motion*:

> There are opportunities at the management level, as mentors, to establish safe relationships and create physical and psychological surroundings for FAW. There are many ways you can demonstrate and build relationships. However, you know, all of them revolve around serving others. As you get closer to retirement, there might be less opportunity (Long, 2022, p. 150).

Fused Environmental Dimensions in the FAW Framework

When the Long (2022) study participants assessed and described their current FAW organizational framework, using the Miller and Ewest (2015) framework as a reference, most fused various environmental dimensions to describe the situation and its effect on SK *in motion*, dimensions included country culture (e.g., Midwestern U.S.A, France, India, Swiss-based, and Japanese-based), company structures such as ownership, their specific work department, and their job or role. [See Long, 2022, pp. 269–275 for more details.] One real-life scenario was Jacob, who worked at a "Faith-Avoiding" military organization and yet had a "Faith-Safe" job/role so he could use his SK and SQ to help others. He explained:

> I was a Psych Tech; my job was never proselytizing, so I never did. [I was] to provide tools to deal with cognitive distortions from the [military environment] uncertainty and help them to take care of themselves holistically. . .accessing body, mind, and spirit activities. . . [including] Faith-Safe medical care routines that do not cross inappropriate boundaries (p. 151).

Theodore, an IT Finance manager, described the environmental dimensions that affected his company's FAW framework and how the company and departmental SK affected his ability to use SQ:

> The entire corporation is Faith-Safe. However, the department in the Midwest U.S. is isolated; our management is hands-off from the company in India and is closer to Faith-Friendly. I follow faith practices within my department more than others but never get pushback for my faith (p. 152).

Pat, who said that she only knows "a small part of the large organization," defines the FAW framework and SK *in motion* as:

> Somewhere between the Safe and Faith Friendly with Faith-Tokenism, they follow the law. . . have spaces for self-directed faith practices, and are undoubtedly inclusive of various things. . .they also tokenize the more obscure, cultural, and religious practices and encourage non-mainstream Faiths (p. 152).

Also, in the Long (2022) study, changes in a company's ownership affect the FAW framework, creating a faith-at-work environment for enhanced SK *in motion*. Theodore explained that "the previous owners were Faith-Avoiding definitely. . . their God was money, definitely wealth. The current business owners are more aware of and have more communications around cultural diversity including religion" (p. 152).

A "family" company culture, as both Joyce and Eve described their organizations in Long (2022), created FAW frameworks and SK *in motion* that were "Faith-Friendly with Avoid Litigation" and "Faith-Fragile," respectively. Both felt affection for their company's family culture but acknowledged significant differences in the organizational SK. Eve described her workplace as:

> We come from different backgrounds. This is a Japanese company, so there are all different types of cultures represented in our workforce. . . it is a dysfunctional family that I love and consider part of a work family regardless of their background and beliefs; I love our differences (p. 153).

Eve said the "family" company culture translated to a FAW framework "based off of the work itself, [with the] *people* excluded, it will be more Faith-Safe." However, when she included the people, it changed the environment and even the level of organizational SK to "Faith-fragile". She explained:

> I think specific individuals within a department, though, can make it not feel Safe. However, it is not Faith-Avoiding either because it is like being attacked by being made fun of. You are being put on a show in front of the department and made to feel less than for believing what you do, which I do not believe is appropriate. . .technically, you could say people are being harassed. It is one person getting away with it, which impacts the environment. . . you feel fragile or vulnerable. You feel like by exposing yourself, you are going to be attacked (p. 153).

On the other hand, for Joyce, the FAW family environment was supportive:

> We are a family. We care for each other. We are a large company, and we must be cautious; we want to avoid litigation. . . the only thing in the Faith-Safe framework that goes along with our company is that they avoid litigation, which is understandable. I am thankful they always think of our safety and security. . .what it does to keep our employees happy and make our job easier (p. 153).

Joyce's company encourages SQ development to enhance SK *in motion* and personal consciousness levels. The FAW framework allows her freedom to discover SQ. She explained a faith-at-work tool on her desk:

> My company would never interfere with how I feel about my faith. . . and gives me time throughout my day to reflect on Who I am. I feel very positive about how I can feel and express my thoughts. I am in the right place. I am in the right company. I am in the right job. Moreover, that never leaves me. . . . Our company wants us to interact with our customers during work hours. . . . It encourages us to be so entuned to the wants and needs of our people, but also outside, outside the box, outside the hours to continue to be that way with our customers; it [the FAW tool] just reminds me that our customers bless us (p. 153).

These real-life examples of employees and managers fusing environmental dimensions of faith-at-work and SQ and SK *in motion* remove abstraction. The last portion of this section discusses how "the place", the work environment, is significant to spiritual knowledge management by using three aggregated figures that will be applied to practical organizational design opportunities in the final section of the chapter.

Places, Plus More Frameworks

In the previous sections, the "who", the employees and managers who experienced faith-at-work, demonstrated their spiritual intelligence and knowledge *in motion* through details of the "what" or spiritual tools, the "how" or spiritual practices, and the "where" or the FAW framework places. The Long (2022) study brings to life the complexity of developing SQ and accessing SK at work. The following three figures from the study further simplify abstractions for organizational planning and design purposes.

First, Figure (7.1). The *External to Internal Context Matters* demonstrate that the study participants acknowledged how their faith-at-work environment consists of multiple layers, including the most external context (Country) to the innermost internal self-perspective (Personal). The research confirmed that the context makes a difference when understanding the faith-at-work environment for spiritual knowledge management purposes.

One example, noted by Amrit working in a collectivist environment, labeled his FAW framework as both a "Faith-Culture" and a "Kind-of Faith-Friendly" company because his organization responded to the workers' values and faith practices rather than the workers needing to respond to the organizational business principles. He said, "Indian faith is known to the world; many different faith systems in India affect the way people work; faith affects productivity, but workers do not care [about the productivity]" (Long, 2022, p. 198).

Secondly, Figure (7.2) *A Spectrum of Faith and Work Organizational Frameworks from Zero to 13* displays the 14 FAW frameworks from the study. This demonstrates the range of possible frameworks using the foundation of Miller and Ewest's (2015) four

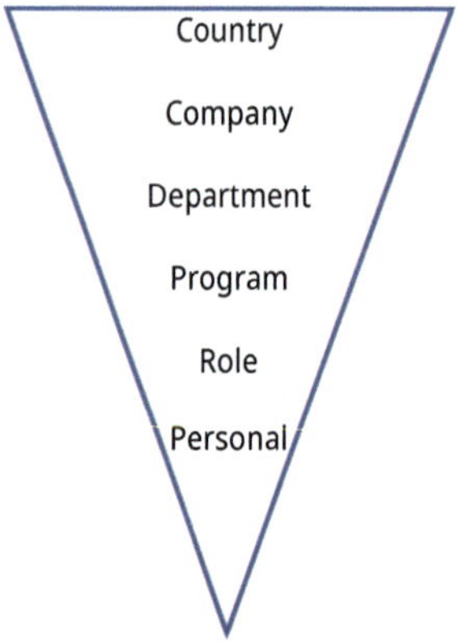

Figure 7.1: The external to internal context matters.
Source: Long (2022)

orientations, plus the added complexity from real-life experiences. The framework names come from In-Vivo and Themeing-the-data codes in Long (2022).

0. Faith-Less
1. Faith-Avoiding
2. Faith-Fragile
3. Faith-Based
4. Possibly Faith-Comfortable
5. Faith-Steward
6. Faith-Safe
7. Seeking Faith-Safe; somewhere between Safe and Friendly with Faith-Tokenism
8. Faith-Safe with Faith-Approachable Services
9. Closer to Faith-Friendly than Faith-Safe
10. Faith-Friendly with Avoid-Litigation
11. Faith-Friendly
12. Faith-Friendly Kind-Of Organization
13. Faith-Culture

Figure 7.2: A spectrum of faith and work organizational frameworks from 0 to 13.
Source: Long (2022)

Then, Figure (7.3) *Graph of Fourteen FAW Frameworks* is a simple graphical illustration of the spectrum in Figure (7.2), including all the FAW organizational frameworks, ranging from zero (Faithless) to 13 (a complete Faith-Culture), totaling 14 frameworks shown together. This representation of the 14 frameworks is also based on Miller and Ewest's (2015) criteria of religious accommodations, formal policies, and fatal dualism but expanded by actual, real-life experiences. [For detailed descriptions and evidence of the extended frameworks, see Long, 2022, pp. 269–275.]

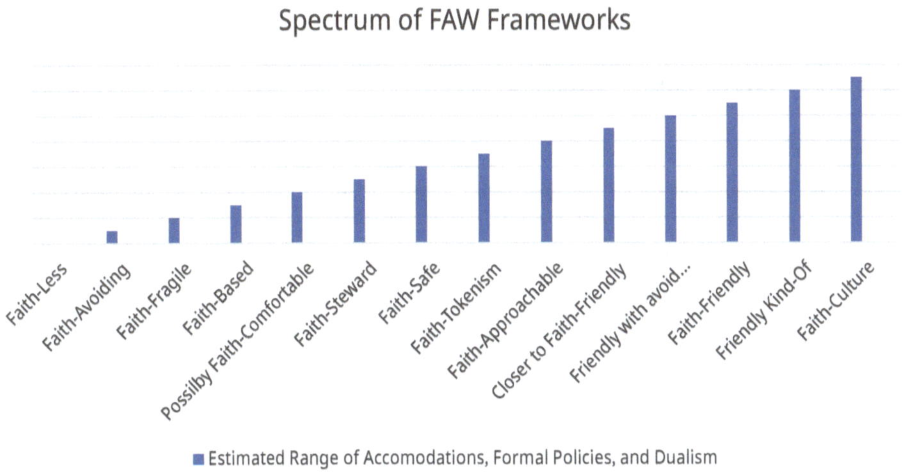

Figure 7.3: Graph of fourteen FAW frameworks.
Source: Long (2022)

According to Long's (2022) research, context matters and for spiritual knowledge management is relatable to Dubow's (2013) contemplation about why context matters:

> We must consider the author's and audience's context in our exegesis whenever we read, interpret, and apply scripture. We do this . . . to faithfully understand and learn from them. . . When we take the time to seek out and understand context, the text becomes alive, vibrant, effective. . .and valuable for teaching, rebuking, correcting, and training in righteousness. (2 Tim 3:16) (para. 10)

Correctly understanding employees' FAW's context is also critical to understanding SQ and SK *in motion* experiences. Thus, the real-life examples and the three figures, (7.1) *The External to Internal Context Matters,* (7.2) *A Spectrum of Faith and Work Organizational Frameworks from Zero to 13,* and (7.3) *Graph of Fourteen FAW Frameworks* can help scholar-practitioners to build operationalized definitions of SQ and SK at work for their organizations. To make a more accurate assessment of each situation, scholar-practitioners may examine or question the external context of the entire company's cultural, historical, and geographical background, as well as the internal context of the employee of their department, program, role, or job. The Long (2022) conceptual models do not claim that all these frameworks would replicate. However, they ask scholar-practitioners to consider the provocative knowledge and practical applications because "the workplace is the dynamic context in which people express themselves and strive for their fulfillment" (Bratianu, 2015, p. 14).

Section 3: Spiritual Knowledge Management (SKM) and Human Flourishing (HF)

This section explains a Spiritual Knowledge Management (SKM) strategic model derived from the previous findings that promote letting people develop their spiritual intelligence (SQ) and access spiritual knowledge (SK) and being able to respond skillfully in real situations by studying and practicing spiritual skills at work. Ideally, as the individual SKM changes, the organizational SKM changes too because the organizational consciousness will grow like personal hierarchical needs grow (Barrett, 2015).

The proposed model responds to the researcher's call for better ways to integrate workplace spirituality as a human resource offering (Moll, 2022). The model highlights human flourishing (HF), in contrast to human resources (HR), and is a practical design from the Long (2022) empirical study. Current Human Resource Development (HRD) processes lack the element of spiritual intelligence, and "HRD programs need to be re-designed and consideration of employees entire being (mind, body, and spirit) would create a climate for the holistic flourishing of the employees" (Poole, 2009, as cited by Ahmed et al., 2016, p. 70). The proposed SKM model embraces faith-at-work experiences, including spiritual intelligence growth and spiritual knowledge attainment, as a consciousness perspective of human flourishing. Scholar-practitioners can revisit HR from this consciousness perspective using the faith-at-work experiences as SQ and SK *in motion* to support employees' and managers' ability to flourish at work.

This section contains specific ways companies can design these human flourishing (HF) strategies, processes, and roles to affect the necessary organizational consciousness growth from survival to unity (Barrett, 2015) to support spiritual, emotional, and rational knowledge management. Consider the following findings from managers and employees in Long's (2022) FAW: PPPT study. First, they often defined a locus of control, like positing a spiritual force of will more significant than one's own, such as God's. Evidence from Long's (2022) study shows that, but is not necessarily generalizable for all people, whether at home or work, in a post-materialism view, "we are free to posit a spiritual force driving the evolutionary arc of life" (Grosso, 2019, as cited in Long, 2022, p. 176). Notable, too, is the importance of personal and organizational fulfillment of purpose at work; both personal and organizational consciousness affect positing a locus of control and purpose fulfillment. One of the six mega faith-at-work experience elements, spiritual discernment, and the associated SQ *in motion* real-life examples, were part of accessing one's locus of control and spiritual forces of will (Long, 2022). Secondly, as shown in the study, the holistic spiritual exercises, the third mega-element, support cultivating spiritual discernment by creating proper relationships with God, self, and others. However, a micro-element called "suffering and testing during challenges" could occur when employees and managers pursue faith-at-work or spiritual knowledge and intelligence *in motion*. These challenges included fear of being atypical, experiences of discrimination, or exclusion from opportunities and relationships due to bringing their whole self to work, including faith. They revealed that employees need support at work to develop SQ and access SK to avoid or reduce the suffering and testing experiences (Long, 2022). Third, as noted in the study, faith-at-work experiences utilizing spiritual intelligence and knowledge can be life-changing. At least three crucial mechanisms support successful changes: a rational framework for SK and SQ to make sense of the environment, an understanding community to support ongoing SKM practices, and a mentor or faithful advisor (Vaughn, 2002). A spiritually intelligent workplace provides these mechanisms to allow people to flourish.

Although not necessarily easy, realignment of organizational consciousness, strategies, structures, and processes is possible with a better understanding of employees' spiritual forces of will, need for purpose fulfillment, reduction of suffering and testing in faith-at-work, and the mechanisms for spiritually intelligent workplaces as Vaughn (2002) describes. The following three sub-sections, HF strategy, HF structures, and HF processes, detail a path for these changes and are practical applications intended for implementation by organizations pursuing SKM. Long's (2022) FAW and HF model, where the faith-at-work experiences include SK and SQ *in motion*, illustrates the strategy, structures, and processes that could move traditional HRD from a transactional to a transformational perspective.

HF Strategy

The proposed model reveals linkages between faith-at-work (and SQ and SK *in motion*) and human flourishing as an operational strategy. See Figure (7.4) *FAW and a human flourishing (HF) Strategy*. In addition, the model addresses the call for creating "a structure and culture in which leaders and followers can respectfully negotiate religious and spiritual diversity" (Hicks, 2002, as cited in Long, 2022, p. 193).

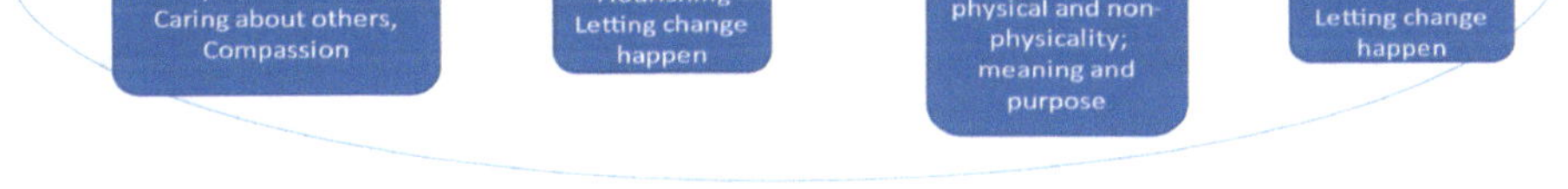

Figure 7.4: FAW and a human flourishing (HF) strategy.
Source: Long (2022)

As noted in the Long (2022) study, the rationale for the model is that faith-at-work experiences involve a variety of SQ and SK *in motion* practices and tools (e.g., prayer and meditation), and these practices embrace certain faith-at-work and spiritually intelligent characteristics of an individual, such as caring about others or compassion. When employees develop spiritually, referred to as "soul-work", it creates opportunities for human development and personal transformation. The key driver is that the organization lets these changes happen for non-materialistic reasons and the common good. The faith-at-work, SK and SQ *in motion* experiences distinguish what is truly valuable to the employees and managers in their day-to-day work (by the interdependence of their physical and non-physical worlds in ways that provide meaning and purpose). As people work together, they share their spiritual experiences and are involved in a human flourishing process (whether consciously or not). Over time, the organization's culture develops and transforms along with the people, as demonstrated in the previous sections, and these changes occur because a deliberate HF strategy is inclusive of non-materialistic reasons and for the common good. A looping, continuous HF strategy reinforces faith-at-work, spiritual intelligence and knowledge experiences, and the continuous experiences reinforce the HF strategy in a hermeneutical circle (Long, 2022). Optimally, moving the organizational consciousness from a survival mode (ensuring physical or economic survival) to a unity mode serving humanity and the planet (Barrett, 2015) and becomes a virtuous learning organization.

HF Structures

Organizational strategies require operational structures, and the following HF structures support the proposed HF strategy. First, the potentially enlightened organization needs to be self-aware of its current culture and FAW framework (or lack thereof) to determine the potential for transforming an HR to an HF strategy that embraces spiritual knowledge management and is intrinsic and non-materialistic for the common good. To assess the possibilities for creating an HF strategy with SKM, the organization can identify its current position on the *Spectrum of Faith and Work Organizational Frameworks* previously shown in Figures (7.2) and (7.3) from "faithless to a faith-culture". The *Spectrum of Faith and Work Organizational Frameworks* oversimplifies the range of possibilities but is based on real-world inputs and is one starting point. [Refer to Long, 2022, Appendix K – FAW Frameworks with Environmental Factors by Respondent Quotes for additional details]. Next, consider using Barrett's (2015) cultural assessment mapping personal, current culture, and desired values because the most successful companies are "able to operate from the full spectrum of consciousness and have a high degree of values alignment" (p. 266). Note that SKM in the workplace requires more than material changes in policies and procedures but may require a conversion of the organization's assumptions, beliefs, and values (Gull & Doh, 2004). To make conceptual changes and reduce any profound ontological barriers to the idea that HF and SKM may be of value to the organization may pose a conflict for many organizations. Creativity is needed. Creativity is the flexibility with which one can think about a component of an ontological category in the context of another ontological category (Chi, 1997). Creativity can help companies "shift across" ontological categories or "re-represent" a concept from one ontological category to another (Chi, 1997). Therefore, when an organization is self-aware of its current faith-at-work framework and culture, it may turn to creative organizational development integrated strategic change processes such as Worley et al.'s (1996) to determine appropriate organizational goals and methods enabling SKM and consciousness.

Roles

Well-defined roles, such as a chief spiritual officer (CSO) and organizational spiritual consultants and coaches (OSC), can lead and operationalize the strategies and structures. These roles specifically address the suffering and testing in FAW experiences mentioned earlier and lead SQ development by techniques such as respectful spirit-sharing and accepting diversity of thought through RPD and SQ conversations. To better understand individualized employee needs, OSCs can use SKM transformational tools, such as a voluntary FAW-IQ or SQ assessment, to identify individual and organizational SQ acedia and growth (Long, 2022). Additionally, they guide the following HF dynamic development processes.

HF Processes

To begin with, these HF processes are based on Long's (2022) fourth mega-element, faith-at-work as dynamic processes, and the corresponding sub-elements of spiritually developing, resulting fruits of how one treats others such as charity, joy, peace, patience, kindness, goodness, gentleness, commitment, and continency or self-control, and specific theological and moral virtues, and character strengths (Long, 2022). Another precept for the HF processes is from Wigglesworth's (2013) notions of SQ development, where SQ is a natural movement of wisdom and compassion towards others, regardless of the context. Moreover, SQ coordinates different perspectives, transforms consciousness, and teaches one to see the value of these qualities in others and oneself (Wigglesworth, 2013). The HF processes recognize researchers' agreement that SQ can be developed; the development requires discipline, attention training, transforming emotions, and cultivating ethical behavior (Vaughn, 2002; Wigglesworth, 2011). Also, just as SQ is related to but different from other types of intelligence (e.g., IQ, EQ, or even physical, PQ) and may grow at different rates, SQ development may be related to but is different from cognition, emotional, and moral development. Lastly, the HF processes accept that unmanaged emotional or ethical issues could interfere with SQ development, and

SQ first requires self-awareness. Therefore, the processes include formalized training, curriculum, soul-work, coaching, and everyday encounters for spiritual knowledge management because it is possible to "design and implement a spiritual actualization learning system within the organization" (Ahmed et al., 2016, p. 68).

HF Training and Development (T&D)

The HF training and development (T&D) processes for SQ development stem from Long's (2022) faith-at-work findings; for example, a common understanding by all people in the study is that faith-at-work is "how one treats others" (p. 140), and "requires that you put yourself inside somebody else's moccasins with empathy" (p. 193). As well as from the aligned research where "SQ is the ability to behave with wisdom and compassion while maintaining inner and outer peace, regardless of the situation. . .*behave* is important because it focuses on how well we maintain our center, stay calm, and treat other people" (Wigglesworth, 2013, p. 447).

Notably, the employees and managers in Long (2022) made repeated conscious efforts to create the right environment for one's faith at work by establishing common grounds with others through respectful pluralism processes. "Under the conditions of respectful pluralism, employees can express, to a significant degree, their religious and spiritual as well as political, cultural, and other commitments within the workplace" (Hicks, 2002, p. 392). They were inclusive while expressing their views; they learned about another's views rather than just finding the lowest common denominator in their relationships. They participated in developing respectful, pluralistic relationships through dialogue, listening, sharing, other communication techniques, personal soul-work, and character growth (Long, 2022). The HF T&D processes also include these because "scholars from various areas of leadership studies have argued that healthy organizational environments allow common ground to be built and that organizations can benefit from respectful, honest conflict (Hicks, 2002, p. 391).

Curriculum

The HF training and development curriculum enhances diversity, equity, and inclusion programs by utilizing some faith-at-work, SQ and SK *in motion*, 24 experience elements mentioned earlier, such as tri-identity (mind-body-spirit), spiritual discernment, and wholistic spiritual exercises. Four potential learning objectives and sample approaches for the curriculum are noted in Table (7.1) *HF T&D Curriculum Objectives.*

Respectful pluralism dialogues and "spiritual intelligence conversations offer a way for people to get a deeper motivation than pay and promotions," and "a spiritually intelligent workplace offers a chance for people to live from their purpose and values, and to bring their best selves to work" (Wigglesworth, 2013, p. 445). Therefore, a predominant part of the HF T&D curriculum is a relational and a wholistic spiritual exercise, the respectful pluralism dialogue, that develops proper relationships, as evidenced in the Long (2022) study. For example, a higher-education professor, Pat, noted that her epistemology of a scientific, material, and rational worldview was a "belief-in" or a "faith-of-sorts" in science and self and was her SQ premise. After journaling for a couple of days for the study, Pat decided to have an RPD or SQ conversation at work and then integrated her "faith" worldview into a work assignment, resulting in feelings of inclusion, finding common grounds with her coworkers, and accessing her "spiritual" knowledge.

Table 7.1: HF T&D curriculum objectives.

	Learning Objectives	Sample Approaches
1	Understand individuals' spirituality Type and unique spiritual expressions.	Use the "Looking at Type and Spirituality" tool by Hirsh & Kise (2016), built upon the Myers-Briggs Type Indicator® instrument, to guide individuals to understand their spiritual direction better and start common ground language for FAW and SQ.
2.	Manage stages of SQ development.	Use the SQ21, a spiritual intelligence self-assessment, diversity-appropriate, and skills-based tool by Wigglesworth (2011;2013). This tool could also help discussions and development about SQ skills and behaviors based on powerful human motivators and success factors.
3	Create a workable spiritual exercise rhythm with the employee.	Match Type and SQ levels and discuss relevant spiritual exercises.
4	Discover how employers could support spiritual exercise rhythms.	Manage spiritual exercises within the existing environmental and work responsibilities and enhance spiritual care support with RPD.

Source: Long (2022)

Respectful Pluralism Dialogue (RPD) & Spiritual Intelligence (SQ) Conversations

Many people in the Long (2022) study found common grounds (i.e., being inclusive while expressing one's views and learning about another's) with respectful pluralism processes. Their life-long, faith-at-work and SK-in-motion experiences of developing respectful, pluralistic relationships resemble extended SQ development documented by their dialogue, listening, sharing, and other communication techniques as well as their soul-work (e.g., Bible study and Mussar training) and character growth. As exhibited by multiple real-life examples, many people tried to create the right environment for their faith at work using spiritual knowledge to establish common grounds with others' spiritual knowledge. The spiritually intelligent allowed the Divine to break through personally but regularly, not to convert a co-worker (Pierce, 2001). This portion of the HF T&D program intends to help people understand context, speak a language the other person understands, and notice each other's spiritual intelligence.

Practical Ways

Suppose the organization is not ready for new HF strategy, structures, or processes, but "finding common ground and practical ways of respectful pluralism. . .is a practical contribution" towards integrating faith-at-work (Long, 2022, p. 196). Inspired by managers and employees who find simple approaches for SQ development and accessing SK in respectful, pluralistic ways are these three practical ways to inspire RPDs shown in Table (7.2) *Practical Ways to Inspire RPDs.*

Table 7.2: Practical ways to inspire RPDs.

	Practical ways	Long (2022) Quotes
1.	Individuals learn to ask this question and listen authentically to the answer.	"Shabbat Shalom", or "What is the state of your peace?" ("Shalom, my friend: A host of meanings," 2010).
2.	Individuals or employers use parts of the Mussar practice for developing character traits and doing intentional soul-work (Mussar Institute, 2020; Mussar Institute, 2021).	Intentional awareness comes from this practical approach [of soul-work]. Miriam recognized, "Sitting in front of my computer and taking yet another phone call will not change my life, but taking care of myself might change someone else's life if I handle them better."
3.	Individuals or employers use an RPD technique to identify the essential supportive roles to create the right FAW environment.	Griffin described an RPD by asking, "Who is your Paul, Who is your Barnabas, and Who is your Timothy? Meaning, who is your mentor, peer, and protégé? Timothy can be a protégé in either a business or a faith walk. Paul is a mentor, and Barnabas is a peer or small group of peers. Barnabas can be a good friend who shares an equal footing spiritually."

HF Coaching

As noted previously, people are not static in their spiritual intelligence of knowledge, and "cultivating SQ seems to call for a commitment to some form of spiritual practice" (Vaughn, 2002, p. 26). Another HF dynamic development process that supports an ongoing commitment is a *voluntary* coaching program called "As Wise as a Serpent and as Gentle as a Dove," offered by the HF department OSCs to managers and employees. Moll (2022) notes, "Participatory design and a voluntary offering design is necessary for a moral and ethical implementation" (p. 209). Spiritual coaching is spiritual care for individual SQ development and a commitment to managing spiritual knowledge and rational and emotional knowledge at work. The coaches are trained business psychologists who expertly support ongoing psychological well-being and related SKM experiences. The HF strategy and structures, along with processes such as the "As Wise as Serpent and as Gentle as a Dove" coaching program, support organizational SKM and potential spiritual transformations at work because if "spirituality infusions in modern organizations are to be successful, they must be introduced effectively and they must be well managed" (Hoover, 2007, p. 324).

Soul-Work

The following dynamic development process, soul-work, further contextualizes and operationalizes faith-at-work and SKM in an HF schema. Managers and employees in Long (2022) identified the fruits or moral actions (i.e., charity, joy, peace, patience, kindness, goodness, commitment, gentleness, and self-control) of how one treats others, the theological virtue of hope, moral virtues of prudence, justice, and temperance, and the specific character strengths comparable to prudence, fairness, as well as transcendence as critical to faith-at-work and flourishing. A person's theological and moral virtues and character strengths in Long's (2022) findings stabilized their moral actions (i.e., fruits – something that inevitably appears on a healthy tree). These fruits are evidence of a flourishing employee. A new manager, Eve, best explained this as "things that I have learned, like the virtues I have, I try to exhibit within the workplace. Patience and love. . .helping and supporting others. If I had no faith, I probably would not exhibit those virtues" (p. 195).

Because "moral virtue is rationally guided. . . a state of character concerned with choice. . .people can train to possess moral virtues. . . ." (Rocha & Pinheiro, 2021, p. 136). An HF dynamic development process called "The Fruits" is a voluntary soul-work program to develop moral virtues and character strengths. "The Fruits" reflect Long's (2022) heuristic, where fruits are the effects of people living a life according to the spirit or the will of God, based on an axiom where the fruits of the Holy Spirit are the good habits, the virtues, and the good deeds that come from living as a child of God (Flader, 2015). Thus, the objectives of "The Fruits" program are to support and develop specific moral virtues, actions, and character strengths as part of the overall spiritual knowledge management system.

Match Employee and Organizational FAW Frameworks to Optimize SKM

Recalling that spiritual knowledge integrates values and beliefs about life and spiritual intelligence addresses and solves problems of meaning and value, employees and organizations need to optimize the management of spiritual knowledge to enjoy long-term success (Bolisani & Bratianu, 2018; Bratianu, 2015). To do inspired work and find meaning in the workplace and the work done, employees must align personal values, beliefs, and practices with the organizational value system (Barrett, 2005; Bratianu, 2015). Additionally, "a company that has a strong alignment between the personal values of the employees and the organizational values, and the top ten values of the organizational culture covering all seven stages of organizational consciousness, will enjoy long-lasting success" (Bratianu, 2015 p. 16). Therefore, the final suggestion for creating a climate for human flourishing is to design additional HF dynamic processes that will match potential employee values and the company's cultural faith-at-work frameworks during the recruiting, talent acquisition, and onboarding processes. Through guided, candid conversations, or even the "Looking at Type and Spirituality" tool by Hirsh & Kise (2016) and the SQ21 assessment by Wigglesworth (2011;2013) overseen by the OSC's in the HF department, the intrinsic merits of considering the whole self – mind, body, spirit – would provide an opportunity to optimize SKM for both individual and organizational consciousness and growth.

Summary

Faith At Work: People, Places, Practices, and Tools by Long (2022) demonstrates real-life examples of developing spiritual intelligence and accessing spiritual knowledge, revealing the richness and significance of what people truly value in their lives at work. Managing spiritual, rational, and emotional knowledge is critical to scholar-practitioners, employees, and organizations because it addresses the meaning and quality of people's working lives (Bratianu, 2015). The explanations of faith-at-work via SQ and SK *in motion* enacting real-life spiritual tools, practices, and the places that impact individual and organizational experiences contribute to the SKM literature. In addition, a deeper understanding of the faith-at-work empirical research with its familiar, similar, or unique experience elements across traditions – even secular ethical philosophies, assists the development of SKM theory and applications that favor the flourishing of humankind at work.

From a non-materialist paradigm, the SKM human flourishing strategy, structures, and processes presented in this chapter provide an upside potential to developing or expressing a person's entire being – mind, body, and spirit. The diverse faith-at-work and respectful, pluralistic approaches to developing SQ and accessing SK *in motion* at work allow shifting to a higher level of organizational consciousness or unity (Long, 2022; Barrett, 2015).

Much gratitude goes to the employees and managers in Long (2022) who wholeheartedly shared their genuine faith-at-work, SK and SQ *in motion* examples, and real-life shifts in individual SQ and organizational SK to create suitable faith-at-work environments. Their experiences enabled the nuanced explanations of various FAW frameworks, leading to the development a practical SKM human flourishing model that can create value.

References

Ahmed, A., Arshad, M. A., Mahmood, A., & Akhtar, S. (2016). Spiritual intelligence (SQ): A holistic framework for human resource development. *Administratie si Management Public, 26*, 60–77.

Alvesson, M. & Gabriel, Y. (2013). Beyond formulaic research: Praise greater diversity in organizational research and publications. *Academy of Management Learning & Education, 12*(2), 245–263. https://doi.org/10.5465/amle.2012.0327

Ashforth, B. E. & Pratt, M. G. (2003). Institutionalized spirituality: an oxymoron? In R.A. Giacalone & C.L. Jurkiewicz (Eds.), *Handbook of workplace spirituality and organizational performance* (pp. 93–107). M.E. Sharpe.

Barrett, R. (2015). Culture and consciousness. Measuring spirituality in the workplace by mapping values. In R.A. Giacalone & C.L. Jurkiewicz (Eds.). *Handbook of workplace spirituality and organizational performance* (2nd ed., pp. 255–275). M.E. Sharpe.

Bolisani, E. & Bratianu, C. (2018). Emergent Knowledge Strategies: Strategic Thinking in Knowledge Management. In Ettore Bolisani & Meliha Handzic (Eds.). *Knowledge Management and Organizational Learning Volume 4.* (pp. 1–218). Springer International Publishing AG.

Bratianu, C. (2015). *Organizational Knowledge Dynamics: Managing Knowledge Creation, Acquisition, Sharing, and Transformation.* Hershey: IGI Global. https://doi.org/10.4018/978-1-4666-8318-1.ch004

Dehler, G. E., & Welsh, M. A. (2015). The experience of work: Spirituality and the new workplace. In R. Giacalone & C. Jurkiewicz (Eds.), *Handbook of Workplace Spirituality and Organizational Performance* (pp. 59–72). Routledge.

Delbecq, A. (2009). Spirituality and business: one scholar's perspective. *Journal of Management, Spirituality, and Religion, 6*(1), 3–13. https://doi.org/10.1080/14766080802648599

Dent, E.B. (2019). MSR 2.0: Spirituality Plus Religion. In J. Marques (Ed.). *The Routledge Companion to Management and Workplace Spirituality* (1st ed., Vol. 1, pp. 74–87). Routledge. https://doi.org/10.4324/9781351015110-9

De Ruyter, D., Oades, L., & Waghid, Y. (2020). Meaning(s) of Human Flourishing and Education. *Research brief by the International Science and Evidence-based Education Assessment. An Initiative by UNESCO MGIEP.*

Ewest, T. & Miller, D. W. (2019). Linking Spirituality to Religion. In J. Marques (Ed.). *The Routledge Companion to Management and Workplace Spirituality* (1st ed., Vol. 1, pp. 67–73). Routledge. https://doi.org/10.4324/9781351015110-8

Farnese, M. L., Barbieri, B., Chirumbolo, A., & Patriotta, G. (2019). Managing Knowledge in Organizations: A Nonaka's SECI Model Operationalization. *Frontiers in Psychology, 10*, 2730–2730. https://doi.org/10.3389/fpsyg.2019.02730

Flader, J. R. (2015). Are the fruits of the Holy Spirit the same as the gifts? The Catholic Weekly. https://www.catholicweekly.com.au/are-the-fruits-of-the-holy-spirit-the-same-as-thegifts/

Fry, L. W., Matherly, L. L., & Ouimet, J. R. (2010). The spiritual leadership balanced scorecard business model: The case of the Cordon Bleu-Tomasso Corporation. *Journal of Management, Spirituality, and Religion, 7*(4), 283–314. https://doi.org/10.1080/14766086.2010.524983

Gull, G. A., & Doh, J. (2004). The "Transmutation" of the Organization: Toward a More Spiritual Workplace. *Journal of Management Inquiry, 13*(2), 128–139. https://doi.org/10.1177/1056492604265218

Hirsh, S. K. & Kise, J. A. (2016). *Looking at type and spirituality*. Center for Applications of Psychological Type, Inc.

Hoover, J. D., (2007). How "Whole" is Whole Person Learning? An Examination of Spirituality in Experiential Learning. *Developments in Business Simulation and Experiential Learning Proceedings in the Annual ABSEL conference, 34*, 324–330.

Koenig, H. (2011). Spirituality and Health Research: Methods, Measurements, Statistics, and Resources. Templeton Press.

Lips-Wiersma, M., & Mills, A. J. (2014). Understanding the Basic Assumptions About Human Nature in Workplace Spirituality: Beyond the Critical Versus Positive Divide. *Journal of Management Inquiry, 23*(2), 148–161. https://doi.org/10.1177/1056492613501227

Long, E. C. (2022) *Faith at work: People, Places, Practices, and Tools*. [Doctoral dissertation, The Chicago School of Professional Psychology]. ProQuest number 28866790. https://tcsedsystem.idm.oclc.org/login?url=https://www.proquest.com/dissertations- theses/faith-at-work-people-places-practic-es-tools/docview/2626052137/se-2

Miller, D. W. & Ewest, T. (2015). A new framework for analyzing organizational workplace religion and spirituality. *Journal of Management, Spirituality & Religion, 12(*4), 305–328.https://doi.org/10.1080/14766086.2015.1054864

Mitroff, I. I., & Denton, E. A. (1999a). *A spiritual audit of corporate America.* Jossey-Bass Publishers.

Mitroff, I. I., & Denton, E. A. (1999b). A study of spirituality in the workplace. *Sloan Management Review, 40*(4), 83–92.

Moberg, D. O. (2002). Religion and spirituality. Forum. *Social Compass, 49*(1), 133–138.

Moll, T. (2022). Exploring Aspects of New Work: Spirituality at Work in Agile Organizations. *Spiritual Care, 11*(3), 203–211. https://doi.org/10.1515/spircare-2021-0017

Moustakas, C. (1994). *Phenomenological research methods*. Sage Publications. online version, published 2011, eight chapters. https://doi.org/10.4135/9781412995658

Ouimet, J. R. (2005). *The golden book: Reconciliation of human well-being with productivity and profits.* Translated from the French by Steven R. Bigham. Ouimet-Cordon Bleu Inc.

Ouimet, J. R., & Semen, Y. (2013). *Everything has been loaned to you: The biography of a transformational CEO.* Society of St. Paul.

Phipps, K. A., & Matkin, G. S. (2014). Same direction, different paths: A phenomenological study of employees who are religious yet open to religious pluralism. *Employee Responsibilities and Rights Journal, (26)*, 279–295. https://doi.org/10.1007/s10672-014-9241-6

Pierce, G. F. (2001). *Spirituality at work: 10 ways to balance your life on the job.* Loyola Press.

Rocha, R. G. & Pinheiro, P. G. (2021). Phronetic Workplace: A Step Forward into a Practically Wise Company. *Open Insight, XII*(26), 130–166.

The VIA Classification of Character Strengths. (2004–2018). VIA Institute on Character. https://www.viacharacter.org/research/findings

Vaughan, F. (2002). What is Spiritual Intelligence? *The Journal of Humanistic Psychology, 42*(2), 16–33. https://doi.org/10.1177/0022167802422003

Wigglesworth, C. (2011). Spiritual Intelligence and Why It Matters. Retrieved on 07 November 2022 from https://deepchange.com/resources

Wigglesworth, C. (2013). Spiritual Intelligence. In Neal, J. (eds). *Handbook of Faith and Spirituality in the Workplace: Emerging Research and Practice,* (pp. 441–453). Springer. https://doi.org/10.1007/978-1-4614-5233-1_27

Zohar, D. & Marshall, I. N. (2000). *SQ: spiritual intelligence: the ultimate intelligence*. Bloomsbury.

Maria Jakubik

Chapter 8
Exploring the Spiritual Dimension of Wisdom Pedagogy

Abstract: This chapter seeks to address the question of *how human development can be shaped with wisdom pedagogy in higher education.* Higher education is in the knowledge business. As leading social institutions of higher education, universities share existing knowledge, do research with knowledge, innovate by combining knowledge, and create new knowledge. Moreover, most importantly, universities focus on developing human beings, human capital that is a vital part of intellectual capital. However, research on intellectual capital has highly ignored the role of the spiritual wealth that gives meaning to human actions. Spiritual capital is difficult to define, and it needs more understanding. It includes the value system of core values, such as a person's responsible attitude, meaningful purpose, motivation, and passion. This chapter argues that the spiritual dimension of wisdom pedagogy needs more understanding. This qualitative research is based on educational literature and empirical data from fourteen Finnish Universities of Sciences. The findings underline the need for evolutionary pedagogies and wisdom pedagogy. The theoretical framework presented here shows the central role of the spiritual dimension of wisdom pedagogy in shaping values, attitudes, authenticity, and responsibility. This chapter contributes to the discourses about the role of universities in the postmodern society. However, since the chapter builds on a limited number of references and quantitative and qualitative data only from one country, it highlights the need for an international perspective and a deeper focus on wisdom pedagogy. The chapter outlines practical implications for university educators, management, and curriculum developers.

Keywords: Attitudes, Authenticity, Higher Education, Responsibility, Spirituality, Values, Wisdom Pedagogy

Acknowledgment: The author thanks Dr. Harriet Zilliacus, Acting Professor of the Educational Sciences Faculty of the University of Helsinki, for her valuable feedback on the first version of this manuscript. She has provided me with further literature to read and suggested improvements that were incorporated into this version.

Maria Jakubik, Eötvös Loránd University (ELTE), Faculty of Education and Psychology, Budapest, Hungary; Ronin Institute, Social Sciences, Montclair, New Jersey, USA; University of Pécs, Faculty of Business and Economics, Pécs, Hungary, e-mails: maria.jakubik@ppk.elte.hu, maria.jakubik@ronininstitute.org, jakubik.maria@pte.hu

https://doi.org/10.1515/9783111010410-009

Introduction

There is an increased demand for being and becoming wise in a complex, highly interconnected world where knowledge is abundant and mostly freely available and where there are global challenges and risks. The global risks, based on their likelihood and impact, are grouped into five categories: economic, environmental, geopolitical, societal, and technological risks (WEF, 2021, p. 12). According to the Global Risks Perception Survey (GRPS), based on their impact, the risks are infectious diseases, climate action failure, weapons of mass destruction, biodiversity loss, natural resource crises, human environmental damage, livelihood crises, extreme weather, debt crises, and IT infrastructure breakdown (ibid.). Based on replies of nearly 1,000 experts to the GRPS in 2022, the top 10 global risks were identified as climate action failure, extreme weather, biodiversity loss, social cohesion erosion, livelihood crises, infectious diseases, human environmental damage, natural resource crises, debt crises, and geoeconomics confrontation (WEF, 2022, p. 14).

The global risk landscape is even more complex. In the social environment, the problems are wars, terrorist attacks, immigration, gender inequality, income inequality, economic crisis, health crisis, COVID-19 global pandemic, food safety, demographic changes, extinction of languages, robotization, end of jobs, unemployment, corruption, and ethical and moral crisis. In the natural environment, the challenges are climate change, global warming, flooding, hurricanes, and the extinction of animal species. The United Nations (UN, 2015) set up a sustainable development agenda for 2030: "They recognize that ending poverty and other deprivations must go hand-in-hand with strategies that improve health and education, reduce inequality, and spur economic growth – all while tackling climate change and working to preserve our oceans and forests." In addition, we are experiencing a moral and ethical crisis. It is challenging to decide what is right and what is wrong. Humanity is facing an overflow of data and information, and it is becoming harder to make decisions and eliminate fake data and information from valid. Existing knowledge and skills quickly become obsolete. Judgments and sense-making are becoming more challenging in this complex and interconnected world.

Higher education (HE) and universities are essential in addressing and solving the world's problems (Jakubik, 2022). It is possible by educating future generations who can act authentically and responsibly for the common good. The role of the university in the postmodern society is discussed broadly in the literature (Barnett, 2018; Jakubik, 2021a; Jorge & Peña, 2017; Kouatli, 2019; Latif, 2018; Maxwell, 2021b; Sousa et al., 2021). Universities are in the knowledge business. The main task of universities is human development; they are responsible for educating people, shaping values, attitudes, authenticity and responsibility of the young generation, producing new knowledge with research, and collaborating and networking with businesses. However, there is a need for a better understanding of *how* universities can shape students' feelings, thinking, knowing, reflecting, and acting. Moral and ethical values and attitudes toward social and natural environments determine the person's behavior. Authenticity is inward-directed (i.e., to personal development), and responsibility has an outward direction (i.e., taking care of others and the environment). Therefore, education has not only epistemological aims, i.e., developing knowledge, skills, and competencies of learners, but it has ontological aims too, such as educating people to *be* in the world, *be* good citizens, able to transfer their knowledge to different contexts for the common benefit of all. Actions based on values, attitudes, authenticity and responsibility make individual learners successful and impact the whole world, other people's lives and the natural environment.

Human capital is vital to intellectual capital (Jakubik, 2020a). Nevertheless, research on intellectual capital has highly ignored the role of the spiritual capital that gives meaning to human actions. Spiritual capital is difficult to define. It shows the value system of core values, such as a person's responsible attitude, meaningful purpose, motivation, and passion. The '*knowing-why*' dimension is the spiritual dimension of human and intellectual capital. Spiritual capital is an essential and forgotten dimension of wisdom pedagogy and the becoming wise journey of persons. During the last four-five decades, wisdom research has intensified in philosophy (Barnett, 1994, 2015, 2018, 2022; Maxwell, 2019a, 2019b, 2021a, 2021b; Müürsepp, 2021; Robinson, 1990); in psychology (Ardelt, 2004; Baltes & Staudinger, 2000; Bangen et al., 2013; Jeste et al., 2010; Karami et al., 2020; Karami & Parra-Martinez, 2021; Sternberg & Karami, 2021); and in management and leadership literature (Bachmann et al., 2018; Banerjee, 2014; Ekmekçi et al., 2014; Jakubik, 2021b; Jakubik & Müürsepp, 2022; McKenna & Rooney, 2005; McKenna et al., 2009; Nonaka et al., 2014; Rooney et al., 2010; Solé, 2017). However, research on wisdom, practical wisdom in HE and research on wisdom pedagogy have been neglected for a long time (Diamond, 2021).

This chapter argues that the spiritual dimension of wisdom pedagogy (i.e., knowing why) is vital for human development in HE. Therefore, this chapter seeks to answer the question:

RQ: *How can wisdom pedagogy shape human development in higher education?*

This chapter applies qualitative research methods. It builds on relevant educational literature (Allan, 2018; Arlin, 1999; Auxier, 2018; Barnett, 2018; Bassett, 2005; Gidley, 2012; Hart, 2001; Henderson & Kesson, 2004; Jakubik, 2020b and 2020b; Kouatli, 2019; Latif, 2018; Lehtonen et al., 2018; Maxwell, 2021a, 2021b; Nixon, 2012; Sternberg, 2001; Wals & Benavot, 2017; Willamo et al., 2018); on educational research (Helin, 2019; Morley, 2012; Nissilä, 2018; Rothblatt, 2012; Standaert, 2012; Ström, 2021; Teittinen, 2020); and on examples of missions, visions, and values of 14 Finnish Universities of Sciences (USCs) (Jakubik, 2021a).

The author of this chapter is highly interested in quality education because she believes that (1) this topic is contemporary and needed (WEF, 2021, 2022; UN, 2015); (2) the future role of the university in the postmodern society needs more understanding; (3) spiritual dimension of wisdom pedagogy has a decisive impact on addressing the global risks and problems in the social and natural environment and on moving toward a better world (UN, 2015), and (4) this chapter has a novel idea and it contributes to a better understanding of the roles of university, roles of educators, and wisdom pedagogy. In addition, the author of this chapter is motivated by this research because it allows her to reflect on her more than two decades of experience in Finnish HE.

This chapter is organized as follows: (1) the global challenges, the need and motivation to explore this topic, and the main research question were presented in the introduction; (2) the research design section covers the theoretical framework, three research sub-questions and objectives, research methodology and methods; (3) next, the main concepts and university pedagogy are introduced; (4) the findings and discussion section explores the three research sub-questions, and (5) the final section answers the main research question by summarizing the findings, outlines the implications for university educators, indicates the limitations of this chapter and suggests future research directions.

Research Design

Theoretical Framework

The theoretical framework (Figure 8.1) presents three dimensions (i.e., body, mind, and spirit) of human capital, and it indicates the four dimensions of wisdom pedagogy: affective, cognitive, behavioral, and spiritual dimensions (i.e., feelings and thinking, knowing, acting and reflecting, and knowing-why). The theoretical framework utilizes the literature on intellectual and human capital (e.g., Goldin, 2016; Roos et al., 1997; Sullivan, 1998). Human capital is defined (Sullivan, 1998, p. 5) as 'know that' (factual, historical, scientific, explicit knowledge) and 'know how' (practical, tacit knowledge), skills and abilities of a person. Roos et al. (1997, pp. 34–41) argue that "the value of human capital originates from competence, attitude and intellectual agility" (Roos et al., 1997, p. 35). They add that competence comprises knowledge and skills, and attitude depends on motivation, behavior, and conduct. Intellectual agility (e.g., innovation, imitation, adaptation, turning an idea into a product or service) is the ability to transfer knowledge. "If competence is the content, intellectual agility is the ability to use the knowledge and skills, building on it, applying it in practical contexts and increasing it through learning" (Roos et al., 1997, p. 39). Goldin (2016), in her essay, focuses on the two main components of human capital, i.e., education and training and health. She defines human capital as "the stock of productive skills, talents, health, and expertise of the labor force, just as physical capital is the stock of plant, equipment, machines, and tools" (Goldin, 2016, p. 83). While education is essential in increasing the capacity and capability of human capital, the author of this chapter argues that Goldin's definition lacks values, attitudes, authenticity, and responsibility of the human capital, which are parts of the spiritual dimension of wisdom pedagogy (Figure 8.1).

The concept of 'spiritual knowledge' described by Bratianu (2015) is connected to the spiritual dimension of wisdom pedagogy (Figure 8.1). According to Bratianu, spiritual knowledge is related to human existence, aspirations, and motivation because it contains possible answers to questions concerning our existence in society, on Earth, and in the Universe; it gives life or vitality to persons' existence; it embraces our most profound sense of existence; it reflects the essence of any human aspiration and the kernel of any strategic thinking, and it embraces our living aspirations and motivations. He also sees a tight connection between spiritual knowledge and values, ethics, decisions, and actions because it embraces the values and ethical principles we live by and ways of embedding these in our lives and work; it is about our values in society and organizations; it is intrinsically related to the vision and values of organization leadership; it is the third fundamental component of the triple helix of knowledge, i.e., it integrates dynamically with rational knowledge and emotional knowledge; it is beyond our biological body and the physical environment of the company, and it influences our decisions and actions.

When knowledge is becoming abundant, there is an increased need for wisdom. Figure 8.1 builds (1) on Ardelt's (2003, 2004, p. 275) three-dimensional wisdom (i.e., cognitive, reflective, affective); (2) on Bangen et al.'s (2013) the most commonly used subcomponents in 24 wisdom definitions (i.e., knowledge of life, prosocial values, self-understanding, acknowledgment of uncertainty, emotional homeostasis, tolerance, openness, spirituality, and sense of humor), (3) on Bassett's (2011) wisdom model of four elements (i.e., cognitive, affective, active, and reflective), and (4) on Sternberg and Karami's (2021) 6Ps model of wisdom (i.e., purpose, problems, person, process, products, press).

Ardelt (2004, p. 275) defines cognitive dimension (cf., the intersection of body and mind in Figure 8.1) as an "understanding of life and a desire to know the truth, i.e., to comprehend the significance and deeper meaning of phenomena and events, particularly about intrapersonal and interpersonal matters. Includes knowledge and acceptance of the positive and negative aspects of human nature, of the inherent limits of knowledge, and of life's unpredictability and uncertainties". She defines reflective dimension (cf., intersection of body and spirit in Figure 8.1) as a "perception of phenomena and events from multiple perspectives. Requires self-examination, self-awareness and self-insight". The affective dimension of wisdom means being sympathetic and having compassionate love for others (cf., intersection of mind and spirit in Figure 8.1).

Bangen et al. (2013) argue that the "most commonly included subcomponents, which appeared in more than half of the definitions are (1) social decision making and pragmatic knowledge of life, which relates to social reasoning, ability to give good advice, life knowledge, and life skills; (2) prosocial attitudes and behaviors, which include empathy, compassion, warmth, altruism, and a sense of fairness; (3) reflection and self-understanding, which relates to introspection, insight, intuition, and self-knowledge and awareness; (4) acknowledgment of and coping effectively with uncertainty; and (5) emotional homeostasis, which relates to affecting regulation and self-control" (Bangen et al., 2013, p. 1256).

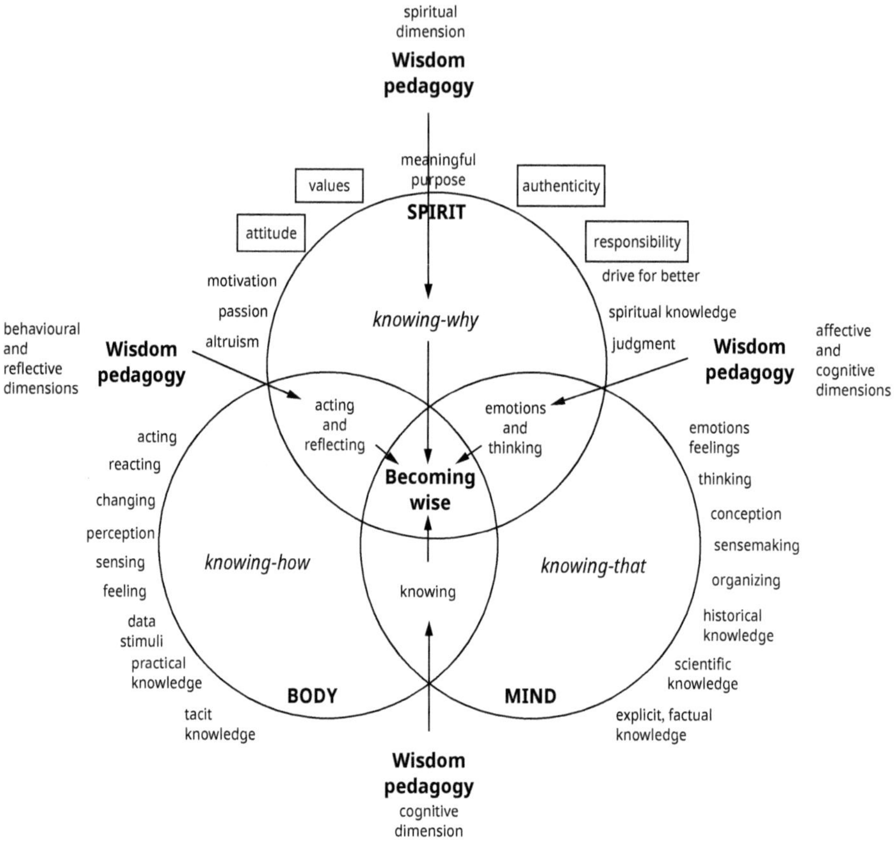

Figure 8.1: Theoretical framework.
Source: Author

According to Sternberg and Karami (2021), the six Ps of wisdom are: "the (a) Purpose of wisdom, (b) environmental/situational Press that produce wisdom, (c) nature of Problems requiring wisdom, (d) cognitive, metacognitive, affective, and conative (motivational) aspects of Persons who are wise, (e) psychological Processes underlying wisdom, and (f) Products of wisdom" (Sternberg & Karami, 2021, p. 4). They also note that the purpose of wisdom is an essential drive of wisdom (Sternberg & Karami, 2021, pp. 6–8); therefore, in the theoretical framework, meaningful purpose (Figure 8.1) is a component of the spiritual dimension of human capital.

The five main concepts of this chapter are values, attitudes, authenticity, responsibility, and wisdom pedagogy. They will be thoroughly discussed in separate sections. In brief, the theoretical framework combines characteristics of human capital, wisdom, and education (i.e., wisdom pedagogy). Figure 8.1 indicates the intersection of body, mind, and spirit as a person is the 'becoming wise' process. This chapter argues that the combination of *knowing-that* (episteme, epistemology), *knowing-how* (techne, ontology) and *knowing-why* (phronesis, practical wisdom, axiology) are the dimensions of wisdom pedagogy. This chapter focuses on the spiritual dimension of wisdom pedagogy, specifically on forming a student's values, attitudes, authenticity, and responsibility (Figure 8.1).

Research Problem, Questions and Objectives

The risks and problems (WEF, 2021, 2022; UN, 2015) in the world push the university to rethink its mission, vision, values, and its future role in society. Moving to a better world (Maxwell, 2021a) depends on how people will prevent and solve societal problems. There is a decisive role of university pedagogy in this process. Because universities mainly focus on enhancing learners' cognitive capabilities, knowledge, skills and competencies, it is time to rethink their existing curricula and pedagogy and focus on shaping learners' values, attitudes, authenticity, and responsibility. Therefore, the main research question is ***RQ***: *How can wisdom pedagogy shape human development in higher education?* The aim is to find out how the spiritual dimension of human capital could be shaped with wisdom pedagogy and to ponder how the university's values impact the values of learners.

The following sub-questions will help to answer the main research question. ***RQ1:*** *Why do universities exist?* – The objectives are to explore the university's missions from the literature and provide examples from the missions of 14 Finnish Universities of Sciences (USCs). ***RQ2:*** *Why is there a need for rethinking the roles of the university?* – The objectives are to explore the '*ecological university*' as a possible form of the future university and to give an example of the vision of 14 Finnish USCs. ***RQ3:*** *How can learners be successful actors addressing wicked social and natural environmental problems?* – The objectives are to explore '*ecological curriculum*' and '*wisdom pedagogy*'. In addition, the aim is to clarify what attitudes and values learners need in a super complex world to act with authenticity and responsibility.

Research Methodology and Methods

The methodology (research philosophy) is interpretivism. The reality (ontology), the phenomenon of this chapter, is socially constructed; it has multiple interpretations, and the social and natural environments as a context of this research are in constant flux evolution. The knowledge about this reality (epistemology) is gained through studying literature, analyzing qualitative data, and personal experience. Axiology is value-bound because the author's values, beliefs, and experience in HE are crucial to her topic selection, understanding, interpretations of the data, contribution, and conclusions.

The research method is qualitative data analysis. First, the missions, visions and values of 14 Finnish USCs were collected based on their web pages (Data Sources).

Then, the keywords were identified from the free texts, and finally, word clouds were created to visualize the most frequently mentioned keywords. The findings and their interpretations are presented in the discussion section. This chapter utilizes HE-related research findings and literature.

Five Key Concepts of the Spiritual Dimension of Human Capital

The five main concepts of this chapter are values, attitudes, authenticity, responsibility, and wisdom pedagogy (Figure 8.1). According to the OECD (2019) Learning Compass 2030, competencies are knowledge, skills, attitudes and values. Values and attitudes augment the earlier definition of competence because they are needed for learners to set a goal, reflect, and act in an evolving environment.

Values

Philosophers Plato, Aristotle, Seneca, Spinoza, Kant, Hegel, and others discussed value and values, good and goodness, and beauty and aesthetics in their works (Durant, 1954). Values are discussed in philosophy, history, religion, sociology, psychology, anthropology, behavioral sciences, business, education, and research. As a concept, 'value' has many understandings and dimensions. It can be defined from different perspectives, such as economic value (financial value, profit, wealth, real estate value, market value, value to customers, value from suppliers, utility value, value networks, value chain), social value (community values, family values), cultural value (historical values, art, religion, believes), and human values (moral values, goodness, loyalty, trust, ethical values, rightness, justice, independence, freedom).

In the 20th century, the theory of value or axiology was developed. Axiology studies the role of value and ethics. Runes (1966, p. 32–33) discusses four problems of axiology: (1) the nature of value experience (pleasure, interest, apprehension, unity of personality, enhancement of life); (2) the types of value (good, true, beauty, holy, bodily well-being); (3) the criterion of value, standards for testing values (quantity of pleasure, rational norms, ideals, wholeness, coherence, inclusiveness, biological survival), and (4) the metaphysical status of value or its relation to the facts in natural sciences (subjectivism, logical objectivism, metaphysical objectivism).

According to work psychologists George and Jones (1997), values have a future perspective, i.e., how things should be in the future; they have a general focus, i.e., human approaches to life, and they are relatively stable over long periods. Values could be quantified from specific perspectives, but we mostly think about 'values' in qualitative terms. People have not one but many values. In the context of this chapter, 'values' are viewed as qualitative human values, as drivers of human behavior, and as something good humans strive for in their lives. Values are formed throughout life by family, friends, school, work, culture, and other social life relationships and experiences. Arnold et al. (2017, p. 242) argue that "values are a person's beliefs about what is good or desirable in life. They are long-term guides for a person's choices and experiences". Ethics defines values as necessary and reasonable, guiding actions and showing how to live a good life. In ethics, they argue that some core values do not change, and some values could change. Ethical values help people make judgments and decide what is good and wrong. Values influence mindset, attitudes and actions (Figure 8.1). Values guide the behavior and actions of persons (Arnold et al., 2017) toward a good life, impacting the social and natural world. This chapter aims to explore the impacts of university pedagogy on the formation of values of learners.

Attitudes

Attitudes are necessary because they help people to make sense of their environment, they help people to interpret situations, and evaluate what is good and what is evil (i.e., the cognitive dimension of attitude). Attitudes help people to act effectively in their social and natural environment (i.e., the behavioral dimension of attitudes). Attitudes help us build and maintain good human relationships, empathize, sympathize with others, and care about others (i.e., attitudes' social and affective dimensions). Attitudes help us understand who we are (self-identity) and our values (self-esteem).

There are attitudes to society, others, education, learning, work, and nature. Arnold et al. (2017, pp. 238–274) discuss attitudes at work and argue that attitudes are not value-free not neutral; they are linked to behavior, can predict behavior, are specific, can change by events, and attitude surveys can measure them. They argue that "attitude' is usually taken to mean the cognitive and affective components. Behavior is often constructed as an outcome of attitudes" (Arnold et al., 2017, p. 241). Interestingly, they believe that attitudes can change values. There is a close interrelation between attitudes and values. It is not generally possible to say the cause of the other. In specific cases and situations, however, it is possible to identify which played a higher role in changing the other. This relationship between values, attitudes, and behavior is presented in Figure 8.1. This chapter focuses on attitudes, values, authenticity, and responsibility because they are integral parts of the spiritual dimension of human capital and influence a person's behavior and actions (Figure 8.1) in the natural and social environment to create a better world.

Authenticity

Authenticity is a complex concept. The "*know thyself*" is one of the three Delphic aphorisms. For people, it is essential to know who they are, their culture, and their roots and values. Knowing ourselves, self-awareness, and being true to ourselves determine our thinking, choices, decisions, and actions. This chapter argues that authenticity is more than knowing yourself. It is a personal characteristic that expresses itself in behavior, actions, and practicing beliefs, values, and principles. It also means permanency, maintaining our true selves in all life situations.

Kernis and Goldman (2006, pp. 283–357) discuss the philosophical and psychological views of authentic functioning. They argue that authenticity from a philosophical point of view is related to ontology and phenomenology. According to them, "authentic functioning is characterized in terms of people's (1) self-understanding, (2) openness to objectively recognizing their ontological realities (e.g., evaluating their desirable and undesirable self-aspects), (3) actions, and (4) orientation towards interpersonal relationships" (Kernis & Goldman, p. 284). They define authenticity as the "unimpeded operation of one's true- or core-self in one's daily enterprise" (Kernis & Goldman, 2006, p. 344), and they describe four components of authenticity such as (1) awareness (i.e., knowing yourself, your motives, emotions, preferences, and abilities); (2) unbiased processing; (3) behavior (i.e., act authentically, consistently with your values and needs, even at the risk of criticism or rejection), and (4) relational orientation (i.e., being in close contact with others, being tolerant, compassionate, accepting of otherness, being truthful and honest) (Kernis & Goldman, 2006, pp. 293–301).

Responsibility

The concept of responsibility is multi-dimensional and it can be viewed as (1) an individual responsibility for family members, friends, and peers; (2) social responsibility means being responsible at work, in relationships, with superiors, employees, leadership responsibilities for people's well-being and safety, managerial responsibility for the results and performance of the organization; (3) universal responsibility that comprises environmental, legal, moral and ethical responsibilities, and (4) as responsibility for science, research, applying valid data, avoiding 'fake' data and information, and for applying knowledge for the benefit of society and people (Jakubik, 2022).

Being responsible in all actions could cause pressure on a person. Work psychologists Arnold et al. (2005) claim that people who face high-level organizational responsibility for employees, people's well-being, health and safety, for physical assets, equipment, budget, financial performance, innovation, trade secrets, and the environment could suffer from a high level of stress and health problems (Arnold et al., 2005, pp. 401–402).

Wisdom Pedagogy

The main goal of HE is human development. University pedagogy plays a direct and central role in human development and indirectly in creating a sustainable future for the natural and social environment. Pedagogy has different approaches regarding learners' age and state (physical, mental, emotional). Pedagogy is applied for children, adults, physically challenged, and learners with disabilities (hearing, seeing, speaking, reading and writing difficulties, neurodevelopmental disorder, and autism). Pedagogy differs also in learning different subjects (natural sciences, physics, mathematics, chemistry, management, social sciences, research, and so on). Pedagogy is influenced by challenges (WEF, 2021, 2022; UN, 2015), culture, trends, developments, and innovations in the social and natural environment (Figure 8.1). The COVID-19 pandemic shifted learning from the physical to virtual space. Therefore, pedagogy must be based on technology with virtual connections for learning. Technology development, artificial intelligence, and robotization influence pedagogy as well. Approaches to learning could be constructivist (reversed classroom, distance assignment, problem-based learning), collaborative (work-based learning, project-based learning, teamwork, guest lecturers), integrative (tutorials, debates, applying concepts, theories in practice), inquiry-based (research problem, scenarios, case study, role play), and reflective (discussion, feedback seminar, sharing learning experiences, giving constructive feedback).

University pedagogy is multidisciplinary. It can be approached from philosophy, educational philosophy, psychology, social psychology, sociology, and many other perspectives (e.g., brain science, technology, AI). This chapter focuses on university pedagogy from an educational philosophy perspective. Philosophy focuses on human development, existence, being and reality (ontology). It explores knowledge (epistemology), learning, intelligence, education, mind, ethics, morals, virtues, goodness, wisdom, truth, courage, beauty, happiness, passion, values, attitudes, and actions. It deals with religion, society, science, art, and human and environmental relationships. In brief, philosophy focuses on the fundamental issues of life (Durant, 1954). Educational philosophy has different orientations, like realism, idealism, and pragmatism. Pragmatic educational philosophy is the most relevant to this chapter. Pragmatism in education means concerns for social problems, exploring challenges and solving/preventing/influencing them, the social construction of knowledge, changing and shaping society and nature, and creating the future. The philosophy of education studies values, norms, educational practices, pedagogy, and their connectedness with the natural and social environment. Therefore, the philosophical approach to education is relevant and suitable to the aims of this chapter.

This chapter explores how the spiritual dimension of human capital can be formed with wisdom pedagogy in HE. Since 2000, wisdom in HE has started to receive more attention (Ardelt & Bruya, 2020; Bruya & Ardelt, 2018a, 2018b; Diamond, 2021; Gidley, 2012; Grossmann & Kung, 2019; Hashim et al., 2014; Henderson & Kesson, 2001; Jakubik, 2020b, 2020b, 2021, 2022; Maxwell, 2012, 2014, 2019a, 2019b, 2021a, 2021b; Nylander, 2015; Sternberg, 2001; Yusoffi et al., 2018). However, wisdom research in HE has been ignored for a long time. Diamond (2021) argues that only a "few modern scholars focus their research efforts on understanding how an individual human comes to apprehend something like wisdom and examining how it can be taught, seeking a solution to the question of whether it is possible to teach the development of *wisdom (pedagogy)*, what might be its constituent parts (curriculum), and if yes, then *how to develop wisdom in the current era*" (Diamond, 2021, pp. 9–10, emphases added). Nevertheless, wisdom pedagogy is just emerging, and its role in human development needs more understanding.

Findings and Discussion

The findings are discussed in the three sub-questions of this chapter. They emerged from the reviewed literature and secondary quantitative data. Examples of the mission, vision, and values of Finnish USCs in Figure 8.2 are created based on qualitative data from earlier research (Jakubik, 2021a, pp. 7–10). First, the mission, vision, and value statements were collected from the web pages of 14 Finnish USCs (Data Sources). Then, the keywords were identified from the free texts, and word clouds (Figure 8.2) were generated by freely available software (https://worditout.com/word-cloud/create).

Why Do Universities Exist?

The objectives were to explore the university's missions from the literature and provide examples. The examples are based on the mission statements announced on the web pages (Data Sources) of 14 Finnish USCs. Finnish USCs were selected based on the author's over two decades of experience in Finnish HE and accessible data availability. In Finland, there are 14 USCs in the HE system, of which ten are multidisciplinary, and four are specialized universities. There are 35 higher educational institutions. "A total of 13 universities and 22 universities of applied sciences operate in the Ministry of Education and Culture's administrative branch" (HEIs, 2022). The 14th USC is the National Defense University, which operates under the defense administration. As of August 2005, USCs and universities of applied sciences (UASs) provide master's degrees. According to the Finnish Ministry of Education and Culture, "to guarantee the freedom of science, the arts and higher education, universities are autonomous actors. Universities are independent legal entities with the right to make independent decisions on matters related to their internal administration" (HEIs, 2022).

Universities are social institutions. "Universities of sciences are multidisciplinary and regional higher education institutions with strong connections to business and industries as well as to regional development" (Laakso-Manninen & Tuomi, 2020, p. 16). They perform four primary activities: education, research, management, and community engagement (Jorge & Peña, 2017). The findings of more recent empirical research correspond with this. Jakubik (2021a) argues that the main features and roles of a university are: (1) to educate, develop, learn, grow, and provide degrees; (2) to be an organization, place, space, and infrastructure for learning; (3) to create knowledge, do research, and (4) to share knowledge with partners in its social community. Universities play essential roles in the learning society. They are closely intertwined with the social and natural environment and are connected. They contribute to all 17 sustainable development goals of the United Nations (2015). The seven dimensions of the university's social responsibility are organizational governance, human rights, work practices, environment, legal practices, consumer issues, community involvement and development (Sousa et al., 2021).

In brief, the objective was to demonstrate how universities see their mission in society and how university practitioners see the current roles of the university (Jakubik, 2021a). The mission, vision, and values of the university answer the following questions: 'Why does the university exist?', 'What does the university hope to achieve?', and 'With what guiding principles does the university act?'. According to the mission statements. Universities exist in society to do research and provide education, focus on knowledge and science, connect to the community and business, and be multidisciplinary and international. As a justification for these concluding remarks, I refer to small-scale, online research (Jakubik, 2021a), where questions like what a university is (24 answers) and what the goal of university education is (17 answers) were asked from university practitioners and higher educational participants. Jakubik writes, "The online research indicated that a university is not only an institution, a place but also a social community with special values. The goal of HE is not only to provide students knowledge, skills, and tools but, most importantly, to develop identities, inspire, and achieve societal impacts by applying knowledge to create a civilized world" (Jakubik, 2021a).

The objectives were to explore the '*ecological university*' as a possible form of the future university and to give an example of the vision of 14 Finnish USCs. Educational researchers (Barnett, 2011, 2015, 2018; Jakubik, 2021a; Morley, 2012; Rothblatt, 2012; Standaert, 2012) are looking for new ideas and possibilities for the university. Morley has set up a research agenda for the university of the future and argues that gender, academic values and standards, environmental sustainability, critical knowledge, and opportunity and wealth distribution topics will need to be addressed (Morley, 2012, pp. 26–35). Rothblatt argues that "the multiversity of the twenty-first century, by definition, is a house of many mansions. No single idea prevails, but many exist" (Rothblatt, 2012, p. 24). Standaert writes that the network society brings a fundamental paradigm shift in HE by shifting learning from place to space. He claims that "universities in the future will not only be places of knowledge "production" or of "virtual communication" but also spaces of encounters. One challenge for networked universities is to become in new ways such privileged spaces of encounters. This supposes an ethos of a renewed attention to "in-betweenness," to concrete places where the actors (teachers, students, researchers) encounter each other by treating each other as subjects" (Standaert, 2012, p. 93).

Educational philosopher Barnett proposes the 'ecological university' concept as a feasible future university formation. It is relevant to this chapter as it seeks to find out how the university of the future can enhance learners' capabilities. The university of the future can have different orientations and forms: the metaphysical university, the entrepreneurial university, the open university, the civic university, the liquid university, the postmodern university, the pragmatic university, the therapeutic university, and the ecological university (Barnett, 2011; Barnett, 2015, p. 67). The most feasible idea of the future university is the '*ecological university*' (i.e., utopian university), which is a developmental university that develops human beings as such; it develops personal transferable skills of learners for the world of work; it develops knowledge in-the-world and for-the-world; it develops life-world becoming competences; it develops emancipatory knowing, self-understanding, and critical view of knowledge; it is an authentic and responsible university; it cares about well-being of humans and the environment; it cares about and for the whole world, and it focuses on the sustainability of the whole world, not only the natural environment (Barnett, 2018).

The '*ecological university*' is socially responsible. Latif (2018) identifies a university's seven social responsibilities: community, philanthropic, ethical, legal, stakeholder, research, and operational responsibility. The university's social responsibility dimensions are stakeholders, organization patterns, community contributions, protecting nature, financial resources, reputation, and sustainability measurements (Kouatli, 2019). Nixon (2012) worries about the responsibilities of universities: "Universities of the future will continue to have multiple responsibilities, and academics will continue to be involved in a wide variety of practices relating to research, teaching, and scholarship. However, central to those responsibilities and practices will be a commitment to providing all students with a space to develop capabilities necessary to flourish as receptive and critical learners" (Nixon, 2012, p. 147). Nixon criticized the bureaucratic regimes of universities. "Universities of the future, then, have a vital part to play not only in sustaining and developing modes of practical reasoning or deliberation but in ensuring that these are not distorted through the imposition of wholly inappropriate bureaucratic requirements" (Nixon, 2012, p. 148).

Why is There a Need to Rethink the University's Roles?

The future roles and tasks of the university are at the center of the attention of educational philosophers and researchers (Allan, 2018; Auxier, 2018; Barnett, 2018, 2022; Jakubik, 2021a; Maxwell, 2021b). In a complex environment, to enable learning for an unknown future, the tasks of university education need to be redefined. Students must learn that they can question everything (e.g., data, information, fake news, knowledge) to understand the world around them. The main tasks of the university are "preparing students for a complex world, for a world in which incomplete judgments or decisions have to be made" and enabling students so that they "can prosper in a situation of multiple interpretations" (Barnett, 2015, p. 223). With all these, Allan proposes that the educators' primary task "should be to nurture neither learned scientists nor talented artists

Figure 8.2: Mission, vision, and values of fourteen Finnish Universities of Sciences.
Source: Author

and artisans, but good citizens" (Allan, 2018, p. 119). A more practical view is provided by Auxier, who has an agenda for educators and says, "Students must be assigned tasks to carry out and to bring back the results. . . . They must be interviewed closely about how they carried out these tasks within the general framework provided. They must be encouraged to think about alternative paths to complete tasks. These tasks must encourage initiative, experimentation with resources, and creativity – as well as patience, critical reflection, and thoroughness. Students must be taught the art and techniques of good judgment" (Auxier, 2018, p. 253).

There is a need to shift the educational focus of the university. Barnett claims that university education should focus more on ontological than epistemological tasks: "The educational task is, in principle, not an epistemological task; it is not one of knowledge or even knowing per se. It is not even one of action, of right and effective interventions worldwide. . . . Amid super complexity, the educational task is primarily an ontological task", i.e., how to be in the world (Barnett, 2015, p. 224). Qualitative research about the visions of the 14 Finnish USCs (Figure 8.2) shows that in the future, universities will seek to focus on research for society and sustainability in the world, with responsibility, education, solutions, and innovation. In the future, the university should have more collaboration and cooperation, less hierarchy, more flexibility, curiosity, new knowledge, and new ideas, and focus on continuous learning and education (Jakubik, 2021a).

To find their focus, universities continuously search for feedback from students. For example, quantitative and qualitative research is based on the feedback of MSc (Econ) graduates from 10 Finnish multidisciplinary USCs operating under the Ministry of Education and Culture. Feedback is regularly collected and analyzed (Helin, 2019; Nissilä, 2018; Ström, 2021; Teittinen, 2020). The research is based on large samples (2,300; 2,356; 2,430; 3,018 in 2017, 2018, 2019, and 2020, respectively). The response rates in each year were 68.7%, 76.2%, 71.9%, and 63.4%. In 2017, feedback from graduates indicated the need for more practical and less theoretical techniques in teaching, more practical business projects, more digital methods, and more feedback and interactions between students and staff (Nissilä, 2018, p. 6). In 2018, 20% of the respondents were not satisfied with the teaching methods, and 28% felt that the feedback from their teachers did not help their studies. However, 88% of the respondents felt satisfied with their studies and liked the excellent atmosphere of the university (Helin, 2019, p. 6). Graduates in 2019 expressed their need for more working life-oriented education, cooperation with companies, and more feedback from course teachers. "Respondents were dissatisfied with issues such as unemployment, current rates of pay, fixed-term employment contracts and the fact that their work does not correspond to their education" (Teittinen, 2020, p. 6). The latest survey in 2021 by Ström (2021, p. 7) indicates that graduates in 2020 were interested in digitalization, more working life orientation, and more cooperation with companies. Respondents mentioned the improvements in the digitalization of education and were satisfied with the offer of online courses. Similar to the earlier years, graduates expressed the need for more university company cooperation, more working life experience, and more feedback from teachers.

In brief, the quantitative surveys of master graduates indicated that the university of the future needs to focus more on (1) the connections with working life, with its social and natural environment; (2) the university pedagogy that helps the learners to develop, and (3) educators' role in providing more feedback to students to help their personal growth and to facilitate their becoming wise journey.

How can Learners Successfully Address Wicked Social and Natural Environmental Problems?

The objectives were to explore the *'ecological curriculum'* and *'wisdom pedagogy'*. In addition, the aim was to clarify what attitudes and values learners need in a super complex world to act with authenticity and responsibility. Pedagogical options for the future university are envisioned by Barnett (2018, p. 228). He presents the idea of the ecological university. He argues that the university is an institution that is intertwined in multiple ecologies, in seven ecosystems (Barnett, 2018, pp. 19, 56): the knowledge ecology, the ecology of social institutions, persons, the economy as an ecology, learning, culture, and the natural environment. Later, Barnett extended the number of ecosystems to eight by adding 'polity' to ecosystems (Barnett, 2022, p. 240). The natural ecosystem is only one of the ecosystems of the university. These eight university ecosystems are dynamic, evolving, changing over time, and interacting with each other.

Sustainability education requires the pedagogy of interconnectedness, which "underlines the essentiality of understanding of the world and humans as relational: recognizing the interdependence of society and nature, the local and global, and seeing the common reality as socially constructed and humanness and learning holistically" (Lehtonen et al., 2018, p. 860). Similarly, Wals and Benavot (2017) claim that education and lifelong learning play a vital role in enhancing learners' diverse viewpoints, crossing learning boundaries, community relationships, indigenous knowledge and practices, skills and competencies for life. They argue that *both* instrumental and emancipatory approaches are needed in education. While the first focuses on developing behaviors, the latter develops autonomous, responsible, reflective citizens with values, principles, and behavior toward solving environmental challenges. The emancipatory approach is supported by action-oriented, collaborative, participatory, and transformative learning (Wals & Benavot, 2017, p. 407).

Sustainability is understood in a broader sense than sustainability of the natural environment. Education has sustainability goals, too. There were 17 sustainable development goals identified by the United Nations (UN, 2015). The goal of quality education, i.e., to be inclusive and to ensure life-long learning opportunities for all, is relevant to this chapter. Concurring with Barnett (2018), the *ecological curriculum* of the university is connected with all ecosystems, not only with the natural ecosystem but also with the whole world. He argues that "the curriculum becomes an educational space for stretching the student into unfamiliar and unsettling spaces. *The ecological curriculum entices the student into venturing across the ecosphere of the university*" (Barnett, 2018, p. 114, emphasis original). The ecological curriculum enhances not only the cognitive capabilities of learners but also provides ethical guidelines and practical experiences. Similarly, Bratianu (2015) argues that business schools should have courses in their curricula related to spiritual knowledge "to make students understand that the real mission of any business is not maximizing the profit but creating value for society"

(Bratianu, 2015). The ecological curriculum is a complex, open system that influences its environment and is influenced by its environment.

The author of this chapter argues that ecological curriculum cannot prescribe a specific pedagogy that educators should apply. It requires educators' academic freedom, creativity and openness to apply pedagogical approaches according to students' learning journey. The ecological curriculum requires complex, multiple pedagogies, a kaleidoscope pedagogy of several approaches. This pedagogy is demanding, as it moves students to an unexplored territory by allowing them to explore new things, criticize, reflect upon and question their old assumptions, attitudes, and values, and see the world with different eyes. This pedagogy requires self-reflection, self-knowledge, complexity, freedom, curiosity, concern for the challenges in the world, wisdom, and courage. To address wicked problems in the world, we need comprehensive approaches to pedagogy that promote comprehensive thinking (Willamo et al., 2018, p. 3). Willamo et al. conclude, "University education focuses too much on specialized skills, making it difficult to promote a more comprehensive research and teaching approach. . . . The ability to think comprehensively is a valuable skill, and it can, and should be, taught and learned as any other academic skill. Therefore, university education should respond rapidly to the increasing need for comprehensive thinking and offer possibilities for students to develop their skills" (Willamo et al., 2018, p. 11).

The author of this chapter concurs with Gidley (2012, p. 50) that we need "a more holistic, creative, multifaceted, embodied and participatory approach" in education. Gidley (2012), as a psychologist and educator, writes that since 2000, several post-formal, postmodern, evolutionary pedagogies have emerged due to the 'megatrends of the mind'. She claims that new thinking patterns, new ways of knowing, and new educational paradigms and approaches significantly impact education. She supports "the need for the transition from formal, factory-model schooling and university education to a plurality of post formal – or evolutionary – pedagogies" because "it does not make any sense to educate in the 21st century for 19th-century mindsets" (Gidley, 2012, p. 48). She presents the 21st-century evolutionary pedagogies such as creative education, social and emotional education, spirituality education, holistic and integral education, critical and postcolonial pedagogies, postmodern and poststructuralist pedagogies, aesthetic and artistic education, ecology and sustainability, imaginative education, futures and foresight, complexity education, and *wisdom education* (Gidley, 2012, p. 51). While all these evolutionary pedagogies, or a particular mix of them, could shape learners' attitudes and values, probably the spirituality education, ecology sustainability and wisdom pedagogies are the most relevant to this chapter because they call for collaboration in solving the global crises of the world (UN, 2015; WEF, 2021, 2022).

There are four pedagogical options presented by Barnett (2015, p. 228) in a two-dimensional framework: educational development and educational transformation, and no risk and high risk. According to Barnett, there are four pedagogical options: (1) *'disciplinary initiation'* where the knowledge field is given (no risk, educational development option); (2) *'disciplinary wonder'* where the knowledge field is uncertain and open to change (high risk, educational development option); (3) *'generic skills'* where there are fixed ontologies for an unknown world (no risk, educational transformation option), and (4) *'human being as such'* where there are open ontologies for an unknown world (high risk, educational transformation option). The most relevant to this chapter is the last pedagogical option, i.e., the transformation of human beings, which allows learners to flourish (Figure 8.1). This pedagogy prepares learners for the uncertain world and its challenges. It also prepares learners to realize that their existing knowledge might not be enough to solve the world's wicked problems; it prepares them to seek new knowledge and learn for life. This pedagogy cares about learners as human beings. It develops not only their cognitive competencies (*what* to know, theories, concepts) and their operational competencies (*how* to know, skills), but most importantly, this pedagogy develops their curiosity, and enhances their values and attitudes, and their reflective competencies (*why* to know, practical wisdom). This is why it could be called *'wisdom pedagogy'*.

Educational scholars (Arlin, 1999; Bassett, 2005; Hart, 2001; Henderson & Kesson, 2004; Jakubik, 2020b; Sternberg, 2001) argue that teaching wisdom is not easy but possible. Arlin (1999) presents her developmental model of teaching. She argues that the six characteristics of a wise person (identified by Sternberg) could be applied to *wise teachers*: an understanding of the meaning and the limits to what is known, the search for the understanding of others' thinking, judiciousness, understanding of ambiguity, interest in understanding what is known and what meaning to attach to it, and an appreciation of context. Jakubik (2020b) presented a model of cultivating practical wisdom in education, and she predicts that a new educational paradigm is evolving (Jakubik, 2020c). Bassett (2005, pp. 4–5) argues that transformative learning pedagogy could help teach wisdom and presents an emergent wisdom model and its characteristics. In this model, wisdom's cognitive, affective, active, and reflective dimensions form a holistic system. However, from this model, the spiritual dimension of wisdom is missing. Concurring with Bassett, the author of this chapter believes that asking questions in teaching situations like: "What guides my actions? To what ends are my actions directed? What means do I use? What are my values? How do I live with them? Who or what is the "I" that I think I am? What am I part of?" (Bassett, 2005, p. 5) facilitates the becoming wise capabilities of students; they could contribute to forming the spiritual dimension of human capital (Figure 8.1).

When everything evolves fast in the contexts (place, space, time), related HE ecosystems, and the social and natural environment, attitudes, values, authenticity, and responsibility should be at the heart of human becoming. This chapter argues that university pedagogy would help learners become authentic, take responsibility, and act in the world for the benefit of all. The Learning Compass 2030 of the OECD (2019) claims that values such as respect, fairness, personal and social responsibility, integrity, and self-awareness make students capable of acting for the well-being of society and the natural environment. Similarly, Barnett (2015, p. 200) argues that values closely related to HE in the learning society are courage, carefulness, resilience, self-restraint, integrity, and respect for others. From the value statements of 14 Finnish USCs (Data Sources), the following primary values emerged: responsibility, openness, courage, well-being, criticality, and diversity. Integrity, appreciation, equality, trust, freedom, integrity, and quality were frequently mentioned (Figure 8.2).

In brief, wisdom pedagogy enhances the spiritual dimension of human capital (Figure 8.1) by focusing on the formation of the whole human beings and the environment, on the values, attitudes, responsibility, and authenticity of persons. The spiritual dimension of wisdom pedagogy contributes to the human journey of becoming wise.

Conclusions and Implications

Based on qualitative and quantitative data, this chapter sought to answer the central question of *how human development can be shaped by wisdom pedagogy in higher education* by exploring the three sub-questions. The key findings are:

1. In postmodern society, the university is not an 'ivory tower' of knowledge. It is an organic, integral, and essential part of the social and natural environment; it is intertwined and highly interconnected with the social and natural ecosystems (Barnett, 2018, 2022; Gidley, 2012; Huang & Do, 2021; Kouatli, 2019; Laakso-Manninen & Tuomi, 2020; Lehtonen et al., 2018; UN, 2015).
2. The future university is an '*ecological university*' that is authentic and responsible; it develops human beings as such; it cares for the whole world (Barnett, 2018; Jakubik, 2020b, 2022; Kouatli, 2019; Latif, 2018).
3. The university is influenced by its ecosystems (Maxwell, 2021a, 2021b; WEF, 2021) while actively shaping its context. The university follows the needs of its students (Helin, 2019; Nissilä, 2018; Ström, 2021; Teittinen, 2020); it follows the social and environmental trends, developments, and challenges (WEF, 2021, 2022). It is shaping the values, attitudes, authenticity and responsibility, i.e., the becoming wise process of learners (Figure 8.1) by applying a mix of evolutionary, participative university pedagogies (Gidley, 2012) and with the wisdom pedagogy (Arlin, 1999; Barnett, 2015; Bassett, 2005; Hart, 2001; Henderson & Kesson, 2004; Jakubik, 2020b, 2021a; Sternberg, 2001). The university helps learners flourish in a complex environment and act for the whole world's benefit.

Implications for Educators, Management and Curriculum Developers

University educators are vital in shaping their students' becoming wise (Figure 8.1) journey. The university's mission, vision and values (Figure 8.2) impact educators and learners. Educators are in close contact with their students; they know their needs, strengths, weaknesses, ambitions, motivation, attitudes, and values. Therefore, educators should be able to turn the 'pedagogy kaleidoscope' of complex, multiple, participative, transformative, collaborative, and evolutionary pedagogies (Gidley, 2012) and apply the mix of appropriate pedagogies for the benefit of their students.

The university curriculum and the university management should support the role of educators. Educators need academic freedom to decide what pedagogical mix is appropriate in what situations. Educators must be educated in evolutionary educational pedagogies to become wise teachers (Arlin, 1999) and teach their students wisdom (Bassett, 2005; Hart, 2001; Henderson & Kesson, 2004; Jakubik, 2020b; Sternberg, 2001). Wisdom pedagogy and practical wisdom are highly needed in our complex, interconnected world with wicked problems to be solved (Jakubik, 2020b, 2022; Maxwell, 2021a).

The role of educators is not to please their students but to challenge them, make them think, motivate them to share and apply their knowledge, enhance their skills, moral, and ethical capacities, increase their curiosity and criticality, lead them to unexplored territories where they can be creative thinkers and problem solvers. In brief, educators should enhance the authenticity and responsibility of students and support their growth as authentic and responsible human beings. Educators have an impact on the future of the world by shaping the values, attitudes, and actions of learners.

The role of educators is changing in the 21st century when new educational paradigms are evolving to replace the formal, factory-type of university education with evolutionary, participative learning pedagogies (Gidley, 2012). Educators are not only teachers who transfer their knowledge but also mentors, counselors, and learning process facilitators (Jakubik, 2020c). They could also be role models for their students. They should not only be accessible but available for their students. Educators need empathy, understanding, and flexibility; they must listen to and learn from the students.

Implications for Educational Researchers

The limitations of this chapter are that it builds on a limited number of references. The qualitative data of missions, visions, and values of 14 USCs are from one country (Figure 8.2). The diversity of the university pedagogies is not fully covered, and empirical data and reflections from students and educators are omitted. These limitations offer future research directions. Educational researchers could further explore the values, attitudes, behavior, and action relationships. The references could be extended by undertaking a systematic literature review. Examples could be brought from other countries and, this way, validate or reject the findings of this chapter. The reflections from students and educators could be collected and analyzed. Furthermore, future research could develop case studies or apply action research and find out how evolutionary pedagogies are applied in practice. The concept of '*wisdom pedagogy*' as an emerging new university pedagogy also requires more understanding.

To conclude, this chapter explored how university educators can shape human development, i.e., the becoming wise process of learners with quality education, ecological curriculum, and wisdom pedagogy. This topic is contemporary because of humanity's global social, environmental, moral, and ethical crises. There is a need to pay more attention to developing learners as human beings, helping them to make the right decisions and act for the benefit of all. The novelty of this chapter is in providing a theoretical framework (Figure 8.1) that presents how the three dimensions (i.e., body-mind-spirit) of human capital together with the four dimensions of wisdom pedagogy (i.e., feeling and thinking, knowing, acting and reflecting, and the spiritual dimension of knowing-why) together lead to becoming wise of persons. This chapter emphasizes the central role of the forgotten spiritual dimension of wisdom pedagogy and draws attention to evolutionary pedagogies and the emerging '*wisdom pedagogy*'. Examples of the mission, vision and values of 14 Finnish USCs (Figure 8.2) underline the need for pedagogical changes. Regardless of its limitations, the author believes that this chapter raises vital issues, and she concurs with Durant, "We are all imperfect teachers, but we may be forgiven if we have advanced the matter a little, and have done our best" (Durant, 1954, p. xv).

Author's note

The first version of this chapter has been presented at the European Academy of Management (EURAM) Conference "*Transforming Business for Good*", at the Trinity Business School Dublin, Ireland, on 14–16 June 2023, and it has been included in the conference proceedings.

Data Sources

Aalto University, https://act.aalto.fi/en/strategy, https://act.aalto.fi/en/our-strategy/our-purpose-values-and-way-of-working (accessed: 28 December, 2021).
Åbo Akademi University, https://www.abo.fi/en/about-abo-akademi-university/ (accessed: 28 December, 2021).
Hanken School of Economics, https://www.hanken.fi/en/about-hanken/hanken/mission-and-vision, https://www.hanken.fi/en/about-hanken/hanken/strategies accessed: 28 December 2021, https://www.hanken.fi/system/files/2021-01/hanken_in_a_nutshell_2020_eng_0.pdf (accessed: 28 December, 2021).
Lappeenranta-Lahti University of Technology (LUT), https://www.lut.fi/web/en/get-to-know-us/introducing-the-university/strategy (accessed: 28 December, 2021).
National Defense University, https://www.ndu.edu/About/Vision-Mission/ (accessed: 28 December, 2021).
Tampere University, https://www.tuni.fi/en/about-us/tampere-university/strategy-and-key-information?navref=liftup-links-link (accessed: 28 December, 2021).
University of Eastern Finland, https://www.uef.fi/en/strategy-2030 (accessed: 28 December, 2021).

University of Helsinki, https://www.helsinki.fi/en/about-us/basic-information (accessed: 28 December, 2021).
University of Jyväskylä, https://www.jyu.fi/en/university/strategy-2030 (accessed: 28 December, 2021).
University of Lapland, https://www.ulapland.fi/EN/About-us/Strategy (accessed: 28 December, 2021).
University of Oulu, Strategy of the University of Oulu | University of Oulu, https://www.oulu.fi/en/university-values (accessed: 28 December, 2021).
University of the Arts of Helsinki, https://www.uniarts.fi/en/general-info/vision-mission-and-values/ (accessed: 28 December, 2021).
University of Turku, https://www.utu.fi/en/university/university-strategy-2030 (accessed: 28 December, 2021).
University of Vaasa, https://www.uwasa.fi/en/university/strategy-and-values (accessed: 28 December, 2021).

References

Allan, G. (2018). The Conversation of a University. In A. Stoller, and E. Kramer (Eds) (2018). *Contemporary Philosophical Proposals for the University: Toward a Philosophy of Higher Education*. Cham, Switzerland: Palgrave, MacMillan, Springer Nature, Chapter 6, pp. 103–121.
Ardelt, M. & Bruya, B. (2020). Three-Dimensional Wisdom and Perceived Stress among College Students. *Journal of Adult Development*, Springer, published online 11 July 2020, https://doi.org/10.1007/s10804-020-09358-w.
Ardelt, M. (2003). An empirical assessment of a three-dimensional wisdom scale. *Research on Aging, 25(3)*, pp. 275–324. https://doi.org/10.1177/0164027503025003004.
Ardelt, M. (2004). Wisdom as Expert Knowledge System: A Critical Review of a Contemporary Operationalization of an Ancient Concept. *Human Development*, 47, pp. 257–285, https://doi.org/10.1159/000079154
Arlin, P. K. (1999). The wise teacher: a developmental model of teaching. *Theory into Practice*, 38, pp. 12–17. Available: https://www.jstor.org/stable/1477202 (accessed: 04 January, 2022).
Arnold, J., Silvester, J., Patterson, F., Robertson, I., Cooper, C., & Burnes, B. (2017). Work Psychology: Understanding Human Behaviour in the Workplace. 4th Edition, Harlow: Pearson Education Limited. Chapter 7, Attitudes at work, pp. 238–274.
Auxier, R. (2018). The coming revolution in (higher) education: Process, time, and singularity. In A. Stoller, and E. Kramer (Eds.) (2018). *Contemporary Philosophical Proposals for the University: Toward a Philosophy of Higher Education*. Cham, Switzerland: Palgrave, MacMillan, Springer Nature, Part V: Future Inquiry: Higher Education in the Coming Century, Chapter 11, pp. 217–260.
Bachmann, C., Habisch, A., & Dierksmeier, C. (2018). Practical Wisdom: Management's No Longer Forgotten Virtue. *J Bus Ethics*, *153*, pp. 147–165.
Baltes, P. B., & Staudinger, U. M. (2000). Wisdom. A metaheuristic (pragmatic) to orchestrate mind and virtue toward excellence, *American Psychologist*, *55*(1), pp. 122–136, https://doi.org/10.1037//0003-066x.55.1.122.
Banerjee, A. (2014). Knowledge and Wisdom Management, Google Scholar, available at: http://www.delhibusinessreview.org/v_2n2/dbrv2n2p.pdf (accessed 25 May 2021).
Bangen, K. J., Meeks, T. W., & Jeste, D. V. (2013). Defining and Assessing Wisdom: A Review of the Literature. *Am J Geriatr and Psychiatry*, Vol. 21, No. 12, pp. 1254–1266. http://dx.doi.org/10.1016/j.jagp.2012.11.020.
Barnett, R. (1994). *The Limits of Competence. Knowledge, Higher Education and Society*. Buckingham: The Society for Research into Higher Education (SRHE) and Open University Press Imprint.

Barnett, R. (2011). *Being a University*. London: Routledge, Foundations and Futures of Education Series, Taylor & Francis Group.
Barnett, R. (2015). T*hinking and Rethinking of University: The selected works of Ronald Barnett*. New York: World Library of Educationalists, Routledge, Taylor & Francis Group.
Barnett, R. (2018). *The Ecological University: A Feasible Utopia*. New York: Routledge, Taylor & Francis Group, Chapter 8, Sightings of an ecological curriculum, pp. 113–125.
Barnett, R. (2022). *The Philosophy of Higher Education. A Critical Introduction*. London: Routledge Taylor & Francis Group.
Bassett, C. L. (2005). Wisdom in three acts: using transformative learning to teach for wisdom. in: Sixth International Transformative Learning Conference, East Lansing, Michigan. Available: https://www.wisdominst.org/WisdomInThreeActs.pdf (accessed: 4 January, 2022).
Bassett, C. L. (2011). Understanding and Teaching Practical Wisdom. *New Directions for Adult and Continuing Education,* 2011(131): 35–44. https://doi.org/10.1002/ace.419.
Bratianu, C. (2015). Spiritual Knowledge. In Constantin Bratianu: *Organizational Knowledge Dynamics: Managing Knowledge Creation, Acquisition, Sharing, and Transformation*. Chapter 4, Hershey: IGI Global. DOI: 10.4018/978-1-4666-8318-1.ch004. Available: https://www.researchgate.net/publication/322235156_Spiritual_Knowledge (accessed: 12 March, 2023).
Bruya, B. & Ardelt, M. (2018a). Fostering Wisdom in the Classroom. A General Theory of Wisdom Pedagogy. *Teaching Philosophy*, 2018, *41*(3), 239–253, https://doi.org/10.5840/teachphil201882889.
Bruya, B. & Ardelt, M. (2018b). Wisdom can be taught. A proof-of-concept study for fostering wisdom in the classroom. *Learning and Instruction*, 58, 2018, 106–114, https://doi.org/10.1016/j.learninstruc.2018.05.001.
Diamond, Z. M. (2021). Old Pedagogies for Wise Education: A Janussian Reflection on Universities. *Philosophies* 2021, 6, 64. https://doi.org/10.3390/philosophies6030064.
Durant, W. (1954). *The Story of Philosophy. The Lives and Opinions of the Greater Philosophers*. New York: The Pocket Library.
Ekmekçi, A. K., Teraman, S. B. S., & Acar, P. (2014). Wisdom and management: a conceptual study on wisdom management, 10th international strategic management", Elsevier. *Procedia – Social and Behavioral Sciences*, Vol. *150*, pp. 1199–1204, https://doi.org/10.1016/j.sbspro.2014.09.135, available at: https://www.sciencedirect.com/science/article/pii/S1877042814051842 (accessed 25 May 2021).
George, J. M. & Jones, G. R. (1997). Experiencing work: Values, attitudes, and moods. *Human Relations, 50*(4), 393–416. https://doi.org/10.1023/A:1016954827770.
Gidley, J. M. (2012). Evolution of education: From weak signals to rich imaginaries of educational futures. *Futures*, 44, pp. 46–54.
Goldin, C. (2016). Human Capital. In C. Diebolt, M. Haupert (Eds.), *Handbook of Cliometrics*, Springer-Verlag Berlin Heidelberg, pp. 55–86, https://doi.org/10.1007/978-3-642-40406-1_23.
Grossmann, I. & Kung, F. Y. H. (2019). Wisdom and Culture. In Handbook of Cultural Psychology, 2nd ed.; Kitayama, S., Cohen, D., Eds. Guilford Press: New York, NY, USA.
Hart, T. (2001). Teaching for wisdom encounter. *Education for Meaning and Social Justice*, 14, pp. 3–16.
Hashim, R., Hussien, S. & Imran, A. M. (2014). Ḥikmah (wisdom) pedagogy and students' thinking and reasoning abilities. *Intellectual Discourse*, *22*(2), Available online: https://www.researchgate.net/publication/289106151_Hikmah_wisdom_pedagogy_and_students'_thinking_and_reasoning_abilities (accessed: 26 August, 2022).
HEIs (2022). Higher Education Institutions. Ministry of Education and Culture. Available: https://minedu.fi/en/heis-andscience-agencies (accessed: 15 January, 2022).
Helin, K. (2019). Vastavalmistuneiden kauppatieteiden-maisterien-palaute 2018. Helsinki: Suomen Ekonomien Julkaisu, available: https://www.ekonomit.fi/wp-content/uploads/2020/06/Vastavalmistu-neiden-kauppatieteiden-maisterien-palaute-2019.pdf (accessed: 10 January, 2022).

Henderson, J. G. & Kesson, K. R. (2001). *Curriculum Wisdom: Educational Decisions in Democratic Societies*. Pearson Education Inc.: Upper Saddle River, NJ, USA.

Henderson, J. G. & Kesson, K. R. (2004). *Curriculum Wisdom: Educational Decisions in Democratic Societies*. Pearson Education Inc., Upper Saddle River, NJ.

Huang, Y-F. & Do, M-H. (2021). Review of empirical research on university social responsibility. *International Journal of Educational Management*, Vol. 35 No. 3, pp. 549–563, https://doi.org/10.1108/IJEM-10-2020-0449.

Jakubik, M. & Müürsepp, P. (2022). From knowledge to wisdom. Will Wisdom Management replace Knowledge Management? *European Journal of Management and Business Economics (EJM&BE)*, Vol. 31 No. 3, pp. 367–389, https://doi.org/10.1108/EJMBE-07-2021-0219.

Jakubik, M. (2020a). Enhancing human capital beyond university boundaries. *Higher Education, Skills and Work-Based Learning*, Emerald Publishing Limited, Vol. 10, No. 2, pp. 434–446. https://doi.org/10.1108/HESWBL-06-2019-0074.

Jakubik, M. (2020b). Educating for the Future – Cultivating Practical Wisdom in Education, *The Journal on Systemics, Cybernetics and Informatics (JSCI)*, *18*(7), pp. 50–54.

Jakubik, M. (2020c). Quo Vadis Educatio? Emergence of a New Educational Paradigm, *The Journal on Systemics, Cybernetics and Informatics (JSCI)*, *18*(5), pp. 7–15.

Jakubik, M. (2021a). Searching for Practical Wisdom in Higher Education with Logos, Pathos and Ethos. Case: Finnish Universities of Sciences. Invited paper to the Special Issue *'From the Acquisition of Knowledge to the Promotion of Wisdom'*, *Philosophies*, 6(3), 63.

Jakubik, M. (2021b). How can practical wisdom manifest itself in five fundamental management and leadership practices? *VILAKSHAN-XIMB Journal of Management, Emerald Insight*, Outstanding Paper 2022 Award, *18*(1), pp. 3–25. https://doi.org/10.1108/XJM-08-2020-0078.

Jakubik, M. (2022). The Role of Higher Education in Solving Global Problems. *International Journal of Management, Knowledge and Learning* (IJMKL), Volume 11, pp. 285–295 https://www.doi.org/10.53615/2232-5697.11.285-295.

Jeste, D. V., Ardelt, M., Blazer, D., Kraemer, H. C., Vaillant, G., & Meeks, T. W. (2010). Expert consensus on characteristics of wisdom: a Delphi method study, *Gerontologist*, *50*(5), pp. 668–680, https://doi.org/10.1093/geront/gnq022.

Jorge, M. L. & Peña, F. J. (2017). Analysing the Literature on University Social Responsibility: A Review of Selected Higher Education Journals. *Higher Education Quarterly*, 71(4), pp. 302–319, https://doi.org/10.1111/HEQU.12122.

Karami, S., Ghahremani, M., Parra-Martinez, F. A., & Gentry, M. (2020). A polyhedron model of wisdom: a systematic review of the wisdom studies in psychology, management and leadership, and education", *Roeper Review*, *42*(4), pp. 241–257, https://doi.org/10.1080/02783193.2020.1815263.

Kernis, M. H. & Goldman, B. M. (2006). Authenticity Inventory. A Multicomponent Conceptualization of Authenticity: Theory and Research. *Advances in Experimental Social Psychology*, 38, pp. 283–357. https://doi.org/10.1016/S0065-2601(06)38006-9.

Kouatli, I. (2019). "The contemporary definition of university social responsibility with quantifiable sustainability", *Social Responsibility Journal*, 15(7), pp. 888–909. https://doi.org/10.1108/SRJ-10-2017-0210.

Laakso-Manninen, R., & Tuomi, L. (2020). *Professional Higher Education Management – Best Practices from Finland*. Helsinki: Professional Publishing Finland Oy.

Latif, K. F. (2018). "The development and validation of stakeholder-based scale for measuring university social responsibility (USR)", *Social Indicators Research*, Vol. 140, No. 2, pp. 511–547.

Lehtonen, A., Salonen, A., Cantell, H., & Riuttanen, L. (2018). A pedagogy of interconnectedness for encountering climate change as a wicked sustainability problem. *Journal of Cleaner Production*, 199, pp. 860–867.

Maxwell, N. (2012). Creating a Better World. Toward the University of Wisdom. In Barnett, R. (Ed.) *The Future University. Ideas and Possibilities*. Routledge, Taylor & Francis Group: New York, USA, Chapter 10, 123–138.

Maxwell, N. (2014). *How Universities Can Help Create a Wiser World: The Urgent Need for an Academic Revolution*. Exeter: Imprint Academic.

Maxwell, N. (2019a). From Knowledge to Wisdom. In *SpringerBriefs in Philosophy.* pp. 69–77.

Maxwell, N. (2019b). How Wisdom Can Help Solve Global Problems. In R. Sternberg, H. Nusbaum, & J. Glueck (Eds.), *Applying wisdom to contemporary world problems.* pp. 337–380. London: Palgrave Macmillan.

Maxwell, N. (2021a). *The World Crisis–and what to Do about it: A Revolution for Thought and Action*. London: World Scientific Publishing Company.

Maxwell, N. (2021b). How Universities Have Betrayed Reason and Humanity – And What's to Be Done About It? *Front. Sustain. 2*, 1–11. https://doi.org/10.3389/frsus.2021.631631. Available at: https://discovery.ucl.ac.uk/id/eprint/10125878/1/Maxwell_frsus-02-631631.pdf (accessed: 21 December, 2021).

McKenna, B., & Rooney, D. (2005). Wisdom Management: Tension between Theory and Practice in Practice, available at: https://www.researchgate.net/publication/37618441_Wisdom_Management_Tensions_Between_Theory_And_Practice_In_Practice (accessed 31May 2021).

McKenna, B., Rooney, D., & Boal, K. B. (2009). Wisdom principles as a meta-theoretical basis for evaluating leadership, *Leadership Quarterly*, *20*(2), pp. 177–190, available at: http://kimboal.ba.ttu.edu/Selected%20writings/wisdom%20principles.pdf (accessed 30 May 2021).

Morley, L. (2012). Imagining the university of the future. In R. Barnett (Ed) (2012). *The Future University: Ideas and Possibilities*. New York: Routledge Taylor & Francis Group, Chapter 2, pp. 26–35.

Nissilä, W. (2018). *Vastavalmistuneiden kauppatieteiden maisterien palaute 2017.* Suomen Ekonomien Julkaisu, No. 2/2018, p. 6, https://ekonomit.emmi.fi/l/NNQDXJxLHjxh (accessed: 14 January, 2022).

Nixon, J. (2012). Universities and the common good. In R. Barnett (Ed) (2012). *The Future University: Ideas and Possibilities*. New York: Routledge Taylor & Francis Group, Chapter 11, pp. 141–151.

Nonaka, I., Chia, R., Holt, R., & Peltokorpi, V. (2014). Wisdom, management and organization, *Management Learning*, *45*(4), pp. 365–376, https://doi.org/10.1177/1350507614542901.

Nylander, C. (2015). Why and How to Upgrade Human Collective Wisdom; Lunds Universitet: Lund, Sweden, 2015. Available online: https://www.academia.edu/21541883/Why_and_How_to_Upgrade_Human_Collective_Wisdom_feb_2016 (accessed: 30 September, 2022).

OECD (2019). Learning Compass 2030. Future of Education and Skills 2030. Conceptual Learning Framework. Available: https://www.oecd.org/education/2030-project/teaching-and-learning/learning/learning-compass-2030/ (accessed: 19 January, 2022).

Robinson, D. N. (1990). Wisdom through the ages. In R.J. Sternberg (Ed.) *Wisdom: Its nature, origins, and development*. Cambridge: Cambridge University Press.

Rooney, D., McKenna, B., & Liesch, P. (2010). *Wisdom and Management in the Knowledge Economy*, Routledge, New York, https://doi.org/10.4324/9780203852798.

Roos, J., Roos, G., Dragonetti, N. C. and Edvinsson, L. (1997). *Intellectual Capital. Navigating the Business Landscape*, MacMillan Press.

Rothblatt, S. (2012). The future isn't waiting. In The Future University: Ideas and Possibilities; In R. Barnett (Ed) (2012). *The Future University: Ideas and Possibilities*. New York: Routledge Taylor & Francis Group, Chapter 1, pp. 15–25.

Runes, D. D. (Ed.) (1966). *Dictionary of Philosophy*. Totowa: Littlefield, Adams & Co.

Solé, J. B. (2017), "Wisdom management, ECKM 2007–20017 review", Proceedings of the 18th European Conference on Knowledge Management (ECKM), 7–8 Sep, 2017, Barcelona, Spain, Vol. 1, p. 55, available at: https://books.google.fi/books?hl5en&lr5&id59k88DwAAQBAJ&oi5fnd&pg5PA55&d-q5%22wisdomþmanagement%22þsource:%22KnowledgeþManagement%22&ots5slzxV9WtF-B&sig54lXUNA1WaRhG6vEhXz4A4yoFK3M&redir_esc5y#v5onepage&q&f5false (accessed 30 May 2021).

Sousa, J. C. R. d., Siqueira, E. S., Binotto, E., & Nobre, L. H. N. (2021). "University social responsibility: perceptions and advances", *Social Responsibility Journal*, Vol. 17 No. 2, pp. 263–281. https://doi.org/10.1108/SRJ-10-2017-0199.

Standaert, N. (2012). Towards a networked university. In The Future University: Ideas and Possibilities; In R. Barnett (Ed.) (2012). *The Future University: Ideas and Possibilities*. New York: Routledge Taylor & Francis Group, Chapter 7, pp. 87–100.

Sternberg, R. J. & Karami, S. (2021). What is Wisdom? A Unified 6P Framework. *Review of General Psychology*, pp. 1–18, https://doi.org/10.1177/1089268020985509.

Sternberg, R. J. (2001). Why Schools Should Teach for Wisdom: The Balance Theory of Wisdom in Educational Settings. *Educational Psychologist*, *36*(4), 227–245.

Ström, C. (2021). Vastavalmistuneiden kauppatieteiden maisterien palaute 2020. Helsinki: Ekonomit, MER, available: https://www.ekonomit.fi/wp-content/uploads/2021/10/Vastavalmistuneiden-kauppatieteiden-maisterien-palaute-2020.pdf (accessed: 10 January, 2022).

Sullivan, P. H. (Ed.) (1998). *Profiting from Intellectual Capital. Extracting Value from Innovation*, John Wiley & Sons.

Teittinen, J. (2020). Vastavalmistuneiden kauppatieteiden maisterien palaute 2019. Ekonomit, MER (2020), https://www.ekonomit.fi/wp-content/uploads/2020/10/Vastavalmistuneiden-palaute-2019_raportti_final.pdf (accessed: 29 September, 2022).

UN, United Nations (2015). Sustainability Development Goals (SDGs): The 17 Goals. UN Department of Economic and Social Affairs, available: https://sdgs.un.org/goals and https://sdgs.un.org/topics/education (accessed: 31 December, 2021).

Wals, A. E. J., & Benavot, A. (2017). Can we meet the sustainability challenges? The role of education and lifelong learning. *European Journal of Education*, 52(4), 404–413. https://doi.org/10.1111/ejed.12250.

WEF (2021). The Global Risks Report 2021. 16th Edition, Insight Report. World Economic Forum, p. 12. Available: https://www3.weforum.org/docs/WEF_The_Global_Risks_Report_2021.pdf (accessed: 21 December, 2021).

WEF (2022). The Global Risks Report 2022. 17th Edition, World Economic Forum, p. 14. Available: https://www3.weforum.org/docs/WEF_The_Global_Risks_Report_2022.pdf (accessed: 15 January, 2022).

Willamo, R., Helenius, L., Holmström, C., Haapanen, L., Sandström, V., Huotari, E., Kaarre, K., Värre, U., Nuotiomäki, A., Happonen, J., & Kolehmainen, L. (2018). Learning how to understand complexity and deal with sustainability challenges – A framework for a comprehensive approach and its application in university education. Elsevier, *Ecological Modelling*, 370, pp. 1–13, https://doi.org/10.1016/j.ecolmodel.2017.12.011.

Yusoffi, W. M. W., Hashim, R., Khalid, M., Hussien, S., & Kamalludeen, R. (2018). The Impact of Hikmah (Wisdom) Pedagogy on 21st Century Skills of Selected Primary and Secondary School Students in Gombak District Selangor Malaysia. *Journal of Education and Learning*, 2018, 7(6), pp. 100–110.

Carla C. T. Neves, Paula F. Marchant-Pérez and Paulo Pinheiro

Chapter 9 Knowledge Management and Spirituality in Higher Education Institutions: A New Challenge

Abstract: Based on the existing definitions in the literature on knowledge management and spirituality for other organizations, this study aims to reflect on how Higher Education Institutions (HEIs) face issues related to knowledge management and spirituality in the workplace. A qualitative methodology was used to achieve the goal with data collected from interviews with higher education teachers. The conclusion shows that, although most interviewees perceive the HEIs' mission, vision and values, these were not explicitly disseminated. In terms of knowledge management, the organizational culture of HEIs should promote the appreciation and recognition of tacit knowledge about corporate spirituality; there is a long way to go in HEIs as a whole. This work aims to present a transparent interconnection between knowledge management and spirituality in the workplace and, through the integration of research carried out by other authors on this matter, offer a sustained analysis of the data. Also, this study implies implications at a strategic management level of HEIs since management should promote more practical knowledge management and develop practices that contribute to a workplace guided by spiritual values, always considering gains in productivity and competitiveness.

Keywords: Knowledge Management, Spirituality, Higher Education Institutions

Acknowledgments: The authors thank Dr. Raysa Rocha for her valuable comments, suggestions, and availability in always answering our questions. This work was supported by the NECE – Research Center in Business Sciences funded by the Multiannual Funding Program of R&D Centers of FCT – Fundação para a Ciência e Tecnologia, Portugal, under Grant UIDB/04630/2020.

Carla C. T. Neves, NECE – Research Unit in Business Sciences, University of Beira Interior, Portugal; School of Technology and Management, Polytechnic Institute of Bragança, Portugal, e-mail: carla.teixeira.neves@ubi.pt
Paula F. Marchant-Pérez, NECE – Research Unit in Business Sciences, University of Beira Interior, Portugal; School of Kinesiology, School of Medicine, University of Valparaíso, Chile, e-mail: paula.marchant.perez@ubi.pt
Paulo Pinheiro, NECE – Research Unit in Business Sciences, University of Beira Interior, Portugal, e-mail: Portugal pgp@ubi.pt

https://doi.org/10.1515/9783111010410-010

Knowledge Management and Spirituality in Higher Education Institutions: A New Challenge

In a rapidly changing, competitive world and in an economy where the only certainty seems to be uncertainty, it is increasingly complex to manage organizations, assuming knowledge as a source that ensures competitive advantage (Biswakarma, 2018; Nonaka, 1991).

When markets change constantly, technologies proliferate, competitors multiply themselves, and products become obsolete overnight, successful organizations stand out as those that create knowledge, disseminate it throughout the organization and incorporate it into new technologies and products (Nonaka, 1991; Lee, 2016). In this context, mainly due to the specificity of their activity, Higher Education Institutions (HEIs) are environments of knowledge creation and sharing. They are the intellectual center of knowledge production and research and are responsible for education, research and knowledge transfer to society, thus contributing to national development (I Ojo, 2016). Thus, according to this author, it is expected that such development will depend on the ability of these universities to produce new knowledge, new technologies and quality graduates.

The interest in researching Knowledge Management at the level of HEIs is relatively recent, even though knowledge creation and dissemination have been the main activities of these organizations since their foundations (Quarchioni et al., 2020). Dhamdhere & Ganeshkhind (2016) called them "Knowledge Houses", where knowledge flows from Professors to Students and new knowledge is created. Therefore, as Rowley (1995) states, one of the main activities of HEIs is knowledge creation and dissemination.

Hence, and as it happens in other organizations, HEIs are increasingly required to have employees with differentiating and unique skills since they are the ones that positively contribute to organizations to maintain competitiveness and distinguish themselves from others. In this context of seeking new skills, spirituality is found. Lakshmi and Das (2021) refer to the present pandemic context, showing that knowledge, ability and attitude are insufficient at individual and institutional levels. Therefore, there is a need to look to the employee as an asset that can contribute to increasing competitiveness and not as a static productive factor. The employee is a human being, and as such, he/she is a rational, emotional and spiritual being, so when he /she performs a job, this must provide some meaning to his life (Rego et al., 2007). According to the authors, if such does not happen, there is an affective and emotional dissociation from the organization, revealing a lower level of effort and commitment.

In this logic, discussing knowledge management and spirituality in organizations is essential. Spirituality can be the employee's primary motivator, leading him to act on his capacity to increase organizational effectiveness and strengthen knowledge management tools and techniques (Lakshmi & Das, 2021). Thus, according to Rocha and Pinheiro (2021), increasing organizational spirituality can be a way to realize a more humanized strategy, making knowledge management an efficient method to spread high-level values to the organization.

Lakshmi Das (2021) highlights that spirituality and its impact on management are still at a research stage, so there is no doubt that contemporary organizations, in general, urgently need employees who are physically and emotionally stable and who can effectively deal with their moods and emotions.

The theoretical contribution of this study, from the existing literature, is to provide insight into how knowledge management and spirituality are crucial for generating and sharing knowledge. Regarding practical implications, this study has strategic management of HEIs to leverage knowledge management and spirituality as implications.

This paper has the following structure: literature review, description of methodology, presentation and analysis of results, conclusions, limitations and future lines of research.

Literature Review

Knowledge Management in Higher Education Institutions

The 21st century is characterized by the growth in the importance of knowledge in organizations and its impact on an organization (Bose, 2004). Thus, organizations must be able to implement a solid knowledge management strategy effectively (Ipe, 2003; Bose, 2004; Halawi et al., 2005; Bolisani & Bratianu, 2018; Kavalić et al., 2021) as well as become knowledge-based organizations, since this is a mandatory condition for their success (Bose, 2004; Lee, 2016; Zheng, 2017; Nasab et al., 2017). Bolisani & Bratianu (2018) point out that it is possible to identify the following knowledge processes in an organization: "knowledge creation, knowledge acquisition, knowledge sharing and distribution, knowledge transformation, knowledge storing and retrieving, knowledge losing, and knowledge using" (p. 37). Organizations successfully prepare themselves through effective knowledge management to face demanding and chaotic circumstances (Kavalić et al., 2021).

Linblon Tikkanen (2010) refers to knowledge management as a conscious strategy of getting the proper knowledge to the right people at the right time and helping them share and put the information into action to improve organizational competitiveness. Therefore, knowledge management is an exciting topic for organizations and all institutions offering education and training. Consequently, HEIs are generally challenged to keep up with the changes in this global business environment (Brewer & Brewer, 2010).

The goals of HEIs are diffuse due to their complex and sophisticated nature (Rodrigues et al., 2004). According to these authors, the value society attributes to these institutions depends on the scientific impact of knowledge it generates (research), knowledge transfer skills (teaching and learning) and the utility of the technology it develops. The nature of HEIs' challenges in structuring their internal value chain and marketing their products and services differs from other organizations. They are higher learning centers, so they must create an environment where all their stakeholders can participate in knowledge management activities (Hoq & Akter, 2012).

Although knowledge management is not recent in HEIs, it is still fragmented and unfocused since Knowledge Management overlaps with other disciplines (Quarchioni et al., 2020). Besides, HEIs cannot be perceived as places where knowledge is merely created and transferred; they must be seen as institutions highly dependent on knowledge resources but simultaneously extremely exposed to its dissipation. They represent a community of students and people where students are intellectually developed in various fields and where high-level research is promoted (Kassaye, 2018). Hence, knowledge management is fundamental in these institutions (Omerzel et al., 2011; Nawaz et al., 2020).

Quarchioni et al. (2020) state that knowledge management for HEIs must take into account their unique forms of accountability and their multi-layered impact on society (e.g., in terms of dissemination of education, industrial innovation, scientific production, etc.), which makes them different from any other organization, both in the private and public sectors. Given that their outputs are precisely knowledge, one might assume that this has always been managed in HEIs (Ratcliffe-Martin et al., 2000). However, studies have shown that knowledge is not easily shared within HEIs and may not stand as learning organizations in the traditional sense of the term.

A fundamental aspect of improving knowledge management in HEIs is involving all employees in knowledge management practices to strengthen university effectiveness and quality (Dei & van der Walt, 2020). Therefore, Baptista Nunes et al. (2017) point out that human resource management practices, fostering employees' trust and promoting collaborative practices positively impact knowledge sharing.

Quarchioni et al. (2020) also refer to intangible factors such as social relationships, shared understanding, and cultural influences to enhance knowledge sharing. Knowledge transfer can be influenced by organizational policies and technological tools that facilitate one's access to knowledge. How knowledge management manifests derives from its integration with organizational systems and the values it is built on. Knowledge management is achieved through creating, sharing, and applying knowledge, but it needs to feed into organizational best practices and the lessons learned in corporate memory (I Ojo, 2016).

It is undeniable that HEIs create knowledge throughout their academic and administrative processes. However, using tacit and explicit knowledge as an integrated central source is still challenging to improve knowledge sharing and decision-making (Baptista Nunes et al., 2017). When sharing knowledge resulting from scientific production, it is "confined" to exchanges within the laboratories or among faculty members (Quarchioni et al., 2020). These authors say academics follow different behaviors and practices in producing scientific knowledge. It is essential to create policies and strategies that ease and improve the use of tacit and explicit knowledge and the sharing of scientific production.

Khari & Sinha (2018) argue that employees who perceive that their organization focuses on their well-being and the well-being of others tend to have a positive attitude concerning knowledge sharing, influencing psychological flourishing and organizational trust. Van den Hooff Huysman (2009) considers that the organizational culture developed by HEIs is crucial to establishing and creating a knowledge-friendly culture that sets a clear knowledge-related vision and goals. This aspect provides beneficial social dynamics for knowledge sharing.

Spirituality in Higher Education Institutions

The concept of spirituality in the workplace has increasingly gained interest in organizational research, which is indicative of its growing importance in organizational terms (McKee et al., 2008; Saks, 2011; Khari & Sinha, 2018; Jurkiewicz & Giacolone, 2004; Gupta et al., 2014; Vasconcelos, 2018; Lakshmi & Das, 2021), leading to the emergence of a new paradigm in organizational sciences (Jurkiewicz & Giacolone, 2004). People spend more and more time at work, so if they want to live well they have to find a way to connect what they do to a broader meaning (Wicks, 2014). In this sense, Karakas (2010) points out that 21st-century organizations must incorporate humanistic and spiritual values in their workplaces.

As in any other organization, employees and managers at HEIs need to think more and more about how to incorporate spirituality, wisdom, reflection, inspiration, creativity and compassion into their work, that is, how to carry out an organizational culture geared to the new values.

Spirituality in the workplace has the same positive impact on HEIs as in other organizations (Mat et al., 2012). In this sense, and particularly in a teaching context, Palmer (2003) states that spirituality "is the eternal human longing to be connected to something greater than our ego" (p. 377). According to Dandona (2013), spirituality is passion, putting our heart, soul and spirit into what we do, so work, in addition to having a deeper meaning, also serves a higher purpose.

Belwalkar et al. (2018) state that it is possible to speak of spirituality at work when the work environment promotes an atmosphere that enables the relationship between mind and soul. This happens when the individual seeks to find meaning for their work and perceives a desire to connect with others. These are factors that produce beneficial consequences for the individual, the organizations, and society as a whole.

While studying workplace spirituality and organizational commitment among HEI faculty members, Thakur et al. (2017) report that, overall, organizations are not only concerned with the skills and qualifications of their staff. They seek employees who feel fully integrated into their workplaces and maintain cordial working relationships. In this sense, education is a sector that can provide the best human capital to organizations (Bell-Ellis et al., 2015). HEIs are essential to provide organizations with appropriately qualified knowledge employees (Kokt & Palmer, 2019). HEIs must be genuinely committed employees, which is accepted by academics and other professionals (Bell-Ellis et al., 2015).

According to Soliman et al. (2021), professors are fundamental key workers in HEIs since they are the ones who represent their institutions and determine the quality of the teaching and learning process. Mat et al. (2012) refer to a growing encouragement for the importance of spirituality at the HEI level. For these authors, there are also emerging conceptual and research bases for assuming that the professor can significantly transmit these spiritual values through student-centered attitudes and teaching methods.

From the perspective of the sustainability of HEIs, Alomar et al. (2022) point out that there are benefits to applying spirituality in the workplace since it inspires more significant innovation, reduces absenteeism and attrition, strengthens relationships, enhances productive work and emotional intelligence, employee engagement and loyalty.

Spirituality in the workplace brings positive results to employees on an individual level (happiness, peace of mind, job satisfaction and motivation). In the workplace, it acts as a need for self-improvement. Therefore, organizations that provide their employees with opportunities for spiritual development have better performances (Konz & Ryan, 1999).

Environments marked by spirituality, such as HEIs, are prone to creating knowledge since, on the one hand, they promote efficient knowledge management, and, on the other hand, spirituality enhances trust and promotes sharing. Knowledge sharing can be enhanced if team members establish and promote trust (Shahzadi, 2017).

In this sense, according to Rocha and Pinheiro (2020), knowledge management facilitates a positive relationship between organizational culture and spirituality in the workplace. If knowledge management is an efficient method to spread high-level values, spirituality plays a vital role in organizational theory and practice (Rocha & Pinheiro, 2021).

Spirituality is an organizational identity resulting from its values, practices and speech, composed of work and individual spirituality, including the spirituality of the leader and employees. The environment influences organizational spirituality, culture and knowledge management and generates value and social well-being visible in the organizational image, mission, vision and values.

Research Methodology

Study Type and Case Selection

To meet the goal set out in this study, a qualitative methodology was used to understand the subject under study better. This provides a deep understanding of people's experiences, perspectives and stories in their context (Spencer et al., 2003). In other words, this methodology allows for exploring human experiences in personal and social contexts and obtaining a greater understanding of the factors that influence these experiences (Gelling, 2015), capturing what is subjective in social phenomena (Silva, 2013). As Lameiras (2016) states:

> Among many distinct characteristics, qualitative evaluation is characterized by a concern with exploring phenomena from the perspective of those being studied; the use of unstructured methods sensitive to the social context of the study; the collection of detailed, rich and complex data; a process that is inductive rather than deductive; and answering questions like 'what is it?', 'how?' and 'why?'. It employs various methods, including exploratory interviews, Focus groups, observation, conversation, discourse and narrative analysis, video and document analysis (p. 3).

Since interviews are essential in case studies, especially in social research (Yin, 1994), this technique was used to extract rich and nuanced information and elements from the interviewee (Quivy & Campenhoudt, 1995). According to Kvale (1996), the interview is a deliberate and informed conversation from which the researcher seeks to understand the context of the interviewees, taking into account their experiences. This is crucial to some types of qualitative research, particularly case study research, where the aim is to study people's understanding of the meanings of their experienced world, describing their experiences and self-understanding.

Analysis Context

The data collection process involved applying interviews with HEI professors in Chile and Portugal (see Table 9.1). The interviews consisted of nine questions (see Appendix A). The interviewees were contacted by telephone to set the day and time of the interview, and if it was not possible to do so in person, to request that it be done by videoconference. These were recorded after the interviewees' consent and later transcribed. The interviews took place in March 2022, each lasting approximately 35 minutes.

Table 9.1: Interviewees characterization.

Code	Age	Gender	Qualifications	Work	Time Working in the Job	Subject Area in Which Works
A1-CL	48	Female	Master Degree	Professor Management Network Coordinator	Ten years	Management
A2-CL	43	Female	Bachelor Degree	Professor Health and physical activity Network Coordinator	Eight years	Physical Exercise and Health Sciences

Table 9.1 (continued)

Code	Age	Gender	Qualifications	Work	Time Working in the Job	Subject Area in Which Works
A3-CL	55	Male	Doctoral Degree	Titular University Professor Cathedra Coordinator Ethics Committee Member	19 years	Health Sciences
B1-PT	45	Male	Doctoral Degree	Professor Civil Construction and Planning Department Coordinator Director of the CTESP of Civil Construction	22 years	Civil Engineering and OHS
B2-PT	66	Male	Doctoral Degree	Professor	36 years	Economy and Management
B3-PT	61	Female	Doctoral Degree	Professor	22 years	Behavioral and Human Resources Management

Results Analysis and Discussion

In order to better analyze the questions asked during the interviews, it was chosen to group them around two main points, as shown in Table 9.2.

Table 9.2: Grouping of the interview questions.

Thematic group	Questions
Knowledge Management	2. Is your organization concerned about making the best use of tacit* knowledge within it? How do you explain it? 4. What are the internal procedures for the organization to disseminate scientific knowledge? 5. Do you consider the research publication and the attendance of seminars and conferences as scientific production? Why or why not?
Spirituality in work	1. As an employee, are you aware of the mission, values and vision of the institution where you work? Do you share and identify yourself with the mission, values and vision of your institutions? To what extent? 3. Do you think the institution is using your skills to contribute to social improvement? How do you feel about it?

Table 9.2 (continued)

Thematic group	Questions
	6. Looking at your organization, do you feel an organizational culture of respect, accountability, cooperation, tolerance, welcoming, and mutual help exists? Moreover, is there solidarity among colleagues? Can you give examples? 7. Do you feel your organization is sensitive to employees' problems? Can you give examples? 8. Does the institution promote an environment of collaboration and team spirit? Can you give examples? 9. Do you feel happy with your work? And with your organization?

Knowledge Management

Knowledge management by organizing, documenting, sharing and storing knowledge helps organizations with a higher level of organizational complexity to decide better, in a lighter way, to provide further effectiveness in solving problems (Hoq & Akter, 2012). In this sense, these authors mention that HEIS needs to build information infrastructures as higher learning centers and create a favorable atmosphere where working staff, teaching and non-teaching staff, students, researchers, patrons and other stakeholders can participate in various knowledge management activities.

According to Rowley (2000), HEIs already have knowledge management activities. They need to consciously and explicitly manage the processes associated with knowledge creation and recognize the value of their intellectual capital to maintain their role in society. They are seen as 'knowledge centers' and 'knowledge houses', where there are carried out different activities that generate, preserve, disseminate and apply knowledge. In this way, professors, students and researchers are crucial and are all engaged in various activities (Hoq & Akter, 2012; Dhamdhere & Ganeshkhind, 2016).

When questioned about the use of tacit knowledge by the different HEIs, responses showed significant differences. Some interviewees point out that the HEIs where they work for and make use of this knowledge, though in an unconscious manner. In this regard, interviewee A2-CL mentions that when she was recruited, the HEI not only considered whether she had a master's or doctoral degree but also analyzed her experience. Hence, she states that she was recruited "because I had the profile they were looking for because I like sports, physical activity, healthy living habits, and these are the aspects, the knowledge, the experience that they want me to pass on to the students". Another interviewee considers that his HEI has not always valued the experience and knowledge acquired by professors. However, this situation has changed over time.

Two interviewees consider that there is still no concern from their HEIs in using their employees' tacit knowledge. Interviewee B3-PT even mentions that "there is still no awareness of the importance of this type of knowledge". Interviewee B2-PT states that his HEI ignores this type of knowledge, pointing out that certain groups have been created, which "leads to neglecting tacit knowledge and thus underutilizing the available knowledge".

Hoq & Akter (2012) point out that HEIs should inspire students, professors and employees to share explicit and tacit knowledge. This can be achieved through regular sessions to solve problems, share ideas, and encourage the exchange of knowledge, information and inspiration. Knowledge sharing is only achieved if institutions have human resources management practices that foster employee trust and promote collaborative practices (Baptista Nunes et al., 2017). According to Ratcliffe-Martin et al. (2000), studies have shown that knowledge is not easily shared, and HEIs may not be *learning houses* in the traditional sense.

When asked about scientific knowledge dissemination in general, all interviewees agree that the HEIs where they work have procedures for disseminating this knowledge, such as official web pages, repositories, conferences, lectures, and platforms for inserting scientific articles. Similarly, they also indicate that their teaching activity is related to knowledge dissemination, and some professors dedicate more hours of their work to research than to the teaching component.

However, interviewee B2-PT states that these procedures are scarce in the HEI, where he lectures. Some scientific knowledge is disseminated in bulletin boards, intranet, and institutional disclosure. But only partially. Not all scientific research is disseminated because not all research is appreciated, welcomed and encouraged. All comes down to guidelines and specific goals of internal groups with negotiating power to impose procedures, rules and norms, depending on the pre-established personal goals.

Most interviewees concur that publishing research articles and attending seminars and conferences come across as scientific production, with the most important aspect being that it is possible to disseminate discussion, generate new knowledge, and improve their lectures. Interviewee A1-CL states, "Everything that can be done in a publication, a conference, a talk, will be a seed to generate new research, new knowledge and, therefore, grow". Interviewee A3-CL indicates that "all that constitutes an activity that generates knowledge, whether quantitatively or qualitatively, is a scientific production, with a methodological design that supports it, a data analysis. . .".

Interviewee B2-PT points out that, at first, the outcome may seem very small. However, there is a solid basis for knowledge production and dissemination from that point forward. Conferences and seminars address topics with incremental innovation. This increases curiosity, interaction and sharing among colleagues, which becomes a gateway for access and dissemination of tacit knowledge. It also disseminates knowledge in progress that could give rise to new or improved knowledge.

Interviewee B1-PT mentions that these are the elements that the institution considers crucial as a publication. However, from a personal perspective, I consider that there are others. For example, what is the point of a professor being perfect scientifically if he/she is not the best when teaching lectures? (. . .) The school wants lectures to be taught, period. Moreover, it does not matter if they are good or bad. With today's demands, there is no time to improve the pedagogical part.

As Omerzel et al. (2011) and Nawaz et al. (2020) point out, knowledge management processes in HEIs are as vital as in any other organization. Doing this effectively can enhance decision-making skills, reduce "product" development cycle time (for example, curriculum development and research outputs), improve academic and administrative services and reduce costs.

Spirituality in the Workplace

In the organizational context, which HEIs are part of, one cannot reflect on knowledge management without considering its relationship with organizational culture (Omerzel et al., 2011). The same is true when referring to the issue of spirituality, and this concept has led to a new paradigm in organizational sciences (Jurkiewicz & Giacolone, 2004). Karakas (2010) states that 21st-century organizations must incorporate humanistic and spiritual values in their workplaces. All employees and all managers need to think more about how to incorporate spirituality, wisdom, reflection, inspiration, creativity and compassion at work, that is, how to carry out an organizational culture oriented to the new values.

In this sense, all employees must comprehend, internalize and identify with the organizational culture of their organization. Regarding the organizational culture in HEIs, in general, and despite not being informed, most interviewees are familiar with their institution's mission, vision and values. However, one of the interviewees (B1-PT) stated that he does not know them and has only an idea of his institution's mission, vision and values. He points out that he has worked in the institution for 22 years and that no one ever told him about them, not even when he was recruited. As he states, the perception he built about these was "based on the demands, where there is something behind, not knowing where you want to go". Corroborating this opinion, another interviewee (B2-PT) said he knows his institution's values, mission and vision because he held a management position. He stated, "I think most of my colleagues do not know that reality". At the heart of this situation is "the institution's poor communication, as well as a very traditional organizational culture".

For such facts, HEIs should communicate their mission, vision and values so that all employees are in tune with the institution. Organizations will only have genuinely engaged employees (Omerzel et al., 2011).

Concerning the identification with HEI values, mission and vision, all interviewees claim to identify with what they know or perceive these to be. They consider them to align with their motivation for teaching and what they can convey to their students. However, interviewee B2-PT mentions that, despite personally identifying with them, sometimes "what is 'thought' and 'written' often diverges from the behavior of agents, which represents a violation of the principles of its mission and goals".

It should also be noted that interviewee B3-PT stressed the students' hard and soft skills regarding the values, vision and mission. The goal of his institution is to teach, inspire and empower its students to add value to society and the organizations where they work. It is also concerned with providing its students with technical skills (hard skills) and the soft skills that the labor market values, such as the ability to lead, undertake, take risks, work in a team, etc.

Rowley (2000) states that norms, values and practices associated with creating, sharing and disseminating knowledge in HEIs are complex. However, several factors may already be challenging traditional values. Along with the importance of knowledge management for organizations, one should also consider the strategic importance of managing organizational spirituality. According to Konz & Ryan (1999), this can be explained as a dynamic process through which individuals express personal values within the organizational context, thus seeking greater meaning and purpose for their lives through connection with others and the community.

When asked whether HEIs are using their competencies to contribute to society's improvement, all interviewees indicated that, in some way, they contribute to this improvement, mainly through the contents and values they transmit to students and which they subsequently apply in a professional context. Interviewee A1-CL mentioned that, although she could not say yes categorically, she believed students leave very well prepared, that they are good professionals and that this is corroborated by society. Interviewee B3-PT mentions that there is a vital concern about training students with a wide range of skills that can impact the development of society. Also, there is an increasing concern of the faculty to train students based on values of intellectual freedom, critical spirit, professional and social ethics, social responsibility, the pursuit of excellence, respect for difference and appreciation of merit.

Interviewee B2-PT stresses that, although there is a powerful concern in contribution to society, "there is a concern to commodify knowledge/help/contribution instead of providing help for the society to build itself up and grow. Therefore, sustainability is precarious".

Professors generally feel good when they see HEIs use their competencies to contribute to society, even if this situation overlaps with their duties. There is no financial reward/ compensation for it. Some interviewees, particularly those who lecture at HEIs in Chile, call attention to this matter since it is evident that HEIs' concern is closely linked to what happens in the society/community where they are located.

Spirituality must be integrated into organizational culture and reflected in daily organizational practices to be effective. This is only possible if management and the board of directors adopt it as a part of their vision (Dandona, 2013). Hence, according to this author, the organization must have a favorable organizational culture to effectively implement spirituality in the workplace. This can increase employee morale, commitment and productivity, reduce stress and burnout at work (Karakas, 2010; Dandona, 2013), enhance creativity, and contribute to personal fulfillment and commitment, ultimately increasing organizational performance (Krishnakumar & Neck, 2002). Jurkiewicz and Giacalone (2004), when addressing spirituality, refer to some values, such as adaptability, commitment, motivation, trust, responsibility, respect, justice, receptivity, integrity, mutuality, benevolence, humanism and generativity. These are the values that have a positive impact on the employee's and organizations' performances. Organizations can exhibit these values through their work processes, policies and practices that constitute their culture.

Reflecting on some values of organizational spirituality present in the organizational culture, all interviewees unanimously consider that there is an organizational culture of respect in their HEIs. Most interviewees feel that solidarity and cooperation occur more within than between groups. One of the interviewees mentions that the lack of cooperation is felt because there is a shortage of time, verified when people meet and ask for help, so it is an aspect to be improved. It is also found that, although collaborative work does not always happen, there is always a desire and an intention to do so.

In this context, it is mandatory that this HEI somehow reflects on some aspects of its organizational culture so that, precisely as far as the collaborative process is concerned, it does not remain just an intention.

Interviewee B1-PT also mentions that these aspects are absent, especially when there is competition to improve their careers. In these cases, people try to "go" over each other and feel that anything is possible. It pains me to say this, but people seem to stop being people and live obsessed with a particular position.

This is the environment where Khari & Sinha (2018) refer that employees who perceive that their organizations focus on their well-being and the well-being of others promote psychological flourishing and organizational trust. When asked whether their HEI is sensitive to employees' problems, the interviewees perceive that this sensitivity exists within their groups, that is, more at the level of people in a team or department and not so much at the organizational level in general. For example, interviewee B2-PT states that current department managers brought new feelings, and there is a tendency to improve the levels of collaboration, respect, and tolerance, among others, towards employees' problems. However, such situations are not yet global, and some try to override the feelings of others, nullifying them, for example, certain attitudes of influential groups, which end up conditioning others.

Although the different feelings of the interviewees converge, there are some differences. An interviewee states that the HEI where he teaches has very close management. According to Konz & Ryan (1999), this perspective puts managers and organizations in a difficult position. A manager is trained in four functions: planning, organizing, leadership and control. They are selected, promoted and rewarded according to their ability to perform these four functions, according to the needs of their organizations. Hence, to this author, to be a spiritual guide and to have this proximity with their employees is a responsibility for which managers are unprepared.

At the same time, when asked whether their institution promotes an environment of collaboration and team spirit, not all interviewees consider that this situation occurs. Some interviewees point out that the institution seeks and has work forms that tend more toward teamwork, such as social events or a work structure in disciplinary networks. However, this collaboration does not always occur because people do not have the will to do so. Interviewee A2-CL states, "As a professor, I think that at the work level, there is no collaboration or team spirit". Corroborating this opinion, interviewee B1-PT points out that "as a director of a Higher Professional Technical Programs (HPTP), when I sometimes suggest a group work in certain subjects, I often get an answer like, "But do I have to work with that person? Why? I would rather work alone because I can articulate things my way".

Interviewee B2-PT states, "Theoretically, there is an effort to declare and emphasize team spirit and group work. However, daily things are different and individual values override group values, negatively affecting the organizational climate and culture".

Hoq & Akter (2012) state that proper coordination and collaboration among 'university family' members are essential for effective knowledge sharing and management. If different members do not spontaneously participate in exchanging information and ideas, many blockages are created, which would frustrate all knowledge management initiatives.

When asked if they were happy with their job and organization, all interviewees said they enjoyed their job, teaching, and student contact.

When facing HEI as an organizations, there are differences between the interviewees. Interviewee B3-PT claims to be happy with the organization, stating, "The perception that I have is that my work is increasingly recognized both by the students and the institutions itself". From a different perspective, interviewee B2-PT points out that, although he feels good about the HEI, they are not in harmony. He adds, "I have learned to live in isolation to get around the setbacks I encountered at school. However, I must confess that today I am respected by my colleagues, regardless of their political, scientific and pedagogical leanings." Finally, interviewee B1-PT mentions that "some things could be better. I consider that, in general, the most 'difficult' and 'boring' work that nobody wants always falls upon the same people. I see people who, despite having the skills, do very little and are not called for anything, and sometimes, when they are called, they do not want it and do not accept it, so they do not have to deal with stress, criticism and the possibility of mistakes and failures."

Given the responses, and in line with the interviewees, Bell-Ellis et al. (2015) state that there is an individual longing for more spirituality in higher education and that most HEIS do not consider this need.

Conclusion

This study reflected on how HEIs view knowledge management and spirituality issues. There was a resort to teachers' perceptions and feelings about their workplace. As well as an attempt to identify the values of the organization's culture based on knowledge and its sharing and dissemination within the HEIs. A study of this nature has some limitations regarding the subjectivity of the questions and themes and the number and type of employees. However, overall, the work allows for some conclusions to be drawn.

It can be concluded that even though the HEIs' mission, vision and values have not been explicitly disseminated, most interviewees have strongly perceived them. Given this reality, it is understood that HEIs should rethink their organizational strategy so that their employees feel genuinely committed and, in parallel, they have knowledge management processes, as argued by Omerzel et al. (2011). As the interviewees revealed, if organizational culture were disseminated more effectively, it would foster all the fundamental organizational values, such as responsibility, cooperation, tolerance, solidarity, and team spirit.

On the topic of knowledge management, specifically in the tacit domain, only two of the six interviewees (A1-CL and A2-CL) mentioned that HEIs take advantage of and value this knowledge. It seems that, once again, the institution's organizational culture at the level of knowledge management is present since it should value and recognize the pre-existing individual knowledge as an asset for the organization. The culture that best suits the knowledge management practices of an organization is where employees do not feel inhibited about sharing knowledge (Hoq & Akter, 2012; Devi Ramachandran et al., 2013).

Although organizational spirituality is fundamental for organizational success, there is still a long way to go for all HEIs. Just as life has no meaning without work, work without spirit also has little meaning, which is why employees who maintain the bonds of spirituality at work exhibit interesting positive values, such as responsibility, justice and reciprocity, as it is argued by Jurkiewicz and Giacalone (2004) and Thakur et al. (2017).

From the answers obtained, one feels that there is, on behalf of those responsible for the respective services, the will to implement improvements at the level of collaborative spirit, mutual help, tolerance and team spirit.

However, it was clear that this is not yet the case globally. The interconnectedness and interdependence of employees experienced through feelings of community and meaningful work lead to more outstanding organizational commitment, job satisfaction, and self-esteem (Milliman et al., 2003). According to Karakas (2010) and Thakur et al. (2017), incorporating spirituality at work provides organizational members with a sense of community and connection, thus increasing their attachment, loyalty, and sense of belonging to the organization.

In general, it is clear that, although professors have different ages, different years of service, and belong to countries with very own particularities, the results converge in terms of answers.

Regarding theoretical implications, this study, at the literature review level, presents a transparent interconnection between knowledge management and spirituality in the workplace. This allows us to sustain concepts and definitions and integrate studies developed by other authors concerning the research goals to develop a more sustained analysis.

Regarding practical implications, this study has some implications at the strategic management level of HEIs since managers should promote effective knowledge management and develop practices that promote a workplace guided by the values of spirituality and always thinking about productivity gains and competitiveness.

This article is not free from limitations. Despite having a small number of interviews and having heterogeneity in the areas of the professors interviewed, we have reached inductive thematic saturation (Saunders et al., 2018). Thus, some issues that could be studied are identified:

- To what extent are the organizational cultures of the HEIs worked on to be endowed with an intensive spirit and oriented spiritually?
- How does the organizational culture help the organization to unify around common goals?
- How does incorporating values of spirituality help HEIs become more competitive and ethical?
- Which values of spirituality should HEIs value most?

Due to its importance for developing HEIs and society overall, this work must be continued.

Appendix A

Interview script

1. As an employee, are you aware of the mission, values and vision of the institution where you work? Do you share and/or identify yourself with your institution's mission, values and vision? To what extent?
2. Is your organization worried about making the best use of the tacit knowledge within it? How do you explain it?
3. Do you think the institution is using your skills to contribute to social improvement? How do you feel about that?
4. What are the internal procedures for the organization to disseminate scientific knowledge?
5. Do you consider the publication of research and the attendance of seminars and conferences as scientific production? Why or why not?
6. Looking at your organization, do you feel there is an organizational culture of respect, accountability, cooperation, tolerance, welcoming, and mutual help? And is there solidarity among colleagues? Can you give examples?
7. Do you feel your organization is sensitive to employee problems? Can you give an example?

8. Does the institution promote an environment of collaboration and team spirit? Can you give examples?
9. Do you feel happy with your function? And with your organization?

Appendix B

Excerpts of interviews concerning knowledge management and spirituality in Higher Education Institutions

Thematic Codes		Excerpts
Knowledge Management	Tacit Knowledge	The institution respects each professor's tacit knowledge or 'cultural baggage'. (A1-CL) This is not always the case. Sometimes, the people selected to perform some tasks are not the ones with the required knowledge nor the ones with the most experience (B1-PT) I do not think so. I am convinced that my organization ignores that! My institution still operates by groups, what we call "chapels". This leads to neglecting tacit knowledge and underutilizing the available knowledge. In terms of technical and administrative staff, the situation is much worse. Even communication and feedback with some of the sectors is non-existent (B2-PT) I do not think there is an awareness of the importance of this kind of knowledge (B3-PT)
	Scientific Knowledge and Knowledge Transference	Everything that can be done in a publication, a conference, or a talk will be a seed to generate new research and new knowledge and, therefore, grow (A1-CL) When we talk about scientific knowledge, there is a formality within teacher training, in training, in what is the progress of the curriculum. Due to the formality of being a scientist, one goes from the state of being an assistant lecturer, then a lecturer and then a professor... which is not only concerned with transmitting knowledge to climb the hierarchy but to generate the respective cases of transmitting scientific knowledge (A3-CL) All that constitutes an activity that generates knowledge, whether quantitatively or qualitatively, is a scientific production with a methodological design that supports it, a data analysis or a proposal that endorses it as quantitative or qualitative. Therefore, it is knowledge. (A3-CL) These are the elements that the institution considers crucial as a publication. However, from a personal perspective, I consider that there are others. For example, what is the point of a professor being perfect scientifically if he/she is not the best when teaching lectures? (...) The school wants lectures to be taught, period. Moreover, it does not matter if they are good or bad. With today's demands, there is no time to improve the pedagogical part. (B1-PT)

(continued)

Thematic Codes		Excerpts
		These procedures are scarce. Some scientific knowledge is disseminated in bulletin boards, intranet, and institutional disclosure... But only partially. Not all scientific research is disseminated because not all research is appreciated, welcomed and encouraged. All comes down to guidelines and specific goals of internal groups with negotiating power to impose procedures, rules and norms, depending on the pre-established personal goals (B2-PT) I would highlight the organization of conferences and lectures. There is a strong incentive for collaboration and cooperation between teams from different areas of knowledge and research groups, informal talks on various topics, and workshops (B3-PT)
Spirituality in Work	Mission, Values and Vision of the Institution	In the case of the school, yes, I know them and have worked with them. In the case of the university in general, not so much. I do not have deep knowledge, but I know them (A1-CL) I know them because usually when we plan the whole structure in the disciplinary issue of plans and programs, the mission and vision are always embodied... (A2-CL) In practice, I do not know. I perceive the institution's mission, values and vision, but not from written information that goes in that direction. (...) I do my part within what I direct, and here, I can say that I identify myself with the perception that I have of them (B1-PT) I know the mission and values of my institution because I was in a management position. However, I think most of my colleagues do not know that reality. This is due to the institution's poor communication and traditional organizational culture. I identify with the essence of those values. However, what is "thought" and "written" often diverges from the behavior of the agents, which violates the principles of the mission and objectives (B2-PT) So far as the HEI to which I belong seeks excellence in training the individuals who choose the institution to obtain their academic qualifications. In terms of vision, my HEI aims to teach, inspire and empower its students to add value to society and the organizations where they work. It is also concerned with equipping its students not only with the technical skills (hard skills) but also with the soft skills that the labor market values so much, such as the ability to lead, undertake, take risks, and work in teams, etc. (B3-PT)
	Organizational Culture: Respect, Responsibility, Cooperation, Tolerance, Welcoming, Mutual Help and Solidarity	Some of the concepts you point out are present. I think there is a good environment, respect, collaborative work, or if that collaborative work does not always occur, at least there is the desire, the intention (A1-CL) We have a perfect working environment, respect, empathy, and tolerance, but sometimes we lack cooperation. This is because our demand is also very high, and we lack time to cooperate normally. (A2-CL)

(continued)

Thematic Codes		Excerpts
		There is competition, a separation between people, helping each other when necessary and not always. There are individual and group interests. For example, if there are prospects of a contest to increase in rank, you can see people trying to "go" over each other and feel that anything is possible. It pains me to say this, but people seem to stop being people and live obsessed with a specific position component at work (B1-PT) At the University, we still live in "little chapels". Tolerance, cooperation, welcoming, and mutual help, among many other values, are found within groups and little between groups. For this very reason, I believe that these values are not lived in the organization (B2-PT) More and more, I feel that there is cooperation and mutual help among my department colleagues. Maybe because we are not a very big department and a Department of Organization and Management, this culture of sharing, cooperation, and solidarity is felt in all the elements. There is a strong concern about integrating new colleagues. (B3-PT)
	Employees' Well Being	If we look at Valparaiso University as a whole, with all the schools, it is not sensitive. But if we focus on one school, yes, and this is because we are less, we are more humane, and we know each other (A1-CL) Roughly speaking, I think so. It is stated that it has been changing, offering training alternatives or workshops to help teachers and involving more social issues, contingency issues, inclusivity, the issue of inclusive language and stress management in the classroom, and mindfulness; that is, they have opened up in a certain way to go to not so classical and traditional in the training of professors and students since they can also participate. (A2-CL) In some cases, yes. Especially health problems in which there is somehow a spirit of solidarity and mutual help and support to employees on the part of the institution. However, the concern to organize activities and demands compatible with family activities does not always happen (B1-PT) I have to recognize that current department managers bring new feelings, and there is a tendency to improve the levels of collaboration, respect, and tolerance, among others, toward employees' problems. But such situations are not yet global, and the feelings of some try to override the feelings of others, nullifying them, for example, certain attitudes of influential groups, which end up conditioning others (B2-PT)

(continued)

Thematic Codes		Excerpts
	Collaboration and Team Spirit	The school where I work is networked, which comprises different subjects within the same line of work. However, it also groups other subjects. (A1-CL) We always talk about interdisciplinary issues between all the faculties. The councils are made between all the schools at the board level, and then it goes to the schools themselves, but it does not happen in practice. Finally, as a professor, I think that at the work level, there is no collaboration or team spirit. The work is seen more from the point of view of production and management and not so much from the work environment and human resources. (A2-CL) Jobs, in general, are collective works, and the structure of our school is always teamwork. Teamwork that depends on the shift direction can be organized in networks, committees, delegates, etc., and it is always promoted. (A3-CL) Not always. Sometimes, the institution promotes it, but people are not always willing or ready. The school asks, but sometimes it is not easy. For example, to define and organize an HPTP with specific rules. Each person thinks about their Curricular Unit and forgets about everything else, not being able or not wanting to see the whole. I do my job, and the next person can close the door. In reality, it cannot be like this. Some teachers cannot approach or relate subjects other than their own when sometimes extracting and complementing these ideas would be interesting. As a director of an HPTP, when I sometimes suggest group work in certain subjects, I often get an answer like, "But do I have to work with that person? Why? I would rather work alone because I can articulate things my way". Perhaps in these aspects, the institution could promote an environment of collaboration and team spirit so that each professor would not look only at their content but at their curricular unit (B1-PT) Theoretically, there is an effort to declare and emphasize team spirit and group work. However, daily things are different and individual values override group values, with adverse effects on the organizational climate and its culture (B2-PT) It organizes some social events for the employees to socialize and promotes some concerts for the community (B3-PT)

References

Alomar, A., Mydin, A. A., & Alaklabi, S. (2022). A Review of Authentic Leadership and Workplace Spirituality & Campus Sustainability in Educational Institutions. *International Transaction Journal of Engineering, Management, & Applied Sciences & Technologies*, *13*(2), 13A20 1–13. https://doi.org/10.14456/ITJEMAST.2022.36

Baptista Nunes, J. M., Kanwal, S., & Arif, M. (2017). Knowledge Management practices in Higher Education Institutions: a Systematic Literature Review. *IFLA WLIC 2017 – Wrocław, Poland – Libraries. Solidarity. Society*, *1994*, 1–16. http://library.ifla.org/view/conferences/2017/2017-08-18/731.html%0Ahttp://www.ncbi.nlm.nih.gov/pubmed/20237272%0Ahttp://www.pubmedcentral.nih.gov/articlerender.fcgi?artid=PMC2852648

Bell-Ellis, R. S., Jones, L., Longstreth, M., & Neal, J. (2015). Spirit at work in faculty and staff organizational commitment. *Journal of Management, Spirituality & Religion*, *12*(2), 156–177. https://doi.org/10.1080/14766086.2014.992355

Belwalkar, S., Vohra, V., & Pandey, A. (2018). The relationship between workplace spirituality, job satisfaction and organizational citizenship behaviors – an empirical study. *Social Responsibility Journal*, 14(2), 410–430. https://doi.org/10.1108/SRJ-05-2016-0096

Biswakarma, G. (2018). Impact of Workplace Spirituality on Employee Productivity in Nepalese Hospitality Organizations. *Journal of Tourism and Hospitality Education*, *8*, 62–76. https://doi.org/10.3126/jthe.v8i0.20011

Bolisani, E., & Bratianu, C. (2018). The Emergence of Knowledge Management. In Knowledge Management and Organizational Learning, 4, 22–37, July. https://doi.org/10.1007/978-3-319-60657-6_2

Bose, R. (2004). Knowledge management metrics. *Industrial Management & Data Systems*, 104(6), 457–468. https://doi.org/10.1108/02635570410543771

Brewer, P. D., & Brewer, K. L. (2010). Knowledge Management, Human Resource Management, and Higher Education: A Theoretical Model. *Journal of Education for Business*, *85*(6), 330–335. https://doi.org/10.1080/08832321003604938

Dandona, A. (2013). Spirituality at Workplace and Job satisfaction. *International Journal of Biosciences, Alternative and Holistic Medicine*; Coimbatore, 4(1), 1–9.

Dei, D.-G. J., & van der Walt, T. B. (2020). Knowledge management practices in universities: The role of communities of practice. *Social Sciences & Humanities Open*, *2*(1), 100025. https://doi.org/10.1016/j.ssaho.2020.100025

Devi Ramachandran, S., Chong, S., & Wong, K. (2013). Knowledge management practices and enablers in public universities: a gap analysis. *Campus-Wide Information Systems*, *30*(2), 76–94. https://doi.org/10.1108/10650741311306273

Dhamdhere, S., & Ganeshkhind, C. (2016). *Knowledge Management Model for Higher Educational Institutes. Journal of Commerce and Management Thought*, *6*(1), 130–161. https://doi.org/10.5958/0976-478x.2015.00010.5

Gelling, L. (2015). Qualitative research. *Nursing Standard*, *29*(30), 43–47. https://doi.org/10.7748/ns.29.30.43.e9749

Gupta, M., Kumar, V., & Singh, M. (2014). Creating Satisfied Employees Through Workplace Spirituality: A Study of the Private Insurance Sector in Punjab (India). *Journal of Business Ethics*, *122*(1), 79–88. https://doi.org/10.1007/s10551-013-1756-5

Halawi, L., Aronson, J., & McCarthy, R. (2005). Resource-Based View of Knowledge Management for Competitive Advantage. *The Electronic Journal of Knowledge Management*, *3*(2), 75–86.

Hoq, K. M. G., & Akter, R. (2012). Knowledge Management in Universities: Role of Knowledge Workers. *Bangladesh Journal of Library and Information Science*, *2*(1), 92–102. https://doi.org/10.3329/bjlis.v2i1.12925

Hsieh, H. F., & Shannon, S. E. (2005). Three approaches to qualitative content analysis. Qualitative Health Research, 15(9), 1277–1288. https://doi.org/10.1177/1049732305276687
I Ojo, A. (2016). Knowledge Management in Nigerian Universities: A Conceptual Model. *Interdisciplinary Journal of Information, Knowledge, and Management*, *11*, 331–345. https://doi.org/10.28945/3607
Ipe, M. (2003). Knowledge Sharing in Organizations: A Conceptual Framework. *Human Resource Development Review*, *2*(4), 337–359. https://doi.org/10.1177/1534484303257985
Jurkiewicz, C. L., & Giacalone, R. A. (2004). A Values Framework for Measuring the Impact of Workplace Spirituality on Organizational Performance. *Journal of Business Ethics*, *49*(2), 129–142. https://doi.org/10.1023/B:BUSI.0000015843.22195.b9
Karakas, F. (2010). Spirituality and performance in organizations: A literature review. *Journal of Business Ethics*, *94*(1), 89–106. https://doi.org/10.1007/s10551-009-0251-5
Kassaye, A. Y. (2018). Contemporary institutional solid waste management practices of Haramaya University, Eastern Ethiopia. *African Journal of Science, Technology, Innovation and Development*, *10*(2), 219–238. https://doi.org/10.1080/20421338.2018.1443412
Kavalić, M., Nikolić, M., Stanisavljev, S., Đorđević, D., Pečujlija, M., & Terek Stojanović, E. (2021). Knowledge Management and Financial Performance in Transitional Economies: the Case of Serbian Enterprises. *Journal of Business Economics and Management*, *22*(6), 1436–1455. https://doi.org/10.3846/jbem.2021.15540
Khari, C., & Sinha, S. (2018). Organizational Spirituality and Knowledge Sharing: A Model of Multiple Mediation. *Global Journal of Flexible Systems Management*, *19*(4), 337–348. https://doi.org/10.1007/s40171-018-0197-5
Kokt, D., & Palmer, E. P. (2019). Strategic priorities for cultivating commitment amongst academic staff: The militating effect of workplace spirituality. *SA Journal of Human Resource Management*, *17*, 1–8. https://doi.org/10.4102/sajhrm.v17i0.1054
Konz, G. N. P., & Ryan, F. X. (1999). Maintaining an organizational spirituality: no easy task. *Journal of Organizational Change Management*, *12*(3), 200–210. https://doi.org/10.1108/09534819910273865
Krishnakumar, S., & Neck, C. P. (2002). The "what", "why" and "how" of spirituality in the workplace. *Journal of Managerial Psychology*, *17*(3), 153–164. https://doi.org/10.1108/02683940210423060
Kvale, S (1996) *Interviews: An Introduction to Qualitative Research Interviewing*. Thousand Oaks, CA: SAGE Publications Inc.
Lakshmi, P. M., & Das, D. V. T. (2021). Exploring the Missing Links of Workplace Spirituality and Knowledge Management: a Conceptual Framework. *EPRA International Journal of Economic and Business Review*, *9*(10), 7–16. https://doi.org/10.36713/epra8688
Lameiras, M. D. (2016). *Análise Qualitativa de Entrevistas Estruturadas*. Universidade de Coimbra.
Lee, M. C. (2016). Knowledge management and innovation management: Best practices in knowledge sharing and knowledge value chain. *International Journal of Innovation and Learning*, *19*(2), 206–226. https://doi.org/10.1504/IJIL.2016.074475
Lindblom, A., & Tikkanen, H. (2010). Knowledge creation and business format franchising. *Management Decision*, *48*(2), 179–188. https://doi.org/10.1108/00251741011022563
Mat, N., Romli, R., & Noor, N. (2012). Modelling Workplace Spirituality and Teaching Effectiveness for Academician in Malaysia. *International Journal of Business and Management Studies*, *4*(1), 157–164. http://www.sobiad.org/eJOURNALS/journal_IJBM/arhieves/2012_Vol_4_n_1/norazuwa_mat.pdf
McKee, M. C., Mills, J. H., & Driscoll, C. (2008). Making Sense of Workplace Spirituality: Towards a New Methodology. Journal of Management, Spirituality & Religion, 5(2), 190–210. doi:10.1080/14766080809518699
Milliman, J., Czaplewski, A. J., & Ferguson, J. (2003). Workplace spirituality and employee work attitudes. *Journal of Organizational Change Management*, *16*(4), 426–447. https://doi.org/10.1108/09534810310484172

Nasab, M. M., Nasab, A. S., Ghaemi, B., Nozari, M. R., Pour, R. G., & Pirzad, A. (2017). New organizational Knowledge Management: Principles, Technics, Concepts, and Strategies. *Helix*, *7*(2), 1323–1332. https://doi.org/10.29042/2017-1323-1332

Nawaz, N., Durst, S., Hariharasudan, A., & Shamugia, Z. (2020). Knowledge Management Practices in Higher Education Institutions – A Comparative Study. *Polish Journal of Management Studies*, *22*(2), 291–308. https://doi.org/10.17512/pjms.2020.22.2.20

Nonaka, I. (1991). The Knowledge-creating company. Harvard Business Review, New York, *69*(6), 96–104, Nov./Dec

Omerzel, D., Biloslavo, R., & Trnavcevic, A. (2011). Knowledge management and organisational innovation in higher education. *Journal for East European Management Studies*, *16*(3), 111–139. https://doi.org/10.2307/23281852

Palmer, P. J. (2003). Teaching with heart and soul: Reflections on spirituality in teacher education. *Journal of Teacher Education*, *54*(5), 376–385. https://doi.org/10.1177/0022487103257359

Quarchioni, S., Paternostro, S., & Trovarelli, F. (2020). Knowledge management in higher education: a literature review and further research avenues. *Knowledge Management Research & Practice*, *20*(2), 304–319. https://doi.org/10.1080/14778238.2020.1730717

Quivy R. & Campenhoudt Luc Van (1995) Manual de Investigação em Ciências Sociais, Gradiva.

Ratcliffe-Martin, V., Coakes, E., & Sugden, G. (2000). Knowledge Management issues in universities. *VINE*, *30*(4), 14–18. https://doi.org/10.1108/eb040770

Rego, A., Souto, S., & Couto, M. P. (2007). Espiritualidade nas organizações, positividade. *Comportamento Organizacional e Gestão*, *13*(1), 7–36.

Rocha, R. G., & Pinheiro, P. G. (2020). Organizational Spirituality: Concept and Perspectives. *Journal of Business Ethics*, *171*(2), 241–252. https://doi.org/10.1007/s10551-020-04463-y

Rocha, R., & Pinheiro, P. (2021). Can Organizational Spirituality Contribute to Knowledge Management? *Management Dynamics in the Knowledge Economy*, *9*(1), 107–121. https://doi.org/10.2478/mdke-2021-0008

Rodrigues, L., Maccari, E., & De Almeida, M. (2004). Knowledge management in higher education. *The Internet Society: Advances in Learning, Commerce and Securuity*, *3*, 309–318. https://doi.org/10.2495/NL040321

Rowley, J. (1995). Management development: New agendas for information professionals. *Library Management*, *16*(1), 5–10. https://doi.org/10.1108/01435129510076178

Rowley, J. (2000). Is higher education ready for knowledge management? *International Journal of Educational Management*, *14*(7), 325–333. https://doi.org/10.1108/09513540010378978

Saks, A. M. (2011). Workplace spirituality and employee engagement. Journal of Management, Spirituality & Religion, 8(4), 317–340. doi:10.1080/14766086.2011.63017

Saunders, B., Sim, J., Kingstone, T., Baker, S., Waterfield, J., Bartlam, B., Burroughs, H., & Jinks, C. (2018). Saturation in qualitative research: exploring its conceptualization and operationalization. Quality & Quantity, 52(4), 1893–1907. https://doi.org/10.1007/s11135-017-0574-8

Shahzadi, I. (2017). Clan Culture and Spiritual Motivation to devise Academicians' Intention towards Tacit Knowledge Sharing in business schools of Pakistan. *Journal of Managerial Sciences*, *XI*(03), 459–484. http://www.qurtuba.edu.pk/jms/default_files/JMS/special_edition/4 GDHEC/24 (AIC-GDHEC 2017) 459–484 Irum Shehzadi GDHEC-777.pdf

Silva, E. A. da. (2013). As metodologias qualitativas de investigação nas Ciências Sociais. *Revista Angolana de Sociologia*, *12*, 77–99. https://doi.org/10.4000/ras.740

Soliman, M., Di Virgilio, F., Figueiredo, R., & Sousa, M. J. (2021). The impact of workplace spirituality on lecturers' attitudes in tourism and hospitality higher education institutions. *Tourism Management Perspectives*, *38*(2021), 100826. https://doi.org/10.1016/j.tmp.2021.100826

Spencer, L., Ritchie, J., Lewis, J., & Dillon, L. (2003). Quality in Qualitative Evaluation: A framework for assessing research evidence A Quality Framework The report was produced on behalf of the Cabinet Office. *National Centre for Social Research, UK*, 3. www.natcen.ac.uk

Stemler, S.E. (2015). Emerging trends in content analysis. In R. Scott and S. Kosslyn (Eds.), Emerging Trends in the Social and Behavioral Sciences. Hoboken, NJ: John Wiley and Sons

Thakur, K., Singh, J., & Kaur, P. (2017). A study of spirituality at work and organisational commitment of university teachers. *Pertanika Journal of Social Sciences and Humanities*, *25*(4), 1501–1514.

Van den Hooff, B., & Huysman, M. (2009). Managing knowledge sharing: Emergent and engineering approaches. *Information & Management*, *46*(1), 1–8. https://doi.org/10.1016/j.im.2008.09.002

Vasconcelos, A. F. (2018). Workplace spirituality: empirical evidence revisited. *Management Research Review*, *41*(7), 789–821. https://doi.org/10.1108/MRR-07-2017-0232

Wicks, A. (2014). Stakeholder theory and spirituality. Journal of Management, Spirituality & Religion, 11(4), 294–306. doi:10.1080/14766086.2014.917984

Yin, R. K., (1994). Case Study Research Design and Methods: Applied Social Research and Methods Series. Second edn. Thousand Oaks, CA: Sage Publications Inc.

Zheng, T. (2017). A Literature Review on Knowledge Sharing. *Open Journal of Social Sciences*, *05*(03), 51–58. https://doi.org/10.4236/jss.2017.53006

Juha Kansikas

Chapter 10
Indicative Typology of Spiritual Entrepreneurs: Spirituality and Its Contesting Ideologies

Abstract: The spirituality and ideologies of leaders and organizations have attracted attention in management science. The study of entrepreneurs from the perspective of spiritual and ideological thinking needs further attention, as conceptual challenges currently beset it. The ideologies of entrepreneurs are typically seen in the current research as political thinking. Therefore, this chapter aims to increase the conceptual understanding of this indicative typology of spiritual entrepreneurs and any conflicting personal ideologies they may hold. Contesting ideologies are defined in this study as the individual cognitive logic meant to explain the world around us. Contesting ideology replaces spiritual thinking with personal egoistic interests. The mindset and values of entrepreneurs that stem from spiritual knowledge are discussed in the context of entrepreneurial reasoning. This study contributes to the literature on how entrepreneurship is affected by spirituality, as well as the values related to it. Using a typological analysis of the selected research literature and applying the classification theme advanced by the cognitive-conative-affective approach, the study shows that the typology of spiritual entrepreneurs consists of societal, family-centric, environmental, religion-centric, anti-social, and opportunistic entrepreneurs.

Keywords: Spiritual Knowledge, Spirituality, Entrepreneurship, Entrepreneur, Typology

Indicative Typology of Spiritual Entrepreneurs: Spirituality and Its Contesting Ideologies

There are multiple research gaps in how spirituality impacts management and entrepreneurship, as it has numerous characterizations and contexts (Rocha & Pinheiro, 2021). It offers explanations that help us understand the world and its multiple entities. These explanations, as personal ideologies, are culturally influenced in every context in which they take place (Alshehri et al., 2021; Henning & Henning, 2021; Nandram, 2016). The ideologies of both leaders and organizations have gathered attention in management science (Arvate & Story, 2021; Kakavelakis & Edwards, 2021). These leader and

---

Juha Kansikas, Jyvaskyla School of Business and Economics, University of Jyvaskyla, Finland, e-mail: juha.kansikas@jyu.fi

https://doi.org/10.1515/9783111010410-011

organizational ideologies offer pathways to understanding the variety of ethical and logical reasoning about the reality of the world around us.

By entrepreneur, we mean a person who owns, manages, and runs a small business. Thus, an entrepreneur is a significant decision-maker and resource holder in a small business (Howorth et al., 2005). Studying entrepreneurs from the perspective of their ideology needs more attention, as this area is not widely understood because of its conceptual ambiguity (Vogel, 2022). In addition, the ideologies of entrepreneurs are viewed in the research as political agendas and political thinking (Jarrodi et al., 2019; Maldonado-Bautista et al., 2021; Mollan & Geesin, 2020), which aim to change social conditions by achieving a political mission (such as Trumpism). This political perspective, however, does not encompass the full conceptual awareness of ideologies. Some entrepreneurs who do not exhibit spiritual knowledge have replaced spirituality with contesting personal ideologies in their thinking. Just as there are spiritually thinking entrepreneurs, some also hold atheistic, materialistic, opportunistic, and egoistic ideologies. These characteristics replace spiritual knowledge as contesting, often highly person-centric, egoistic, and narcissistic ideologies. Spiritual thinking enables ethical awareness and values. Thus, the spiritual thinking of entrepreneurs is personal. The values guiding their business decision-making vary according to these individual preferences.

A belief in God, multiple Gods, or no God are examples of different forms of spiritual thinking. Both religiousness and spirituality can be influenced by person-specific ideologies, which stem from cognitive, conative, and affective constructs based on the previous experiences of entrepreneurs. Cognitive constructs reflect the thoughts, worldviews, and mindsets of spiritual entrepreneurs. Motivating an entrepreneur and being willing to run a business reflect conative aspects (Masele, 2019). These business experiences influence entrepreneurs' mindsets and ideological thinking. Affective experiences reflect entrepreneurs' emotions and emotional knowledge, influencing spirituality (Lim & Kim, 2020). Cognitive, conative, and affective perceptions are personal experiences reflecting subjective reasoning (Lee et al., 2022).

The research question addressed in this chapter is: *What is the indicative typology of spiritual entrepreneurs?* Entrepreneur spirituality should be typologized using the classification theme of cognitive-conative-affective constructs. As the spirituality of entrepreneurs is analyzed in this chapter, contesting ideologies of spirituality are debated to create a more comprehensive view of entrepreneurial logic. This is accomplished using this typology to describe distinct types of entrepreneurs (Smith, 2017).

Methodology of the Typological Analysis

The typological analysis conducted in early entrepreneurship research suffered from multiple classifications. These studies contained overlapping labels of entrepreneurial concepts. Thus, Woo et al. (1991) suggested a consistent style of analysis and critical consideration of the conceptual labels, types, and integrated typologies in entrepreneurship. Rigorous typological analysis in entrepreneurship research aims for conceptual clarity in classification fit and interpretation. Accountability in analysis demands similar entrepreneur typologies even when different researchers analyze the same material multiple times. Another way to solve conceptual challenges is to understand the different types of entrepreneurs through a theoretical lens when developing such a typology (Nikolaou et al., 2018), which is the path that this study follows by understanding the cognitive-conative-affective classification theme in spiritual entrepreneurship and its corresponding contesting ideologies.

Typological analysis can be conducted through a conceptual approach or by collecting empirical data, which leads to the development of a typology of entrepreneurs (Erpf et al., 2019; Nulleshi, 2022; Pandey & Amezcua, 2020; Salamanca & Alcaraz, 2022). Both methodological choices are valid in creating a typology in entrepreneurship research. This study's typological analysis of the selected research literature was conducted through a conceptual approach (Dahlke et al., 2021). The research literature was chosen using a keyword search in Scopus.com. The keywords and their combinations used in this research include typology and entrepreneur, typological and analysis and management, values and entrepreneur, spirituality and entrepreneur, spiritual knowledge and entrepreneur, spirituality and spiritual knowledge, and ideology and leader. First, their scientific journal ranking (based on the quality of the outlets) was prioritized in selecting research articles for the analysis. Conference papers, theses, political reports, and other nonrefereed and unpublished publications were removed from the analysis. Second, publications from the analysis that did not contain relevant content for the analysis were excluded. Thus, researcher interpretation was conducted. Such interpretation aims to develop new conceptual entities and conceptualizations regarding the entrepreneur's spiritual typology. New conceptualizations are typical for typology-based methodology and contain new information based on conceptual understandings and the prior literature or empirical evidence (Bunduchi et al., 2022).

We can divide the typological analysis steps into the categories of authors, typology bases, and entrepreneur types. In the category of authors, we recognize those scholars who have defined entrepreneurs in their study. The category of typology base refers to the data collection methodology used to create definitions and entrepreneur typologies. This can be a concept-based (such as the preferences of entrepreneurs) or a data collection-based (such as interviews) approach. The categorical types of entrepreneurs serve as a starting point for a typology by creating labels for entrepreneurs and contributing to our understanding of what kinds of entrepreneurs there are (Risker, 1998; see also Pisani et al., 2017). This study adopts the Risker (1998) concept-based approach by first understanding spirituality. This way, the types of entrepreneurs related to spirituality will be understood.

Spirituality and Spiritual Knowledge in Entrepreneurship

This chapter focuses on recognizing the concepts behind spirituality and spiritual knowledge, particularly from the perspective of entrepreneurship. Thus, this chapter provided details regarding what spirituality is in entrepreneurship and how it differs from other spirituality. Entrepreneurship is a value-driven activity, and entrepreneurs see value directly influencing business success (Morris & Schindehutte, 2005). These types of results have been achieved as the values of spirituality have been studied in the context of career development in business (Campanario et al., 2022). Values in business are individual values held by entrepreneurs that are business-specific and related to the environment and context of the business in which decisions are made (Sotiropoulou et al., 2021; Wiid et al., 2013). These personal values stem from ideologies on competing, surviving, growing, and behaving in a business environment. Ideology refers to a cognitive view of the world around us that influences our way of thinking. Ideologies contest those explanations of existence typically held by spiritual and religious mindsets.

According to Zsolnai and Illes (2017), connectedness is an essential element in the spirituality of humankind. It creates a need to be connected to a superior force and to communicate somehow with the power of God (or gods). This need for connectedness creates spirituality and belongingness in communities such as churches. This causes interconnectedness among people, which reflects social and mutual belonging together. Interconnectedness is essential not only for churches or other spiritual or religious movements but also for workplaces and organizations that try to improve their working conditions and work satisfaction (Long & Driscoll, 2015; Pardasani et al., 2014). Individual spirituality has consequences for the values that organizations represent and maintain (Vasconcelos, 2018). Negative and positive leadership practices like corporate governance reflect organizational spirituality and values. Spirituality is not just for personnel value management in business. It can improve personnel well-being and, thus, the psychological assets of organizations needed in times of crisis and change (Ihl et al., 2022).

Spirituality stems from mental human experiences, making us believe in values and ethics. Values are connected to entrepreneurs' religiousness, influencing entrepreneurial behavior, decision-making, and actions (Gursoy et al., 2017). Spirituality and religiousness influence each other in ethical decision-making, as their purposes are, in some parts, like each other about connectedness, interconnectedness, and beliefs (Alshehri et al., 2021).

Belief in supernatural forces and magics is one expression of spirituality. Belief in magic is, in many societies, anti-religious – and sometimes personal – thinking. As Ganzin et al. (2020) mention, belief in magics can offer tools for entrepreneurs in future predictions and thus for preparing for the uncertain future. In that context, magics are a tool for spiritual entrepreneurs to cope with uncertainty and unpredictable future business. This personal ideology of believing in the supernatural is culture-specific and takes multiple forms worldwide.

Spirituality and religiousness in business are based on a subjective mixture of work ethics, decision-making, and social-financial gains (Vu, 2021). Nandram (2016) highlights intuition as a form of entrepreneurial spirituality. As intuition is based on gut feelings about earlier experiences, it reflects the spiritual thinking of entrepreneurs. It influences the vision of business, rapid decisions on customer service, and operational decisions. Intuition in entrepreneurship is integral to decision-making and being proactive and agile in changing environments with scarce resources available (Baldacchino et al., 2015; Mitchell et al., 2005). Intuition is not necessarily a positive factor in entrepreneurship, as it can also lead to adverse outcomes and contain false impulses in a situation. Thus, ideas and initiatives for decision-making stemming from intuition need critical assessment and analysis before any action will be taken.

According to Kauanui et al. (2008, p. 170), spirituality in entrepreneurship is characterized by personal self-expressions regarding actions, work, ethics, and the passion to work. As an ideologically opposing factor, few ethical entrepreneurs focus on maximizing wealth accumulation regardless of the causal outcomes or potential moral dilemmas that may be involved. Spirituality reflects ethical thinking (Breidenstein, 2020) as a form of thinking, behavior, and action aiming at reasonable and fair decisions. Thus, spirituality in entrepreneurship reflects meaningful work, honesty, and integrity. Spiritual knowledge that stems from entrepreneurs' work, actions, and experiences shapes their thinking. Therefore, spirituality in entrepreneurship takes multiple forms. Kauanui et al. (2010) suggest that spiritual entrepreneurs seek to combine play and work. Some entrepreneurs who maintain and develop spiritual knowledge may aim to increase their happiness and fun in life and business. Thus, the goal of work is not simply profit, and goal setting and goal achievement are related to work rewards. Work contains elements of humor, entertainment, amusement, and happy moments. Spirituality-based decision-making and actions can increase the harmonious and positive experiences that occur in entrepreneurship (Chu, 2007); thus, spirituality affects both the well-being and success of entrepreneurs.

One of the dilemmas related to spiritual entrepreneurship is whether material motives are more important than moral motives. Focusing on ethics and morality can result in financial losses in the business environment, which favors profit maximizing-based thinking positioned in competition with others (Cheung & King, 2004). Thus, spirituality in entrepreneurship reflects decision-making, actual decisions, and the causal consequences of those decisions (Fernando & Jackson, 2006). Moral decision-making reflects ethical thinking and leads to a chain of behavior, actions, and causal outcomes that result from those decisions. Spirituality in business decision-making creates beliefs for entrepreneurs. This includes believing in a higher power, being interconnected with society and its goals, and engaging in ethical and legal thinking. These beliefs can be an asset for entrepreneurs in the output creation of business operations (Rashid & Ratten, 2022). Beliefs offer moral codes that help entrepreneurs to understand or express their spirituality. They reflect experimental decision-making based on earlier transactions and negotiations by confirming or rejecting personal beliefs. These beliefs are connected to entrepreneurs' identities, formulated by identity-based roles, creativity, and previous experiences in business (Zhan et al., 2022).

Interpretative Assumptions on Spirituality in Entrepreneurship

Spirituality takes multiple forms in entrepreneurship. Religious entrepreneurs are only one type of spiritual entrepreneur. Spirituality in entrepreneurship is not simply institutionally oriented but contains work- and decision-making-related perspectives. Spiritually alert entrepreneurs combine play and work in creative and innovative contexts. Allowing resources to be used for arts, music, games, sports, hobbies, family issues, informal social events, and unstructured timeslots devoted to thinking and reading increases the opportunities for creative ideas and renewed thinking in business. Creating a new business vision often results from this playful spiritual knowledge.

Playing with ideas and generating new worlds of thoughts through creative processing in a business context reflects the intuitions of entrepreneurs. Intuitions are emotion- and experience-based thoughts on business that reflect earlier customer transactions, customer service feedback, competition, product launches, sales, HR recruiting, investments, and many other business aspects that have been commonly encountered. Intuitions are based on a gut feeling about something. Intuition involves spiritual and immaterial thinking that could be documented as calculations, plans, pictures, and drawings. Intuition in entrepreneurship is personal and reflects entrepreneurial identity, experiential learning and the entrepreneurial journey that has taken place.

Ethical thinking as an entrepreneur leads to seeing spirituality as an essential part of decision-making and causal thinking. Recognizing possible moral dilemmas and the ethical reasoning related to them increases spirituality in entrepreneurship. Moral thinking – what is right and wrong for the entrepreneur, the company and its multiple stakeholders, and society – creates a value-based mindset in entrepreneurship. These values reflect longitudinal personal norms. Values can also be organizational, as in the case of family businesses, which could remain in the same family for generations. Therefore, family entrepreneurs and their businesses might contain long-lasting values shaped through multigenerational experiences, concepts, and decision-making. Thus, the values of family entrepreneurs might be more collectively and organizationally born than those of self-employed, solo entrepreneurs.

Values are an aspect of ethical thinking, decision-making, behavior, and the actions occurring in the sociocultural context in which entrepreneurs operate. Values create beliefs containing immaterial and intangible tacit knowledge as competitive advantages that reflect what we represent and who we are. This identity-building process in entrepreneurship takes a long time. Spirituality in entrepreneurship is based on believing – and trusting – in the right decision, action, and business operation from the perspectives of ethics, profitability, and entrepreneurial identity. Beliefs are reflections of spirituality and spiritual knowledge processing (see Table 10.1). The table illustrates these concepts to reflect the conceptual preunderstanding prevalent in the entrepreneurship literature on spirituality and spiritual knowledge.

The theoretical preunderstanding in Table 10.1 shows that conceptual and empirical research on spiritual entrepreneurship is still in its infancy and contains multiple research gaps. Spirituality is a socio-cultural concept with religious and historical roots in controlling and governing society and its members. Spirituality takes institutional forms, such as normative and legislative power in society. The doctrines and viewpoints of religion are taught and nurtured at the institutional church, then become a part of human cultural and historical heritage.

Connectedness, a conative motivation to belong somewhere and connect with others, is typical for collective and individual spirituality. Spirituality can be an individual part of personal identity and an institutionalized concept. In that case, connectedness can be connected to the supernatural – or gods or God – in multiple ways, such as prayer. Collective spirituality – a need to connect with other spiritual or religious people – can occur as belonging to a church. Interconnectedness, as a need to participate in social and spiritual events and to be interconnected with multiple people, events, and organizations, creates a network for spiritual entrepreneurs.

Connectedness and interconnectedness increase spiritual knowledge and the opportunities to benchmark and compare personal spirituality to the surrounding world. As spiritual thinking increases the well-being of entrepreneurs, it is worth studying whether both connectedness and interconnectedness serve as integral mechanisms of the positive health impact of spirituality in future entrepreneurship research. Having social contexts for spiritual thinking might expand spiritual knowledge and foster the spiritual experiences and thoughts that entrepreneurs encounter in their daily business operations.

Classifications of Spiritual Entrepreneurship and its Contesting Ideologies: Cognitive, Conative, and Affective Aspects

Next, this study will analyze the classification theme of entrepreneurs' cognitive, conative, and affective constructs to delineate spirituality and its contesting ideologies. Conative, cognitive, and affective aspects are interlinked and thus offer a framework to help understand entrepreneurship (Johannisson, 2016; Keller & Kozlinska, 2019; Kyrö et al., 2011; Lomberg et al., 2019). These aspects have also been studied in education sciences, as individuals combine cognitive-conative-affective aspects by selecting past, present, and future knowledge, motives, thoughts, and feelings (Longva & Foss, 2018; Neergaard et al., 2021).

Table 10.1: Interpretations of spiritual entrepreneurship and its theoretical preunderstanding.

Concept	Author	Interpretation based on article content	Interpretative assumption
Spirituality	Rocha and Pinheiro (2021)	Conceptual definitions of spirituality are still vague and in their infancy.	More conceptual and empirical research on spirituality in the contexts of management and entrepreneurship are needed.
Spirituality and its characteristics	Alshehri et al. (2021); Ganzin et al. (2020); Ihl et al. (2022)	Spirituality positively influences well-being. Spirituality and religion are not synonyms with each other, but rather influence each other and contain some overlapping elements. Elements such as the belief in magic and supernatural forces are considered anti-religious by some institutional religions.	Spirituality is a sociocultural concept that takes multiple forms depending on the research questions derived from empirical evidence.
Spiritual entrepreneurship	Breidenstein (2020); Chu (2007); Fernando and Jackson (2006); Kauanui et al. (2008, 2010)	The individual perspective on spiritual entrepreneurship is more typical than the organizational or regional perspectives. Spiritual entrepreneurship is a self-expressed construct which combines ethical decision-making with a passion toward work. Spiritual entrepreneurship is about combining play and work in creative and in innovative ways. Spiritual-related decisions increase positive entrepreneurship experiences. They reflect the causal consequences of business operations.	Spiritual entrepreneurship is an individual-level topic; therefore, more case studies are needed to understand the types of spiritual entrepreneurs. Creative entrepreneurial ecosystems and individuals reflect multiple contexts for spirituality in work and for the creation of novelty for customers and markets.
Values of spirituality	Campanario et al. (2022); Cheung and King (2004); Gursoy et al. (2017); Vasconcelos (2018).	The values related to spirituality positively influence career development. They impact entrepreneurial behavior, decision-making, and actions. Spirituality impacts the values of organizations and individuals. Ethical values in decision-making do not necessarily aim for profit maximizing, but also for social results.	Ethical or unethical values influence the spirituality and cognitive-conative-affective constructs of entrepreneurs. Ethical thinking explains spirituality and its contesting ideologies.

Connectedness and interconnectedness	Long and Driscoll (2015); Pardasani et al. (2014); Zsolnai and Illes (2017)	Connectedness creates the need for spirituality in terms of a desire to connect with spiritual or religious experiences and events. Interconnectedness creates a need to actively participate in social events related to institutional organizations like the church.	Connectedness reflects spirituality and spiritual knowledge sharing in social contexts. Interconnectedness explains spiritual and religious movements in history. The organization of institutional religion and voluntary work reflect interconnectedness with spirituality and religion.
Intuition	Nandram (2016)	Intuition refers to entrepreneurial spirituality and spiritual thinking as vision building, agile decision-making and operative actions.	Intuition reflects the mindset of spiritual entrepreneurs who use spiritual knowledge in business design. Experiential learning is typical for entrepreneurs, and intuitive decision-making reflects the use of these earlier experiences.
Beliefs	Rashid and Ratten (2022); Zhan et al. (2022).	Spirituality in business creates beliefs that serve as psychological capital for entrepreneurs in business operations. Beliefs do not simply influence business its related and decision-making but also impacts the identities of entrepreneurs.	Beliefs and spirituality influence each other. They both act as important motivators for entrepreneurial behavior and actions.

Source: Author

The classification style used in the typological analysis is adopted by Pret and Cogan (2019), who use this classification strategy to analyze the types of entrepreneurs and reveal their underlying typology. Thus, the main emphasis of classification methods is the analysis of conceptual identities and their characteristics. Classification themes increase knowledge of how various types are positioned about each other and what distinct types of entrepreneurs there are (McLaughlin et al., 2022; Pret & Cogan, 2019). By classifying the types of entrepreneurs related to spirituality and its contesting ideologies (Serres et al., 2022), this study contributes to the spiritual knowledge literature by increasing the understanding of spiritual entrepreneurs. The implications for entrepreneurship research based on typology are related to the literature on spirituality and management (Abebe et al., 2020). Thus, classification leads us to understand how various types of entrepreneurs might differ from each other or overlap with each other in terms of their identities (Lubberink et al., 2018; Mair et al., 2012; Müller & Korsgaard, 2018). The classification theme of cognitive, conative, and affective constructs is used to delineate entrepreneur typology, which assigns different labels to the different types of entrepreneurs (Candeias & Sarkar, 2022; Kibler et al., 2021).

Cognitive constructs are learned, experienced, and adopted from the environment. Thus, they are highly personal human assets influencing new venture creation and entrepreneurship (Sriyakul & Jermsittiparsert, 2019). They are a conglomerate of recognition processes, identification, understanding, thinking, reasoning, and conclusion-making (Moore et al., 2021; Muñoz, 2018; Politis et al., 2019). Cognitive processes lead to concepts that influence entrepreneurial mindset (Larsen, 2022) and, therefore, behavior, decision-making, and actions (Benevolo et al., 2021). Affective aspects are combinations of feelings that create long-term emotions, determining how we feel about something (Cristofaro, 2020). Temperament and mood are also part of the affective aspects of the human mind. Affective assets can be positive or negative about something, and they reflect our past experiences and our learned and adopted ways of thinking (Kurczewska et al., 2018). Conative aspects are human personal constructs of will and motivation. These conative aspects impact our interests and efforts to achieve our goals.

Cognitive aspects reflect entrepreneurs' thinking, understanding, and reasoning (Costin et al., 2019). Cognitive logic is subjective due to the unique experiences and learning events that have taken place in human life. Thus, cognitive logic is personal regarding its reasoning processes concerning business, opportunities, risks, resources, and other entrepreneurial processes. Conative constructs reflect the will and motivation to do something, participate, and make decisions related to the action (Rooney et al., 2021). Conative constructs are meaningful to entrepreneurial intention and the personal motives behind pursuing entrepreneurship. They possess, together with cognitive aspects and affective assets, a combination of items that lead to either engaging in a new business start-up or not. This study does not focus on metacognitions, metacognitions, and meta-affections, defined as meta-competencies. These are needed to manage and control behavior and its outcomes (Ustav & Venesaar, 2018).

Indicative Typology and Its Characteristics

Connectedness (Zsolnai & Illes, 2017) and interconnectedness are typical for spiritual entrepreneurship (Long & Driscoll, 2015; Pardasani et al., 2014). They take multiple forms in the spiritual thinking of entrepreneurs (see Table 10.2). Society and its goals offer multiple opportunities for belonging and mutual understanding. Family, which is not essential only to family businesses but can be just as impactful for other entrepreneurs, creates possibilities for solid ties that can last forever. This interconnectedness plays a role for environment-oriented entrepreneurs and religion-oriented entrepreneurs. The need for connectedness and interconnectedness with other people, society, and the environment creates types of spiritual entrepreneurs.

Table 10.2: Indicative typology of spiritual entrepreneurship and its contesting ideologies (classification style cognitive-conative-affective constructs).

	Reasoning, understanding, and thinking	**Willpower and motivation**	**Examples of possible emotions**
Types of spiritual entrepreneurs	**Cognitive aspects**	**Conative aspects**	**Affective aspects**
Societal Entrepreneurs	Society and social value in business	Change, mission, social acceptance	Optimistic, pleased, satisfied
Family-centric entrepreneurs	Family and its interests in business	Continuity, family heritage	Tender, Intimate, loving, devoted, passionate
Environmental entrepreneurs	Saving the environments and its resources, proactive thinking	Causing change, motives to act and to influence society	Enjoyment, satisfaction, peace
Religion-centric entrepreneurs	The God (or gods) and institutions like church can guide and help people	Common good, The will of God or the gods, status quo of society	Conservativeness, control
Contesting ideologies			
Anti-social entrepreneurs	Legislation and ethics prevent business operations, cruel and hostile thinking toward others	Victory, whatever it costs, revengeful behavior	Angry, bitter, mad, desperate, unhappy, miserable, hopeless, narcissistic, psychopathic or Machiavellian behavior (or a combination of these three)

Table 10.2 (continued)

	Reasoning, understanding, and thinking	Willpower and motivation	Examples of possible emotions
Types of spiritual entrepreneurs	**Cognitive aspects**	**Conative aspects**	**Affective aspects**
Opportunistic entrepreneurs	Maximizing profit whatever the cost	Disrespect toward others, motivation to damage others and gain personal profits	Egoism, selfishness, and narcissistic, psychopathic or Machiavellian behavior (or a combination of these three)

Source: Author

Societal entrepreneurs feel connected to societal goals and social missions. Spirituality stems from social context, social relationships, and the aim of achieving the common good. Societal entrepreneurship is not a synonym for social entrepreneurship, which refers to the business model and types of operations an entrepreneur applies. Societal entrepreneurship as a form of spiritual entrepreneurship can encompass both social entrepreneurship and fully commercial entrepreneurship. Thus, it contains socially enterprising, hybrid organizations, and commercially oriented businesses that also partly aim to achieve social goals (Lehner & Kansikas, 2012, 2013).

Environmental entrepreneurs differ from societal entrepreneurs because their spirituality is based on environmental health, resource recycling, and environmental management. A future orientation and active approach toward recognizing societal issues related to environmental problems is typical for environmental spirituality. Environmental spirituality reflects the relationship between humans and nature and looks to nature as a source of inspiration, relaxation, and the common good. Religion-centric entrepreneurs follow in their spirituality gods, the God or churches as institutions of authority. Conservative values are typical of institutional religiousness. These values influence spiritual entrepreneurship, which is religion-centric (Gursoy et al., 2017).

Connectedness and interconnectedness, typical goals of societal, family-centric, environmental, and religion-centric spiritual entrepreneurs, diminish, even disappear entirely in some cases, when contesting ideologies overtake a spiritual mindset. Thus, spiritual entrepreneurship has contested ideologies challenging spiritual knowledge from ethics, legislation, norms, and intuitions regarding proper action. In contrast to socioenvironmental cognitions, conations, and affections, subjective materialistic and egoistic purposes compete with spiritual knowledge for some entrepreneurs. These antisocial and opportunistic entrepreneurs replace spirituality with ideologies positing superior personal knowledge and direction and the effectuation of being more critical than others. Narcissism, as self-love and hate of others, leads to the everlasting cognition of superior position and knowledge (Leung et al., 2021). It also prevents learning from failure in entrepreneurship (Liu et al., 2019). A lack of spirituality in decision-making leads to psychopathy and Machiavellianism. Psychopathic personality does not recognize other people's emotions, and people who suffer from this lack the empathy and intelligence related to the recognition of the emotions of others. Machiavellianism is a manipulative leadership style designed to influence and control personnel and customers to fulfill their unethical goals (Wu et al., 2019), influencing entrepreneurs' cognitive-conative-affective mindset.

One assumption derived from this research setting is that types of spiritual entrepreneurs can overlap, and one person can change their type of spirituality or contesting ideology depending on the situation and context. Thus, an individual's types of spirituality do not remain consistent throughout their personal history. Instead, they disappear, change, transform, and overlap with each other as one's personal life changes. The types of spiritual entrepreneurship can also be transformed according to social situations, and thus, spirituality can become altered when talking with customers, family, employees, or media. Hybrid types of spiritual entrepreneurship can occur as combinations of the characteristics of the entrepreneurship types presented in this paper. Therefore, spirituality and its contesting ideologies in entrepreneurship are subjective because long-lasting values and norms can influence them. Some of the characteristics of personal spirituality can be unchangeable. In that case, they become a part of a person's identity. Therefore, we should study these types of spiritual entrepreneurs empirically, mainly using a qualitative research setting, to understand the traits of spiritual identities. Some entrepreneurs do not belong to any of the types presented as the indicative typology, and they may not hold any spiritual knowledge or contesting ideologies. A study of the behavior and anti-spiritual mindset of these types of entrepreneurs offers new research opportunities.

Discussion and Conclusion

The spiritual dimensions of entrepreneurship do not just cover value-based ethical questions. Thinking of spiritual entrepreneurs only as religious businesspeople gives a limited understanding of spiritual entrepreneurship. As religious institutions contain influential and well-known entrepreneurs locally and globally, they represent a visible sample of spiritual knowledge in entrepreneurship. Spirituality and its contexts are diverse, and therefore, spirituality in entrepreneurship is not confined to just decision-making, actions, and behavior but also references the techniques to create novel opportunities through play, intuition, creativity, and innovativeness.

The chapter's research question is: *What is the indicative typology of spiritual entrepreneurship?* As suggested earlier, some of the types of spiritual entrepreneurs might overlap. Societal and environmental entrepreneurial archetypes provide an example of this interdependence from the perspective of the entrepreneurial identities of spiritual businesspeople. Environmental entrepreneurs are motivated to contribute to society, which may be a point of differentiation from societal entrepreneurs who focus on environmental problem-solving and tools to save resources efficiently (Lehner & Kansikas, 2012, 2013). This can be accomplished through developing and testing new technology related to manufacturing, incremental innovations that make minor improvements to current products and services, recycling management, and customer-chain improvements. Environmental entrepreneurs motivate themselves by finding solutions to difficult and complex problems that are partly unsolvable with the currently available technology.

Family-centric entrepreneurs teach us how to manage the same business through subsequent generations and how to control a family-fun business. Spirituality as related to the family is conservative in that the values that are typical for family-centric entrepreneurs focus on continuity, family culture cultivation, multigenerational work and consensus-style decision-making (Long & Driscoll, 2015; Pardasani et al., 2014; Zsolnai & Illes, 2017) and long-term control of the business and its gains. Family-centric entrepreneurship is culturally diverse, including families with conflicts, feuds, and lengthy disputes and thriving and well-known family businesses that are part of national identity and heritage. Family-centric entrepreneurs are, in some cases, very talented regarding brand performance because they nurture well-known brands. Family serves as a concrete group of family members engaged in owner management and the corporate governance of family business. It also contains a spiritual legacy that the family creates, including intangible legends, myths, unwritten stories, routines, and sociocultural constructs.

Religion-centric entrepreneurship is based on a spirituality that follows the constructs of religion and the institution of the church or other organizations that practice religion. Religion offers socioeconomic resources for entrepreneurs, as belonging to institutional organizations provides opportunities for networking and social capital accumulation. Naturally, religion is a testimony of spirituality, and it offers multiple channels and activities to practice religion and increase the level of spiritual knowledge related to it (Vu, 2021). Religious ceremonies, events, and meetings foster religiousness and religious beliefs. As religion-centric entrepreneurship takes multiple forms, it covers exceptionally conservative and doctrine-based entrepreneurs and entrepreneurs who practice religion more selectively and occasionally. Standard features of religion-centric entrepreneurship are trust, loyalty, and spiritual knowledge based on religion and its teachings. We can learn from religion-centric entrepreneurship that spirituality can be a positive asset in times of struggle. Spiritual thinking can help maintain a positive mentality through complex decision-making and an entrepreneur's intuitive vision-building (Nandram, 2016).

Anti-social and opportunistic entrepreneurs hold alternative ideologies to spirituality. Instead of spiritual thinking, these entrepreneurs motivate themselves with materialism and egoism (Leung et al., 2021) without thinking about consequences, society, or the environment. This type of thinking shows not only a lack of ethics in the form of spiritual knowledge but also a lack of empathy and moral thinking (Wu et al., 2019). These cases teach us about the dark side of entrepreneurship with all its accompanying psychological disorders and symptoms. Avoiding sadness, bitterness, miserable or revengeful behavior, and aggressiveness toward other people in entrepreneurship is one of the learning lessons necessary for antisocial and opportunistic entrepreneurship.

The current research literature that helps us to understand more types of spiritual entrepreneurs can be divided into multiple sections (see Table 10.3). The literature on social venturing and social entrepreneurship can help us to understand societal entrepreneurs and their mindset about the world. Interpretation is needed, as social entrepreneurs are not synonymous with societal entrepreneurs. Studies on ethics, ethics in management and ethics in entrepreneurship offer pathways to understand the roots of spirituality in the context of societal and environmental entrepreneurs. Sustainable research on entrepreneurship and environmental management increases the understanding of environmental entrepreneurs' motives and operational behavior. This topic is multidisciplinary, and thus, studies conducted in other areas might also be helpful to the study of spiritual entrepreneurship.

Table 10.3: Future research initiatives.

Types of spiritual entrepreneurs	Future research initiatives on spiritual entrepreneurship	Entrepreneurship literature related to the topic	Data collection orientation (suggestions)
Societal Entrepreneurs	How do societal entrepreneurs manage their social capital? How do societal entrepreneurs enter business society and pursue a career in it?	Not just social entrepreneurship but also for-profit entrepreneurs with social awareness, like social venturing, mission-driven entrepreneurship, and ethical decision-making in entrepreneurship	Selecting well-known societal entrepreneurs. Snowball-type interviews in which each interviewee suggests new interviewees
Family-centric entrepreneurs	What advantages and disadvantages does family-centric entrepreneurship create for entrepreneurs and their families? What are the types of mindsets that family-centric entrepreneurs have?	Family business, business history, family studies, gender studies	Selecting positive and negative cases of family-centric entrepreneurship. Case study technique with multiple data sources, interviews, business histories, written documents, company archives
Environmental entrepreneurs	What motivates environmental entrepreneurs? What are the differences between environmental and hybrid business models?	Environmental entrepreneurship, sustainable entrepreneurship	Interviews with stakeholders and the informants themselves; focus group suitable

Table 10.3 (continued)

Types of spiritual entrepreneurs	Future research initiatives on spiritual entrepreneurship	Entrepreneurship literature related to the topic	Data collection orientation (suggestions)
Religion-centric entrepreneurs	How does religion influence entrepreneurial decision-making? What are the ethics that are typical for religion-centric entrepreneurs?	Spirituality in management and entrepreneurship, religion and entrepreneurs, religion and economics	Case study technique with multiple data sources, interviews, written documents, archives
Contesting ideologies			
Anti-social entrepreneurs	What explains anti-social behavior among entrepreneurs? What are the motives behind anti-social behavior? How do anti-social entrepreneurs enter into business society and pursue a career in it? Does anti-social behavior change, and if so, under what conditions and why?	Entrepreneurial behavior, Machiavellianism in management literature, psychology, and entrepreneurship, "dark side of entrepreneurship."	Stakeholder and eyewitness interviews (and document or media research) in the case that entrepreneurs refuse to be interviewed, long-term approach on what and why
Opportunistic entrepreneurs	What are the typical motives for opportunistic entrepreneurs in business? What are the impacts opportunistic entrepreneurs create around themselves? How do opportunistic entrepreneurs manage their business in times of crisis?	Entrepreneurial behavior, Machiavellianism in management literature, psychology, and entrepreneurship, "dark side of entrepreneurship."	Stakeholder and eyewitness interviews (and document or media research) in the case that entrepreneurs refuse to be interviewed, long-term approach toward what and why

Source: Author

Family-centric entrepreneurs are not a source of family business management and family entrepreneurship research, but fields such as gender studies also offer approaches to funning family businesses. Family businesses are the cradle of female managers in many countries; through inheritance and career development, gender studies can be used as a source for family-centric entrepreneurship. Naturally, the history of family businesses extends the understanding of this topic. The research literature on religion and economics has extended our understanding of the role of religion in economic development. Religion-centric entrepreneurship might be selectively studied through extant publications in economics. Perhaps even more helpful to the extension of this understanding is the concept of spirituality in management, especially regarding those studies that reflect religious institutions and their role in management. Anti-social and opportunistic entrepreneurship are multidisciplinary topics; therefore, psychology offers studies conducted in the context of this type of behavior and businesspeople. The latest entrepreneurship research has also studied entrepreneurial behavior from the perspective of the "dark side of entrepreneurship" by understanding the disorders experienced by entrepreneurs.

These literature sources offer much to think about and study. They offer pathways to understand the distinct types of spiritual entrepreneurs. Why have societal entrepreneurs chosen the path to becoming socially oriented and society-friendly? How do societal entrepreneurs enter business society? What motivates environmental entrepreneurs? What are the types of business models that they have? Answering these questions increases our understanding of societal and environmental entrepreneurship. Further, they can be applied to all types of spiritual entrepreneurs.

The study of family-centric entrepreneurship increasingly benefits family business research. Family-level spirituality in family business refers to the perspective that legitimizes family-centric entrepreneurship. Whether this spirituality derives from the founder's legacy, family impact in business, family myths, or something else remains a focus of future research. Religion and its meaning for entrepreneurs in business is an exciting research initiative. As economics has begun to study the intersection of religion and economics from multiple perspectives, entrepreneurship research can actively pursue the same approach in religiousness and entrepreneurship.

Anti-social entrepreneurship and opportunistic entrepreneurship reflect contesting ideologies to that of spirituality. Spirituality in entrepreneurship is about cultivating spirit and mindset from the perspective of cognitive-conative-affective constructs. However, its contesting ideologies reflect a lack of values and empathy toward other people and societies. Societal and environmental entrepreneurship and family-centric and religion-centric entrepreneurship are not necessarily positive. Families or some of their members can be maladjusted, which can influence family-centric entrepreneurship by prioritizing personal ideologies over spiritual thinking. Environmental entrepreneurs can make unethical decisions. Societal entrepreneurs might aim to work for the good of society but instead produce social profit only for a tiny elite within society rather than for the whole of society. Thus, the types of spiritual entrepreneurs are not inherently good or bad but have different cognitive-conative-affective connotations that make them distinct. Anti-social and opportunistic entrepreneurs can cause (without any conscious attempt) good outcomes, such as high employment rates and tax revenues for society that result from unethical business operations. Thus, spiritual entrepreneurship contains multiple paradoxes.

As mentioned earlier, the types of spiritual entrepreneurs can overlap and change over time. Spirituality is not constant or unchangeable. It takes multiple forms and different flavors as life changes. Studying this evolution of spiritual entrepreneurship through a longitudinal study could be exciting and necessary if we want to understand why it takes so many forms and the processes behind it.

References

Abebe, M. A., Kimakwa, S., & Redd, T. (2020). Toward a typology of social entrepreneurs: The interplay between passionate activism and entrepreneurial expertise. *Journal of Small Business and Enterprise Development*, *27*(4), 509–530. https://doi.org/10.1108/jsbed-08-2019-0279

Alshehri, F., Fotaki, M., & Kauser, S. (2021). The effects of spirituality and religiosity on the ethical judgment in organizations. *Journal of Business Ethics*, *174*(3), 567–593. https://doi.org/10.1007/s10551-020-04614-1

Arvate, P., & Story, J. (2021). Leaders affect business creation: Evidence from Mayoral Elections. *The Leadership Quarterly*, 101577. https://doi.org/10.1016/j.leaqua.2021.101577

Baldacchino, L., Ucbasaran, D., Cabantous, L., & Lockett, A. (2015). Entrepreneurship research on intuition: A critical analysis and research agenda. *International Journal of Management Reviews*, *17*(2), 212–231. https://doi.org/10.1111/ijmr.12056

Benevolo, C., Penco, L., & Torre, T. (2021). Entrepreneurial decision-making for global strategies: A "heart-head" approach. *Management Decision*, *59*(5), 1132–1157. https://doi.org/10.1108/md-10-2019-1495

Breidenstein, J. I. (2020). Cartesian philosophy as a spiritual practice. *Metaphilosophy*, *51*(2–3), 244–258. https://doi.org/10.1111/meta.12408

Bunduchi, R., Crișan-Mitra, C., Salanță, I.-I., & Crișan, E. L. (2022). Digital product innovation approaches in entrepreneurial firms – the role of entrepreneurs' cognitive frames. *Technological Forecasting and Social Change*, *175*, 121343. https://doi.org/10.1016/j.techfore.2021.121343

Campanario, S. C., Bikos, L. H., & Kendall, D. L. (2022). Ignatian spirituality and career development: New evidence for age-old practices. *Journal of Career Development*, *49*(3), 647–665. https://doi.org/10.1177/0894845320957086

Candeias, J., & Sarkar, S. (2022). Entrepreneurial Ecosystems and distinguishing features of effective policies – an evidence-based approach. *Entrepreneurship & Regional Development*, *34*(5–6), 343–375. https://doi.org/10.1080/08985626.2022.2045634

Cheung, T. S., & King, A. Y. C. (2004). Righteousness and profitableness: The moral choices of contemporary Confucian entrepreneurs. *Journal of Business Ethics*, *54*(3), 243–257. https://doi.org/10.1007/s10551-004-6405-6

Chu, E. (2007). Spiritual capitalism: The achievement of flow in entrepreneurial enterprises. *Journal of Human Values*, *13*(1), 61–77. https://doi.org/10.1177/097168580601300107

Costin, Y., O'Brien, M. P., & Hynes, B. (2019). Developing cognitive and non-cognitive entrepreneurial competences through business simulation games. *Journal of Enterprising Culture*, *27*(4), 471–498. https://doi.org/10.1142/s0218495819500171

Cristofaro, M. (2020). "I feel and think, therefore I am": An affect-cognitive theory of management decisions. *European Management Journal*, *38*(2), 344–355. https://doi.org/10.1016/j.emj.2019.09.003

Dahlke, J., Bogner, K., Becker, M., Schlaile, M. P., Pyka, A., & Ebersberger, B. (2021). Crisis-driven innovation and fundamental human needs: A typological framework of rapid-response COVID-19 innovations. *Technological Forecasting and Social Change*, *169*, 120799. https://doi.org/10.1016/j.techfore.2021.120799

Erpf, P., Tekula, R., & Neuenschwander, J. (2019). Clustering social enterprises: An empirically validated taxonomy. *Social Enterprise Journal*, *15*(3), 397–420. https://doi.org/10.1108/sej-12-2018-0081

Fernando, M., & Jackson, B. (2006). The influence of religion-based workplace spirituality on business leaders' decision-making: An inter-faith study. *Journal of Management & Organization*, *12*(1), 23–39. https://doi.org/10.5172/jmo.2006.12.1.23

Ganzin, M., Islam, G., & Suddaby, R. (2020). Spirituality and entrepreneurship: The role of magical thinking in future-oriented sensemaking. *Organization Studies*, *41*(1), 77–102. https://doi.org/10.1177/0170840618819035

Gursoy, D., Altinay, L., & Kenebayeva, A. (2017). Religiosity and entrepreneurship behaviours. *International Journal of Hospitality Management*, *67*, 87–94. https://doi.org/10.1016/j.ijhm.2017.08.005

Henning, H., & Henning, M. (2021). Reflections on the nature of spirituality: Evolutionary context, biological mechanisms, and future directions. *Journal for the Study of Spirituality*, *11*(2), 174–181. https://doi.org/10.1080/20440243.2021.1955453

Howorth, C., Tempest, S., & Coupland, C. (2005). Rethinking entrepreneurship methodology and definitions of the entrepreneur. *Journal of Small Business and Enterprise Development*, *12*(1), 24–40. https://doi.org/10.1108/14626000510579626

Ihl, A., Strunk, K., & Fiedler, M. (2022). Interpretations of mindfulness practices in organizations: A multi-level analysis of interpretations on an organizational, group, and individual level. *Organization*, *29*(6), 1099–1132. https://doi.org/10.1177/1350508420968195

Jarrodi, H., Byrne, J., & Bureau, S. (2019). A political ideology lens on social entrepreneurship motivations. *Entrepreneurship & Regional Development*, 31(7–8), 583–604. https://doi.org/10.1080/08985626.2019.1596353

Johannisson, B. (2016). Limits to and prospects of entrepreneurship education in the academic context. *Entrepreneurship & Regional Development*, *28*(5–6), 403–423. https://doi.org/10.1080/08985626.2016.1177982

Kakavelakis, K., & Edwards, T.J. (2021). The impact of structure and corporate ideology on leader-follower relations in the bureaucratic organization: A reflection on moral mazes. *Journal of Business Ethics*, 181, 69–82. https://doi.org/10.1007/s10551-021-04919-9

Kauanui, S. K., Thomas, K. D., Sherman, C. L., Waters, G. R., & Gilea, M. (2008). Exploring entrepreneurship through the lens of spirituality. *Journal of Management, Spirituality & Religion. An International Refereed Journal*, *5*(2), 160–189. https://doi.org/10.1080/14766080809518698

Kauanui, S. K., Thomas, K. D., Sherman, C. L., Waters, G. R., & Gilea, M. (2010). An exploration of entrepreneurship and play. *Journal of Organizational Change Management*, *23*(1), 51–70. https://doi.org/10.1108/09534811011017207

Keller, P. G., & Kozlinska, I. (2019). Entrepreneurial affect and emotions in entrepreneurship education impact research: A systematic review and research agenda. *Entrepreneurship Education and Pedagogy*, *2*(4), 281–307. https://doi.org/10.1177/2515127419860303

Kibler, E., Mandl, C., Farny, S., & Salmivaara, V. (2021). Post-failure impression management: A typology of entrepreneurs' public narratives after business closure. *Human Relations*, *74*(2), 286–318. https://doi.org/10.1177/0018726719899465

Kurczewska, A., Kyrö, P., Lagus, K., Kohonen, O., & Lindh-Knuutila, T. (2018). The interplay between cognitive, conative, and affective constructs along the entrepreneurial learning process. *Education + Training*, *60*(7/8), 891–908. https://doi.org/10.1108/et-09-2016-0148

Kyrö, P., Seikkula-Leino, J., & Mylläri, J. (2011). Meta processes of entrepreneurial and enterprising learning: The dialogue between cognitive, conative, and affective constructs. In O. J. Borch, A. Fayolle, P. Kyrö, & E. Ljunggren (Eds.), *Entrepreneurship research in Europe: Evolving concepts and processes* (pp. 56–84). MPG Books Group.

Larsen, I. B. (2022). Fostering an entrepreneurial mindset: A typology for aligning instructional strategies with three dominant entrepreneurial mindset conceptualizations. *Industry and Higher Education*, *36*(3), 236–251. https://doi.org/10.1177/09504222211038212

Lee, C.-C., Yeh, W.-C., Chang, H.-C., Yu, Z., & Tsai, Z.-Y. (2022). Influence of individual cognition, satisfaction, and the theory of planned behavior on tenant loyalty. *Frontiers in Psychology*, *13*, 882490. https://doi.org/10.3389/fpsyg.2022.882490

Lehner, O. M., & Kansikas, J. (2012). Opportunity recognition in social entrepreneurship. A thematic meta analysis. *The Journal of Entrepreneurship*, *21*(1), 25–58. https://doi.org/10.1177/097135571102100102

Lehner, O. M., & Kansikas, J. (2013). Pre-paradigmatic status of social entrepreneurship research: A systematic literature review. *Journal of Social Entrepreneurship*, *4*(2), 198–219. https://doi.org/10.1080/19420676.2013.777360

Leung, Y. K., Franken, I., Thurik, R., Driessen, M., Kamei, K., Torrès, O., & Verheul, I. (2021). Narcissism and entrepreneurship: Evidence from six datasets. *Journal of Business Venturing Insights*, *15*, e00216. https://doi.org/10.1016/j.jbvi.2020.e00216

Lim, S. H., & Kim, D. J. (2020). Does emotional intelligence of online shoppers affect their shopping behavior? From a cognitive-affective-conative framework perspective. *International Journal of Human–Computer Interaction*, *36*(14), 1304–1313. https://doi.org/10.1080/10447318.2020.1739882

Liu, Y., Li, Y., Hao, X., & Zhang, Y. (2019). Narcissism and learning from entrepreneurial failure. *Journal of Business Venturing*, *34*(3), 496–512. https://doi.org/10.1016/j.jbusvent.2019.01.003

Lomberg, C., Thiel, J., & Steffens, P. (2019). The hare and the tortoise: The impact of action- versus state-orientation on entrepreneurial progress and persistence. *International Small Business Journal: Researching Entrepreneurship*, *37*(6), 604–625. https://doi.org/10.1177/0266242619836615

Long, B. S., & Driscoll, C. (2015). A discursive textscape of workplace spirituality. *Journal of Organizational Change Management*, *28*(6), 948–969. https://doi.org/10.1108/jocm-12-2014-0236

Longva, K. K., & Foss, L. (2018). Measuring impact through experimental design in entrepreneurship education: A literature review and research agenda. *Industry and Higher Education*, *32*(6), 358–374. https://doi.org/10.1177/0950422218804912

Lubberink, R., Blok, V., van Ophem, J., van der Velde, G., & Omta, O. (2018). Innovation for society: Towards a typology of developing innovations by social entrepreneurs. *Journal of Social Entrepreneurship*, *9*(1), 52–78. https://doi.org/10.1080/19420676.2017.1410212

Mair, J., Battilana, J., & Cardenas, J. (2012). Organizing for society: A typology of social entrepreneuring models. *Journal of Business Ethics*, *111*(3), 353–373. https://doi.org/10.1007/s10551-012-1414-3

Maldonado-Bautista, I., Klein, P. G., & Artz, K. W. (2021). The role of political values and ideologies of entrepreneurs and financiers. *Entrepreneurship Theory and Practice*, *47*(1), 172–205. https://doi.org/10.1177/10422587211010496

Masele, J. J. (2019). Top management team's green entrepreneurial attitude and its influence on green ebusiness adoption: Empirical evidence from tour operators in Tanzania. *Small Enterprise Research*, *26*(1), 78–104. https://doi.org/10.1080/13215906.2019.1572030

McLaughlin, C., Bradley-McCauley, L., & Stephens, S. (2022). Exploring entrepreneurs' business-related social media typologies: A latent class analysis approach. *International Journal of Entrepreneurial Behavior & Research*, *28*(5), 1245–1272. https://doi.org/10.1108/ijebr-10-2020-0715

Mitchell, J. R., Friga, P. N., & Mitchell, R. K. (2005). Untangling the intuition mess: Intuition as a construct in entrepreneurship research. *Entrepreneurship Theory and Practice*, *29*(6), 653–679. https://doi.org/10.1111/j.1540-6520.2005.00102.x

Mollan, S., & Geesin, B. (2020). Donald Trump and Trumpism: Leadership, ideology and narrative of the business exectuive turned politician. Organization, 27(3), 405–418. https://doi.org/10.1177/1350508419870901

Moore, C. B., McIntyre, N. H., & Lanivich, S. E. (2021). ADHD-related neurodiversity and the entrepreneurial mindset. *Entrepreneurship Theory and Practice*, *45*(1), 64–91. https://doi.org/10.1177/1042258719890986

Morris, M., & Schindehutte, M. (2005). Entrepreneurial values and the ethnic enterprise: An examination of six subcultures. *Journal of Small Business Management*, *43*(4), 453–479. https://doi.org/10.1111/j.1540-627x.2005.00147.x

Müller, S., & Korsgaard, S. (2018). Resources and bridging: The role of spatial context in rural entrepreneurship. *Entrepreneurship & Regional Development, 30*(1–2), 224–255. https://doi.org/10.1080/08985626.2017.1402092

Muñoz, P. (2018). A cognitive map of sustainable decision-making in entrepreneurship. *International Journal of Entrepreneurial Behavior & Research, 24*(3), 787–813. https://doi.org/10.1108/ijebr-03-2017-0110

Nandram, S. S. (2016). How do spirituality, intuition and entrepreneurship go together? *Philosophy of Management, 15*(1), 65–82. https://doi.org/10.1007/s40926-016-0029-7

Neergaard, H., Robinson, S., & Jones, S. (2021). Transformative learning in the entrepreneurship education process: The role of pedagogical nudging and reflection. *International Journal of Entrepreneurial Behavior & Research, 27*(1), 251–277. https://doi.org/10.1108/ijebr-04-2020-0235

Nikolaou, I. E., Tasopoulou, K., & Tsagarakis, K. (2018). A typology of green entrepreneurs based on institutional and resource-based views. *The Journal of Entrepreneurship, 27*(1), 111–132. https://doi.org/10.1177/0971355717738601

Nulleshi, S. G. (2022). How do women entrepreneurs influence the strategic orientation of family businesses? A typology of Swedish decision-making in Småland community. *Journal of Enterprising Communities: People and Places in the Global Economy.* https://doi.org/10.1108/jec-06-2022-0091

Pandey, S., & Amezcua, A. S. (2020). Women's business ownership and women's entrepreneurship through the lens of U.S. federal policies. *Small Business Economics, 54*(4), 1123–1152. https://doi.org/10.1007/s11187-018-0122-5

Pardasani, R., Sharma, R., & Bindlish, P. (2014). Facilitating workplace spirituality: Lessons from Indian spiritual traditions. *Journal of Management Development, 33*(8/9), 847–859. https://doi.org/10.1108/jmd-07-2013-0096

Pisani, M. J., Guzman, J. M., Richardson, C., Sepulveda, C., & Laulié, L. (2017). Small business enterprises and Latino entrepreneurship: An enclave or mainstream activity in South Texas? *Journal of International Entrepreneurship, 15*(3), 295–323. https://doi.org/10.1007/s10843-017-0203-6

Politis, D., Gabrielsson, J., Galan, N., & Abebe, S. A. (2019). Entrepreneurial learning in venture acceleration programs. *The Learning Organization, 26*(6), 588–603. https://doi.org/10.1108/tlo-04-2018-0082

Pret, T., & Cogan, A. (2019). Artisan entrepreneurship: A systematic literature review and research agenda. *International Journal of Entrepreneurial Behavior & Research, 25*(4), 592–614. https://doi.org/10.1108/ijebr-03-2018-0178

Rashid, S., & Ratten, V. (2022). Spirituality and entrepreneurship: Integration of spiritual beliefs in an entrepreneurial journey. *Journal of Enterprising Communities: People and Places in the Global Economy, 16*(6), 876–899. https://doi.org/10.1108/jec-12-2020-0199

Risker, D. C. (1998). Toward an innovation typology of entrepreneurs. *Journal of Small Business & Entrepreneurship, 15*(2), 27–41. https://doi.org/10.1080/08276331.1998.10593282

Rocha, R. G., & Pinheiro, P. G. (2021). Organizational spirituality: Concept and perspectives. *Journal of Business Ethics, 171*(2), 241–252. https://doi.org/10.1007/s10551-020-04463-y

Rooney, D., Küpers, W., Pauleen, D., & Zhuravleva, E. (2021). A developmental model for educating wise leaders: The role of mindfulness and habitus in creating time for embodying wisdom. *Journal of Business Ethics, 170*(1), 181–194. https://doi.org/10.1007/s10551-019-04335-0

Salamanca, E., & Alcaraz, J. (2022). A typology of Mexican highly educated immigrant entrepreneurs in the United States. *Thunderbird International Business Review, 64*(6), 647–663. https://doi.org/10.1002/tie.22304

Serres, C., Hudon, M., & Maon, F. (2022). Social corporations under the spotlight: A governance perspective. *Journal of Business Venturing, 37*(3), 106192. https://doi.org/10.1016/j.jbusvent.2022.106192

Smith, R. (2017). Examining the characteristics, philosophies, operating practices and growth strategies of village entrepreneurs. *International Journal of Entrepreneurial Behavior & Research, 23*(4), 708–725. https://doi.org/10.1108/ijebr-10-2016-0350

Sotiropoulou, A., Papadimitriou, D., & Maroudas, L. (2021). Personal values and typologies of social entrepreneurs. The case of Greece. *Journal of Social Entrepreneurship*, *12*(1), 1–27. https://doi.org/10.1080/19420676.2019.1668827

Sriyakul, T., & Jermsittiparsert, K. (2019). The mediating role of entrepreneurial passion in the relationship between entrepreneur education and entrepreneurial intention among university students in Thailand. *International Journal of Innovation, Creativity and Change*, *6*(10), 193–212.

Ustav, S., & Venesaar, U. (2018). Bridging metacompetencies and entrepreneurship education. *Education + Training*, *60*(7/8), 674–695. https://doi.org/10.1108/et-08-2017-0117

Vasconcelos, A. F. (2018). The lack of spiritual perspective of organizations: an exploratory study. *International Journal of Organizational Analysis*, *26*(5), 915–940. https://doi.org/10.1108/ijoa-02-2018-1345

Vogel, S.K. (2022). "Neoliberal Ideology and the Myth of the Self-Made Entrepreneur", Eberhart, R.N., Lounsbury, M. and Aldrich, H.E. (Eds.) *Entrepreneurialism and Society: New Theoretical Perspectives* (*Research in the Sociology of Organizations, Vol. 81*), Emerald Publishing Limited, Leeds, pp. 77–99. https://doi.org/10.1108/S0733-558X20220000081005

Vu, M. C. (2021). Sensemaking and spirituality: The process of re-centring self-decentralisation at work. *The International Journal of Human Resource Management*, 1–31. https://doi.org/10.1080/09585192.2021.1991977

Wiid, J. A., Cant, M. C., & Rooyen, N. v. (2013). The ethical conundrum of entrepreneurs: Is there a difference between personal and business values? *Corporate Ownership and Control*, *11*(1), 360–371. https://doi.org/10.22495/cocv11i1c3art7

Woo, C. Y., Cooper, A. C., & Dunkelberg, W. C. (1991). The development and interpretation of entrepreneurial typologies. *Journal of Business Venturing*, *6*(2), 93–114. https://doi.org/10.1016/0883-9026(91)90013-4

Wu, W., Wang, H., Zheng, C., & Wu, Y. J. (2019). Effect of narcissism, psychopathy, and machiavellianism on entrepreneurial intention-the mediating of entrepreneurial self-efficacy. *Frontiers in Psychology*, *10*, 360. https://doi.org/10.3389/fpsyg.2019.00360

Zhan, S., Uy, M. A., & Hong, Y.-y. (2022). Missing the forest for the trees: Prior entrepreneurial experience, role identity, and entrepreneurial creativity. *Entrepreneurship Theory and Practice*, *46*(6), 1469–1499. https://doi.org/10.1177/1042258720952291

Zsolnai, L., & Illes, K. (2017). Spiritually inspired creativity in business. *International Journal of Social Economics*, *44*(2), 195–205. https://doi.org/10.1108/ijse-06-2015-0172

Maria Angeles Iniesta-Bonillo, Felipe Andrés-Ruiz
and Alberto Valiente-Fitzsimons

Chapter 11
Spiritual Entrepreneurship: ACIM Social as a Tool for Spiritual Networking and Sharing

Abstract: Framed in the third axis of knowledge, the spiritual, this text describes the story of 3 people dedicated to self-knowledge and spiritual growth, whom life brought together in a moment of space and time. Their initial purpose was to share their reflections on A Course in Miracles. Subsequently, it evolved into an *inner calling to create something defined as spiritual entrepreneurship.* Its scope was unknown, but intuition showed them that it was *geared to serve, to become instruments in the service of God's Light and Love, to provide a context from which to facilitate others to connect with their true Self, bringing value to the world.* Since then, they have been walking together along a path, sometimes serene and sometimes more rugged. Currently, they are materializing part of that purpose by designing an app, ACIM Social. It responds to an inner call to bring the Course closer to other brothers and sisters, facilitate its practice comfortably and straightforwardly, and transmit spiritual knowledge. Thereby, what a priori could be understood as an instrument to carry out an activity in the outside world, such as the development of an app on a mobile phone, became, for them, an element aimed at facilitating learning and the will to focus their gaze inwards through sharing.

Keywords: A Course in Miracles, ACIM Social, App, Spirituality, Spiritual Entrepreneurship, Spiritual Knowledge, Knowledge Management

Antecedents

After a weekend workshop on A Course in Miracles (hereafter ACIM or the Course) at Ryo's[1] house in December 2012, four of the attendees, Filocasto, Ryo, another friend, and myself, Ángeles, had the desire to create a Course study group. I was urged to call a meeting at the beginning of the year and choose a topic to start working on. For me, it

1 The names of the people who are developing this project are fictitious, except for the person speaking in the first person, to preserve their anonymity.

M. Angeles Iniesta-Bonillo, University of Almería, Spain, e-mail: miniesta@ual.es
Felipe Andrés-Ruiz, Senda Hirdaya Association, Spain, e-mail: ryoandruiz@gmail.com
Alberto Valiente-Fitzsimons, Servicios Valiente, Spain, e-mail: albertojosevaliente@gmail.com

https://doi.org/10.1515/9783111010410-012

was an exciting challenge! Up to that point, I had been studying the Course alone. Paradoxically, the non-dual perspective offered by ACIM states that "I am one Self, united with my Creator" (ACIM, 2018: L.95). However, in the dual world of manifestation, that path inward is a path to be traveled and from oneself, through the relationship with others. However, I found it precious to have the opportunity to share concerns and reflections on the spiritual path I had begun.

At that time, I had been studying ACIM for about a year. I met it through a Mindfulness course at the University of Almeria (Spain), where ACIM facilitators and people dedicated to self-knowledge and the spiritual path participated. At that time, I was in full mourning for the breakdown of my marriage in 2010. Until then, my transcendent vision came from the Catholic religion, and I was plunged into the only crisis of faith I have ever experienced. I did not understand why life was bringing me this painful experience. Nothing made sense to me. I did not know that it was part of a path that, more unconsciously than consciously, I longed to walk. It was through this experience that I began to move from blind faith in the dogmas of Catholicism to a spiritual vision which, as the Dalai Lama (1999) points out, is based more on the qualities of the human spirit, such as love, forgiveness, compassion, responsibility and others, which bring happiness to both oneself and others. I consciously began a journey home to God.

However, it was a different concept of God from the one I had grown up with: God as the Origin, the Source, the Life, the all-embracing One, the Universal substance in which everything Is. In the face of my surrender, Life wisely and naturally led me to take a few steps in that direction. Moved by love and compassion, love that I did not know where it came from, the desire that my children would not suffer from our separation; surrendered to the reality of the facts, I was pushed to let go of the idea of how things should be, from forgiveness, love, and without judgment. As everything has its raison d'être, if we are open to "listen", that rupture helped me to find meaning in life. I found help and guidance from various people and trainings. I bought the ACIM version from the Foundation for Inner Peace (FFIP) in 2011 (ACIM, 2007), but it was not until a year later that I started reading it. Since then, I have not stopped my journey toward this God-One through a process of self-inquiry, both psychologically and spiritually. I see everything that happens to me as an opportunity to keep questioning the idea of myself as an individual ego and open myself to discovering my true nature in God.

At that meeting at Ryo's house, we agreed to meet a few weeks later at mine. The topic we started with was judgment, a great topic! From that meeting, situations already arose on which to practice the review observation. Ryo and I started a relationship as a couple, which we consecrated to God to guide us in stripping ourselves of all egoic forms before each other. Throughout the time we were a couple, there were many scenarios in which we could practice everything we were learning theoretically in the Course. There were several break-ups and reconciliations. Even today, not being a couple, our relationship remains a good training ground for uncovering the traps of the ego. After that first meeting, the friend who had attended left the group. She did not accept the beginning of the relationship between me and Ryo. She judged it inappropriate, given our circumstances. Eventually, the connection with her was reestablished, and although we went our separate ways, we had much affection. Therefore, we could observe the judgments and practice forgiveness from the beginning.

Filocasto, Ryo and I continued to meet one weekend a month for years. We met in the name of Jesus and felt inspired and guided by Him. We meditated, philosophized and discussed the Course of life. . . and a beautiful brotherhood was forged over time. At that time, we also met with another committed couple on the inner journey. Our purposes converged towards devotional service, *becoming instruments in serving God's Light and Love in the world.* Each time we met, we felt we were called to do something together, *to create a space, a context to share and to facilitate others to connect with their true Self.* We wanted to share the devotion and love we felt and our own experience and knowledge with the rest of the world. We did not know how, but we were always convinced that our meeting was not by chance and that we had something to create and give to the world. From this, a name was born: *The Abode of the Creator*.

The Abode of the Creator symbolizes the place or space to dwell and reconnect with God-Love. It is a place of healing and rest for the soul, of disidentification from the individual body-mind separate from others, with an associated name, psychology and personal history that gives it an identity. At first, we visualized that place as a physical space with specific physical characteristics; in time, we realized that this idea did not need to be in a particular area in space-time. The Abode of the Creator is within each of us; it is an inner state of connection with the One and with All. The rest would follow. . . as an effect of this internal state. However, we do not rule out that one day, there may be a physical place where this cherished ideal can be realized.

During these years, we have followed our path towards the Light. We have carried out a personal work of self-knowledge and consciousness, both from ACIM and other spiritual philosophies (e.g., Vedanta-Advaita by Ramana Maharshi, Nisargadatta Maharaj, Aurobindo and Mother, Mooji, yoga, Buddhism, mindfulness and different currents). All this has been producing a significant transformation in each one of us. Sometimes, the three of us have walked together, sometimes separately, sometimes with more resistance, and sometimes with less, according to the emotional and psychological moments of each one. During this time of inner work, many faces of the ego have surfaced, represented by attachments, resistances, and opposition to the freedom of the Self. Moreover, they continue to appear. We have experienced many joys through deep connection with the transcendent. We have also experienced much pain and suffering resulting from attachments and lack of acceptance. Sometimes, the conflict stemmed from personal issues, misunderstandings and misinterpretations.

We have lived, as every human being lives, experiencing the two opposing thought systems that ACIM speaks of: that of the ego, expressed through fear, attachment to personal identity, the inner wounds this causes, and the refusal to heal those wounds; and that of the Holy Spirit, manifested as forgiveness, the recognition of the immutable innocence that permeates all Creation, and the oneness from which both come. As a result of the cyclical surrender to one of these two opposing systems of thought, there have been times when one of the three has needed to walk away. However, the other two have always remained together with Jesus, preserving the purpose.

However, What a Course in Miracles is?

A *Course in Miracles* is a non-dual spiritual teaching to remember our true nature, oneness with God-Love. Since reality is defined in ACIM as God or Heaven (which is our true Self as Christ, the state of perfect Oneness), unreality is anything outside of Him (Wapnick, 2022). As it states, "The journey to God is merely the reawakening of the knowledge of where you are always and what you are forever. It is a journey without distance to a goal that has never changed" (ACIM, 2021: T-8.V.12:6–7).

This is summarized as follows (ACIM, 2018: T-In.2:2–4):

Nothing real can be threatened.
Nothing unreal exists.
Herein lies the peace of God

A Course in Miracles is not a religion. It does not claim to convey a universal theology, which it considers impossible (ACIM, 2018: C-In.2:5; Preface.2.3). Although the terminology and focus of the Course are Christian, it is a learning program, a mental training, leading to a universal experience. It teaches that the way to remember Love and Peace, our real Identity, is based on undoing guilt through forgiveness. The practice setting is relationships, which, once healed, become holy (FFIP, n.d.). Through its study, however, one becomes aware that the only possible relationship to be healed is the relationship with God.

The Course resulted from the transcription of an inner voice identified as coming from Jesus by Dr. Helen Schucman, a clinical and research psychologist and tenured Associate Professor of Medical Psychology. Dr. William Thetford, her department chair and Professor of Medical Psychology at the Columbia University College of Physicians and Surgeons (New York), assisted her in transcribing the inner dictation. The Course materialized thanks to the request for help and commitment to find another way of relating from two co-workers who seemed trapped in a problematic relationship. United in that purpose, the relationship between them was redirected, and they could work in harmony (Skutch, 2010). It was, therefore, love that brought the relationship between them back on track. The text states, "Miracles occur naturally as expressions of love. The real miracle is the love that inspires them. In this sense, everything that comes from love is a miracle" (ACIM, 2018: T-1-I.3:1–3). Some versions of ACIM exist (Shawley, 2014). The most widely known at this time is the one of the Foundation for Inner Peace (cited in this text as ACIM, 2018). However, other versions are the Circle of Atonement (ACIM, 2021) or the Sparkly or Thetford Edition (2012). The URtext is the earliest ACIM version available, which has not been edited (ACIM, 2001).

This learning system based on non-dual forgiveness, or miracle, consists of the Text, Workbook for Students, and Teachers Manual. It also clarifies Terms and Supplements (Psychotherapy and The Song of Prayer). The workbook consists of 365 lessons, one for each day of the year. It aims to train the mind to correct erroneous perceptions based on the belief in separation, guilt and fear by transforming the dualistic thought system.

The Sense of Making ACIM Social App: Sharing the Spiritual Experience

Origin of ACIM Social: Purpose

In 2021, as a result of his own experience with ACIM, Ryo thought of a way of studying the Course that would help students maintain the necessary consistency in practicing the lessons in the workbook. The lessons of the Course are conceived as a daily practice. The student meditates at certain times of the day and recalls different spiritual ideas and thought forms at specific frequencies for each lesson. He believed that it was possible, and would be helpful, to design an automated alert system for mobile devices through an app, which would help to maintain the necessary attention and consistency. He found that the existing apps in the Apple and Android app stores only incorporated a basic alert system. However, none offered the complex system of alerts that the Course proposes. He also thought about possibly creating a global community of ACIM students.

Since the spirit of The Abode of the Creator was still very present in us, he shared his idea with Filocasto and me, and we were both inspired to participate. We began what could be called our spiritual venture, whose purpose is the development of projects oriented towards the awakening of Consciousness, thus creating value for society. The primary motivation is not the economic benefit of its promoters but the experience of its development and the desire to promote spiritual advancement in the world.

Figure 11.1 shows the image associated with the ACIM Social app.

ACIM Social

Figure 11.1: ACIM Social logo.
Source: Author's elaboration

Building a Community to Share the Experience

As the App took shape, we discovered that it could become a new expression of the Abode of the Creator that would extend beyond us. From our personal experience studying the Course and that of people close to us with the version edited by the FFIP, we can say that, a priori, it is not a simple teaching. Its study can be complex, even leading to misinterpretations of its ideas. One can feel very lonely and lost at times. A Course in Miracles proposes to change the thought system of the world, or of the ego, which is inevitably painful for it (ACIM, 2018: T4.II.5:1), to a new thought system. Such a change generates much resistance in our mind, which tends to cling to what is known so that reactivity can arise.

Having access to other people with the same interests, who can make the understanding and practice of ACIM easier, and sharing feelings, concerns, or doubts with them can be exceptionally comforting for an ACIM student. This can be a great help and a determinant for further study. The App could become a meeting place between ACIM students, teachers, or Course facilitators. The facilitators are people who have been studying the Course for longer or have reached a higher level of understanding and experience of its postulates. In this way, a network or community could be created to share their doubts, experiences, and content linked to this teaching system to help each other. The system of thought proposed by ACIM is very particular and is in the process of expansion. For this reason, it seemed interesting to offer a space that would make it easier to share its study with other people and available to everyone since nothing like this exists so far.

The ACIM Social App is prepared to search for students, show which other users are studying the same lesson and section of the text, and contact them via chat. In addition, it also makes it possible to search for facilitators (Figure 11.2). Any user can be a facilitator; however, it is requested that they have studied ACIM in-depth and have practiced all lessons at least once. In any case, users can indicate the years they have studied the Course. It also allows you to search for groups by name or that go by the same lesson or section of the Text and the most popular groups.

To facilitate sharing between students, facilitators, or both, the App allows the creation of study groups (Figure 11.3). These can be public (any user can join freely), private (closed groups to which access can be requested) or closed (access cannot be requested). The group administrator can mark the lesson or section of the Text to be studied. The group also has a chat for private communication among its members. Additional text or multimedia information can also be shared and made available to group members.

The App becomes a kind of spiritual, social network of ACIM, where knowledge can be created within groups and open to the community (Figure 11.4); they may or may not be associated with a lesson or section of the Text (only open to facilitators). Any user can publish posts, comment on and like them, and other users can be followed. However, since its purpose is to share, not compete, only each user can know their number of followers. It is not possible to see the number of followers other users have.

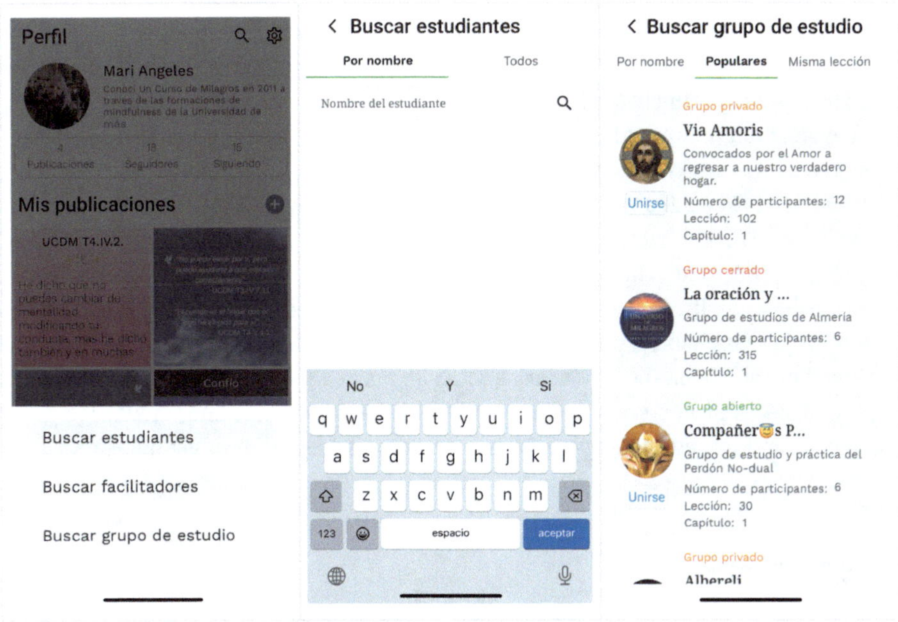

Figure 11.2: Search possibilities of ACIM Social.
Source: Author's elaboration

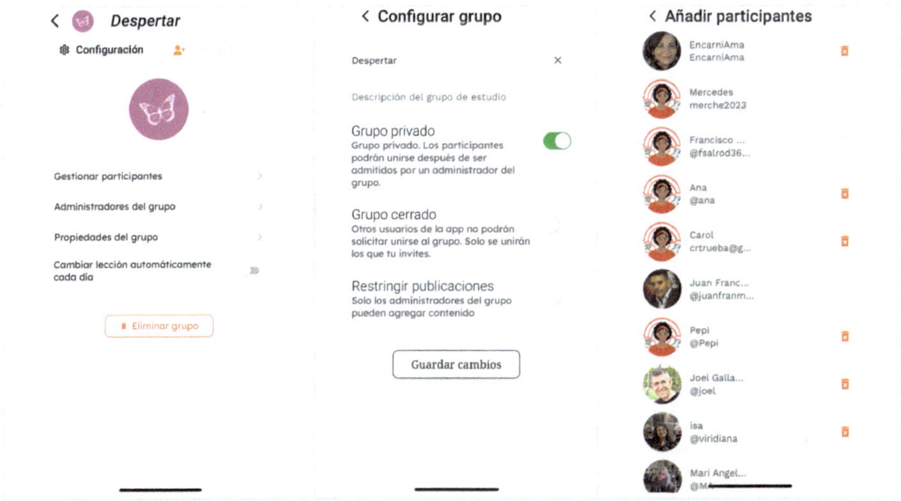

Figure 11.3: Groups functionality.
Source: Author's elaboration

From that moment on, we considered approaching the strategic planning of the App from a professional point of view. The mission and vision of this project, framed in the third component of the triple helix of knowledge, spiritual knowledge (Bratianu, 2015), are beyond our comprehension. Its elaboration obeys an inner calling. What comes out of it, how far the App will go and who will benefit from it, will depend on whether there is a real need for such a creation. Although a priori, we would say there is, we do not know it now. The App's development was not preceded by market research but inspired by the Holy Spirit, to Whom we directed our steps. Moreover, when we surrender to Him, the most significant benefit has already been obtained; giving our time and energy to this project has had very positive consequences in terms of personal fulfillment and satisfaction, which, on their own, are enough to make it worth having developed. Even so, the project's promoters have extensive business experience and knowledge of the Course. Therefore, everything we do is focused on adequate product development in the market.

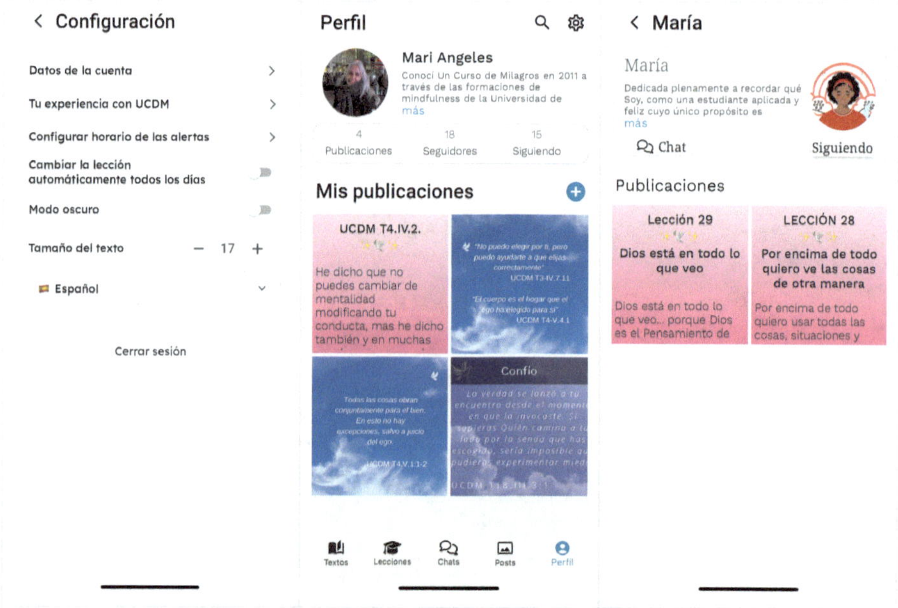

Figure 11.4: User profile and posts.
Source: Author's elaboration

Implementing Acim Social

From a professional perspective, the project's mission is *to create a space for ACIM students to come together and meet through the ACIM Social app; on the one hand, facilitating their study and practice comfortably and, on the other hand, incorporating specific tools not yet available on the market, such as the Course study groups, a spiritual, social network, and a system of individualized alerts per lesson.* Our vision is *to be an instrument of transformation at the service of the God-Love-Self.*

Starting Point: Internal Analysis

To implement the project, we divided the tasks: Ryo would program the app, Filocasto would take care of the content and the configuration of the complex alert system, and I would record the audios of the lessons and the Text, giving voice to the Voice that speaks for God. The initial idea for the project grew, and with it, the complexity and level of programming required. Ryo's brother Dante, a very experienced programmer, joined the project. Defining himself as an atheist, he inexplicably volunteered to collaborate in developing the app.

Therefore, the app's promoters are Filocasto, Ryo, Dante and myself. We all have professional or academic experience in entrepreneurship and business management. We have two programming experts with experience in app programming, and three of us have been practicing A Course in Miracles for over ten years. Together, we have the necessary skills to develop this spiritual entrepreneurial project.

The development of the App incorporates very new technologies, which are enabling a global creative explosion. On the one hand, cloud-based information storage and sharing systems developed by Google (Firebase) are being used. These systems allow a single person, in a very efficient way, to do sets of tasks that used to require entire teams of people. On the other hand, an emerging programming language, "flutter", created by Google, is being used, which allows apps to be developed for the IOS platform and Google simultaneously, without duplicating programming efforts. In addition, Ryo is programming on a platform called Flutterflow that allows the app's source code to be generated in Flutter without coding directly, which generates the native code for both iOS and Android. In addition, a client-server architecture has been designed for the alert system. All these systems are installed in the cloud, facilitating their interconnection. The App is a terminal that displays the information stored and shared in the cloud. An audio recording and editing system incorporated into the Audacity program is being used, allowing professional work to be done using tools available to everyone.

The Environment: The Need to Return to the Inner Self

The most developed societies have been focused on "having" for many years and moving to another based on "doing". Rushing, stress, and no time to do and do and do and do. . . are the general tone of behavior and a consequence of focusing attention on the "outside". It is well known that this, in turn, triggers physical and psychological health problems (DeLongis et al., 1988; Reinecke et al., 2017), as well as depression and many other mental problems (Thoits, 2010). Losing the illusion of living or not finding meaning in life generates the most internal suffering a human can experience. In fact, according to psychiatrist Gutiérrez Rojas, suicide occurs when people believe there is nothing left to do (Sánchez León, 2023). Moreover, this happens from an increasingly early age. We learn to live with our consciousness captured by an infinity of external stimuli. We forget to look at and listen to ourselves and pay attention to what we think, feel, desire or experience at any moment. People who live this way are unaware of the purpose of their behavior, forgetting that, ultimately, we all seek the same thing, and we all seek it because it is inherent to human nature itself. We are all embarked, conscious or not, on the same longing: the longing for "Being", which has nothing to do with "doing" and "having". In our consciousness, we translate it as the desire to be happy. One day, either because we have reached the limit of our physical or mental possibilities, or because some event happens in our life that shocks us, or simply because of a flash of consciousness, we stop. Moreover, in doing so, we are likely to ask ourselves: What am I doing? Why am I doing what I am doing? Why am I running so much? Why am I working so hard? Where do I want to go? What purpose led me to orient my life in this direction? Well, the answer to these questions, although it seems to take particular forms in the conscience of each individual, usually has, in all of them, a very similar background: "There must be another way of doing things, another way of thinking and approaching life, another way of living".

This response is growing collectively in society. It is a natural response to information overload, to the increasing complexity of society and to the growing presence of collective thinking that blurs the consciousness of individuals. This is increasing interest in self-knowledge, personal growth and a return to spirituality, a more secular spirituality, less pigeon-holed into a particular dogma. More and more people need to find the meaning of their lives, to look inward and reconnect with the essential part of themselves that they can only find by turning the focus of awareness within. Around this need, a growing industry is emerging, offering products and services related to self-knowledge, spirituality and the inner path. From this purely economic or material point of view, the creation of an app that can meet this need seems, in itself, appropriate. At the macroeconomic level, there seems to be no brake on its development. At the microeconomic level, there is an expanding market for this spiritual teaching of ACIM worldwide. It is now translated into 27 languages (FFIP, n.d.), with practitioners of the Course in several languages. In particular, there is a vast market of people studying the Course in Spanish in Spain and Latin America. Many people facilitate their learning through study groups, videos, courses, retreats, workshops, etc. However, as far as we know, there is no community of students and facilitators of the course where everyone can meet and share. Many people study it and follow specific teachers, but there is no space where everyone can converge and share.

As a consequence of our own experience and contact with the experience of many other people studying ACIM, we are aware of the difficulty many find in grasping and deeply understanding its postulates. In this sense, the availability of specific didactic tools such as audio texts, summarized instructions on what to do in each lesson, alerts, information related to ACIM, study groups, and forums to ask questions and share life experiences, which are sometimes difficult, etc., can facilitate learning and internalization, and be very useful. An analysis of the different ACIM apps on the market shows both free and paid apps. In general, they provide access to the text and lessons. The alert systems are generally fundamental. Some have standard lesson alerts; most do not show lesson title notifications unless configured by the user daily. Moreover, only one of them shows the meditation time. The most advanced alert is that of the FFIP, which has customized lesson alerts, but the visual presentation and functionality are fundamental.

Therefore, we concluded that there is a target market for this product and no product with the characteristics of ACIM Social.

Management Summary: SWOT Analysis

A summary of the main strengths, opportunities, weaknesses, and threats associated with this project is presented in Table 11.1.

The main weakness observed is related to the personal transformation processes that team members are undergoing, which sometimes makes communication and decision-making difficult. However, even these tiny stops are learning opportunities that positively impact our joint project.

The project also has some strengths. Firstly, the developers have a great deal of experience in software development. They are currently developing other apps in larger companies, so all their experience in this work area is being applied to the development of ACIM Social. Secondly, they are using newly created tools that multiply the efficiency of what one person can do. This reduces the cost of App development. It also improves the value for money compared to other apps developed with inferior technologies. Thirdly, the developers have a long history of spiritual work and have been practicing ACIM for over a decade. Therefore, as a fourth strength, it can be mentioned that the developers know from the user's perspective and as facilitators what the needs of the course students and those who want to facilitate their study.

About threats, the main problem we may have is that the royalties requested by the FFIP in order to use their version of ACIM may not be financially bearable for the project. However, if this is the case, we would consider including another of the existing versions. On the other hand, it is possible that other apps that already have a market

Table 11.1: SWOT analysis.

WEAKNESSES	**THREATS**
- Some occasional difficulty in communication and decision-making due to the personal processes of the promoters.	- Some existing apps with a market share may imitate ACIM Social content. - The Course is accessible in pdf format and on different websites. - The FFIP is developing an ACIM App and website. - We have not yet agreed with the FFIP to use the texts of the Spanish version of ACIM, which could lead us to consider other versions of the Course.
STRENGTHS	**OPPORTUNITIES**
- Extensive experience of the developers in software development. - Innovative tools for app development that multiply efficiency and improve value for money. - Great knowledge and practice of ACIM. - Knowledge of the needs of the course learners and facilitators.	- At the moment, there is no spiritual or social network of the Course nor a community of learners and facilitators. - The App is designed from the perspective of the student and the facilitator. - Innovative organization and systematization of the app's content. - App with a wide variety of functionalities.

Source: Author's elaboration

share could incorporate some of the innovations presented in this one, although this process requires time and investment. Moreover, the Course is freely available online in PDF and other formats. However, they do not have the characteristics of this app, although they do allow free dissemination and are therefore competitive in terms of price. The fact that the FFIP is also developing an app and a web platform to study the text could also be identified as a threat.

As opportunities, it should be noted that the organization and systematization of the app's content follows an approach that does not exist in any existing Course apps. These, moreover, do not offer as many functionalities together. On the other hand, the App includes a spiritual, social network that enables the creation of a community of ACIM students and facilitators. This is something that does not exist so far. The App has also been designed from the student's perspective and adapted to their needs. It also considers facilitators' needs, making it a handy tool for those who generate content and value around the original text.

Marketing Planning

As described above, the purpose of ACIM Social is twofold. On the one hand, it aims to facilitate the internalization of the system of thought of the Course, providing tools to make the study of the Text and the practice of the exercises easier. On the other hand, it seeks to enable communication of experiences or doubts by creating a spiritual community or network.

By mid-2023, the ACIM Social App was practically finished and ready to be added to the Google Play Store and Apple Store. Its launch, initially in Spanish, was the first objective from a business point of view. However, for this to be possible, we still have to decide which version of ACIM will finally be incorporated into the App. Although all the material in it is currently the FFIP version, if the royalty proposal is not economically viable for the project to be developed, we would assess the feasibility of including another version of the Course or making our translation of the royalty-free version. In this sense, the first objective to be addressed is to decide which version of ACIM can be incorporated into the App.

Once this issue is resolved, we will proceed to launch the App. The next objective would be disseminating the App by implementing different actions (Table 11.2). They are intended to achieve the third objective: to reach between 800 and 1000 subscribers in the first year and 2000 in the second year. To this end, among other actions, we intend to give free access to between 200 and 500 users. As a fourth objective, new content will be added to the App for its continuous improvement: audios of the chapters of the Text, improvements in reminders and notifications, guided meditations for the lessons, summaries, offering in English all the content available in Spanish to extend the App to the entire English-speaking world, or access to content about ACIM published by Course facilitators, such as YouTube videos. Finally, it is a goal of each of us to enjoy the work done, to share on a personal level the experience of use and to let destiny happen for us.

Table 11.2 provides a summary of the future actions to be developed for each of the objectives.

Table 11.2: Linking actions to objectives.

Objective	Action
1. Decision on the version of ACIM to be incorporated into the App.	Contact the editors of the different editions to determine if they are open to collaborating with the project.
	Assess which option is more economically viable.
2. Incorporate the App in the Google Play Store and Apple Store.	Start the process of activating subscriptions for new users.
	Complete the debugging phase during February. The four promoters, plus the 25 current test users, will be involved.

Table 11.2 (continued)

Objective	Action
3. Disseminate the App in the main networks	Develop a website that explains the project and allows ACIM facilitators to contact our spiritual project.
	Create ACIM Social App profiles in the most widespread social networks.
	Develop a strategy for generating content on networks that, on the one hand, makes people with suitable characteristics aware of the App's existence and, on the other, provides added value via messages, posts, etc.
	Advertising on Google and Meta.
4. Reach 800–1000 subscribers in the first year and reach 2000 in the second year.	Free access to several users between 200–500.
	Plan the process of recruiting and involving ACIM facilitators throughout the Spanish-speaking world.
	Word-of-mouth communication and sharing of user experience.
5. Add new content	Complete the audio recording of all sections of the text.
	Add specific new or existing content (e.g., YouTube videos), organized and systematized, to the different lessons and chapters.
	Offer in English all the content available in Spanish in order to extend the App to the whole English-speaking world.
	It improved reminders and notifications.
	Guided meditations.
	Brainstorming on new possibilities of the App.

Source: Author's elaboration

Technical Characteristics of Acim Social

ACIM Social App is a smartphone application intended to be offered through Apple's App Store and Android's Play Store. It includes many specific functionalities, some of them still under development at the moment (Table 11.3). Nevertheless, others will continue to be added due to experience using the app. To this end, suggestions from the users themselves will be considered.

Table 11.3: ACIM Social App functionalities.

Linked to the lessons
Lessons in text and audio are presented consecutively and accessible from various search tools: Index, search by content, and search by number.
Adjustable audio speed.
A specific alert system for each lesson can be activated or deactivated. It allows setting the alerts' start and end times and changing lessons automatically every day.
Programmable timer.
Summary with the particular specifications of the practice of each lesson.
Linked to the Text (book chapters)
The content of the Text is organized in sections, following the same layout as the printed edition of the book. In this way, the user can access all the contents in an easy and organized way.
Audios for each section of the Text (under development).
Bookmark for the Text.
Linked to the ACIM community-network
Chats: to contact people studying or facilitating the Course worldwide.
Search for students, facilitators and study groups.
Study groups. These can be created by ACIM facilitators or by anyone who wants to share the study of the Course with others. They can be public, private, or closed; the latter are by invitation only. Groups have lesson and text indexes, which the group leader marks.
Possibility to share ACIM content, such as images, videos, texts, YouTube videos, links to web pages, etc. Content can be public for the whole community or private within a group. Such content can be associated with specific lessons or chapters of the Text.
Possibility to see the posts linked to a specific chapter or lesson.
Possibility of sharing a lesson or section of the Text.
Ability to know who is studying the same lesson or section of the Text.
Ability to follow other users, whether they are facilitators or other learners. However, users can only see their followers and the number of people they follow, not others.
Other functionalities
A notepad for jotting down ideas or things to remember in lessons and the Text.
Selection of favorite lessons or text sections.
Display in light or dark mode.
Possibility to switch from individual profile to group profile.

Source: Author's elaboration

In Figure 11.5, different parts of the App can be physically visualized. Examples are incorporated, both in light and dark format.

About the Costs

As mentioned, the primary motivation of this spiritual entrepreneurial project is not financial profit. However, its development is associated with various costs that, so far, are being assumed by the promoters. The primary investment is in time. Each promoter contributes his or her time, adapting the project's progress to the rhythm and individual availabilities. However, the project is already requiring dedication with a certain constancy. If it is eventually launched, there will be an increase in the costs of maintaining the systems promoting the app and the human costs linked to all of this. This makes it unfeasible to carry out a project of this scale without a small cost to the user. Even the time contribution of the promoters, which until now has been done altruistically, needs a profit to compensate for the opportunity cost of giving up alternative sources of income. For all these reasons, it is necessary to establish a price.

As part of the promotion strategy, however, it is planned to provide free access to a certain number of users. The aim is to acquire a sufficient volume of users for the social and community part of the App to provide added value. New users would have a two-month trial period, after which they would have to subscribe to the App to continue using its content. The facilitators would be financially involved in disseminating the App among their contacts. The users they provide would, in turn, obtain a commercial advantage over those who download the App on their own on the platforms.

The price is not yet determined, as operational costs will vary depending on the version finally included in the App and its associated costs, the average use of the App by each customer, the facilitators involved in disseminating the project, and other variables. After the launch, it will take some time to determine how much these costs will be. However, we propose the cost of the annual subscription between 6 and 10 euros (per year), depending on the measurement of average costs per user. The duration of the course study is indefinite. This price level is based on the assumption that the theoretical study of the Text may take one or two years and the practice of the exercises another year.

Overall, the user would make a similar or lesser outlay than buying the text physically but would obtain a much more comprehensive range of services. This undoubtedly makes it attractive for all the complementary services it provides. Break-even is expected to be reached when between 600 and 800 users join the app. Once this is achieved, the operating margin will be used to increase the developers' time commitment.

Figure 11.5: Text and lesson functionalities.
Source: Author's elaboration

Final Considerations

This project has become the materialization of an inner call to share our spiritual path with others, The Abode of the Creator. We are doing this by creating networks to share and accompany each other in the standard process of awakening Consciousness through the teachings of a particular curriculum, A Course in Miracles. We have called it a spiritual entrepreneurship project, characterized by the fact that the search for financial gain is not the primary motivation. Just a year ago, we would not have imagined that a social app for A Course in Miracles would be coming out and that we would be the promoters. Today, it is already a reality.

On an academic level, this study provides the literature with the first steps of a confirmed case of applying spiritual management through the development of a spiritual entrepreneurship project. Spiritual entrepreneurship, as a particular form of entrepreneurship, is proposed in this work due to personal experience and is, therefore, a novel concept. In terms of management implications, although we are still taking the first steps, this project is an example of another form of entrepreneurship based on spiritual knowledge and sharing. The primary motivation for this form of entrepreneurship is an inner feeling to move in a specific direction and create something beyond personal interest.

As a line of future research, given that no previous studies have addressed the concept of spiritual entrepreneurship, it is necessary to develop further studies to validate this concept. The term needs to be conceptualized, delimiting its scope and differentiating it from related concepts, such as social entrepreneurship. It should also be studied at an empirical level, proposing measures of the spiritual entrepreneurship orientation of companies and providing guidelines with the principles on which this type of entrepreneurship is based. It would also be interesting to monitor the project presented here and extract indicators of its performance in its different aspects, especially regarding user experience and building a spiritual network.

This work is not without limitations. On the one hand, it is an isolated, personal experience that may differ significantly from other experiences related to the generation of spiritual knowledge. We intend to continue working on this project, as it has yet to be launched and put on the market. In parallel, we will continue to improve the app, adding content and functionalities aimed at better meeting the needs of current and potential users. In this sense, some of the improvements that will be addressed in the future are creating open groups and workshops to delve into specific areas, such as forgiveness, judgment, love, unique and holy relationships, etc. Another action not contemplated in the planning is the generation of more audio content, such as guided meditations for each lesson, the audios of the rest of the book (Teacher's Manual, Prayer Song. . .), and multimedia content. There is already much audiovisual material on networks such as YouTube, Facebook, and Instagram, and we would like some of it to be offered through the App by its creators.

The following steps as a team and the form that the service to which we will be called next will take we do not. What is a reality is that we will remain fully committed, on the one hand, to our purpose of drawing back the veils that blind our "vision" to remember the Truth that Already Is, and on the other hand, to the service of the Holy Spirit, to assist in the awakening of other brethren who feel the same inner call to return Home. As the Course tells us, "There is no order of difficulty in miracles" (ACIM, 2018: T-1.I.1).

References

ACIM (2001). *A Course in Miracles. URText.* Vol. 1. The Illuminate Brotherhood Edition.

ACIM (2018). *A Course in Miracles*, 2ª ed., Ed. Foundation for Inner Peace.

ACIM (2021). *A Course in Miracles: Based on The Original Handwritten Notes of Helen Schucman--Complete & Annotated Edition*. Circle of Atonement.

ACIM (2012). *Course in Miracles: Sparkly Edition.* The Borderland Foundation.

Bratianu, C. (2015). *Organizational Knowledge Dynamics: Managing Knowledge Creation, Acquisition, Sharing, and Transformation*. Hershey: IGI Global. DOI: 10.4018/978-1-4666-8318-1.ch004

Dalai Lama (1999). Ethics for the millennium. New York, NY: Putnam.

DeLongis, A., Folkman, S. and Lazarus, R.S. (1988). The Impact of Daily Stress on Health and Mood: Psychological and Social Resources as Mediators. *Journal of Personality and Social Psychology*, *54* (3), 486–495.

Foundation for Inner Peace (FFIP) (n.d.). ACIM – A Course in Miracles. Recovered the 28th January 2023 in https://acim.org/

Reinecke, L., Aufenanger, S., Beutel, M.E., Dreier, M., Quiring, O., Stark, B., Wölfling, K. and Müller, K.W. (2017). Digital Stress over the Life Span: The Effects of Communication Load and Internet Multitasking on Perceived Stress and Psychological Health Impairments in a German Probability Sample, Media Psychology, 20:1, 90–115, DOI: 10.1080/15213269.2015.1121832

Sánchez León, A. (2023). Luis Gutiérrez Rojas: "Las personas más felices han tenido la inteligencia, la virtud y la suerte de desear cosas buenas, *ACPrensa*, 17 january. Recovered 24 january in https://www.aceprensa.com/la-entrevista/luis-gutierrez-rojas-las-personas-mas-felices-han-tenido-la-inteligencia-la-virtud-y-la-suerte-de-desear-cosas-buenas/

Shawley, B. (2014). *A Course in Miracles -Different Versions Explained*. Miracles of Mind Blog. http://miraclesofmind.weebly.com/blog/a-course-in-miracles-different-versions-explained

Skutch, R. (2010). *Journey without distance*. Ed. Foundation for Inner Peace.

Thoits, P.A. (2010). "Stress and Health: Major Findings and Policy Implications. *Journal of Health and Social Behavior*, *51*(S), S41–S53

Wapnick, K. (2022). *What It Says: From the Preface of "A Course in Miracles"*, Ed. Foundation for A Course in Miracles.

List of Figures

https://doi.org/10.1515/9783111010410-013

List of Tables

https://doi.org/10.1515/9783111010410-014

List of Contributors

Alberto Valiente-Fitzsimons is an entrepreneur and a student of non-dual philosophies. From an early age he felt called to serve God. At the age of 17 he began his spiritual path under the guidance of a teacher who guided him in his early years. He learned about the I Am teachings of the Ascended Masters, which he practiced for many years. He later delved into other spiritual teachings such as the Gnostics, Buddhism and others. On his life path of surrender and helping others, in 2012 he learned about the teachings of A Course in Miracles, and since then he has been dedicated to its study, as well as accompanying others in the transmission of its principles. His life purpose is to be an instrument at the service of Awakening.

Alexander Kaiser is a professor at the Vienna University of Economics and Business and head of the Department of Knowledge Management. He is also the founder and managing director of a small company specializing in coaching, training, and consulting, focusing on vision development processes. His research interests are knowledge-based management, spiritual knowledge management, vision development, and organizational learning. Alexander is the author of numerous scientific articles in journals and at all major conferences in the field of knowledge management. Over the last 10 years, Prof. Kaiser has been responsible for numerous organizational development projects in various organizations. His vision is to develop and push deep learning processes for both individuals and organizations so that more and more people and organizations get closer to their best version.

Carla Neves, is a PhD student in Management at the University of Beira Interior (UBI). She has a master's degree in Human Resource Management. Additionally, she works full time in Consultua – Ensino e Formação Profissional, where she coordinates training projects. Besides, she teaches at IPB the Curricular Unit "Psychosociology of Organizations" of the bachelor's degree in Management and in Accounting. https://orcid.org/0000-0003-2527-799X

Constantin Bratianu is Professor Emeritus of Strategic Management and Knowledge Management, UNESCO Department for Business Administration. He has been Visiting Professor at universities in USA, Japan, Austria, Italy, Poland, Hungary and Egypt. He published over 30 books, and 200 papers in international journals and volumes of international conferences. He published several books in knowledge management: Organizational Knowledge Dynamics (2015), IGI Global, USA; Emergent Knowledge Strategies (2017) together with Ettore Bolisani, Springer, Germany; Knowledge Strategies (2022), Cambridge University Press; Knowledge Translation (2024), together with Alexeis Garcia-Perez, Francesca Dal Mas, and Denise Bedford, Emerald. His academic interests are: knowledge strategies, knowledge dynamics, knowledge management, intellectual capital, and strategic management.

Nitika Sharma, who earned her PhD in Marketing from Delhi University in 2021, is currently pursuing post-doctoral studies at the University of Beira Interior, Portugal, specializing in sustainable marketing and pro-environmental behaviour. She is an Assistant Professor at IMI New Delhi, teaching CRM, sustainability marketing, and marketing foundation courses. Her work, including the awarded paper "The Impact of Eco-Innovation on Green Buying Behavior: The Moderating Effect of Emotional Loyalty and Generation," received the Outstanding Paper Award in the 2023 Emerald Literati Awards and was published in the esteemed journal Management of Environmental Quality. Dr. Sharma has published numerous papers in reputable journals, presented at national and international conferences, received awards from institutions like IIM-Bangalore, and served as a guest editor for a special issue in Taylor & Francis. She has also undergone Innovation Ambassador training by the Ministry of Education.

Duncan Cryle is a founding member of Clear Sky Center www.clearskycenter.org. He was Board Chair from 2008 to 2014 and is an associate teacher and creator of Clear Sky's Integrating Mindfulness and

https://doi.org/10.1515/9783111010410-015

three-month residential intensive programs. He is a Senior Director at SS&C Technologies, a global software company with 25K employees, where he leads a company-wide mindfulness program. He was one of the pioneers of IBM's mindfulness community, which grew to over 10000 members. His mindfulness work in the corporate setting is based on 30+ years of study with his meditation teachers Qapel and Catherine Sensei. Since 2004 he has co-developed Clear Sky as a "living lab" for awareness-based approaches to team learning, communication, organization development, and personal transformation. He and the Clear Sky team now coach other organizations and communities. He also holds a Ph.D. in philosophy from the University of Liverpool.

Edwina Pio, Recipient of an Officer of the New Zealand Order of Merit, Te Rangi Hiroa Royal Society medal, and Duke of Edinburgh Fellowship, Fulbright alumna, Edwina is New Zealand's first Professor of Diversity. A prolific writer, her research is published in leading international journals, books and media outlets. A woman of peace and prayer, a scholar of colour, a passionately engaged educator with networks in Oceania, South Asia, Europe, UK and USA, Edwina brings grace, gratitude, courage and thoughtfulness to governance, teaching, research, doctoral supervisions, and stakeholder engagement.

Elaine C. Long is an Organizational Psychologist, accomplished consultant, coach, researcher, adjunct faculty for The Chicago School, and published author. She earned a Ph.D. with distinction from TCS as well as an MBA from the prestigious J.L. Kellogg School of Management at Northwestern University. With forty years of professional experience and a Life Fellow of the American College of Healthcare Executives, Dr. Long embraces rigorous academic training and practical business acumen. Dr. Long's scholarly pursuits intersect organizational development, workplace spirituality and religion, knowledge management, positive psychology, and healthcare. As a dedicated Faith-at-Work scholar-practitioner, she uncovers the intricate relationships between these domains and their impact on human flourishing. Dr. Long's impactful teachings, publications, and presentations consistently demonstrate a dedication to pioneering novel ideas and facilitating meaningful relationships that bridge theory and practice. To learn more about her contributions and endeavors, see ORCID, and ResearchGate: https://orcid.org/0000-0002-2011-4879 and https://www.researchgate.net/profile/Elaine-Long-3.

Felipe Andres-Ruiz is a businessman with more than 30 years of experience in the financial sector. His interest in spiritual matters arose since he was a child, having always shown great interest in self-knowledge at a psychological and spiritual level. He has been involved in teachings such as those of the Ascended Masters. He has also studied Buddhism, and other non-dual philosophies such as Advaita-Vedanta and A Course In Miracles. He leads spiritual teaching groups of A Course in Miracles. He is a mindfulness instructor (Mindfulness based on the Buddhist Tradition) and yoga teacher. His inner calling towards the awakening of consciousness has led him to be in charge of a yoga association where he helps others to find their own path to the Self.

Juha Kansikas, Senior lecturer, acts as an academic director of the international bachelor (B.Sc.) programme at the University of Jyväskylä School of Business and Economics in Finland. He co-leads Council of Science research project on executive education and business elite formation (2020-2024). In 2021 he worked as a researcher for the Council of Education at the University of Jyväskylä by developing entrepreneurship education. He has post-doc qualification both in business and in education sciences (docent). His research interests are entrepreneurship, business elite, executive education, and family business. Dr. Kansikas has published his research at the journals such as Technological Forecasting and Social Change, Business History, Enterprise and Society, International Journal of Entrepreneurial Behavior and Research, Journal of Social Entrepreneurship, Science and Public Policy, and Journal of Entrepreneurship.

Ludmila Mládková works at the Prague University of Economics and Business, Czech Republic, Faculty of Business Administration. Her primary topics are management and knowledge management. She teaches courses on general management, advanced management, leadership, knowledge management and management of knowledge workers at Czech and abroad universities. Her theoretical knowledge and her experience from practice give her a unique opportunity to look at the problems of management and knowledge management from a systemic view. As for the research, Ludmila sees a significant research gap in the relationship between new management models and knowledge management. She is interested in how new management models work, the prerequisites of their success and how they influence knowledge sharing among employees. She understands spirituality as an inevitable factor of work in such organisations.

Marcia Juliana d'Angelo is an Associate Professor at Fucape Business School in the areas of Strategy and Organization. PhD and Master's in business administration (with distinction) from Presbyterian Mackenzie University. She also holds a Master in Business Administration (MBA) from Warwick Business School in England. Conducts research in the areas of strategy, sustainability, ESG, people management, and diversity. She is an associate editor of Brazilian Business Review, Mackenzie Management Review, and Academia Latin American Administration Journal.

María Angeles Iniesta-Bonillo is an associate professor of marketing and market research at the University of Almería (Spain) and head of the "Science, Consciousness and Development" research group. She has long researched the field of consumer behavior (relational variables such as commitment, perceived value, and perceived sustainability....). Her most recent interests focus on the role of mindfulness in purchasing and consumption behavior, mindful consumption, slow tourism, and digital communication. She is a specialist in personal development and mindfulness, a mindfulness instructor (Mindfulness based on the Buddhist tradition), a yoga teacher, and a neurocoach. She teaches mindfulness courses and leads groups of meditation and study of non-dual philosophies. Dedicated to the experience of the Fullness of Being, her life purpose is to be an instrument in the service of Peace and Love.

Maria Jakubik is an Honorary Associate Professor of the University of Pécs, Hungary and a member of The Hungarian Academy of Sciences' External Public Body. She has more than two decades of experience in Finnish higher education. She is an active research scholar of the Ronin Institute, USA, and member of the International Council on Knowledge Management (ICKM), Austria, and the Philosophy and Theory of Higher Education Society (PaTHES), UK. As a doctoral researcher, she is affiliated with Eötvös Loránd University (ELTE), Faculty of Education and Psychology, Budapest, Hungary. Her current research focuses on higher education, and wisdom pedagogy.

Paula F. Marchant-Pérez, PhD student in Management at the University of Beira Interior (UBI), Portugal. She has a master´s degree in Comprehensive Quality Management and in Community Physiotherapy Care. Also, she is researcher at NECE-UBI Research Centre for Business Sciences and is Associate Professor at Kinesiology School in University of Valparaíso, Chile, in Management Disciplinary Network. Her research lines include strategic and organizational management, and health management. https://orcid.org/0000-0002-5962-1157

Paulo Pinheiro (PhD) is an Assistant Professor at the University of Beira Interior (UBI), Business & Economics Department, and a researcher at the Research Group on Enterprise Science (NECE). His teaching activities are mainly on knowledge management and comprehending undergraduate, master, and doctoral students. He is a Ph.D. in Management and the author of several publications. https://orcid.org/0000-0003-2397-6463

Raysa Geaquinto Rocha (PhD) is an Organization Studies and Human Resource Management lecturer at the University of Essex and a Researcher at the NECE-UBI Research Center of the University of Beira Interior. She teaches Business Ethics and Organizational Behavior at Essex. Her research has been published in journals such as the Journal of Business Ethics and Corporate Social Responsibility and Environmental Management. Raysa's scholarly portfolio includes over fifty publications, encompassing articles, book editions, chapters, proceedings, and presentations at renowned conferences. She is Representative-at-Large for Research of the Management Spirituality and Religion division of the Academy of Management. Her research interests center on individual behavior and organizational practices that promote knowledge dynamics and spirituality, resulting in a humane strategy for long-term sustainable performance.

Vanessa C.M. Englert works as an organization development professional and engages as a PhD scholar at Vrije Universiteit Amsterdam at the overlap of Management and Spiritual Studies. She applies qualitative methods to discover the nature of shared spiritual experiences in organizational settings such as the office, class room, in doctor's consultation, etc. – also termed "collective spirituality in organizational settings". From an integrative perspective, she desires to contribute to answering: How can organizations be designed to serve human kind to live their full Self?

Welmoed van Hoogen is a current Master in Philosophy in Indigenous Studies student at UiT, the Arctic University in Norway. She holds a BSc in Sociology and a MSc in Diversity and Change Management and is interested in diverse societal phenomena, such as spirituality and organizations, authenticity in experiences, and the Indigenous tourism sector.

Index

https://doi.org/10.1515/9783111010410-016